The Psychoanalytic Study
of the Child

VOLUME XVII

The Psychoanalytic Study

of the Child

VOLUME XVII

INTERNATIONAL UNIVERSITIES PRESS, INC.

New York   New York

CONTENTS

Contributions to Psychoanalytic Theory

Aspects of Normal and Pathological Development

Clinical Contributions

Applied Psychoanalysis

CONTRIBUTIONS TO PSYCHOANALYTIC THEORY

ON THE METAPSYCHOLOGY OF THE PRECONSCIOUS

A Tentative Contribution to Psychoanalytic Morphology

K. R. EISSLER, PH.D., M.D. (New York)

The concept of the preconscious has once more moved into the center of theoretical discussion since Ernst Kris made it the subject of a paper in 1950. He then wrote (p. 304): "The introduction of these new [structural] concepts has never fully been integrated with the broad set of propositions developed earlier." Today one feels tempted to paraphrase this statement and wish to integrate concepts such as the preconscious into existing ego psychology. The trend toward discarding parts of psychoanalytic theory in favor of structural psychology is unquestionably strong in the present phase of psychoanalysis.

In the center of research there now stands the attempt to clarify and purify psychoanalytic concepts. Indeed, the heritage of Freud's lifework is so rich (and overwhelming) that several generations will probably have to devote their principal effort to such tasks as ordering, verifying, redefining, briefly digesting, the wealth of discoveries and theories Freud left to posterity.

The clinical, theoretical, and experimental work of psychoanalytic validation, though certainly a wholesome process, involves certain dangers. In the effort to establish the desired harmony of theories and conceptual exactness, the baby may be thrown out with the bath, that is, clinical facts may be overlooked or misinterpreted. One may fear lest there be fulfilled Kant's critical statement about the "overnice sagacity of those who exaggerate, wrench, and refine established and useful concepts in their retorts for such a long time that they evaporate in fumes and volatile salts [*überfeine Weisheit*

*derjenigen welche sichere und brauchbare Begriffe in ihrer Schmelz-
küche so lange übertreiben, abziehen und verfeinern, bis sie in
Dämpfen und flüchtigen Salzen verrauchen]"* (Kant, 1763, p. 126).

It is heartening to observe that such cliffs have been successfully
doubled. What perhaps can actually be observed in one or another
instance is an exaggeration of the differences that allegedly exist
among Freud's theories, as they arose in the course of his development. Thus Brenner, in his attempt at clarifying the history of the
concept of repression in Freud's writings (1957, p. 42), states that
Freud made an essential change in his view of primal repression
inasmuch as he came to consider this part of the repressed also as the
consequence of defense, whereas I believe that related passages in
Freud's *Moses* (1937-1939, p. 155) and in his *Outline* (1938b, p. 43)
may serve to demonstrate that in the last phase of theory formation
too Freud preserved the view that primal repression is a process
prior to the institution of defense.

It may have been a continuation of the same way of thinking
when recently Arlow and Brenner (1960)[1] went a step further and,
applying the scalpel of logical analysis (without neglect of clinical
considerations) to the concept of the preconscious, concluded that
this concept should be discarded altogether. The occasion of this
suggestion prompted me to publish some views about the preconscious which I have been harboring for a long time. As the reader
will see, in view of my emphasis on the topographical aspect, what
I have to say will sound like an anachronism and, indeed, when a
paper like that by Klein (1959) with its brilliant exposition of the
structural view of consciousness is compared with topographical
deliberation, preference would have to be given to the former, if the
two metapsychological aspects were really incompatible. But in
Freud's opinion, as I understand it, they are not.

Metapsychology comprised initially three points of view or frames
of reference: the dynamic, the economic, and the topographic. The
dynamic point of view conceives psychic phenomena "as brought
about by the play of forces in the mind, as expressions of tendencies

[1] Paper read to the New York Psychoanalytic Society on November 24, 1959. I owe
particular thanks to Dr. Charles Brenner for having given me the opportunity of
reading the manuscript.

striving towards a goal, which work together or against one another"
(Freud, 1916-1917, p. 60).

The economic point of view takes into account the quantities
involved in psychic processes and the laws of quantity distribution,
such as pleasure-displeasure principle, constancy principle, etc.

The topographic point of view is concerned with the division of
the personality, with the parts the psychic apparatus consists of.
In particular, it ascertains the pathways psychic processes have to
travel in order to form the phenomena under observation.

Originally, the psychic apparatus was divided by Freud into three
systems: conscious, preconscious, and unconscious (*Cs., Pcs., Ucs.*).
Later, the structural point of view was added by Freud's introducing
ego, superego, and id into the psychoanalytic theory.

I am concerned with the fact that many authors disregard the
full consequences of Freud's having introduced the concept of ego,
superego, and id. Brenner, for example, in his textbook (1955, p.
44f.) presents a formulation that may easily be understood as meaning that Freud intended to replace the topographical aspect with the
structural. Arlow and Brenner suggest "that the two hypotheses
[topographical and structural] are incompatible and that the structural hypothesis is superior, accounting for all the facts explained
by the topographical hypothesis, and others in addition" (1960, p.
447). Without prejudice to the authors' views, I wish to emphasize
here only that this was not, at least, Freud's view. From his writings
it becomes clear that:

(1) the topography of the personality is a metapsychological
frame of reference that per se is not put in question, no matter how
the concepts of conscious, preconscious, or unconscious are defined.

(2) The introduction of the triad (ego, superego, id) not only led
to the structural frame of reference but also had its bearing on the
topographical aspect. That is to say, according to the present status
of psychoanalytic theory, the basic conceptions of the topographic
aspects are ego, superego, and id. When Freud indicated that he
wanted the terms conscious, preconscious, and unconscious understood as no longer designating psychic systems (subdivisions of the
psychic apparatus) but as designating the psychic qualities of the
mind (1932, pp. 100-104; 1938b, pp. 33-45), they lost their standing
as topographical terms but were automatically replaced by ego, id,

and superego, which are simultaneously the focal conceptions of the structural point of view.[2]

Thus Freud says (1926a, p. 266): *"Topographically,* psycho-analysis regards the mental apparatus as a compound instrument, and endeavours to determine at what points in it the various mental processes take place. According to the most recent psycho-analytic views, the mental apparatus is composed of an *'id'* . . . , of an *'ego'* . . . , and of a *'super-ego.'* " Also, in the *Outline* Freud speaks of "the topographical division of the mental apparatus into an ego and an id" (1938b, p. 44). The only way in which the terms conscious, preconscious, and unconscious will appear in topography is in reference to the distribution of the three qualities within the psychic apparatus: all processes within the id, for example, are characterized by the quality of unconscious, whereas some processes in the ego are conscious, others preconscious, and others, in turn, unconscious (Freud, 1932, pp. 102-104; 1938b, pp. 40-43).[3]

That topography and structural points of view operate with the same terms should not be surprising. In anatomy the topographical relations of the liver are studied and in physiology, its functions. Freud's introduction of the structural viewpoint may be compared with the discovery of new organs, which, of course, would have a bearing on physiology as well as on topographical anatomy.

Having set forth which concepts Freud regarded as basic to the topographical frame of his metapsychological system, we can now turn toward our subject, namely, whether the new topographical and structural points of view really make Freud's earlier idea of unconscious, preconscious, and conscious systems superfluous. In other words, do we discover in the human personality anything that would indicate the existence of configurations that resemble what

[2] I am gratefully following Dr. Heinz Hartmann's suggestion when I quote the following passage from Freud's *New Lectures:* "We have . . . also attributed to the word 'unconscious' a topographical or systemic meaning" (1932, p. 101). This may sound as if Freud had equated system and topographical aspect, with the resultant abolition of the latter when the former is excluded. However, further reading of the paragraph as well as the quotations that follow in the text shows that the innovation concerned the dismissal of the term "unconscious" as signifying a system, but by no means the topographical aspect as such, as the very title of Freud's thirty-first lecture (1932, pp. 82-112), *Die Zerlegung der psychischen Persönlichkeit,* literally, "The Dissection of the Psychic Personality," amply demonstrates.

[3] Cf. Freud (1926a, p. 266): "The quality of consciousness, too, has a topographical reference."

was meant by Freud in his earlier writings by *Cs., Pcs.,* and *Usc.?* Freud's final opinion in this respect I have just cited: Conscious, preconscious, unconscious, are qualities of psychic phenomena or processes.

From past writings, it is noticeable that Freud tested a new theory by delineating its maximum explanatory potential, and only later, after having set forth the maximum of possible consequences, did he put the new *mansion,* if I may use the term, into the right proportional relation to the whole house. Thus in 1920, when he introduced the superego into analysis, Freud felt inclined to attribute the function of reality testing to it (p. 114), but later revised this suggestion and once more assigned this function to the ego (1920, p. 114, n. 2; and 1923, p. 28, n. 2).

Closer scrutiny will show that even at a time when Freud assumed conscious, preconscious, and unconscious to be nothing more than qualities, he occasionally used the terms indirectly in a sense that was systematic, as he manifestly did in the case of the symbol *Pcpt.-Cs.,* meaning the perceptual-conscious system, "the most superficial portion of the mental apparatus" (1932, p. 105).

It is my contention that ego, id, and superego do not suffice to outline the whole area of psychoanalytic topography and that on clinical and theoretical grounds it is necessary to assume the existence of something that comes close to, without being identical with, what Freud meant by *Cs., Pcs.,* and *Ucs.* in the seventh chapter of his *Interpretation of Dreams* (1900). The present topographical division of ego, superego, and id to a certain extent leaves unaccounted for a fundamental question, namely, what the pathways of communication are among the three provinces of the personality.

In order to come closer to an answer, I must discuss a pair of concepts that are relevant not only in psychology, where it was discussed first, but in any science that deals with or investigates processes, that is to say, movement.

In investigating movement of any kind, one has to differentiate between conveyed, medial movement, on the one hand, and central, spontaneous movement on the other (see Heider, 1926, 1930). The light waves that reach the eye are typically medial in character. They convey a property of things. They obey strictly the structure of the things that reflected them. They have given up their individuality, so to speak, in favor of becoming pure messengers. The underlying physical laws are well known. The sun is a nucleus that produces white light. By means of medial processes white light reaches the surfaces of objects, where new nuclei rearrange the pattern of the white light that has reached them and medial processes convey these new patterns to the retina of the human eye. Here we can readily distinguish between nuclear and medial processes. Our sense organs are geared to the perception of nuclear processes. The medial processes are imperceptible. Of course, the medium may acquire nuclear-like properties, as when haze or fog interfere with communication between object surface and eye. The medium then asserts its individuality.

Nuclear (central) and medial processes can, of course, be easily ascertained in social relations. The ideal slave, being always at his master's beck and call, is an ideal medium. Here too the medium asserts, though minimally, its individuality. Even the ideal slave needs nutriment and sleep. Psychic processes can also be ordered, at least theoretically, according to their nuclear and medial character. The ideal perception is a medium of the world of objects, with whose properties it is strictly correlated. The drives are nuclear forces that are inherent in a psychobiological unit and set into motion processes that are significant of the carrier.

If we now apply the concept of nucleus and medium to psychoanalytic topography, we easily recognize ego, id, and superego as the three centers of powerful forces. They are the sources of nuclear processes. I suggest that the communication among these nuclei is established by specially adapted medial systems which correspond to consciousness and preconsciousness.

If the terminology were not pre-empted, I would differentiate between nucleus or structure and system, but ego and superego are often called systems, and I am therefore at a loss to find the proper generic terms. In analogy with neurohistology one may think of the nerve cell and its axon and speak of nuclei and tracts, the latter serving medial purposes, but the term *tract* does not appear suitable for a psychic formation.[4] Accordingly, the reader may permit me in

---

[4] The comparison with the structure of the nervous system may evoke a scheme of the nuclei being embedded in the depth of the psychic apparatus and the medial systems leading to the surface. It is questionable whether a schematic presentation of

this article to use the term *system* for a psychic configuration of a nonnuclear (medial) nature.

When speculating on the evolution of consciousness, Freud actually described consciousness as an ideal medial system. He looked upon it as a phenomenon that arises instead of a memory trace. According to his construction, the superficial layer of the living organism, pictured as an undifferentiated vesicle, would bear the brunt of external stimulation that constantly impinges upon it. This ceaseless impact would cause a permanent modification, "a crust . . . so thoroughly 'baked through' by stimulation that it would present the most favourable possible conditions for the reception of stimuli and become incapable of any further modification" (Freud, 1920, p. 26). The modification of elements, brought about by excitatory processes, depends on whether these elements are capable of putting up a resistance. (This at least was Freud's metapsychological assumption of 1900, p. 539.) Since the elements of the system *Cs.* were so modified that they had lost any resistance to excitatory processes, the system *Cs.* is the result of a process of gradual transformation of a nucleus into an ideal medium, nucleus being defined in this instance by the capacity to put up a resistance to stimulations.

Of course, this metapsychological description of the ideal type of the system *Cs.* covers only one aspect of consciousness. Observation and experience clearly show that consciousness never operates in this ideal fashion.

My proposition thus is as follows. The personality consists of three nuclei which initiate processes (movement in physical terminology; demands, tasks, impulses, or what not, in psychological terminology). The movements they initiate cause, aside from intranuclear changes, processes in medial systems, two of which have been mentioned: the systems *Cs.* and *Pcs.* Of course, excitations that originate in the outer world also pass through these systems. The perceptive apparatus appears to be a nuclear part of the ego structure that is in broad communication with the system *Cs.*, but also in direct connection with the system *Pcs.*, from where it may reach the id without

the psychic apparatus has any great heuristic value at present. If one is inclined toward visualization, two different models suggest themselves: medial systems may be thought of as providing connections between nuclei and the surface, or internuclear connections may be tentatively visualized as peripheral medial adaptations at the surface of nuclei so located that two or more nuclei share in them.

the ego's awareness. The possibility of remote effects from one nucleus to another without the intermediary of interconnecting systems is not excluded by this proposition. Neurological analogies of this kind are known.[5]

My proposition does not exclude the qualitative nature of conscious and preconscious, since the quality of consciousness and preconsciousness would be among the characteristics of the processes that occur in either of the two systems.

These two systems would be, according to my proposition, adaptations of the psychic apparatus for the purpose of establishing communications between nuclei. We find sometimes id derivatives and sometimes superego derivatives in them; that is to say, they border nuclei which have access to them. Or one may imagine that nuclei have given up in fringe portions part of their nuclear structure and changed into media. Of course, ego material such as memories, knowledge, and what not, also has access to both.

In turning now specifically toward the system *Pcs.*, I quote Kris (1950, p. 311), who speaks of "two continua, one reaching from solving problems to dreamlike fantasy, and one reaching from logical cohesive verbal statements to dreamlike imagery," both of which occur in preconscious mental processes. We may assume that there are afferent and efferent tracts in the system *Pcs.* as well as *Cs.*, one, for example, leading from the ego and particularly the perceptual apparatus to the superego and the id, the other carrying impulses, emitted by the id, and derivatives from repressed imagery, both traveling on efferent tracts of the *Pcs.*, ready to incite processes in the ego or superego.

The *Cs.*, as mentioned before, was described at one point by Freud as the ideal medium. It is the medium not only of external excitations, but also of ego, superego, or id. From Freud's tentative diagram of the personality (1932, p. 111), it is known that only the border between the ego and the repressed part of the id is heavily guarded by countercathexis. Outside of this border, ego and id communicate freely. The system *Cs.* is very close to the ego and the

[5] One may feel tempted to assume for such instances interconnecting systems between id and ego on the one hand, and id and superego on the other, following Freud's account, according to which ego as well as superego gradually emerge from the id. However, it may be advisable here to assume something like a fusion of nuclei along a limited area.

perceptual system. Most of the time of wakefulness it is kept busy, so to speak, by this nucleus or nuclei. The opposite extreme is a state in which the system *Cs.* is flooded by the id and the ego recedes, as happens during orgasm.

There can, of course, be only a theoretical answer to the question of the energy with which these systems work. According to a remark by Freud, a system is in a state of potential functioning, or can be activated only when it is cathected. Freud called this "the principle of the insusceptibility to excitation of uncathected systems" (1917, p. 234, n. 2). The idea is probably taken from the physiology of muscles. A muscle has its own tonus even when not active, without which nerve impulses would not succeed in activating the muscle fibers. Likewise a system that is decathected cannot be activated.

Depending on whether one agrees with the concept of neutralization of energy, one may assume that the working efficiency of the system *Pcs.* depends per se on the degree of neutralization (Hartmann, 1950, p. 86) of the energy with which the system proper is cathected.[6] Since I doubt the validity of the concept of neutralization, I feel more inclined to correlate system efficiency with quantitative factors of system cathexis.[7]

It is no less difficult to form a suitable opinion about the nature of the energy of processes that take place within a system. When id derivatives enter the *Pcs.*, are they cathected with energy different from those that originate in the ego and superego? In other words, is the cathexis of the contents of a system accomplished with the energy of the system proper, or with the energy of the nuclei from which they originate?

[6] See among the extensive literature on neutralization, Hartmann, Kris, and Loewenstein (1949).

[7] The principle of insusceptibility, obvious as it may appear on closer reflection, harbors some challenging problems. Freud himself discovered two situations in which it did not seem to operate. (1) Dreaming occurs when the system *Cs.* has been emptied of cathexis (1917, p. 234). (2) When reality testing has been suspended, as happens in amentia, the patient is still conscious of hallucinatory wish fulfillments (1917, p. 233). This contradicted Freud's assumption that the patient's break with external reality is caused by a withdrawal of energy from *Cs.* Both situations made additional hypotheses necessary: (a) Only a *"partial* removal of cathexis" occurs during sleep or the perceptual system operates in accordance with energic laws different from other systems (1917, p. 234, n. 2); (b) the ego "withdraws *a* cathexis, the special nature of which may be the subject of further enquiry" (1917, p. 233; italics by Freud), an argument most favorable to the theory of neutralization.

To a certain extent, this question is reminiscent of the one Freud raised in his metapsychological paper on "The Unconscious" (1915a). There, however, the problem was a purely topographic one, namely, whether when a content changes from *Ucs.* to *Pcs.* or *Cs.*, it actually changes its topographic location, that is to say, whether the transposition from *Ucs.* to *Pcs.* or *Cs.* requires "a second registration, in a fresh psychical locality" or consists just in a change of the state of the content (1915a, p. 174). The entrance of a content into a system, I presume, may require in principle some change in intensity or quality of cathexis, but it is not probable either that the nucleogenic cathexis necessarily disappears and is replaced with that of the system or that the nucleogenic cathexis is preserved. Both eventualities are equally feasible and, last not least, it is one of the tasks of psychoanalysis to study just the vicissitude of cathexes within the psychic apparatus before they reach the end stage of discharge.

I wish to suggest at this point an answer to the question why, under certain conditions, the *Cs.* may be excited even when the system is emptied of its own cathexis, as happens in dreams. It is feasible that when contents charged with cathexis of high intensity invade a decathected system, the cathexes of these invading contents spread out within the system as a whole and thus effect transient susceptibility of an otherwise decathected system. I do not wish to pursue the consequences of such an assumption any further.

I return now to the contradiction which Arlow and Brenner, in their afore-mentioned paper, assert exists between earlier and later definitions of the preconscious as a system. If there were indeed such a substantive contradiction, it would add weight to their proposal that the concept of the preconscious be dropped altogether.

As a matter of fact, Freud, in 1932, as earlier, defined the preconscious as only latently unconscious and as easily becoming conscious (p. 101), whereas in the *Outline* he gave—besides the customary definition—a more complete description of the preconscious, which may seem to contradict earlier statements. Thus he remarked that some processes, however highly organized they may be, may remain preconscious, "although as a rule they press forward, as we say, into consciousness" (1938b, p. 38). When Freud refers to the occasional, temporary inaccessibility of preconscious material caused by resistance, as in passing forgetfulness, or to its temporary submergence in the unconscious, as happens in the formation of jokes (1938b, p. 40), he is dealing with special instances that are familiar to the analyst. However, the third of Freud's references that are relevant in this context is ambiguous. He asserts that access to consciousness and linkage with verbal residues are not sufficient to characterize the preconscious. "The proof of this," he continues, "is that large portions of the ego, and in particular of the superego, which cannot be denied the characteristic of being preconscious, none the less remain for the most part unconscious in the phenomenological sense of the word" (1938b, p. 42f.). Whether Arlow and Brenner are right in interpreting these statements as meaning that Freud believed that part of the preconscious may be inaccessible to consciousness (1960, p. 448) may be questioned, but there is no doubt that the readiness with which a content becomes conscious is no yardstick of its belonging to the preconscious, as Freud had already stated in 1915(a). There he set forth in unmistakable terms that part of the *Pcs.* cannot become conscious—at least spontaneously. About derivatives of the *Ucs.* that had reached the *Pcs.* he had the following to say: "On the one hand, they are highly organized, . . . have made use of every acquisition of the system *Cs.* and would hardly be distinguished in our judgment from the formations of that system. On the other hand they are unconscious and are incapable of becoming conscious. Thus *qualitatively* they belong to the system *Pcs.*, but *factually* to the *Ucs.*" (p. 190f.).[8] What can be stated with certainty is that clinical evidence demonstrates that some unconscious contents are only temporarily unconscious and become conscious with ease, and others only after resistances have been overcome. Quite rightly, Freud subsumed the two groups of phenomena under different names, that is to say, attributed them to two different systems. However, Freud indicated at the very start that a preconscious content can enter consciousness *only when certain conditions are fulfilled.*[9] The contradiction in what purports

8 It is surprising to find here the concept of the *Pcs.* linked with "quality"; cf. Freud (1938b, pp. 33-45). In 1915, I believe, one would rather have expected the formulation that these derivatives belong topographically, to the *Pcs.* and dynamically to the *Ucs.*

9 Cf. Freud: ". . . the excitatory processes occurring in it [the preconscious] can enter consciousness without further impediment *provided that certain other conditions are fulfilled*" (1900, p. 541; italics mine).

to be the definition of the same system, namely, the fact that the intersystemic communication between *Cs.* and *Pcs.* is most of the time free but at times impeded by resistance, requires the formulation of a different definition, which actually can be found in Freud's work.[10]

The two groups of statements about the preconscious singled out by Arlow and Brenner are irreconcilable if viewed in isolation, but in principle I do not see why the censoring agency whose operation is to be assumed at the threshold between *Pcs.* and *Cs.* should not function in a way that would include the extremes Freud postulated: namely, either to permit the passage of contents that at the respective moment are in demand by the ego, or to prevent their appearance in *Cs.*, depending on special circumstances. Two essentially different situations are to be distinguished: (a) A preconscious content may be debarred from *Cs.*, although its conscious representation is needed and wanted by the self; or (b) a preconscious content may be debarred because of the direct displeasure its becoming conscious would arouse. Freud had the following to say about the latter situation:

> . . . we find that many preconscious formations remain unconscious, though we should have expected that, from their nature, they might very well have become conscious. Probably in the latter case the stronger attraction of the *Ucs.* is asserting itself. . . . The *Ucs.* is turned back on the frontier of the *Pcs.* by the censorship, but derivatives of the *Ucs.* can circumvent this censorship, achieve a high degree of organization and reach a certain intensity of cathexis in the *Pcs.* When, however, this intensity is exceeded and they try to force themselves into consciousness, they are recognized as derivatives of the *Ucs.* and are repressed afresh at the new frontier of censorship, between the *Pcs.* and the *Cs.* Thus the first of these censorships is exercised against the *Ucs.* itself, and the second against its *Pcs.* derivatives [1915a, p. 193].

[10] Here a point which may easily cause confusion must be straightened out. If metapsychological formulations were to be completely exact, they would have to be quite cumbersome. Therefore, abbreviated formulations have become customary. Thus Freud made it quite clear that in his view a content had to be preconscious before it could become conscious. Nevertheless, he at times raises the question of (a) how an unconscious content becomes conscious, and (b) how a preconscious content becomes conscious. What is meant then is: (a) how an unconscious content becomes preconscious, and (b) how do contents which genuinely belong to the *Pcs.* and do not originate in the *Ucs.* become conscious.

Accordingly, preconscious contents that are ego syntonic generally become conscious with ease. Preconscious contents, however, that originated in the *Ucs.*, and have not yet been sufficiently purified of the taint attached to the repressed, are rejected by the second censor.

The question will be asked why the second censor works here with greater accuracy and sensitivity than the first one. Speculation may set forth a variety of possible explanations, aside from those mentioned by Freud. Under the impact of the psychoanalytic process, the repressed may obtain an unusually strong upsurge sufficient to provide its derivatives with additional cathexis facilitating their penetration into the *Pcs.*, but resulting in an increase of a second-line defense. Also, the effect of a censor may depend on the cathectic proportion between the systems separated. Disarrangements of system cathexis may lower or increase censor cathexis. Thus the total tension within the psychic apparatus may decrease if a content is temporarily permitted to change from the repressed to *Pcs.;* this new equilibrium may, however, become disturbed if there is further progress toward *Cs.* Thus Freud's definition, *Pcs.* is what becomes conscious with ease, requires the reservation: unless it carries "the hall-mark of repression, a certificate of origin—like, let us say, 'Made in Germany' " (Freud, 1925, p. 236), a phrase Freud used when explaining negation.

The instance in question is of general interest. The topographical marking per se evidently does not suffice to predict the vicissitude of a particular content. The functioning of a system in an individual instance is determined not only by the laws characteristic of this system but also by the history of the particular element. A similar situation is also encountered in the definition of the repressed. It is generally correct to say that the repressed becomes conscious after the removal of resistances. However, this does not hold true of the primal repressed, which, because of its particular history, does not become conscious even after the removal of resistances. I do not see any particular theoretical or practical difficulty here and will leave the matter at that.

However, there are instances when a preconscious content does not become conscious, although a subject is searching for it and it does not seem that its appearance would arouse particular displeasure. Such an instance would constitute a dysfunction of the second censor. Here, however, it is necessary to remember that the adequate functioning of the system *Pcs.* also requires the continuous activation of a censor. We have only to think of a remark Freud made in a seemingly different context: ". . . a normal person uses concentration to keep away not only what is irrelevant or unimportant, but, above all, what is unsuitable because it is contradictory" (1926b, p. 121).[11] Consequently, a huge number of preconscious contents have to be kept away from *Cs.*, and for this purpose alone a censoring agency is required.

The function of the censors may be described as follows. In the repressed is stored that which would arouse displeasure under all circumstances and the censor has to protect the self against it; the *Pcs.* is the carrier of contents that under certain circumstances would arouse displeasure:[12] When someone tries to recall the year when Rome was founded, but that of the first Olympiad comes to mind instead, this arouses displeasure, but in a different context this very datum may be the one looked for and then its appearance in *Cs.* will satisfy. In view of the continuous operation of a censor between *Pcs.* and *Cs.*, it is not surprising that at times it misfunctions and a content needed by the self remains inaccessible in the *Pcs.* Thus the censor may selectively debar the ego syntonic, that is to say, hold back the supply that would fill the demand of the present situation. Yet if the whole area were covered by Freud's frequent definition that preconscious is the latently unconscious, that which becomes conscious with ease upon demand, we would possess a reliable clinical index with which to recognize preconscious contents. Freud's additional remark, that this is not always so, deprives us of a generally valid clue that would inform us of the preconscious quality.

However, such an index or clue can be found. It seems that the processes involved when a content changes from *Pcs.* to *Cs.* are different from those of change from *Ucs.* to *Pcs.* The former occurs

---

[11] There are also passages in Freud's book on jokes which demonstrate that a censoring agency between *Pcs.* and *Cs.* is requisite for effective functioning of the psychic apparatus. See Freud (1905a, p. 225, and particularly p. 220): ". . . processes, which run their course in the preconscious but lack the cathexis of attention . . ."

[12] I omit here the case of id derivatives just discussed.

by hypercathexis (1915a, p. 194), the latter by a decrease of counter-cathexis.

A historical remark is necessary here. At one point, Freud also used the term *hypercathexis* in describing the *Ucs.*'s becoming *Pcs.* "A representation which is not put into words, or a psychical act which is not hypercathected, remains thereafter in the *Ucs.* in a state of repression" (1915a, p. 202). Yet in my opinion, hypercathexis does not refer here to the cause which effects the (topographical) change from *Ucs.* to *Pcs.*, but to the change which the content undergoes when it rises from *Ucs.* to *Pcs.* ". . . these hypercathexes [that is, word presentations] . . . bring about a higher psychical organization" writes Freud (1915a, p. 202). However, here it can only be a matter of bringing together the unconscious thing presentations with the preconscious hypercathexes (word presentations), the two being sep-arated by a censor. When the censor is weakened by sleep or disease, or reduced by the analytic process, the two are united. Yet in becom-ing conscious the preconscious cathexis receives an additional cathec-tic charge.

Accordingly, the more comprehensive definition is as follows: *Pcs.* is what becomes actually or potentially conscious by hyper-cathexis; *Ucs.* is what becomes *Pcs.* by decrease of countercathexis. In most instances hypercathexis is quite sufficient to change pre-consciousness into consciousness, that is to say, to overcome the censoring guardian between the two systems; in some instances, as mentioned before, this hypercathexis fails in accomplishing this task; yet this has no bearing on the fact that it is only by means of hyper-cathexis that these contents also are potentially capable of becoming conscious.

There is also a phenomenological difference between the way in which a preconscious content appears in consciousness and the way a repressed content does so, as I shall now set forth by citing two extreme instances.

A patient who was traveling abroad had the unpleasant experi-ence of being unable to recall the name of a colleague whom he knew very well. It was important that he recall the name, for he had to leave a message for him. As happens in such instances, a few words came to his mind that he was sure sounded almost like the name he sought, but he knew that none was exactly it. Since he felt ashamed to write home in order to obtain the name, he tried to analyze the apraxia. In the course of his free associations, he discovered to his surprise a flood of intense invectives, all of which were directed against the person whose name he had forgotten and centered in an advantage this colleague had obtained by a fortunate accident. Evidently the patient harbored the secret claim that fate should have given him preference. The patient was aware of the irrationality of his anger, of which he had not had the slightest inkling before his attempt at self-analysis. Yet, again to his surprise, despite the progress he made in understanding what was inhibiting his memory, the name he sought did not return. There was nothing for it but to write home. As soon as he was apprised of the colleague's name he, of course, immediately acknowledged it as the name he was looking for. It is this well-known feeling of recognition, of immediate awareness that a content is identical with one previously acquired that one has been searching for, that, in my opinion, provides a phenomenological index of a preconscious content. It may not be superfluous here to be quite exact in the phenomenological description. The subject was aware of a gap in the ideational continuum. He was eager to fill that gap but was unable to do so. He was never incapacitated in determining whether a suggested content was different from, similar to, or identical with the one he was in search of. When by communication from the outside he was provided with the erstwhile forgotten name, his situation was marked by three features that are relevant: (1) an immediate insight that this was the correct name; (2) a recollection of the past state when he was in possession of the temporarily forgotten name; (3) the absence of any feeling that he had incorporated something new. There was only the feeling that he had recovered a past content which had been part of his regular stock.

This is an example of what seems to be a substantial resistance against a preconscious content. "Resistance" is not quite the correct term. One has to assume that the colleague's name was debarred from consciousness by the bearing which the repressed had upon it. It fell victim to the attraction of a repressed impulse. This does not necessarily mean that it actually entered the area of the repressed; it only lost its mobility, its potential ability to ascend to consciousness. The difference is comparable to that between being held incommunicado and being imprisoned.[13]

It is interesting to speculate upon why this patient did not recover his colleague's name, even after having made a relevant step toward the analysis of his apraxia. There are two possibilities. (1) He was close to sixty and had the difficulties in remembering usual at that age. Thus an organic component not conquerable by self-analysis may have been at work.[14] (2) The necessity of having to write home to ask for the name was definitely experienced as a humiliation. Since a forbidden aggressive impulse had been the primary reason for his forgetting, the masochistic self-punishing tendency may have gotten the better of him (cf. Freud, 1916-1917, p. 69; Eidelberg, 1944). It was probably this repressed wish for punishment that held the preconscious element incommunicado.

The clinical situation just described is not without a noteworthy implication. The successful self-analysis brought an aggressive impulse to his attention. The unconscious feeling of guilt and need for punishment were apparently intensified by this insight, so that his chances of recovering the name fortuitously, as so often happens, were actually diminished. To be sure, the patient was unaware of the masochistic, self-punishing component and the infantile sources of his anger at the colleague. His insight had thus remained incomplete, despite the revealing associations that had come to his mind. Under less complicated circumstances, however, the kind of associations he had produced would have increased the likelihood of his recovering the forgotten name.

An opposite extreme to this situation is the following. A patient reports during the analytic session that on the previous day an image suddenly and unexpectedly came to his mind, of which he immediately had the feeling (or, better, the conviction) that it referred directly to a very early childhood recollection. It was the picture of a menstruating woman standing in a bathtub. Although he was certain that it must have referred to a recollection, he called it a "picture" because some formal traits were reminiscent of illustra-

13 However, the metapsychological description of true repression in a case of forgetting would be equivalent.

14 About psychophysiological factors in the forgetting of names, see Freud (1916-1917, p. 67).

tions in a cheap book of which he had been fond in latency. Together
with the image there came to his mind a sentence spoken in baby
talk which he also apprehended as words he must have spoken as
a child. This sentence, by the way, he later again forgot, but the
printlike picture remained with him. Furthermore, although in the
course of analysis it did not lose its initial isolation, he never doubted
its character as a reproduction of a reality observation which he must
have made in his first year of life, around the age of nine months,
as he was reasonably certain. Here is an instance of the sudden
upsurge of an archaic, deeply repressed memory. I was unable to
ascertain the factors responsible for the recall. It was certainly not
characteristic of the patient, and remained the only instance of its
kind in his analysis.

At the start of his treatment he had a recollection of about half
a dozen childhood memories dating from the first four years of his
life. His treatment contributed much insight into the meaning of
these recollections, but no new memories appeared aside from the
one reported; that is to say, despite a considerably better understanding of his early childhood, the infantile amnesia persisted
essentially unbreached. Thus, it would have been all the more important to understand the sudden giving in of the defense, but the event
remained as enigmatic as it was at the time when it occurred.[15]
Whether it is to be assumed that in such instances the repressed
enters directly into the *Cs.*, or whether under all circumstances the
repressed can communicate with the *Cs.* only through the passage
of the *Pcs.*, is not relevant here. If the latter is correct, then in this
instance the *Pcs.* had certainly been caught napping. I feel inclined
to assume that, in view of the ego's gradual transition into the id
outside of the repressed, and the practical indiscernibility of ego and
id under healthy conditions (Freud, 1926c, p. 201), direct commu-

[15] It may be worth while to add a few remarks about the sudden return of the
patient's early childhood memory. He had been told earlier in his analysis that he
might have made an observation referring to menstruation in his infancy. The patient
had admitted that such a possibility existed, but the matter remained peripheral. The
trend of his analysis did not converge upon this trauma or indicate that any particular
recollection was to be expected at that time. The recollection came like lightning from
a blue sky and remained isolated as it was initially. In view of all these factors it
seems to me reasonable to surmise that preconscious elaboration was minimal in this
instance.

nication between the repressed id and consciousness may be possible under special conditions.[16]

The essential point of my bringing this incident to the reader's attention is the way it struck the patient at the time of its appearance. Despite the full conviction of its reality character, there was not the slightest indication of insight that the suddenly rising image was identical with a previous event. That is to say, the feature of recognition of the identity of two conscious contents, such as appears when a forgotten name is remembered, was absent. There was only a feeling of conviction that the image came from infancy. I stress here the difference between the two meanings of the term *to recognize*. On the one hand it refers to the acknowledgment that a content is identical with a known previous experience (*wiedererkennen*); on the other, a fact is realized (*erkennen*).[17] The former is characteristic of the recall of preconscious contents, the latter of repressed ones. The reaction of Freud's patient to the recall of repressed contents: "As a matter of fact I've always known it" (Freud, 1914, p. 148), seems to fall into the latter category. Thus it is to be weighed that the two indices, actual or potential hypercathexis and recognition (*wiedererkennen*) are two clinical marks of preconscious contents.

Metapsychologically the difference between processes that make unconscious contents preconscious and preconscious contents conscious is comparable to that in a comparison Freud used occasionally, namely, the difference between the artist's work *per via di porre* and that *per via di lavare* (1905b, p. 260). In one instance something is added; in the other, something removed. When a repressed content is to rise to the *Pcs.*, a defense (countercathexis) has to be removed or weakened. When a preconscious content becomes conscious, cathexis has to be added. This hypercathexis is nothing else but what is called attention, to which Kris has attributed a special function in states of concentration (1950, p. 313f.).[18]

16 See, however, Kris (1950, p. 306), who suggests that the id can reach consciousness directly only by a pathological detour.

17 See also Kris (1950, p. 309). However, the context does not always make it clear which of the two meanings of recognition Kris had in mind.

18 In 1900 Freud wrote that *Pcs.* can only become *Cs.* when " 'attention' is distributed in a particular way" (p. 541), and later: "Becoming conscious is connected with the application of a particular psychical function, that of attention—a function which . . . is only available in a specific quantity" (p. 593). On this occasion Freud also wrote of dropping "the cathexis of attention" as if it were a conscious act or at least one that

Besides the points of differentiation I have so far enumerated, others can be found when two kinds of recall are considered. If I try to remember a telephone number or a name or any piece of information, I make efforts, I search, I think. My efforts, more frequently than not, are rewarded immediately. If not, there is dysfunction. The situation is quite different in most instances of the recall of dreams. We may wake up with a dream on our minds or with an immediate recollection of the dreams that were dreamed. Or we may wake up with the knowledge that we had a dream but be unable to remember it.[19] When the dreamer tries to recall the dream the way he tries to remember a name or piece of external information, he usually fails. A frequent report is that a certain event suddenly brought forth the recollection. The subject then usually does not have the feeling that *he* recalled it but rather that the *event* brought it to his mind (cf. Grotjahn, 1951). Typical is the recall of dreams while the subject is brushing his teeth (cf. Lewin, 1953), or, in the case of men, while shaving. Then we hear sometimes that the subject was not thinking of anything in particular, and suddenly the whole dream stood before his inner eye; sometimes the subject may be able to give the specific point of his ideation at which the dream recollection shot up. Of course, the instance is well known in which the subject during the analytic hour suddenly recalls a dream or complements a reported dream by the recall of a forgotten part (Freud, 1900, p. 518). All these instances are accompanied with a feeling of passivity, in contrast to the active effort of the recall of other information (by hypercathexis). The mode of dream recall is quite reminiscent of (though not identical with) the way Freud recommends a subject should proceed when he has forgotten a name that stubbornly refuses to return to memory. In this instance too the subject feels

---

occurs in the system *Cs.* And, further: ". . . a train of thought . . . is capable of attracting the attention of consciousness to itself and . . . , through the agency of consciousness, receives a 'hypercathexis' " (p. 594). Yet in a later section Freud wrote: "The system *Pcs.* . . . has at its disposal for distribution a mobile cathectic energy, a part of which is familiar to us in the form of attention" (p. 615). On the other hand, in 1911 attention was described by Freud as a function of consciousness (p. 220). Another passage (1915a, p. 192) about attention is debatable. I do not feel quite as certain as Mr. Strachey (*ibid.*, n.) that Freud there ascribed attention to *Pcs.*, but the passage is ambiguously worded and Mr. Strachey, of course, may be correct, particularly in view of the passage (p. 615) in the *Interpretation of Dreams.*

19 The instance of remembering a dream although there was no previous recollection of having dreamed I omit.

passive at the moment when the transitory amnesia is ended.[20] Notwithstanding the effect of repressive forces which come to the fore in the case of the forgetting of dreams, I believe that forgetting and recall of dreams deserves a more specific comment. When we recall dreams, are we lifting a preconscious content to Cs., or are we obtaining a repressed content? There is a general peculiarity about the recall of dreams which I believe has not been discussed before. To my best knowledge, there is no instance known in which the analytic procedure brought a past dream to consciousness that had not been recalled at least once by the subject within two days after it was dreamed.[21] That dreams are recalled within forty-eight hours, then forgotten for years and again recalled in analysis is by no means rare. But my observation refers to the fact that psychoanalysis is incapable of recovering a dream unless it has been redeposited in Cs. within a short span after having been dreamed. Are we dealing here with a peculiarity of the defense apparatus, with a peculiarity of counter-cathexis when directed against dream memories, or does this phenomenon depend on the vicissitudes of dream memories per se that are not subjected to secondary processes within a limited time?

Freud reported the observation that occasionally a dream that awakes the sleeper and is adequately analyzed by him, may, when the dreamer has fallen asleep again, never again return to memory afterwards (1900, p. 520). It is most surprising that the chains of associations that come into play during the analysis of a dream are also drawn into the act of forgetting. This observation of Freud's confirms the general peculiarity of dream recall. Is it possible that dreams not reproduced by the subject a short time following the

[20] Some of the situations favorable to recall of dreams I have mentioned here have one factor in common, namely, that attention is kept freely suspended; this favors the chance of free associations.

[21] According to Freud, a forgotten dream can be recalled "after three or four, or even more days" (1900, p. 520). I wonder whether a period of four days is not a rather rare occurrence and whether a special inquiry might not show that the dream had been recalled at least once before. Be this as it may, I take Freud's statement as a proof that dreams cannot be recovered by psychoanalysis unless they have been recalled at least once within a relatively short period of time after their occurrence. This is in distinct contrast to the recall of reality events or fantasies. Cf., however, Freud about the Wolf Man (1918): "There was another dream, which . . . I mention because it was forgotten [by the patient] until its appearance during the treatment" (p. 69). Yet it is not clear from this passage whether this is to be taken as meaning literally that the dream had never been remembered by the patient before.

dream are actually dissolved? This would be an example of the actual destruction of psychic material, so to speak, on a nonorganic basis.[22] This gives me the impression that the dream if not made fast by *Cs.* shortly after its recurrence is repressed. Its further vicissitude is a matter of speculation. What is of importance here is the mode of its first recall when the dream is made fast by *Cs.*, after which it may become part of *Pcs.* or it may be repressed again, yet apparently without forfeiting the possibility of later recovery. This first recall is a passive one; the phenomenological indices of hypercathexis are absent. The first release of the dream memory (unless present at the moment of awakening) is not under the control of the subject but depends on accidental constellations that may or may not lead to a relative weakening of countercathexis, such as is brought about by free associations or attention in free suspension. When the first dream recollection is evoked through an external stimulus, it is to be assumed that the attraction of the *Pcs.* has increased to such an extent that the energy balance between repressed and *Pcs.* has swung in favor of the latter, which amounts again to a relative weakening of countercathexis. We here encounter, however, an exception to previous propositions. The awakened dreamer who cannot recall the dreams of the past night experiences the absence of the recollection as a gap, and the first return of the memory is accompanied with a recognition that the memory is identical with the past dream (*wiedererkennen*), both being phenomenological indices I have postulated earlier for the return of temporarily debarred preconscious contents. We will also recall here that the return of repressed material is not always accompanied with isolation and strangeness, as I reported on the occasion of the afore-mentioned clinical example. Frequently, the return of a repressed memory is accompanied with recognition (*wiedererkennen*).

In order to evaluate the state of affairs I have to resort to a general statement which probably will not be accepted by most. The analytic process creates dynamic conditions that are contrary to the natural functioning of the psychic apparatus. In the psycho-

[22] That injury to brain substance may destroy psychic elements such as memories, etc., is well known. Freud's paper, "The Dissolution of the Oedipus Complex" (1924) is sometimes understood to make the same claim on a purely psychic basis. Be this as it may, in *Civilization and Its Discontents* (1930) Freud postulates for the psyche a law that is the equivalent of the physical law of conservation of energy or mass (pp. 69-71).

analytic situation we try to create a situation that may be called a dream with open eyes.[23] The access to motility is blocked and the state of free associations weakens the *Ucs.-Pcs.* censor as happens during sleep. No wonder that we have so much trouble in determining the indices of *Pcs.* and *Ucs.*, since our observations are obtained under conditions which flatten out the difference between the cathectic levels of the two systems. Yet not only is the cathexis of censors between systems reduced but so also is the tension between nuclei. It is not always easy to determine to which nucleus the individual association ought to be attributed when the patient is approaching a state of free association with concomitant lowering of resistance pressure. When the patient is in resistance, the various gradients of tensions become quite steep and then the metapsychological orientation is greatly facilitated. Yet the more the patient is drawn into the analytic process and the resistances become only little hills along a freely meandering path, the more the *Ucs.*—as far as it is convertible into words at all—approaches indices of *Pcs.*, yet without ever becoming identical with it. When a recollection returning from the repressed and appearing in *Cs.* is flavored by the quality of recognition (*wiedererkennen*) and is devoid of strangeness and isolation, it shows that the *Pcs.* has been adequately prepared for its reception. If Freud's technical advice to combine analysis of resistance with the creation of anticipatory ideas[24] is heeded, the appearance of a repressed recollection finds a preconscious content that is equivalent to and not very different from the repressed one. The merger of the two consequently gives the content emerging from the repressed the appearance of a preconscious product.

The psychoanalytic process puts a demand upon the psychic apparatus that is contrary to its natural functioning. The subject, inasmuch as he cooperates, naturally approaches the *Ucs.* as if it were *Pcs.*, and we encounter therefore during the psychoanalytic

23 Cf. Anna Freud: "The dreamer's psychic state differs little from that of the patient during the analytic hour" (1936, p. 15).

24 I prefer here the outdated terminology *Erwartungsvorstellung* that Freud used in 1909 (p. 104) and in his *Lectures* (1916-1917, p. 379) at a place where later he would have used the term *construction* or *reconstruction* (1938a). The constructions which the psychoanalyst conveys to the patient are, if correct, conscious ideational contents that should be confirmed by recollections which will later come to the patient's mind. Correct constructions, if properly timed, create in the patient ideas of what some of the repressed contents are.

process atypical phenomenological indices of the *Pcs*. It is appropriate to recall here an inference Freud drew: "the maintenance of certain internal resistances is a *sine qua non* of normality" (1938b, p. 39). The closer the subject is to the ideal state of free associations, the more these internal resistances become reduced. In other words, a subject in psychoanalysis does not find himself in a normal situation, and in so far as he lives up to the requirements of the analysis he moves away from a normal psychic state. It may be this deviation from normality that impedes a clear insight into certain aspects that are now in the center of psychoanalytic discussion.

In taking up the initial suggestion that the two systems *Cs*. and *Pcs*. are medial adaptations of the psychic apparatus for the purpose of communication between nuclei, I want to make a historical remark. Freud compared the diagram he devised of the psychic apparatus in the *Interpretation of Dreams* with a set of lenses in a microscope (1900, p. 536). When he introduced the structural aspect and divided the personality into ego and id, he compared the two with a rider on a horse (1923, p. 25). The lenses of a microscope are media; horse and rider, however, are nuclear concepts. It is noteworthy to observe that the metapsychological theory in Chapter VII of the *Interpretation of Dreams* lagged behind the actual achievement of the preceding chapters, inasmuch as the dream was correctly described as the result of a conflict between the nuclei of the personality, whereas the theory still depicted the personality as a set of media. Actually, after Freud described the personality as a set of nuclei in the *Ego and the Id*, a rewriting of *The Interpretation of Dreams* in accordance with the functional aspect would have required only a revision of Chapter VII. The clinical part of the book on dreams was not affected by this new step in metapsychology. Freud, in my estimation, had in 1923 brought metapsychology into harmony with his clinical investigations of 1900. But, by dropping *Cs*. and *Pcs*. entirely as systems, Freud, I believe, went too far. Not everything in man's personality is nuclear.[25] There are also medial agencies, as Freud so clearly set forth in his evolutionary idea of consciousness (1920, pp. 25-27). These systems are the stages on

[25] The difference between academic and psychoanalytic psychology can be described in molar terms by saying that the former investigates medial and the latter nuclear processes.

which important psychic processes take place. All three nuclei send their impulses into them. The conditions under which one or two of the nuclei dominate the systems to the exclusion or near exclusion of the rest, how the nuclei that are prevented from direct discharge into the systems circumvent obstacles and find new ways of discharge, all this is constantly under psychoanalytic surveillance.

The differentiation between system and nucleus may facilitate molar clinical descriptions. In the neuroses, the nuclei per se remain intact and the dysfunctions are caused by the unresolved counter-actions of nuclei, the battlefield probably being the systems. In the psychoses, however, the nuclei themselves are the victims of disease. The differentiation between nucleus and system may also help illu-minate why clinical syndromes that are similar, if not identical, nevertheless may prove to be caused by quite different disease proc-esses. Is it possible that the disparity between syndrome and under-lying disease processes stems from topographic differences? If a disease process occurs in a system, the resulting syndrome may show similarity with that of an equivalent process in a nucleus. Yet the dynamics of a nuclear disease must necessarily be quite different from one that affects a tract (system) only.

It is my impression that psychoanalytic metapsychology requires complementation by the phenomenological aspect. Of course, germs of such an aspect are strewn throughout psychoanalytic literature in large numbers, but they have never been systematically presented. It is to be expected that a psychoanalytic phenomenology, which probably would differ essentially from that of academic psychiatry, may show that the triad ego, id, superego does not suffice and that medial concepts, such as *Cs.* and *Pcs.*, are also necessary for a frame of reference that would do justice to the multifariousness and diver-sity of psychic phenomena.

But, in my opinion, there can be no doubt that present psycho-analytic metapsychology is direly lacking in what should be part and parcel of the structural aspect. Structure, after all, is not function alone, but function and form. It is the absence of a psychoanalytic morphology that impedes the development of essential theoretical potentialities. The functional hierarchy that is observed in the organization of the psychic apparatus has its equivalent topographical hierarchy, but the correlation between the two is not necessarily a close one.

A principal remark about the term *unconscious* must be added. The variety of meanings of the concept is well known: (1) Descriptive: everything that is not conscious is unconscious; (2) dynamic: everything that becomes conscious against resistance, or everything that is neither conscious nor preconscious, is unconscious; (3) topographical: the *Ucs.* is a psychic system dominated by the primary process; (4) structural: unconscious is a psychic quality of all processes that occur in the id and of some processes in the ego and the superego.

I will add another meaning, which will be accepted or rejected depending on whether or not psychic functions per se are considered to be conscious. As is well known, opinion is divided on this question.[26] Clinical observation seems to suggest that psychic functions themselves are not conscious even during the periods of their activity and, of course, not when at rest.[27]

Even if it should turn out that this cannot be claimed for all functions, it seems justified of the two principal groups of ego functions, perceiving and thinking. "That I perceive I know from the content of my perceptions; that I am thinking, I know from the sequence of thoughts" would be a summary of this view. Yet whether such functions, when operative, are represented by conscious indices as functions beyond the contents activated by them, is a question left moot in psychoanalytic literature. Since the psychoanalytic theory stresses so strongly that even the contents of those functions, i.e., perceptions, images, thoughts, may occur without being brought to awareness, the problem of functional representation has not aroused the interest it may deserve. If it is true that ego functions such as thinking and perceiving are not represented in consciousness, the indisputable fact that the function of defense is unconscious loses most of its metapsychological relevance. Indeed, even the best-analyzed person is not aware of repressing. He can only be aware of the result, and, at best, may take notice of the gaps created by repression.

26 Freud, as far as I know, never made a statement related to the problem.

27 Cf. Carl Stumpf in his famous paper of 1906. The crudest form of the question he raised would be: "Can we see our seeing?"

If another defense mechanism, projection, is considered, it is to be observed that as Freud pointed out, projection is biologically performed in the visual act, for retinal processes are projected into the visual world surrounding us (Freud, 1913, p. 64). Even subtle and refined self-analysis will fail to discover anything in the conscious mind that could be taken as a representational index of the biological process of ejecting the retinal image upon the source of visual stimulation. When projection, the mechanism of defense, is interpreted, its source, an unconscious impulse, and its result, a conviction allegedly based on perceptive or intellectual evidence, and their connections are brought to the patient's attention. But the mechanism or function of projection as such cannot possibly be experienced consciously. Thus the unconsciousness of the defense mechanism does not render it different from perceiving or thinking. The difference between the two lies in the unconsciousness of effect or relation. I know that I look at a thing, because I see it, but the subject does not know that he perceives a certain element because he projects it into a percept. If the proposition of some psychologists that most functions are unconscious while they are operative turned out to be correct, then some reformulation of structural propositions would in psychoanalysis become necessary. The unconsciousness of repression (defense), or countercathexis, or resistance would no longer be a distinguishing mark, but the unconsciousness of motives, impulses, and further the unawareness of the sources of potential displeasure, would become features which characterize the unconscious part of the ego versus its preconscious and conscious ones.

At first it will seem that not much is to be gained by this descriptive subtlety. However, if the proposition proved correct, it would emphasize the medial aspect of the system *Cs.* all the more. It would reduce further the assumed relevance of the system *Cs.* to the ego. It would adduce additional evidence that the ego is endowed to accomplish most of its achievements preconsciously, a proposition which figures so importantly in Freud's theory of the personality. However, in view of the many findings that seem to favor a debunking of consciousness either as a system or as a quality, one is inclined to ask: Is consciousness necessary at all? Disturbances of consciousness often have grave consequences and immediately threaten the subject's survival. However, disturbances of consciousness usually are not isolated but involve sundry other functions, although this does not occur with the regularity that might be expected. As a matter of fact, it is surprising how well a subject may function in what is called a state of "blackout." I had once an opportunity to observe a subject at a time during which, as it later turned out, she was in a twilight state. I do not believe that any observer would have guessed her state of reduced or even absent consciousness in view of her perfectly rational speech and activities. This condition lasted about ten days and ended in an attempt at suicide, but those ten days or so were not marked by any signs of irrationality.

In view of what the ego accomplishes without consciousness one may doubt its telic usefulness. No doubt, the ego needs an ideal medium, as Freud described it, and a system serves as a conveyor of stimuli during a twilight state too; only the quality conscious is absent. One may be tempted to deduce from Freud's evolutionary hypothesis of consciousness that consciousness was a price to be paid for the acquisition of an ideal medial system, and that the psychic apparatus would better serve its functions if it could operate unencumbered by the quality conscious. Appealing as this proposition may be, there is an observation that quickly proves its utter fallaciousness. All the surprising achievements of which the self is capable without resort to consciousness are only possible in the adult. An infant with even the slightest permanent defect which has a bearing on the evolvement of consciousness will show marked defects in its development, and thus the paramount importance of consciousness is well proved. But it is to be admitted that we are still ignorant of what there is in the quality conscious that makes it one of the mainstays of human existence.[28]

Recent psychoanalytic experimentation in the perception field may open up the possibility of more reliable formulations. I have a particular experiment of Fisher's in mind. Revising the experiments of Allers and Teler (1924) he investigated (1957) the subject's imagery after tachistoscopic exposure of pictures and found an unmistakable bearing of the pictures on the subject's subsequent

---

[28] In one instance Freud called *Bewusstheit* (the fact of consciousness) a symptom (1915a, p. 193), a far-reaching view whose depth has not yet been exhausted by psychoanalytic theory.

free-floating imagery. He states that "the memory images of the preconscious percepts derived from the tachistoscopically exposed picture appear in the images that develop during the period of free imagery" (p. 37). Yet the imagery Fisher studied subsequent to the tachistoscopic exposure emerges from the preconscious, and it is difficult, therefore, to accept the assignment of the tachistoscopic percepts to the same system. We may look at the situation as a miniature conflict. The memory traces of the tachistoscopically exposed pictures apparently show a trend toward ascending to the higher systems, but a barrier pervents them from full realization and all they can effect is to give preconscious productions a certain coloring. On a smaller scale there is repeated here a situation well known in psychoanalysis, when in the preconscious the derivatives of a repressed content are observed. Therefore, the memory traces of the tachistoscopically exposed pictures are to be assigned to the repressed. In a later paper Fisher and Paul (1959) assign sensory registration outside of awareness to the unconscious (p. 73).[29]

Fisher's afore-mentioned experiment is of incalculable importance because it follows, in my estimation, exactly the structure of what Freud designated by the term *primal repression*. Freud postulated two kinds of repressed. The archaic and older one consists of that part of the repressed that never was conscious. Fisher's experimental technique apparently manages to get a content into the unconscious (repressed) without its ever passing through the ego; in accordance with Freud's theory it can then by no means be brought to consciousness.[30] The authors report: "It must be emphasized that in our experiments the subject never recovers the memory of the actual event of sensory registration outside of awareness. When he compares the drawings of his dreams and images to the tachistoscopically

[29] However, the authors qualify this statement by wishing *unconscious* to be understood in the context "in the somatic sense suggested by Schilder" (Schilder, 1924, Ch. V, 12). It is not clear why the authors make this reservation at this point. I am not cognizant of any necessity to assume the nature of the unconscious to be different in this instance from the other instances which we call unconscious. For reasons against using the term *preconscious perception*—reasons that are probably even more valid regarding *unconscious perception*—see Klein (1959, p. 31).

[30] Cf. Fisher (1957, p. 43): "They [the percepts] could not have been repressed from consciousness because they were not capable of entering consciousness in the first place." Yet this is also true of the primal repressed. Dynamically it acts just like the repressed, but it does not owe its coming about to an act of repression.

exposed picture, there is still no conscious memory of the experience of sensory registration" (Fisher and Paul, p. 73).[31]

In other words, there is no *Wiedererkennen* possible and in principle the subject would have to accept any picture the experimenter showed him as the one he had registered without awareness. This, however, is not correct of all perceptions that occur without awareness. I may remember suddenly that I saw something hours ago which had totally escaped my attention. In the eidetic experiment, too, details the subject had not noticed can be recovered, as happens also in hypnosis. Consequently, one may draw the conclusion that three forms of registration occur most of the time while the perceptive apparatus is fully or approximately fully activated: (1) registration with awareness; (2) registration without awareness but recoverable spontaneously or under special conditions; (3) registration without awareness that can under no conditions be recovered but may or may not have effects upon subsequent psychic processes.[32]

It is apparently the third form of registration that is still active even when the perceptive apparatus has suspended the two other modes of functioning. Freud, at least, reported a dream sample that speaks strongly in favor of unrecoverable registration without awareness even during sleep. When he had dreamed that the Pope was dead, he was unable to find an explanation of the dream until his wife asked him whether he had heard "the dreadful noise" caused by the early ringing of all the church bells in the vicinity (1916-1917, p. 84f.). It is reasonable to assume that even deepened analysis would not have unearthed the recollection of the auditory disturbance which no doubt had been registered and given color to the subsequent dream. The subliminal registration during sleep helps the ego to prolong its sleep, thus favoring the gratification of a biological need. It is difficult to speculate upon the function of registration without awareness in the tachistoscopic experiment. A teleological view would emphasize that stimulation of such short duration

[31] It would be an interesting experiment to see whether a subject in deep hypnosis might be able to recover the original tachistoscopically exposed pictures (or whether a subject when in such deep hypnosis possesses the capacity of registering tachistoscopically exposed pictures with awareness). If recovery in hypnosis occurs, this would obviate a comparison with the primal repressed.

[32] It may not be without consequences that in the perceptive area also we encounter three "qualities" that fairly coincide with Freud's ideas about *Cs.*, *Pcs.*, and *Ucs.*

as occurs in this sort of experiment may perhaps not be taking place under natural conditions and that such short exposure is therefore not ego-relevant, at least in terms of survival.

Be this as it may, the recent experiments demonstrate abundantly that the perceptive apparatus functions in a twofold way, namely, in the service of the ego which has to be provided with environmental data, and also in the service of the repressed. It seems that the insatiable id sucks in all that on which the ego does not or cannot lay its hands; automatically an undetermined number of registrations are pumped into the repressed.[33] If one likes teleological deliberations, one may speculate upon an attempt at preventing an overloading of the integrative capacity. On the other hand, the ever-present buoyancy of the repressed may exert attraction upon stimuli of whatever source that are disregarded by the ego.

To come back to the subject matter, I believe that these experiments permit that one postulate an unconscious connection between the perceptive apparatus and the id, that is to say, that there are apparently also media connecting nuclei that work in a way that is comparable to Freud's earlier description of the system *Ucs*.[34]

We come close here to the question of whether or not all perceptions go through a stage that is outside of consciousness, a problem Fisher has so ably discussed (1957, pp. 44-54). In my opinion, both positions are compatible with Freud's views on the working of the psychic apparatus. There is, no doubt, an area where experiment, in the narrower sense of the word, will legitimately adduce an answer which observations in the psychoanalytic situation can hardly supply.

BIBLIOGRAPHY

Allers, R. & Teler, J. (1924), On the Utilization of Unnoticed Impressions in Associations. In: *Preconscious Stimulation in Dreams, Associations, and Images* [*Psychological Issues*, Monogr. No. 7]. New York: International Universities Press, 1960.

Arlow, J. A. & Brenner, C. (1960), The Concept 'Preconscious' and the Structural Theory. Abstract by Walter A. Stewart in *Psa. Quart.*, XXIX.

Brenner, C. (1955), *An Elementary Textbook of Psychoanalysis*. New York: International Universities Press.

[33] This may be used as an experimental proof of Freud's observation that every act of repression is one of *Nachdrängen* (afterpressure) (1915a, p. 180f.; 1915b, p. 148).

[34] Cf. Freud (1915a, p. 194): "Normally all the paths from perception to the *Ucs*. remain open."

—— (1957), The Nature and Development of the Concept of Repression in Freud's Writings. *This Annual*, XII.

Eidelberg, L. (1944), A Further Contribution to the Study of Slips of the Tongue. *Int. J. Psa.*, XXV.

Fisher, C. (1957), A Study of the Preliminary Stages of the Construction of Dreams and Images. *J. Amer. Psa. Assn.*, V.

—— & Paul, I. H. (1959), The Effect of Subliminal Visual Stimulation on Images and Dreams: A Validation Study. *J. Amer. Psa. Assn.*, VII.

Freud, A. (1936), *The Ego and the Mechanisms of Defense*. New York: International Universities Press, 1954.

Freud, S. (1900), The Interpretation of Dreams. *Standard Edition*, IV & V. London: Hogarth Press, 1953.

—— (1905a), Jokes and Their Relation to the Unconscious. *Standard Edition*, VIII. London: Hogarth Press, 1960.

—— (1905b), On Psychotherapy. *Standard Edition*, VII. London: Hogarth Press, 1953.

—— (1909), Analysis of a Phobia in a Five-year-old Boy. *Standard Edition*, X. London: Hogarth Press, 1955.

—— (1911), Formulations on the Two Principles of Mental Functioning. *Standard Edition*, XII. London: Hogarth Press, 1958.

—— (1913), Totem and Taboo. *Standard Edition*, XIII. London: Hogarth Press, 1955.

—— (1914), Remembering, Repeating and Working-Through. *Standard Edition*, XII. London: Hogarth Press, 1958.

—— (1915a), The Unconscious. *Standard Edition*, XIV. London: Hogarth Press, 1957.

—— (1915b), Repression. *Standard Edition*, XIV. London: Hogarth Press, 1957.

—— (1916-1917), *A General Introduction to Psycho-Analysis*. New York: Garden City Publishing Co., 1938.

—— (1917), A Metapsychological Supplement to the Theory of Dreams. *Standard Edition*, XIV. London: Hogarth Press, 1957.

—— (1918), From the History of an Infantile Neurosis. *Standard Edition*, XVII. London: Hogarth Press, 1955.

—— (1920), Beyond the Pleasure Principle. *Standard Edition*, XVIII. London: Hogarth Press, 1955.

—— (1921), Group Psychology and the Analysis of the Ego. *Standard Edition*, XVIII. London: Hogarth Press, 1955.

—— (1923), The Ego and the Id. *Standard Edition*, XIX. London: Hogarth Press, 1961.

—— (1924), The Dissolution of the Oedipus Complex. *Standard Edition*, XIX. London: Hogarth Press, 1961.

—— (1925), Negation. *Standard Edition*, XIX. London: Hogarth Press, 1961.

—— (1926a), Psycho-Analysis. *Standard Edition*, XX. London: Hogarth Press, 1959.

—— (1926b), Inhibitions, Symptoms and Anxiety. *Standard Edition*, XX. London: Hogarth Press, 1959.

—— (1926c), The Question of Lay Analysis. *Standard Edition*, XX. London: Hogarth Press, 1959.

—— (1930), Civilization and Its Discontents. *Standard Edition*, XXI. London: Hogarth Press, 1961.

—— (1932), *New Introductory Lectures on Psychoanalysis*. New York: Norton, 1933.

—— (1937-1939), *Moses and Monotheism*. London: Hogarth Press, 1951.

—— (1938a), Constructions in Analysis. *Collected Papers*, V. London: Hogarth Press, 1950.

—— (1938b), *An Outline of Psychoanalysis*. New York: Norton, 1949.

Grotjahn, M. (1951), The Inability to Remember Dreams and Jokes. *Psa. Quart.*, XX.

Hartmann, H. (1950), Comments on the Psychoanalytic Theory of the Ego. *This Annual*, V.

—— Kris, E., & Loewenstein, R. M. (1949), Notes on the Theory of Aggression. *This Annual*, III/IV.

Heider, F. (1926), Thing and Medium. In: *On Perception and Event Structure, and the Psychological Environment* [*Psychological Issues,* Monogr. No. 3]. New York: International Universities Press, 1959.

—— (1930), The Function of the Perceptual System. In: *On Perception and Event Structure, and the Psychological Environment* [*Psychological Issues,* Monogr. No. 3]. New York: International Universities Press, 1959.

Kant, E. (1763), Der einzig mögliche Beweisgrund zu einer Demonstration des Daseins Gottes. In: *Immanuel Kant's sämtliche Werke in sechs Bänden.* Leipzig: Insel verlag, 1912-1921, IV:113-232.

Klein, G. S. (1959), Consciousness in Psychoanalytic Theory: Some Implications for Current Research in Perception. *J. Amer. Psa. Assn.,* VII.

Kris, E. (1950), On Preconscious Mental Processes. In: *Psychoanalytic Explorations in Art.* New York: International Universities Press, 1952.

Lewin, B. D. (1953), The Forgetting of Dreams. In: *Drives, Affects, Behavior,* ed. R. M. Loewenstein. New York: International Universities Press.

Schilder, P. (1924), *Medical Psychology.* New York: International Universities Press, 1953.

Stumpf, C. (1906), *Erscheinungen und psychische Funktionen* [*Phenomena and Psychic Functions*]. Berlin: Reimer, 1907.

NOTES ON THE SUPEREGO

HEINZ HARTMANN, M.D. and
RUDOLPH M. LOEWENSTEIN, M.D. (New York)

I

It has been said that in psychoanalysis today we find two trends, one of which tends to underestimate the role of the superego compared to that of the ego, while of the second the opposite is true. We think there is some truth in this statement, but we ought to see it in perspective. First of all, we will not be misled into concluding that the isolated study, for certain purposes, of only the one or the other area of the psychoanalytic field means a neglect or an underrating of others. A certain degree of specialization is, today even more than in the past, not only legitimate but has actually proved very fruitful, in analysis as in other sciences. We may also remind you here that Freud found it necessary to object repeatedly to the misunderstanding that his concentration on certain aspects of mental life meant he overlooked or underrated the importance of others which he had not yet, or not yet as carefully, studied. However, what we do ask of every specializing study in analysis, whether it concentrates on the ego, the id, the superego, or any other partial subject, is that it is seen in the framework of the data and theories of psychoanalytic psychology as a whole. At this point, we do not propose to go deeper into the methodological question except in so far as it has an immediate bearing on the themes discussed here.

Theories which set the formation of the superego at a much earlier stage than Freud did—and many do—show a tendency, in contrast to what we just said, to disregard observations and

Paper read at the XXIInd Congress of the International Psycho-Analytical Association in Edinburgh, August 2, 1961.

We want to acknowledge that this paper was first outlined at a time when we still enjoyed the participation of Ernst Kris in our work.

hypotheses in ego psychology that we consider as valid. Some of those constructions seem even more questionable today than they could appear in the past, since a more differentiated knowledge of the development and the functions of the ego has evolved. In a general way, we should think it incompatible with what we know about ego development today to attribute to the superego—as has been done here and there in the psychoanalytic literature—already in the earliest development of the child everything that opposes his instinctual drives from within. These views do not explain the defensive tendencies and capacities of the ego itself, or the role reality plays in their development. You remember what Freud said about the risk we run of overestimating the role of the superego in repression. And, of course, we will think here of A. Freud's (1936) findings on the primary enmity of the ego vis-à-vis the drives; furthermore, of the fact that many inborn apparatus that serve the ego actually are of an inhibiting character (Hartmann, 1952). The picture of the relative roles of ego and superego in child development is also easily distorted—and in the same direction—if in extrapolating our analytic experience to the earliest developmental stages, one fails to consider the processes of both maturation and learning.

We do not suggest that those phenomena or processes that some have described as early forms of the superego are actually without any relation to it. Quite apart from the fact that there is often an analogy of function (sometimes, it is true, a rather vague and superficial one), there is also frequently a true genetic connection between these early phenomena and the superego. Still, we propose to distinguish clearly such genetic determinants from the system superego. It seems preferable to reserve the term superego, as Freud did, to that momentous step in structuralization which is linked with the resolution of the conflicts of the oedipal phase. While this gives the superego its place in the developmental continuum, its definition rests on its functions (e.g., conscience, self-criticism, the function of holding up ideals). Such a definition of the substructures of personality in terms of their functions corresponds to a dominant trend in Freud's later thinking which appears to be the most adequate way of accounting for some essential problems of a structural psychology. It has been emphasized repeatedly (Hartmann, 1955; and elsewhere) that the lack of a clear distinction between function and genesis tends to create confusion not only in the special chapter of analysis we are discussing now. The concept of secondary autonomy in ego psychology is a direct outcome of stressing the difference between the functional and the genetic approach, and we shall see that an analogous concept suggests itself also with respect to the superego.

Freud spoke sometimes of the superego as a differentiated grade "within the ego." We consider the superego, as is commonly done, as a system in its own right. Freud's occasional term *"Stufe im Ich"* might have referred to the genetic connections between ego and superego. But we will not discuss the possible implications of that phrase. Whatever they might be, we want to make it quite clear at this point that Freud certainly never tended to overlook or underrate the genetic connections which link the superego to the id.

We may mention here, too, that we consider the superego, as Freud did, as *one* system of personality, despite its various aspects. We would not, as has occasionally been suggested, consider the ego ideal as a separate system—separate from another system that would comprise other superego functions such as, e.g., conscience. As will be discussed later, the connections between the ego ideal and the prohibitive aspects of the superego are so close that both should be considered as aspects of one and the same system.

Genetic determinants of the superego have often been termed its forerunners, or forestages, or primordia. There is nothing to be said against any of these terminological distinctions, as long as one keeps in mind the differences between function and genesis to which we have just referred; and as long as one sees these factors only as genetic determinants and not as parts of the system superego. To make these distinctions appears particularly necessary in those instances, mentioned before, in which the determinants seem to be in some way or other "similar" to what we recognize as superego function. It is very likely that a genetic tie leads from what Ferenczi called "sphincter morality" to the later superego; but the word "morality" is misleading in this context because it neglects the difference we have in mind. A similar question is familiar from the history of biology: it has long been assumed that the grown form of the organism is preformed in its earliest beginnings. It has taken quite some time before the notion of epigenesis, which is opposed to this view, was generally accepted. In psychoanalysis we face a problem somewhat akin to this one. (For its role in Erikson's work [1950a, 1950b], see, e.g., Rapaport, 1958; see also Bibring, 1947.)

II

For some time it has partly been known and partly been surmised that the oedipal situation as well as preoedipal development, the phallic phase as well as the prephallic phases, and also the maturation and development of the ego influence the formation of the superego. In Freud's classical presentation of the subject the accent is on the immediate and decisive causes: on the oedipal situation, on the fear of castration, and on those key identifications which form the core of the superego. His essential statements on the role of these factors are as valid today as they were at the time when he first formulated them.[1] Later, a broader and in some respects more specific knowledge of the earlier determinants has been added, both from direct observation and from analytic reconstruction. However, we think that this additional knowledge in no way contradicts Freud's basic theses. Some of the results of later research we consider to be well established, while at certain points question marks are in order.

We spoke of the fact that the early general prerequisites, or more specific early psychic determinants, of superego formation can be found in the object relations, or in the development of the ego and the instinctual drives. In this context we might briefly mention another point (to which we do not propose to return): one might wonder whether or not we can speak of inherited traits of the superego—as we do in the cases of the ego and the id. Biologists know that inherited characteristics may make their appearance not at birth but often at a much later time. Moreover, it is true that maturation may proceed without the guidance of function as such (Weiss, 1949). But we want to state that, in our opinion, present knowledge does not provide us with any cogent reason to speak of inheritance in the case of the superego. What one might be tempted to explain as inheritance can also be traced to tradition, to processes of identification, and to inherited characteristics of ego and drives. With respect to the first group of these phenomena, some authors speak of "social

[1] To the historical aspect see also J. Strachey's notes to *The Ego and the Id* (1923).

inheritance," but this concept can easily be misunderstood. More-over, we think it advisable not to use the term maturation with respect to the superego, though this term correctly applies to certain early determinants of the superego which belong partly to the ego and partly to the drives.

There is no doubt that the ways in which the child's developing ego deals in the first years of life with danger from the outside world and danger from the side of the instinctual drives influence the later superego development. The individual history of the child's reac-tions to the earliest sequence of typical anxiety conditions leaves an imprint on castration anxiety and is significant for the individual formation of the superego. The choice of defense mechanisms and their synergisms are, of course, also clearly relevant in this respect. Even those earlier apparatus of the ego which are likely to be forerunners of later defense have to be taken into consideration. Among the defenses Jacobson (1954) emphasizes particularly, and probably rightly, the role of reaction formation as a determinant of the superego. Actually, Freud referred to the ego ideal as "partly a reaction formation against the instinctual processes in the id" (1923). Other defense mechanisms, such as identification, projec-tion, denial, and so on, play a role in the formation of the system superego. Furthermore, we consider it probable that among the determinants which the ego contributes, its early intrasystemic con-flicts are also important. The disposition to intrasystemic conflicts in the ego may well be one of the factors that prepare for the later superego-ego conflicts.

In a general way, the degree of maturity which the child's ego has reached at the time his superego is formed appears to be relevant. More specifically, the level of intellectual development (Hartmann, Kris, and Loewenstein, 1946) and the development of language, for instance, must be considered. It is hardly necessary to remind you of the relations between the auditory sphere and the superego which Freud (1923) suggested (see also Isakower, 1939). The capacity for self-observation (we consider it a function of the ego and will have more to say about it later), the faculty of part of the ego to make mental phenomena the objects of its perception, is another precon-dition of superego development. Another essential factor is the degree of objectivation achieved in inner and outer perception and in thinking. Not really quite independent from the determinants we just mentioned, we must consider the potential for sublimation or, more generally put, for neutralization, and this partly in relation to identification and partly independent of it. We say this without wanting to imply that the energy commonly used by the superego is neutralized to the same degree to which, e.g., the energy feeding intellectual processes is. Furthermore, different aspects of the super-ego (let us say the ego ideal on the one hand, conscience on the other) do not necessarily work with the same degree of neutralization. Finally, we want at least to mention the possibility that the cathexes of superego contents may differ in this respect from the cathexes of superego functions.

Such a somewhat dreary enumeration of ego dispositions and activities that actually do influence or might influence the formation of the superego is of necessity unsatisfactory, in more than one respect. We know very well that each one of the points we make here in a cursory way calls for a special study. For the purpose of presen-tation we have isolated what can be fully understood only in the context of object relationships and of the development of the child's own body and his perceptions of it. We also note that some of the determinants we referred to are in the nature of rather general preconditions, while others show a more specific relation to the spe-cific features of the superego. Furthermore, it appears that some of them seem more relevant for the evolution of one aspect of the superego, the ego ideal, whereas others seem to determine primarily another aspect (self-criticism or conscience).

Some of the influences we mentioned may suggest the hypothesis that the degree of autonomy which the ego has achieved at the height of the phallic phase is an important factor also in regard to the system superego. And beyond this, we may ask whether the ego's autonomy is, more specifically, one of the determinants of the super-ego's independence (or autonomy). This is, no doubt, a highly com-plex question to which we have no ready answer. But we consider it not unlikely that this hypothesis could shed some light on a prob-lem which has always been controversial in psychoanalysis, namely, the particular characteristics of the feminine superego (Sachs, 1928; Jacobson, 1937; Greenacre, 1948). Some of the features often attrib-uted to it might be easier understood if we keep in mind not only that its origin is less climactic than in the boy and that its formation extends over a longer period, but also that in the girl the ego ideal tends to set in earlier, that is, at a time when integration and objectivation, and their autonomous functioning, are, comparatively speaking, less developed (Hartmann's discussion of Greenacre's paper, 1948).

The role which identifications play in the superego structure itself is an essential part of Freud's clinical and theoretical conceptions; it is generally accepted among psychoanalysts. More uncertain is our knowledge of the extent and the ways in which earlier identifications in the ego determine superego formation. A. Reich (1954) has studied this question in a thoughtful paper, and her views are in many respects close to our own thinking on the subject. More recently Beres (1958), Spitz (1958), Sandler (1960), and Ritvo and Solnit (1960) have approached various aspects of this problem—the last-named authors by using observations in a longitudinal study. Each one of these studies contains some findings and thoughts which we consider important. But in this paper we cannot do more than discuss a few selected facets of the intriguing superego problems in which so many questions of concept formation and of theory seem to converge.

III

Before proceeding further in this direction, we feel we should say at least a few words about some analytic terms commonly used in this context, that is, internalization, identification, incorporation, and introjection. While all these concepts are sometimes used interchangeably in our literature, some of the authors quoted before have suggested a differential use of these terms. We would speak of *internalization* when regulations that have taken place in interaction with the outside world are replaced by inner regulations (Hartmann, 1939). The development through which trial activities in the outside world are gradually replaced by thought processes is an example of what we have in mind. In this as in most cases of this kind, it is easy to see the difference between these processes and, let us say, identification. But we admit that there are also instances in which it is less easy to draw the line.

Not all analysts assign exactly the same meaning to the term *identification;* and we have already stated that there are certainly different kinds of identification. Some questions as to its metapsychology are under discussion. But we all agree that the result of identification is that the identifying person behaves in some ways like the person with whom he has identified himself. The likeness may refer to the characteristics, features, attitudes of the object, or to the role the object plays in reality (or to the role it plays in reality according to the fantasy of the person who makes the identification): it may mean to "take the place" of the other person. Freud (1921) describes it also as "moulding oneself" after the fashion of the object that has been taken as a model. We use the term both for the process and for the result. Freud usually describes it as taking place in the ego; but there are, of course, also the identifications he described as forming the superego. There are also different degrees to which what had been part of an object representation becomes, through the process of identification, part of a self-representation.

Incorporation we call an instinctual activity, belonging primarily to the oral phase. It is considered a genetic precursor of identification; and the latter is formed after its model. Clinically, we often find incorporation fantasies connected with identification. And actual identification processes may through a kind of appeal to their genetic forerunners reactivate such fantasies. Despite their genetic relationship, it is not advisable to use the term incorporation as a synonym of identification, which is indubitably not just an instinctual activity.

When Freud began to use the term *introjection,* he attributed it to Ferenczi and occasionally also put it in quotation marks. But soon it was used quite generally both by him and by other analysts. It is questionable that the meaning commonly attributed to the concept today is really identical with the one Ferenczi had in mind, but we do not propose to discuss this historical issue in the context of this paper. At present, we find introjection used as synonymous with identification, sometimes with incorporation, and even with internalization. Some emphasize the defensive character of introjection; that is, they connect this character more closely with introjection than with the other concepts under discussion. Others call introjection the process by which identifications are built. In addition, we encounter the statement that introjection represents a

regression to the oral stage, though this has also been said of identification. We just spoke of the appeal to the genetic instinctual
precursors which identification may induce. But this does not mean
that identification, or introjection, *is* a regression. The extent to
which identification may lead to regression depends, as it does in the
case of other ego functions, on the degree of the ego's autonomy.

In looser connection with our topic, we would like to repeat
what we have said elsewhere (Hartmann, 1939): we do not consider
it justified to describe perception as such as introjection or identification (nor, for that matter, as projection), though it is true that
particularly in early stages of development perception tends to lead
to identifying imitation (to this latter point, see Fenichel, 1945).
What seems comparable, in perception, to introjection or to projection is actually not its psychological character but the physiological
process connected with it. The development of object representation,
of images of the objects, certainly creates an "inner" representation
of the outside world, but here, too, we would hesitate to speak of
identification or introjection. It might be more appropriate to attribute this process to internalization, though this does not seem to be
quite satisfactory either—and we shall leave this very complex problem here. But we want to emphasize at this point that object representations obviously must be described, in common terminology, as
parts of the "inner world."[2] Still, and this is equally obvious, one
cannot say, as is sometimes implied in discussions of this subject, that
this character of the object representations of being part of the inner
world effaces their distinction from the self-representations; or that
this character is the result of something that could be equated with
introjection or identification. This would clearly blur the latter
concepts in a way which we would consider confusing. This distinction, it is hardly necessary to stress, does not imply that the parts of
the inner world which we call object representations do not influence
both our identifications and our relationships to the real objects.
These and related points are more comprehensively discussed in a
recent important paper by Sandler (1960).

The terminological aspects of these problems—or more precisely, the question of the expediency of these terms—are not easy

2 We use this concept (Hartmann, 1939) in a broader sense than does Freud in his
Outline (1938).

to decide. In some instances we should know more about the psychological processes involved before the questions of appropriateness of terms can be decided in a more definite way. Some of the hints we give here should therefore be considered to be of a tentative nature. The uncertainties of definition seem to be particularly marked in the case of introjection. The term, as we have said, is often used as a synonym of identification, or as a process through which identification is being brought about, so that one would come to question the necessity of introducing this concept. But there are clear, and probably good, reasons why the word continues to be used; one reason being that we can derive from the word introjection the terms "introjected" and "introject"—we speak of introjected objects, also of "introjected restrictions," and so on. There is no word derived from the word identification which is equally well suited to designate that which in the process or as a consequence of the process is "taken in" and more or less integrated. A more important reason is that for many the distinction between identification and introjection has come to refer to differences in the degree to which this "taking in," this integration, has been accomplished. We would also consider the relation between the degree of integration and the degree to which self-representation has been substituted for object representation. These two factors vary partly independently. We further want to add that Sandler, in the paper just quoted, considers it the specific feature of the introject that it has the capacity to substitute for the real object as a source of narcissistic gratification. What we say here does not exhaust the actual differences of the two terms in analytic usage (see also Knight, 1940; and Axelrad and Maury, 1951).

IV

It is true that already in early ego development we find some identifications which are not fully integrated in the ego (A. Reich, 1954) and which may remind one of those in the superego which "stand apart." But we have said before that we prefer to regard the former as genetic determinants, without classifying them as "early forms" of the superego. At any rate, the role which such early identifications in the ego play in the mental life of the child of one or two years of age is rather different from the role which the later identifications that become part of the superego are called on to play—in their interaction with the features of the phallic phase and with the passing of the oedipus complex. That is to say, the role of identification depends, at least partly, upon the developmental level on which it takes place. If we knew more than we actually do about the ontogenesis of identification, we would be in a better position to approach the question whether at different stages of growth and development there are differences not only in the psychic milieu in which identification takes place, but also in the processes of identification itself. It is likely that the term identification covers a variety of phenomena, as Greenson (1954) and Jacobson (1954) have suggested, differing at least as to the degree to which this or that aspect of the process is in the foreground. This variety is certainly not limited to the familiar distinction of "total" and "partial" identifications. Some forms have been thoroughly studied, particularly "identification with the aggressor" which A. Freud (1936) has explicitly described as one normal step determining superego formation (see also Spitz, 1957). Identifications (and projections) made at a time when the demarcation of self and object is not yet fully established are not quite the same as those on a higher level. Identification made at the stage of the need-satisfying object may well differ from that made at the stage of object constancy. Some identifications deal with reality problems, others master primarily actual anxiety situations, some serve the mastery of instinctual demands. There is a long way from the primitive imitative forms that mostly serve the mastery of reality, to the role play, and to the momentous changes we see in the case of superego formation. One major distinction certainly lies in the degree of independence from the objects which the process brings about. What in the pre-superego child (and even at the beginning of true superego development) is brought about by identification still depends as to function and reliability of function very much on the child's actual relationship to the objects (A. Freud, 1926). That is to say, depending upon the situation, object relationship, level of development, there are variations in the degree to which what has been "taken over" from another person by way of identification becomes an independent possession of the child. Critical situations will reveal the thresholds of integration; i.e., the degree to which the results of identification have become part of "one's own." To avoid misunderstandings we have to add that even at the level of greater independence more primitive identifications can be used; some do survive from earlier days. Nor should we forget that after the passing of the oedipus complex has led to the identifications which represent the core of the superego, the child still develops new identifications with the parents. These, however, are of a different kind and mostly—though not exclusively—affect the ego without influencing the superego (Freud, 1932).

There is another respect in which early ego identifications differ from those later ones which become part of the superego. Freud (1923) states that identification results in desexualization. This is probably true of both forms of identification we are considering here. In addition, Freud introduced a second economic hypothesis concerning identification. It assumes that in the process aggression is set free. We do not propose to discuss at this point whether Freud meant this assertion to be generally valid; we rather think that he would not have intended it to include those identifications which he has described as preceding object relationships. We may state—and this is the point relevant to our present argument—that we are inclined to consider Freud's hypothesis valid in so far as it refers to superego formation. We are not equally convinced of its validity in the case of the earliest identification we just mentioned, or in the case of the somewhat later but still pre-superego identifications in the ego. It is our impression that this setting free of aggression is definitely less evident in these cases than in the case of the formation of the superego.[3] Both comments we just made are intended to facilitate a better understanding of the special position we attribute to those identifications which form parts of the superego.

V

Turning now to determinants on the side of the drives, we will have to limit severely the presentation of this vast subject. We mentioned before that on the side of the drives, the phallic phase as well as the earlier oral and anal libidinal phases influence the general and individual features of the system superego. The latter do this in two

[3] In the case of identification with the aggressor, it seems unconvincing to assume that the child's aggression is set free as a consequence of desexualization.

ways: first, by their effect on the phallic phase and thus also on the oedipal situation and the way in which it is resolved; second, indirectly by the modeling of ego functions after oral and anal patterns, and by the reaction formations which oral and anal tendencies provoke from the side of the ego. In this context we must also take into consideration the resulting ratio of active and passive, and of male and female components. This ratio helps to shape in a definite way the form which the oedipus complex takes, and thus also the type of superego that emerges. In this context one might expect also a discussion of the contributions which the vicissitudes of narcissism make to superego formation, and particularly of the role which some of them play among the forerunners of the ego ideal. But we decided to deal with these questions later, when we shall take a closer look at this aspect of the superego.

Furthermore, among the vicissitudes of the instinctual drives described by Freud, one, the "turning upon the self," looks very much like a potential forerunner of the superego's turning aggression against oneself. Some authors have explicitly stated this possibility. We think it could well be one of the frequent cases in which a characteristic of the drives is used as a prototype also of noninstinctual functions. On the other hand, we do not know much about it clinically and would at any rate not assume a simple and direct correlation.

Generally speaking, we should expect the history of earliest aggressions to be relevant to our understanding of the superego. This becomes especially true if we also add what we know or surmise of the vicissitudes of neutralized aggression. Nor will we forget that according to one of Freud's late ideas (1937), the amount of free aggressive energy contributes to the disposition to mental conflict, and this theory, too, might come to add to our knowledge of superego-ego relations. However, this is again an idea which unfortunately has so far not been widely applied to clinical thinking, nor, for that matter, to the direct observation of children. Another Freudian hypothesis (1930) which fared better in this respect says that from a certain age on aggression resulting from frustration can be taken over by the superego. This is true once the superego has been formed, but it is also true already for the formation of the superego. However, there also exist situations in which aggression provoked by frustration can be used in a more neutralized mode for building countercathexes (Hartmann, 1953). We are then confronted with the question why in some cases the one and in others the other way of dealing with aggression is used. Most of the time we are far from being able to answer this question.

We briefly alluded to the hypothesis of the preferential use of neutralized aggressive energy in countercathexes (Hartmann, 1950). This hypothesis is relevant to our topic also because, if it proves correct, it would mean that the turning of more or less neutralized aggression by one part of the personality against another part, and the contribution of neutralized aggression to structure formation, does not begin with the superego, but is already earlier a regular occurrence in the ego's building of defense mechanisms. What we said before about early defenses as determinants of superego formation thus gets a more specific economic foundation.

In a paper such as this one, we may claim the right to fall short of a systematical presentation.[4] Thus we will not discuss here, or only in a peripheral way, what is certainly the most important factor in the development of the superego: its being "heir to the Oedipus complex." The complicated relations that this word covers have been stated mainly by Freud (1923), in great detail and with incomparable clarity. We will not repeat the fundamental insights into the subject which he presented in *The Ego and the Id* and elsewhere. These relations find their expression also in the fact that the superego does not reach its full development if the overcoming of the oedipus complex "has not been completely successful" (Freud, 1932). We may just remind you of what has since been learned about the preoedipal object relationships and their developmental impact also on the superego; about the influence of "good" object relations, but also of frustrations and narcissistic wounds, on structure formation, first in the ego and then as a determining factor in superego development. Today we know somewhat more about the effects of environmental factors, and the range of adaptational processes, with respect to the earliest object relations. We should add that constant object relations promote neutralization, and that on the other hand

---

[4] Within the scope of this paper we could not utilize the rich material contained in the Superego Manual of the Index of the Hampstead Child-Therapy Clinic, nor could we discuss some recently published papers on the superego.

neutralization benefits the formation of object constancy (Hartmann, 1952).

There is, of course, also the anticipation of danger and the objectivation of outer and inner reality. Both factors play a role in the
resolution of the oedipal conflicts and in the formation of the superego. The child has learned to relate the means to the ends; and in
his relations with the objects, he takes into account what the evolving
reality principle has taught him about the world outside, but also
his own pleasure and unpleasure experiences and pleasure and unpleasure expectancies. The "siding with the objects," to use Anna
Freud's term, brings about a certain degree of independence from
the instinctual demands long before the superego has developed
as a separate agency, and at a stage when many techniques of the ego
have already become automatized. The decisive step, however, is
made by the erection of the superego which in a unique way strength-
ens the independence of the child, while at the same time it gives the
demands and prohibitions of the parents a definite place in the
child's own mental life.

VI

Before dealing with the functions of the superego, we propose
to make a distinction which promises to be helpful in clarifying a
number of theoretical and clinical questions. We all speak of "contents" of the superego (see, e.g., Freud, 1932); we also speak of superego functions. We expect that the approach to these questions will
be facilitated if we follow a suggestion made by one of us (Hartmann,
1953) in regard to the ego: we should differentiate contents and
functions more clearly than is commonly done; in addition, it is
advisable to distinguish, from the economic point of view, the
cathexes of contents from the cathexes of functions. A thought
content can be cathected, but so can the activity of thinking as such;
it seems relevant to distinguish the cathexis of the self-image from
the cathexis of ego functions, etc. To make the same distinction in
the case of the superego seems promising in regard to developmental
issues, but also for a better understanding of questions of pathology,
e.g., of the so-called "superego regression"—about which point we
shall say a few words later.

Tracing the development of the superego concept in Freud's work (see recently Beres, 1958; Sandler, 1960) we find a high degree of consistency in the different stages of theory formation succeeding one another. But there are also certain activities which at one time are described as ego functions, and at other times as superego functions. We assume that the main trends in the history of Freud's thinking on the subject are generally known among analysts; we shall therefore confine our discussion to a few issues only. Freud had originally assigned reality testing to the superego as one of its functions. Later, in *The Ego and the Id* (1923), he says this is "a point which needs correction" and he adds: "It would fit in perfectly with the relations of the ego to the world of perception if reality-testing remained a task of the ego itself" (p. 28). This, of course, does not mean that the superego cannot influence reality testing. We mention this point only because the distinction between "being a function of" and "being accessible to the influence of" has not always been clearly made in the issue at stake here. Freud himself has given a convincing example (1936) of the case in which the superego interferes with reality testing. Freud's change of mind in attributing reality testing first to the superego and later to the ego belongs into the chapter we mentioned briefly in the beginning, that is, to those changes in the conception of the superego that are the direct outcome of the development of ego psychology.

But we have mentioned the passage from Freud's *The Ego and the Id* with another thought in mind. We feel that a similar argument can be made for the suggestion offered by one of us some time ago (Hartmann, 1950; see also Jacobson, 1954), to assign to the ego still another one of the functions which Freud had originally attributed to the superego. We are speaking of internal perception, of the perception of one's own mental processes. We may remind you of the fact that Freud himself has sometimes spoken—and we think convincingly—of inner perception as a function of the ego. On the other hand, it is also true that even as late as in the *New Introductory Lectures* (1932) he allocated self-observation to the superego as one of its main functions.

Again, as we just said in the case of reality testing, the fact that we attribute internal perception to the ego certainly does not imply that internal perception could not come under the influence of superego functions. In fact, the superego may both stimulate and interfere with self-observation and with the knowledge of inner reality. Self-deceptions—more often than deceptions about the outside world, though these too, can be observed—can in many cases be traced to activities of the superego. What we said about self-observation does not mean that we disagree with assigning the functions of self-criticism, self-reproaches, etc., to the superego. It is possible, though by no means well established, that the frequent confusion or equation of self-perception and self-condemnation is due, among others, to the fact that the self-deceptions we observe so frequently have their origin in the superego.

We may, in this context, also touch on a different, though related topic. Can to "know" something be a function of the superego? We read in Freud (again in *The Ego and the Id*, 1923): "Thus in this case the superego knew more than the ego about the unconscious id" (p. 51), and we can find similar statements elsewhere. They would, in fact, attribute to the superego a capacity of "knowing." It is clearly demonstrable clinically that psychic events or processes can act upon the superego though they are hidden from the ego. However, we would maintain that "reacting to something" should not be construed to imply "knowing" it, at least not in the usual sense of the word. Actually Freud states, two sentences before the one we just quoted: "Analysis . . . shows that the super-ego is being influenced by processes that have remained unknown to the ego." We consider this formulation sufficient to cover the findings we referred to, and preferable to the other one, because we should hesitate to ascribe to the superego anything that could be termed "knowledge." It seems hard to decide whether Freud meant to convey precisely the same meaning in the two sentences quoted, or whether he intended by the use of the word "knowing" to give the second additional significance, beyond what he stated in the first.

Above we employed the term self-criticism which is now generally used to refer to a function of the superego. We realize, however, that it is not quite free of ambiguity. It means clearly that the object of criticism is the self. And what is the relation of that part which does the criticizing to the self? As we said before, the term "self" is not too well defined in analysis, or rather only some of its aspects are well defined (e.g., "self-representation"). While this is not the place to go more extensively into this subject, we must at least mention the fact that we do not, as some analysts do, consider the "self" as a separate psychic system, to be conceptualized in the same way as ego, id, and superego. In this context we want to emphasize that the active agent in self-criticism is represented in the self-image of different individuals in different degrees. These differences do not necessarily parallel the differences in degrees of superego development or of the independence of its functions. Furthermore, in some children the representation of that active aspect of self-criticism in the self-image occurs rather early, while in others there is a considerable time lag between the formation of the superego and the appearance of these phenomena. The representation of both the active and the passive aspects of self-criticism in the image of one's self is strikingly formulated in an aphorism by Nietzsche: *"Wenn man sich selbst verachtet, achtet man sich doch immer noch dabei als Verächter."*[5]

Among the functions which Freud attributes to the superego he also mentions in the *New Introductory Lectures* (1932) the *"Ideal-funktion."* What is, then, the relationship between "ego ideal" and "superego"? There was a time when Freud considered these terms to be synonymous. Several historical presentations have emphasized this point. In the analytic literature we frequently find the ego ideal described as a structure that develops early in the mind of the child, while the structure we call superego is said to develop later. There is no question that idealization not only of the self but also of the objects occurs before the superego is set up. The question is whether or not such early idealizations, like the other early determinants, take on that special character which permits us to describe them as a "system" or "agency," or as a part of it only in the turmoil of the passing of the oedipus complex and in interaction with other developments which had their main origin in this situation. To us it seems reasonable to view the specific character of the ego ideal which is part of the superego in close relation to those other developments which originate in the oedipal conflicts and to distinguish the resulting "ego ideal" from earlier idealizations. We meet here again an issue which is ubiquitous in psychoanalysis and on which we

---

[5] The English translation reads: "He who despises himself, nevertheless esteems himself thereby as despiser."

briefly touched before, namely, the distinction of genetic continuity and functional characterization.

But let us go back to Freud's statement in which he attributes the *Idealfunktion* to the superego. This term is not common in analysis and could be misunderstood. The English translation calls this function "the holding up of ideals," which states in a clear way and, we think, correctly what Freud had in mind. We quote another passage from the same work: "We have now to mention another important activity which is to be ascribed to the super-ego. It is also the vehicle[6] of the ego-ideal, by which the ego measures itself, towards which it strives, and whose demands for ever-increasing perfection it is always striving to fulfil" (pp. 92-93). In the same context we also want to mention: "For us the super-ego is the representative of all moral restrictions, the advocate of the impulse towards perfection . . ." (p. 95). All this we take to mean that, at least at this stage of the development of his theoretical thinking, Freud conceived of the system superego as an agency among whose functions or activities he included the ego ideal. He saw the moral prohibitions and the strivings toward the "ideals" as closely related, and said that together they are what "we have been able to apprehend psychologically of what people call the 'higher' things in human life" (p. 95). We may mention here that not all analysts accept our view according to which the ego ideal is one of the functions of the superego. But we feel reasonably sure that this is what Freud meant and, moreover, that his is the most plausible answer to the question concerning the structural position of the ego ideal. To attribute to one psychic system functions which in some ways are different, though they all have something essential in common, is analogous to our view which considers perception, thinking, defense, and so on, as functions of the ego. Still another comment may be to the point here: we have often spoken of the activity of "the ego" in a global way, neglecting the differences of the various ego functions and the intrasystemic conflicts, in cases where today we believe a differential approach is called for. At present we can observe a similar development in our approach to the superego. In neither case does the concern with specific functions disagree with Freud's basic tripartite model of psychic structure.

[6] The German word is *Träger*.

We have already mentioned that there are differences in the determinants of the various aspects of the superego. In regard to the ego ideal, we have discussed elsewhere that magic thought is among its precursors and that the idealization of strength or power precedes the idealization of moral behavior (Hartmann, Kris, and Loewenstein, 1946). As a consequence of his encounters with reality the child is bound to relinquish a considerable part of his original "omnipotence" of hallucinatory wish fulfillment and magic thinking. Much of this is then projected upon the parental objects and accounts for their idealization. To mitigate the narcissistic loss implied in this process, the child then identifies himself with the idealized parents. But, of course, this is not to deny that parts of the original self-idealization do survive. At any rate, it is well known that narcissistic wounds and frustrations may contribute toward a compensatory cathexis of the precursors of the ego ideal. Looked at from this angle, the setting up of the ego ideal can be considered a rescue operation for narcissism. This is developmentally important and remains significant also for the role the ego-ideal aspect plays in the mental economy once the superego as a system has developed. In this context, another point might become relevant, though little is known about it so far, namely, the habitual or situational representation of the various localizations of narcissism in the self-image.

In the development of the ego ideal both self-idealization and the idealization of the parents play a role. These two processes gradually become integrated (see also A. Reich, 1954), but certainly not always completely integrated. The degree to which the ego ideal is determined more by early self-idealization or more by idealization of the object later becomes more important for both normal and pathological development. Of significance for future pathological development might also be the persistence of early forms of self-aggrandizement or of overvaluation of parents that may stand in the way of the formation of later types of idealizations. Another typical factor which is developmentally relevant is the child's disappointment in the parents. It may lead to a growing independence of the child. But if this disappointment occurs at the wrong time or in the wrong form, the child sees himself deprived of an important support in his dealings with his instinctual drives. In some cases the abolishment of the idealization of the parents will also interfere with, instead of strengthening, the child's self-esteem and ego-ideal development. In later life the loss of ideals, related either to objects or to factors of a more impersonal nature, may lead to what one usually terms cynicism—behind which, however, another set of ideals may be hidden (frequently, e.g., truth values). Something similar may well happen already in childhood, though probably not in early childhood.

The ego ideal's precursors, which are transformed during and after the passing of the oedipal phase and which as a consequence merge with other aspects of the developing superego, then lead to what we consider the ego ideal in a strict sense, namely, the ego ideal as a function of the superego. The contents of the ego ideal and the contents of the moral prohibitions are brought into close contact. The ideal aims and directions of the ego ideal and the moral restrictions are gradually being integrated and assume under the organizing influence of the ego the central position in what has been called a person's "moral system." Once this integration has taken place, to act according to a given set of standards comes to mean not only a reduction of guilt feelings but also a narcissistic gratification. ". . . if the ego has successfully resisted a temptation to do something that would be objectionable to the superego, it feels its self-respect raised and its pride increased" (Freud, 1938, p. 122). To this we may add, with E. Jacobson (1954), that the degrees of self-esteem reflect the harmony or discrepancy between self-representation and the wishful concept of the self. But we shall point out later that in the adult, this "wishful concept" does not fully represent the aim-setting function of the ego ideal. "Pride" should certainly be more carefully studied than has been done so far, particularly in its relation to the ego ideal. It would also be interesting to understand why the moral evaluations of pride itself vary so widely in different value systems. In the case Freud had in mind, we may say that frustration interferes less with narcissism, because a detour to its gratification has been found. This case belongs into the large and important chapter of how new pleasure possibilities are being opened up through structural development (see also Hartmann, 1956). Pride does not necessarily remain tied, as a kind of recompense, to specific instances of resisting temptation. It can become a lasting and characterologically significant aspect of a personality. Also, pride is clearly not limited to moral pride. But we must resist the temptation to pursue this subject further.

The impact of the ego ideal's demands is strengthened by its integration with other elements of the superego which have powerful sources of energy at their disposal. The "ought nots" lend their energy to those positive aims which are their correlates and which are contents of the ego ideal. In turn these add their energies to strengthen the prohibitions. We do not want to imply that all contents of the ego ideal are of this kind, and we should mention that these contents may well go beyond the realm of moral demands. Ideals of perfection are not necessarily of a moral nature. Justice, wisdom, courage, and temperance, the four "cardinal virtues" which were for a long time acknowledged aims of the ancient Greeks, are ideals of perfection that we would include among the aims set by the ego ideal; though they have moral implications, they are not limited to what we would call moral demands. We want to remind you that the great systems of moral thought which humanity has developed very often show the ego-ideal aspect and the aspect of moral restrictions side by side; as the "good" on the one hand, and the "ought not" on the other (Hartmann, 1960).

VII

With these remarks we might have created the impression that we can expect a state of peaceful coexistence between the various aspects of the superego. What we observe certainly does not often conform to this picture. Contradictions between conscious and unconscious morality, between the demands of the ego ideal and the moral taboos, and between various parts of the individual value systems are frequent, and may be the rule. Contrasting tendencies in the superego do exist and can be compared to the intrasystemic conflicts in the ego. Still another analogy with the ego suggests itself. Some of these contradictions may be compared to what Freud (1924b) has termed ego distortions or ego deformations. He speaks of cases in which the ego is "deforming itself, by submitting to encroachments on its own unity and even by effecting a cleavage or division of itself" in order to escape more severe pathology. This thought of Freud's seems to be a major contribution, one, however, which in the scheme of psychoanalytic theory has not yet found its due place. Without going into details at this point, it is our impression that similar occurrences take place in the superego, and that they serve the same purpose. We would therefore refer to these processes as "superego distortions."

It may very well be that in some people early precursors of the ego ideal are preserved without leading to any form of pathology, but beyond a certain individually variable threshold they then tend to become clinically significant, as A. Reich (1954), for instance, has convincingly demonstrated. However, some persisting determinants may counteract the superego after the latter is formed. Of the many questions one could ask at this point, we shall in this context deal with only one. While no doubt there is genetic continuity between the precursors which we have described and the developed ego ideal which is more or less integrated with the other aspects of the superego, there is in the development of the ego ideal "something new," something very important, which we may well describe as or attribute to a "change of function," a term used in describing ego development (Hartmann, 1939). As we said, what is added is that the "striving after perfection" of the ego ideal becomes dynamically a partly independent direction-giving function, which is relatively independent of the objects, and relatively independent also of the instinctual precursors. The aims of the ego ideal are then to a considerable extent no longer identical with the primitive wishes which played a role in its formation.[7]

We spoke of "relative" independence because there can be no question of "absolute" independence in this or in the other forms of autonomy we know in psychoanalysis. At this stage the ego ideal no longer is essentially an agent of wishful thinking. The "ideals" or "ideal aims" we find at that level cannot be rightly termed "illusions"—while the belief that they have been reached or realized and, in some instances, also the belief that they can be reached may, of course, be an illusion. In the place of wishful thinking and of the distortion of inner reality—a distortion which is connected with the more primitive forerunners of ego-ideal functioning—we later find that the contents of the ego ideal are recognized not as aims

[7] About the three types of aims we distinguish, see Hartmann, 1960.

that have been magically reached, but as demands and as direction giving. These demands are at a later stage also recognized as inner demands. If we want to use this terminology, we may say: the previous state was "nonrealistic," while this cannot correctly be said of the later one; on the contrary, the recognition of inner demands broadens the field of objective cognition of inner reality, of self-knowledge, and thus it may also contribute, though indirectly, to the dealings with outer reality (Hartmann, 1947).

The development we just described, together with comparable developments in other parts of the superego, e.g., what Freud observed about a gradual detachment of moral imperatives from the original objects, can well be called a developmental trend toward growing "autonomy" of the superego's functions (Hartmann, 1952)—that is, autonomy from the objects on the one hand and from the drives on the other. But it would be quite difficult—and we do not propose to attempt it here—to define clearly a developmentally extending "autonomy of the superego" from the ego, at least in the sense of the superego's growing independence from the ego. One could try to describe it in relation to specific ego functions, as a growing independence, for instance, of the superego-centered moral motivations from social anxiety, or from self-interest. But any generalizing attempt runs into difficulties. Not only does early superego development depend on ego development, but once the superego as a system is set up, its normal functioning is constantly bound to certain activities of the ego; and the further evolution of the superego does not diminish the developing ego's influence, but tends to increase it. We consider, then, the superego as a dynamically partly independent center of mental functioning with aims of its own. But we do not assert that once the superego has been formed, its further development generally tends to go in the direction of a growing detachment from ego influence. One speaks occasionally of the "autonomy" of a person's "moral system." Here the term autonomy designates something that is related to the subject we just discussed, but that is not really identical with it. It usually refers only to the relative independence of the "moral system" from sociocultural pressures.

The tension between superego and ego is, according to Freud, perceived as guilt feeling.[8] Though the tensions between ego ideal and ego are not independent from the tensions between other aspects of the superego and the ego, they nevertheless vary partly independently from one another. Even if they are not perceived, these tensions lead to a state which is very much like guilt in its dynamic and economic aspects, and which Freud, with some hesitation, termed "unconscious guilt feeling." You all know that this concept came to play an important role in the development of his later theories. In earlier works (1913) Freud had tried to derive the feeling of guilt from ambivalence—a factor which, besides others, may well contribute to the explanation of pre-superego guiltlike feelings in the child (see also the work of M. Klein [1948] and others on "reparation"). But Freud's earlier hypothesis cannot explain "conscience." This can be done only by using that layer of Freud's theory formation on which this paper is based.

We should mention here the thoughtful work of Piers and Singer, *Shame and Guilt* (1953), though this is not the place to review or criticize it as carefully as it deserves. For them, the tension between ego ideal and ego accounts for a feeling of shame, while guilt feeling is the result only of the tension between other parts of the superego (they call them "the superego") and the ego. There is no reason to object to a descriptive distinction between "guilt" and "shame," but it is very difficult to account for this difference in terms of analytic psychology. One may well see a difference between acting contrary to an imperative and not reaching an ideal aim one has set for himself. Actually, it is possible to classify ethical systems according to whether the accent is on the one or the other (Hartmann, 1928). It seems unlikely to us that one can, as these authors assume, distinguish between shame and guilt in terms of outer or inner sanction. The authors connect shame with the fear of abandonment, and guilt with the fear of castration. Such a link seems to us to represent primarily a distinction in terms of developmental level. Shame as well as guilt are reactions to the danger of loss of love, to ridicule, or to anger. It also appears that the difference between "guilt" and "shame," in common as well as in scientific usage, is rather vague,

8 In quoting Freud, we follow of course his terminology; we have stated elsewhere (Hartmann, 1950) why and in what instances we would speak of "self," "self-representation," "self-image" rather than of the "ego" (see also Loewenstein, 1940).

though it is true, as the authors state, that there are cases in which one term is much more frequently used than the other: e.g., *Scham*, in German, in connection with the exposure of the nude body. But such an appeal to the child as "You should be ashamed of yourself," or, in German, "*schäm' Dich*," is quite generally used also when parents expect or wish the child to feel guilty; one just does not say to children: "You should feel guilty." In terms of psychoanalytic theory, we are reluctant to overemphasize the separateness of the ego ideal from the other parts of the superego, and it is, partly, the question of separateness on which the structural opposition of guilt and shame hinges. As we said before, we want, without neglecting the functional differences, to see more clearly what connects, contentwise but also economically, the "ideal demands" with the moral "ought nots."

If a "tension between superego and ego" results in the ego's submitting to the demands of the superego, this is in itself not a phenomenon to be classified as "masochism" as has occasionally been suggested (Loewenstein, 1938, 1940). Freud's argument against what he called a "sexualization" of the concept of repression is valid also in regard to the superego relationships. Their normal relationships are not to be considered as sexual in nature. However, with Freud, we will often have to classify the need for punishment as masochistic. There is, then, a regressive sexualization of morality which is an essential characteristic of moral masochism. The question that often arises, whether the submission to the superego has to be attributed to its strength or to the "masochism of the ego," is not always easy to decide. We are referring to Freud (1924a) and to a paper by Jeanne Lampl-de Groot (1937).

The ego often accepts and integrates demands of the superego without opposition. Superego demands, like instinctual demands, may or may not be ego syntonic. There are also cases in which some of the superego's directions or prohibitions may run parallel with tendencies of the ego. The demand for truthfulness and the prohibition of lying are widespread in many civilizations; they may well bolster the ego's attempts toward objective acceptance of reality. But the willing acceptance of superego demands can often also be traced to the organizing or synthetic function of the ego, which accounts for the coordination of the psychic agencies. In many instances, the result is clearly a compromise formation. Finally, there are situations in which the ego rebels against the pressures of the superego. Frustration often results in a generalized rebellion against superego demands, and instinctual tendencies of self-interest prevail over morality. The ego defends itself by such activities as repression, denial, isolation, rationalization, and so on. Many other methods, some of them not easy to describe, are used for the same purpose. It may happen that an ego aim borrows, on the basis of some relatedness of content, the dignity of a superego command and uses the force thus acquired to combat imperatives it is unwilling to acquiesce in. Many examples come to mind; e.g., the frequent cases in which an idealizing stress on "realistic" attitudes, in the sense of "accepting the world as it really is," is put into the service of a defense against some pressure from the superego. Methods such as this one are relevant in the development of a person's "moral system" in which both ego and superego participate. But in less favorable cases, it may also happen that a kind of ataxia develops between the two systems. We do not propose to treat this subject in any detail, but we cannot omit to add one point. As Freud (1923) found, some features of the conflicts with the mental images of the parents are often continued in the basic forms of the ego's fights against the superego.

Rather frequent are the situations in which, at first, the superego does not succeed in impressing its prohibitions of instinctual action or thought on the defense mechanisms of the ego. In some instances this prohibiting function of the superego seems to be absent, so that only in a second act, as it were, the superego regains its power and punishes the ego after the deed. But there are also cases in which the ego anticipates danger from the superego and uses the feeling of guilt as a signal in an attempt to forestall the danger situation (see also Glover, 1949; Jacobson, 1954). Alexander (1927) described the "bribing of the superego by the id." The opposite can be observed when the superego induces the id to unwanted demands for purposes of self-punishment (Loewenstein, 1945). Ernst Kris termed it "the bribing of the id by the superego." Different again is the mechanism we might call "tentative temptation." Here the ego allows itself a small dose of gratification which then serves to set in motion the forces of the superego.

While the essential features of superego development show us its impact on the instinctual drives, there also appears to be an ego aspect which has been less carefully studied, perhaps because it has less significance for our understanding of neurosis. There are both ideals and positive and negative imperatives which oppose not the drives but clearly specific ego functions (Hartmann, 1947). A more subtle demarcation of one's "rights" and "duties" in relation to those of other people is one of the results of superego formation. In this context the position of "self-interests" assumes importance. Some will prove superego syntonic, and others not. At any rate, we all know that the conflicts between moral demands and the pursuit of self-interests loom large in a great number of moral systems. Thinking of ontogenesis, we can add that among the prohibitions which the parents impose on the child from early childhood on, there are many that concern the child's self-interests.

We often observe projections of the superego, or of certain superego demands, onto the outside world. This may mean relief if what a great preanalytic psychologist said is true: that "to be alone with one's conscience is terrifying" (Nietzsche). If social anxiety is substituted for superego anxiety, this can mean two things: either it is based on a realistic evaluation of dangers threatening from outside, or it is an irrational fear that is wholly or partly due to projection of the superego.

VIII

Freud's derivation of the superego from the oedipal situation explains not only its contents but also its economic aspects. Something of both the loving and the aggressive relations to the parents is preserved in this agency. In particular, this agency offers one of the main avenues for dealing with one's own aggression, by turning it against oneself. Of course, there is the generally known aspect that criticism by the parents is turned into self-criticism, and that their implicit or explicit standards become the child's own ideals or imperatives. As Freud said, the child's superego is built not so much on the model of the parents but on that of the parents' superego (1932). This accounts for the strong element of tradition in moral systems. But perhaps we should add that another possibility exists. The contents of the superego may reflect not only the criticisms of the parents but also the criticisms which the child had directed against the parents (possibly in a way similar to what we mentioned before: early forms of self-idealization may survive together with object idealization in the ego ideal). However, there is not yet sufficient evidence for proving this hypothesis.

What we said so far is only one aspect of Freud's ideas on the origin of conscience: that the critical function of conscience derives directly from the criticism of the parents. He added another when observation had convincingly shown that the severity of the child's superego does not simply reflect the severity with which the child had been treated. The child's superego can be strict even in cases where education has been lenient or tolerant. The later aspect of Freud's theory (1930) does not so much refer to the contents of the superego as it decisively contributes to the economic side of its functioning. This theory says that the child is bound to develop aggression against the adults in a position of authority in consequence of the frustrations they impose; this aggression can, as a rule, not be satisfied; the way out of this "difficult economic situation" is that the child develops a severe superego—the severity in this case originating in the fact that the aggression that he would have liked to turn against the adults is being turned against his self. Freud's theory allows us to include among the genetic determinants of "conscience" also the history of the preoedipal vicissitudes of aggression.

Freud has repeatedly spoken of the superego's closeness to the id. This can have different meanings. At this point we are concerned with its economic meaning. We think one may assume that the aggression which the superego uses—though it is not unmodified free aggression—is in general still closer to instinctual energy than the more fully neutralized energy which the ego functions use (Hartmann, 1955; Beres, 1958). There are degrees in the "severity" of the superego; the economic side of this concept refers to both the amount of aggressive energy at the superego's disposal and to the mode of energy used—its closeness to or distance from the instinctual mode. These factors, we assume, are correlated, though not in a simple way, with the power of the superego to enforce its demands and to punish transgressions of the "thou shalt not." ("Severity" of the superego is occasionally also used to denote something else: the strictness of the demands themselves—independent of the power to enforce them. And there are indeed people with very strict moral codes whose superegos have very little power to enforce these codes.)

Neutralization takes place through the ego. Thus we again are faced with a factor which clearly shows that superego functions depend on ego functions. We do not wish to imply that the ego tends to maximize neutralization of all psychic functions. This is certainly not true; different degrees of neutralization are commonly provided for different ego functions—and the same may be the case in regard to the relations between ego and superego. It is not unlikely that the direction-giving function of the superego works with a higher degree of neutralization of aggression than its enforcing function. But we want to emphasize here that if our assumption is correct, we would expect impairment of the ego's capacity of neutralization to have a definite effect on the superego. Actually, we think that the "cruel," the "overpunitive" character of the superego found in certain psychoses can at least partly be explained by this kind of impairment of ego function (Hartmann, 1953).

This approach to the economic aspect of the superego promises to shed some light on still another question. In the works of Freud and other analysts, we sometimes find the assertion that the aggressive energy of the superego works in a self-destructive fashion. However, if we assume superego aggression to be modifiable, we would expect that these assertions will not necessarily always prove to be correct. A similar question arose in regard to the aggressive energy in the ego. The neutralized aggression active in various functions of the ego is not self-destructive. There is certainly the case, often mentioned by Freud, in which aggression "turned backward" increases self-destructiveness. But this case is different from that in which neutralized aggressive energy is used in the service of ego functions (Hartmann, 1948). The ego—we remind you of a passage in Freud's *Outline* (1938)—"sets itself the task of self-preservation which the id seems to neglect." We would assume, then, that not every activity of aggression which is not directed toward the outside world but works in the mental systems, or between them, is "self-destructive"—and that this is true not only of energy in the ego but also in the superego. The superego, too, has—or can have—survival value, though not in the specific sense in which this is true of the ego.

The hypothesis that not only libidinal but also aggressive energy can be neutralized (Hartmann, Kris, and Loewenstein, 1949) was put forward also by other analysts (e.g., Menninger, 1942; Lampl-de Groot, 1947). Freud, in his works, considered the sublimation of libido in the sense of desexualization, but he did not consider the possibility of an analogous process with respect to aggression—or so we thought. We were, then, happy to discover in one of his letters to Marie Bonaparte, which was published eighteen years after his death (Jones, 1957), a passage that is to the point here. After writing about sublimation, Freud adds: "One must then admit that similar deviations from the goal of destruction and exploitation to other achievements are demonstrable on an extensive scale for the instinct of destruction." But again, there remains a question mark: did Freud think only of the displacement of aims or also of a change in the mode of energy used, as he did in the case of sublimation of libido?

Freud assumed that in repression the energy of countercathexis is the one that had been withdrawn from the drives—but he did not state this widely accepted hypothesis in a very definite way: he rather said, "it is quite possible that it is so" (1915). Because of reasons put forward elsewhere, we hold that other sources of energy are at the disposal of the ego in its defensive activities. We also assume that there is an affinity between inner conflict and aggression and think that the defenses of the ego are most likely fed by a neutralized mode of aggressive energy. What, then, is the relation between the aggressive pressure of the superego on the ego and the aggression used by the ego in defense against the id? That different degrees of neutralization are involved in the two processes is probable, as we said before. In the cases in which it is the superego that stimulates repression, we could describe this economically as "dependence of one form of aggressive relations (between ego and id) on another one (between superego and ego) and possibly as a shift of aggressive cathexis combined with an increase in neutralization," under the influence of the ego (Hartmann, 1953).

Continuing our speculations along these lines, there is another problem which calls for our attention. If outer frustration provokes aggression which cannot be discharged, this aggressive energy can be "made over" to the superego and increase the feelings of guilt. We have quoted this discovery of Freud's before. However, we suggest that an alternative outcome is possible: the undischarged aggression may be used in countercathexis in the ego (defenses). We are impressed by clinical observations that seem to indicate that the increase of guilt, as a consequence of frustration, while certainly often observable, is not a regular occurrence. It is likely that guilt can be avoided if the alternative to which we just referred predominates. Whether it does, may depend on the relative strength of ego and superego and on the ego's capacity for the neutralization of aggressive energy. Freud once also suggested the formulation that if an instinctual tendency is repressed, its libidinal parts lead to symptom formation, its aggressive components to feelings of guilt (1930). He added that this hypothesis may not be generally true, but it nevertheless deserves our attention. We suppose that in other cases, as we said, the aggressive component may find a place in the defensive action itself.

IX

One sometimes speaks—not quite correctly—of "early forms of the superego" surviving in the system superego. These are then commonly called "archaic." What this terms refers to are actually those preoedipal identifications and early drive derivatives and ego activities which, in an unmodified form, survive in the superego system. Some misunderstandings could be avoided if one were to designate them as such (Wexler, 1952). That elements of earlier phases persist "side by side with, and behind, later organizations" Freud has explicitly stated for the phases of libidinal development (e.g., 1932). But it is also true of other aspects of personality development and often very clear in regard to the superego. Clinically relevant is the question, how much of the antecedents survive and, in connection with this, the problem of regression.

The superego "has not been there from the beginning" (Freud), while the instinctual drives and the ego have. This is one reason why regression is harder to conceptualize with respect to the superego than with respect to the drives and the ego. Sometimes "superego regression" is caused by a regression of the instinctual drives—as is probably the case in obsessional neurosis. As a result of "superego regression" we see early identifications and early object relationships taking the place of the contents and the functions of the superego.

We remind you again of Freud's description of moral masochism in which sexual relationships at the time of the oedipal phase are regressively substituted for superego functions. As a rule, the contents of the ideal aims, or the imperatives, or both, have undergone a change, though something of their structure is preserved in superego regression. But we also think of the possibility that there exist variations, partly independent of the contents, in the mode of energy used by the superego—a "regression," that is, to a form of energy closer to the pure instinctual mode, in which case the changes of content are of a secondary nature. It is commonly accepted that the severe or punitive character of the demands and the expected punishments which we find in at least some forms of "superego regression" is to be considered a consequence of early object relations taking the place of the later ones. Of course, this does not mean that the real objects of those earliest stages of development have been as cruel as the regressed superego is. It reflects also the child's fantasies and fears and the ways in which he is dealing with his own aggression. We think that in the extreme forms of superego regression, a change from a more to a less neutralized mode of aggression used by the superego should be considered as an additional causative factor.

As we mentioned before, this again points to the role which the ego plays in this process. During recent years, a lively discussion has taken place on whether or not defective superego formation and (or) superego regression play a central role in the pathology of schizophrenia (Pious, 1949; Wexler, 1951; Hoedemaker, 1955; Brody, 1958; Modell, 1958). What we want to say about it here does not amount to more than a few footnotes. We have attributed the essential role in the pathology of schizophrenia to the impairment of certain ego functions. This is also the opinion of Bak (1952). What is often called the "disintegration" of the superego in schizophrenia is, to our minds, at least partly traceable to the deficiencies in the ego. What we just said about different degrees of neutralization of the aggressive energy active in the superego is a case in point. In close connection with the ego's impaired capacity of neutralization is another aspect of the "disintegrated" superego: the fact that the "brutality" of the schizophrenic's superego is endowed with very little power to enforce its commands. The decisive factor here is again to be found in the pathology of the ego: its reduced capacity to neutralize aggression makes it impossible, or difficult, to set up those stable defenses on whose function the enforcement of superego commands depends (Hartmann, 1953). The "brutal" superego is not a "strong," or at least not a consistently strong, superego. Furthermore, we surmise that much of what has been described as characteristic of the schizophrenic's superego is due to the low level of integration between ego and superego, to the lack of that coordination which is normally established, at least in the adult, between ego and superego functions.

While the role of the superego in schizophrenia is still highly controversial, this is not true—or at least not to the same extent— of its role in neurosis. In this context we propose to discuss only one aspect of the superego's role in neurosis. It is generally accepted that the strictness of the superego, or rather the sense of guilt resulting from that strictness, often considerably increases the suffering of the neurotic. This is true of conscious but also of unconscious guilt feelings. We quote Freud (1923): "In fact it may be precisely this element in the situation, the attitude of the ego ideal, that determines the severity of a neurotic illness" (p. 50). Freud (1924a) noted that in some cases in which an unconscious sense of guilt predominates, the neurosis "may vanish if the subject becomes involved in the misery of an unhappy marriage, or loses all his money, or develops a dangerous organic disease." This finding is theoretically as important as it is clinically striking. The "one form of suffering," Freud continues, "has been replaced by another; and we see that all that mattered was that it should be possible to maintain a certain amount of suffering" (p. 166). Certain observations lead us to suspect that something similar—a considerable decrease of the sense of guilt, in this case also without the help of analysis—occasionally happens where not the ego's masochism but the superego's severity had been the dominant factor. Powerful identifications as they sometimes are made even by adult persons can produce such changes in individuals whose capacity for neutralization is unimpaired, and whose superego has remained more open to change than is commonly the case— that is to say, when the demarcation line between ego identifications

and superego identifications is less strictly drawn than we usually
find it in grown-up people. (In this context one must also consider
what has been described as "parasites of the superego.")

At this point we should like to mention some other observations,
though they are only loosely connected with our present topic. We
are used to finding somatic symptoms in the place of psychic conflicts. It has long been known that mental pain can be converted
into physical pain. In persons with a marked sense of guilt something
in contrast to conversion may come about. It is our impression that
in some persons, guilt is not only added to but also partly substituted for physical symptoms (e.g., for physical pain). But limitations
of time as well as of the plan we devised for this paper prevent us
from the attempt to survey what is partly known and partly surmised
on this subject.

With the setting up of the superego as a separate agency, its
development has not come to an end. Later objects the person takes
as his models and the value systems of his cultural environment leave
their imprints on it. The further development of the ego tends to
integrate the superego with the value systems of a person's cultural environment (Loewenstein, 1951). This raises the question,
how far the influence of sociocultural factors is retained by the ego,
and how far by the superego. Some sociologists, especially T. Parsons
(1952), have strongly emphasized the role of the superego in this
respect. In recent years there have been many studies of the vicissitudes of the superego in adolescence (recently by Spiegel, 1958; A.
Freud, 1958; Geleerd, 1958; Jacobson, 1961), and you are no doubt
familiar with these investigations. The formation of the superego
frequently causes radical changes in the self-image. But the influence of the superego on the self-image does not end at this point.
It extends far beyond it, is very marked in adolescence, and can
be observed even later. But beyond adolescence, we do not know
much about how long and in what respects the superego remains
accessible to modifications; we would not be able to indicate what
is the average relation between age and the decrease of that accessibility. It is quite possible that the correlation is not a simple one.
There may be postadolescent periods in which the trend is temporarily reversed—that is to say, in which the plasticity of the super-

ego increases, possibly in response to instinctual changes.[9] It seems obvious that there exist considerable individual differences in regard to the continuance of superego development after adolescence. The main characteristics of the superego structure are in general, as we know, laid down rather early. But its cathexes and contents can undergo changes much later; this applies particularly to the integration of both its contents and its functions which occur under the influence of the ego and the exigencies of reality acting through the ego. Even in normal people some archaic precursors of the ego ideal or of the prohibiting superego are retained through all these developments. But this statement certainly does not deny that pathology may result in cases where these archaic elements become dominant (Weissman, 1954)—or, on the other hand, that the dominance of these elements can be a sign of pathology.

Let us return to the differences in duration of the superego's postadolescent evolution. We consider protracted ego development a characteristic feature of man. It is not unlikely that the protracted development of the superego serves humanization as well. What happens in the course of prolonged superego development is that the mutual adjustment of ego and superego is promoted and that a workable equilibrium is established between them. However, this conception of a workable equilibrium may easily be misinterpreted, therefore we want to add a few clarifying remarks. Of course, we do not mean that the tension between the two systems tends to become constant, or that these tensions are abolished. We rather assume that the scope of these tensions tends to become a characteristic of the individual—as long as the individual does not get involved in neurotic or psychotic disease. This factor of greater or lesser habitual tensions can also be considered in relation to specific features of cultural systems. What matters above all is the degree to which the two agencies can collaborate, while at the same time preserving the optimum tension between them. This optimum can be defined in several respects: in relation to mental health, to social adjustment, to realistic, and to moral behavior, and so on. Derangement of optimum tension may be due to the impact of the instinctual drives; or, on the side of the ego, to a disturbance of

---

[9] Goethe's well-known statement that geniuses, unlike other people, have repeated puberties, may be significant also in this context.

those functions which make a stable balance of the agencies possible (e.g., impairment of the organizing function or impairment of neutralization). This derangement may result if the superego is too rigid in its relations with the ego and makes all influences from that side impossible; or, on the other hand, if the ego's defiance of the superego does not allow integration to take place—a factor which may also cause the precocious interruption of full superego development. In terms of the points of view mentioned above, it also follows that we regard as an "optimum" neither a maximum preponderance of superego regulations over ego regulations, nor of ego regulations over superego regulations.

X

The transvaluation of values which takes place in ontogenesis presents us with a promising approach to the study of how ego and superego aims come to be integrated.[10] Valuations may be genetically traceable to the gratification of instinctual aims, but also to their renunciation. What provided gratification as well as what prohibited it can become models of what later will make its appearance as part of a value system.

Beyond this, there are obviously also cases in which to act according to some standard of values may at the same time gratify an instinctual tendency. On the other hand, valuations may be used as rationalizations. Then, again, in one and the same action there may be an overlapping of motivations issuing from the ego ideal or the prohibitive part of the superego, or both, with tendencies of the ego (e.g., with self-interest). In certain instances there may be a genetic connection between the two groups of motivations. The reason for this is that demands of security, of health, of self-preservation are so often impressed on the child as his "duties."

Every moral value system—and we shall limit ourselves to this type of values—represents, in different degrees, the ideal demands or directions of the ego ideal, and the "ought nots" of the prohibiting aspects of the superego; the two aspects, as we said before, are closely interrelated. These processes and interactions are usually partly conscious, though many important elements are not. At any

10 What we summarize here is presented more extensively in Hartmann (1960).

rate, on the way from the early idealizations and the interiorizations of parental prohibitions to the moral codes of the adult a factor becomes relevant which reflects the activities of the ego: a process of integration and generalization. Another contribution of the ego is "value testing," that is a scrutinizing procedure which refers to the degree of authenticity which moral valuations have with respect to their individual psychological background. In the processes of integration, the taking over by the individual of the organized value hierarchies of the culture he lives in becomes decisive in the formation of his moral codes. The dynamic relevance of the taking over depends, however, among other factors, on the degree to which such a value hierarchy can become "authentic," in the sense just outlined, for the individual. Despite the influence of sociocultural factors, there remains the fact that the personal moral codes testify to the characteristics of the personality who holds them, in the same way as his instincts and his ego do. The contributions of ego functions to the moral codes we mentioned tend to eliminate contradictions and to bridge the gap between the monolithic ideals and prohibitions of earlier stages and the actual thinking and behavior of the adult. But they do not as a rule—we repeat—abolish the tension between superego and ego.

BIBLIOGRAPHY

Alexander, F. (1927), *The Psychoanalysis of the Total Personality*. New York & Washington: Nervous and Mental Disease Publishing Co., 1930.

Axelrad, S. & Maury, L. (1951), Identification As a Mechanism of Adaptation. In: *Psychoanalysis and Culture,* ed. G. B. Wilbur & W. Muensterberger. New York: International Universities Press.

Bak, R. C. (1952), Discussion of Dr. Wexler's Paper. In: *Psychotherapy with Schizophrenics: A Symposium,* ed. E. B. Brody & F. C. Redlich. New York: International Universities Press.

Beres, D. (1958), Vicissitudes of Superego Functions and Superego Precursors in Childhood. *This Annual,* XIII.

Bibring, E. (1947), The So-called English School of Psychoanalysis. *Psa. Quart.,* XVI.

Brody, E. B. (1958), Superego, Introjected Mother, and Energy Discharge in Schizophrenia. *J. Amer. Psa. Assn.,* VI.

Erikson, E. H. (1950a), *Childhood and Society*. New York: Norton.

—— (1950b), Growth and Crisis of the Healthy Personality. In: *Identity and the Life Cycle* [*Psychological Issues,* Monogr. 1]. New York: International Universities Press, 1959.

Fenichel, O. (1945), *The Psychoanalytic Theory of Neurosis*. New York: Norton.

Freud, A. (1926), *The Psycho-Analytical Treatment of Children*. New York: International Universities Press, 1959.

—— (1936), *The Ego and the Mechanisms of Defense*. New York: International Universities Press, 1946.

—— (1958), Adolescence. *This Annual*, XIII.

Freud, S. (1913), Totem and Taboo. *Standard Edition*, XIII. London: Hogarth Press, 1955.

—— (1915), The Unconscious. *Standard Edition*, XIV. London: Hogarth Press, 1957.

—— (1921), Group Psychology and the Analysis of the Ego. *Standard Edition*, XVIII. London: Hogarth Press, 1955.

—— (1923), The Ego and the Id. *Standard Edition*, XIX. London: Hogarth Press, 1961.

—— (1924a), The Economic Problem of Masochism. *Standard Edition*, XIX. London: Hogarth Press, 1961.

—— (1924b), Neurosis and Psychosis. *Standard Edition*, XIX. London: Hogarth Press, 1961.

—— (1930), Civilization and Its Discontents. *Standard Edition*, XXI. London: Hogarth Press, 1961.

—— (1932), *New Introductory Lectures on Psychoanalysis*. New York: Norton, 1933.

—— (1936), A Disturbance of Memory on the Acropolis. *Collected Papers*, V. London: Hogarth Press, 1950.

—— (1937), Analysis Terminable and Interminable. *Collected Papers*, V. London: Hogarth Press, 1950.

—— (1938), *An Outline of Psychoanalysis*. New York: Norton, 1949.

Geleerd, E. R. (1958), Borderline States in Childhood and Adolescence. *This Annual*, XIII.

Glover, E. (1949), *Psycho-Analysis*. London: Staples Press.

Greenacre, P. (1948), Anatomical Structure and Superego Development. *Amer. J. Orthopsychiat.*, XVIII.

Greenson, R. R. (1954), The Struggle Against Identification. *J. Amer. Psa. Assn.*, II.

Hartmann, H. (1928), Psychoanalyse and Wertproblem. *Imago*, XIV.

—— (1939), *Psychoanalysis and the Problem of Adaptation*. New York: International Universities Press, 1958.

—— (1947), On Rational and Irrational Action. In: *Psychoanalysis and the Social Sciences*, I. New York: International Universities Press.

—— (1948), Comments on the Psychoanalytic Theory of Instinctual Drives. *Psa. Quart.*, XVII.

—— (1950), Comments on the Psychoanalytic Theory of the Ego. *This Annual*, V.

—— (1952), The Mutual Influences in the Development of Ego and Id. *This Annual*, VII.

—— (1953), Contribution to the Metapsychology of Schizophrenia. *This Annual*, VIII.

—— (1955), Notes on the Theory of Sublimation. *This Annual*, X.

—— (1956), Notes on the Reality Principle. *This Annual*, XI.

—— (1960), *Psychoanalysis and Moral Values*. New York: International Universities Press.

—— Kris, E. & Loewenstein, R. M. (1946), Comments on the Formation of Psychic Structure. *This Annual*, II.

—— —— —— (1949), Notes on the Theory of Aggression. *This Annual*, III/IV.

Hoedemaker, E. D. (1955), The Therapeutic Process in the Treatment of Schizophrenia. *J. Amer. Psa. Assn.*, II.

Isakower, O. (1939), On the Exceptional Position of the Auditory Sphere. *Int. J. Psa.*, XX.

Jacobson, E. (1937), Wege der weiblichen Überichbildung. *Int. Z. Psa.*, XXIII.

—— (1954), The Self and the Object World. *This Annual*, IX.

—— (1961), Adolescent Moods and the Remodeling of Psychic Structures in Adolescence. *This Annual*, XVI.

Jones, E. (1957), *The Life and Work of Sigmund Freud*, III. New York: Basic Books.

Klein, M. (1948), *Contributions to Psycho-Analysis*. London: Hogarth Press.
Knight, R. P. (1940), Introjection, Projection, and Identification. *Psa. Quart.*, IX.
Lampl-de Groot. J. (1937), Masochismus und Narzissmus. *Int. Z. Psa.*, XXIII.
—— (1947), On the Development of the Ego and Superego. *Int. J. Psa.*, XXVIII.
Loewenstein, R. M. (1932), D'un mécanisme auto-punitif. *Rev. Franç. Psa.*, V.
—— (1938), L'Origine du masochisme et la théorie des instincts. *Rev. Franç. Psa.*, X.
—— (1940), The Vital and Somatic Instincts. *Int. J. Psa.*, XXI.
—— (1945), A Special Form of Self-Punishment. *Psa. Quart.*, XIV.
—— (1951), *Christians and Jews*. New York: International Universities Press.
—— (1957), A Contribution to the Psychoanalytic Theory of Masochism. *J. Amer. Psa. Assn.*, V.
Menninger, K. A. (1942), *Love Against Hate*. New York: Harcourt Brace.
Modell, A. H. (1958), The Theoretical Implications of Hallucinatory Experiences in Schizophrenia. *J. Amer. Psa. Assn.*, VI.
Parsons, T. (1952), The Superego and the Theory of Social Systems. *Psychiatry*, XV.
Piers, G. & Singer, M. (1953), *Shame and Guilt*. Springfield: Thomas.
Pious, W. (1949), The Pathogenic Process in Schizophrenia. *Bull. Menninger Clin.*, XIII.
Rapaport, D. (1958), A Historical Survey of Psychoanalytic Ego Psychology. Introduction to *Identity and the Life Cycle*, by E. H. Erikson. *Psychological Issues*, I. New York: International Universities Press, 1959.
Reich, A. (1954), Early Identifications As Archaic Elements in the Superego. *J. Amer. Psa. Assn.*, II.
Ritvo, S. & Solnit, A. J. (1960), The Relationships of Early Identifications to Superego Formation. *Int. J. Psa.*, XLI.
Sachs, H. (1928), One of the Motive Factors in the Formation of the Super-Ego in Women. *Int. J. Psa.*, X, 1929.
Sandler, J. (1960), On the Concept of Superego. *This Annual*, XV.
Spiegel, L. A. (1958), Comments on the Psychoanalytic Psychology of Adolescence. *This Annual*, XIII.
Spitz, R. A. (1957), *No and Yes*. New York: International Universities Press.
—— (1958), On the Genesis of Superego Components. *This Annual*, XIII.
Weiss, P. (1949), The Biological Basis of Adaptation. In: *Adaptation*, ed. J. Romano. Ithaca: Cornell University Press.
Weissman, P. (1954), Ego and Superego in Obsessional Character and Neurosis. *Psa. Quart.*, XXIII.
Wexler, M. (1951), The Structural Problem in Schizophrenia: Therapeutic Implications. *Int. J. Psa.*, XXXII.
—— (1952), The Structural Problem in Schizophrenia: The Role of the Internal Object. In: *Psychotherapy With Schizophrenics*, ed. E. B. Brody & F. C. Redlich. New York: International Universities Press.

BLINDNESS AND ISOLATION

GEORGE S. KLEIN, PH.D. (New York)

The 1961 volume of this Annual contains a moving and sensitive report by Eveline B. Omwake and Albert J. Solnit on the treatment of a congenitally blind child. The case is unusual in a number of respects that earn it close study, not the least of which are the fresh and innovative features of a therapeutic strategy which was able to surmount extraordinary obstacles to communication. But it is the ramifications of the case to basic issues of affect and cognitive development that concern me here, for it is one of the valuable, not-to-be-passed-up dividends of a profound case history or of the rare experiment that successfully joins hitherto elusive variables in artful manipulation, that they bring theoretical issues into sharper focus. Giving the present case added interest and importance is the coincidence that the child's twin sister is normally sighted. Of immediate pertinence to my remarks, however, is the relevance of the sensory handicap to the child's symptomatology (including an extreme inhibition of touch and erotization of sensory experience), the relation between sensory deficit and stimulus deprivation that is vividly pointed up by the circumstances of the child's environment, and the implications of both handicaps for ego development generally and for affect and cognitive development in particular.

In order to make my points explicit, a certain distinction is necessary. Omwake and Solnit at times refer to the case as showing the effects of *blindness* on ego functioning. This tends, I think, to obscure the fact that the case illustrates two varieties of deprivation: a specific sensory restriction or deficit; and, in addition, an isolation from the environment—a drastic reduction of opportunities for

Prepared for a meeting of the Western New England Psychoanalytic Society, November 4, 1961, and revised for publication.

From the Research Center for Mental Health, New York University.

assessing environmental facts and signals having serious consequences for adjustment. The second seems to be an assault on the
synthetic function of the ego itself, whereas sensory deficit alone is
not. Examples of sensory deficit are blindness and deafness. Examples
of stimulus isolation are psychoses of solitary confinement, and of
language-isolated refugees (Solomon et al., 1961; Lifton, 1961). The
two classes of handicaps are not to be confused. Of course, perceptual
deprivation is to some extent always concomitant to isolation, one
reason being that the human voice is such a significant part of total
external stimulation. But the distinction is still there: interpersonal
isolation *without* sensory interference can produce symptoms; sensory deficit alone, without affective and interpersonal isolation, need
not.

What is at stake in the second, more critical "deprivation" is the
integrity or organizing rules or "transforms" that, on the one hand,
make it possible to accommodate and conserve the redundant structure of the environment, and, on the other, that take part in the
intrapsychic structuring of drives and of drive controls.

Thus the question faces us: to what extent are the evidences of
retardation and deficit in the present case due to a form of psychological seclusion, and to what extent to sheer alteration of sensory
input?

As for the latter, it can, I think, be safely said that blindness itself
does not necessarily produce cognitive or affective stunting. There
is very little to support the idea that blindness imposes an upper
limit on the potential development of the synthetic functions of the
ego, nor on the construction and differentiation of intrapsychic
structures of the environment that enable the organism to act and
think effectively and creatively. Very likely this development is
somewhat harder to achieve for the congenitally blind than for
others. By and large, however, the cognitive achievements of blind
people lead us to conclude that vision is a *medium* or *carrier* of
informational input, but not an indispensable medium.

There is, indeed, good grounds for believing, contrary to the
popular idea, that blindness, even congenital blindness, is by no
means as pervasive a handicap as deafness, for instance. Leona Tyler,
summarizing the main trends of evidence concerning intellectual
deficits in these handicaps, concludes: "Deafness, when it is con-

genital and complete, constitutes more of an intellectual handicap than blindness" (1956, p. 428). Of course, exact comparisons are difficult to make between the I.Q.'s of blind and deaf children, and those of children generally, because of unavoidable modifications of test materials and procedures. However, on educational tests in all subject matter fields, there seems little doubt that deaf children fare more poorly. Even here, however, deafness seems to be a handicap because of a factor other than the modality restriction alone. As Tyler puts it: "A person who is completely deaf is most handicapped because of his failure to acquire language at the time most children are learning it. That there can be outstanding individual exceptions to these trends—Helen Keller for example—goes without saying" (p. 428).

In short, we can surmise from the work on the relationship of physical defects to intelligence that nature has safeguarded the central nervous system's hegemony over intellectual functioning through structural arrangements that reduce its dependence on particular modalities. The sense modalities are carriers of input for high-order integrative achievements, but they are mainly carriers, not the indispensable organizers of this input. The synthetic function and its products in cognitive development are in this sense *relatively* autonomous of sensory modality. It is true, of course, that blindness is an extreme sensory handicap in that it cuts away a useful, perhaps even the most advantageous, avenue of information. But we should not confuse this with the cutting off of contact with events and objects of the environment and with opportunities for obtaining reliable feedbacks of action and perception, deprivations of which could threaten the organism's integrity. The general conclusions are that only a physical condition that acts on the central nervous system itself will have a debilitating effect upon intellectual development, and that only a developmental handicap that severely curtails the individual's opportunities for contacting his environment and for mastering language will have an irreversible, deleterious effect on intellectual performance.

Thus, it is in relation to the second kind of deprivation—restrictions of environmental contact—that the effects of blindness and of any other physical defect are to be assessed, these effects being not a direct consequence of blindness itself, but reflections of an environmental insufficiency which in one way or another does not allow the individual to utilize compensatory input channels to sustain the synthetic function.

This second, more fundamental, "deprivation" has to do with impairing the organism's opportunities of building up and sustaining intrapsychic structures that subserve cognition, affect, action, and motivation. In general, an impoverished environment, one with diminished heterogeneity and a reduced set of opportunities for manipulation and discrimination, produces an adult with reduced abilities to discriminate, stunted strategies for coping with requirements for detour and delay, and generally less taste for exploratory behavior. Environmental opportunity, provided through stimulation of appropriate frequency and quality, is critical not simply for sustaining the functional efficiency of structures; it is the "nutriment" of their development and differentiation. Appreciation of the stimulus context, its appropriateness and insufficiency, is centrally important too in the differentiation of drive structures, and their ever-more refined attunement to environmental possibility, a consideration that has made for important modifications in psychoanalytic drive theory by Hartmann (1950), Erikson (1959), and Rapaport (1960). All signs point to the conclusion that unless certain forms of stimulation-with-learning take place at certain as yet unknown critical periods of a child's life, it is likely that very intractable consequences for adulthood will result. It is this impoverishment, rather than the effects of sensory restriction per se, that is highlighted by the present case.

In this light, Omwake's and Solnit's contention that a blind child might develop a different "perceptual identity" than a sighted child needs qualification. I believe conceptual clarity would be better served by linking the issue of "perceptual identity" to cognitive style, meaning a high-order organizational tendency that is represented *through* perception, but is not synonymous with sensory *modality*. This is not to minimize the handicap of visual deficit, but I do not see anything to preclude the emergence in a blind child of a cognitive style that would correspond in essential ways with that of a seeing child's. On this point, it is to be hoped that further studies of the child's development will include a comparison of the perceptual styles of the sighted and blind twin. Such a comparison could be a long step toward clarifying the autonomous status of synthetic capacities of the ego in relation to sensory limitation. I will come back to this point.

Now, if we separate the matter of *modality* from that of *isolation*, it becomes understandable to say that the visual apparatus is by no means indispensable for ego functioning. That highly developed models of spatial organization and of environmental constancies can be achieved by the blind requires no demonstration, a fact that alone speaks for such a conclusion. By the same token, the existence of total blindness does not get us very far in accounting for the evidences of ego defects and arrested ego development. I do not believe that blindness was a primary determinant of symptoms in the present case; rather blindness became implicated in pathology because of a more fundamental threat to the synthetic function. The nature of the isolation or deprivations that may have been involved in this assault is by no means clear, but that is where our discussion should center.

As a starting point in this direction, it seems to me important to recognize, first, that blindness is a challenge not only to the child who has to cope with the deficit but to the child's *environment*. The consequences of blindness reflect the manner in which the challenge was met. Blindness occurs in a world of sighted individuals, creating an obligation for the latter to provide the necessary information— and language—to available channels to sustain the *intact* synthetic functioning of the ego. The emergence of adequate conceptual systems is vitally mediated by language. Given the tools of designation and language structure, tailored to modality capacity, a whole world of conceptual possibility and control is opened. Helen Keller *cum* Anne Sullivan is vivid testimony to this fact.

This argues for the special importance to the blind of adequate ego surrogates, in the person of the mother and those generally in closest physical contact with the child. Adequate ego surrogates at critical periods are vital for all children; for the blind and deaf their absence can be especially catastrophic to the development and maintenance of workable schemata of reality and of cognitive representations of drive tensions, the consequences of drive discharge, and drive control. I agree that there is probably a propensity in the blind child for unusual sensitivities, as the authors emphasize; an additional modality offers more *protection* as well as more *information*.

I agree, too, with Omwake's and Solnit's impression that the libidini-zation of hearing is probably more a danger in a blind child than in a sighted child. But I would emphasize that the essential factor here is not the blindness, but maladjustive consequences of a vacuum created by inadequate ego surrogates. In the present case, clearly vital in the creation of this vacuum, were the mother's depression and the withdrawal of the nursemaid who, while sharing responsibility for the twins' care, was clearly disposed to favor the sighted child with *active* ministrations. These difficulties would have been a heavy burden even for a sighted child to bear. Given adequate ego surro-gates, a blind child can develop into a much more sturdy adulthood than a sighted child reared in a context of affect deprivation. The unfortunate fact of the present case is the coincidence of both deprivations.

But now we come to the heart of the matter. What was the critical isolation or deprivation in the present case? What is the nature of the nutriment—the appropriate stimuli—that the child was deprived of? In what specific and critical respects were the mother's depression and the rejective behavior of the nurse implicated? Is the key con-sideration activity and passivity? But passivity or activity in what respects? Perhaps the critical failure of these figures was an uncom-municated lovingness. But why *should* this be crucial? In what specific ways is loving behavior vital for cognitive and drive develop-ment? And just what is "loving *behavior*" in precise detail? These questions demand a level of detailed observation that would be unfair to ask of the case report, and we must retreat to speculation.

To begin with, it seems to me useful to assume that an important nutriment for structure-building consists of stimulus opportunities that permit the child to obtain informational returns of contacts with his environment—*a continuing feedback-evaluation process by means of which the child develops ideas of an anticipatable and predictable reality*. Through such a process, and the structures it gives rise to, there develop highly differentiated distinctions between self and other and self and environment. There are plenty of indica-tions that such a feedback-evaluation process is critical in learning recurrent regularities of the environment and the perceptual con-stancies (Anokhin, 1961). Surely the mother, as the environment's representative who ordinarily affords the most secure opportunities of trial contacts, is an important ancillary of the child's ego in this process. By precept, example, admonition, and assertion, as advance scout and guide, she has a large hand in enlarging a cognitive repertory that would otherwise be severely limited by an insufficient motility.

The importance of the feedback process, generally, can be experimentally demonstrated. Disrupt, for example, the auditory feedback of speech by delaying for a fraction of a second the return of speech to the speaker's ear. Or have people wear lenses that invert the visual field. These circumstances set off an anxious battle for adequate feedback. The latter fact suggests that one of the prime sources of anxiety, in addition to drive eruptions and drive conflict, is in such states which threaten the adequacy of the synthetic function in respect to the feedback-evaluation process—states in which conception and perception do not fit the environment in a manner that makes action possible or effective.

All this, I think, it is safe to assert about the importance of feedback for intrapsychic structuring of the environment. The feedback-evaluation process is even more critical, however, in a second respect, about which we know little, but which is, in my opinion, more profoundly implicated in the deprivations suffered by the child —in the development of fine shadings of affect and of drive control.

One of the important implications to be drawn from the psychoanalytic theory of affects (Rapaport, 1953) is that the *informational* components of affect experience—its "signal" aspect—are critically important to *drive differentiation* and *drive control*. It is through affective reverberations that drive tension is known, and it is through affects produced by drive-generated contact with the environment that the *consequences* of such contacts are in part recorded in structures of action and thought.

Say, for instance, that the child's action momentarily provokes irritability in the mother. This, in turn, reverberates in the child in an affective response that is pointed toward both the action itself and the affective consequences it had in the parent. A process of this nature seems to me at the heart of what is meant by affect differentiation and the building of affective structures. Through the modeling of such affective structures is parental control internalized. It is easy to see, furthermore, that affect signals so developed can become an important, even indispensable, means of monitoring drive tensions. And in thus influencing the control and directions of drive discharge, affect structures would participate in altering the character of the drive itself and be an important medium of drive differentiation.

Thus, the utility of affect feedback seems to me in essential ways coordinate with exteroceptive and proprioceptive feedback. Internal means of monitoring the *fittingness* of affect signals to the control of drive are essential to drive development, in the same sense that there must be adequate monitoring of the fittingness of percepts and cognitive structures for action and thought. Together, these seem to me the principal stabilizers of adjustment.

Here, then, lay perhaps the insufficiency of the mother and also of the nurse: in the deleterious effect they had on the differentiation of the child's affective experience, a differentiation ordinarily made possible through the fine shadings of mutual responsiveness that are involved in the physical contacts of active, unambivalently loving behavior. From the muted or gross responsiveness of the mother surrogates there emerged no clear informational returns regarding the consequences of drive-generated actions; no language of affect developed between them and the child, which could serve the child in checking and guiding drive tension. I suggest that erotization of the child's tactile experience and hearing are to be referred to this failure of responsiveness. Note, for instance, the inert permissiveness of the mother to the tactile scanning of her breasts by the child. In short, the depression and guilt of the mother were serious for their effect in retarding the development of a language of affect helpful to drive differentiation and drive control.

At this point, speculation breaks off completely with data and even theory, for little is known of the subtle language of affect communication through body contact that is implied in this picture of a reverberatory interplay of drive tension and affect feedback. I believe, however, that the successes of therapy achieved thus far with this child have consisted in providing, through the transference on the one hand, a means of monitoring affect and drive tension, and, on the other hand, in the person of another ego surrogate, the teacher, greatly enriched opportunities for perceptual and cognitive control. It is interesting that in the course of time the child herself very carefully drew the distinction between these surrogates and seemed increasingly to recognize her need for both, neither substitutable for the other.

Because of these considerations, it also occurred to me that understanding in the present case would profit less from studies of sensory isolation that have involved radical, temporary alteration of exteroceptive inputs, than from Harry Harlow's studies of monkeys who were reared with artificial, e.g., cloth and wire-mesh "mothers" (Harlow and Comstock, 1961; Harlow and Harlow, 1961). Though it is altogether speculative to say so at the present time, it seems to me that Harlow's studies exemplify the importance of the active, affective contact I am trying to emphasize. Monkeys develop a fierce dependence upon their lifeless "mothers," of a sort not unlike the desperate clinging of our blind child, coming to prefer them to their real mothers. However, the gratification and security gained from such a "dependable," always available, unpunitive "mother" far from guarantee an untroubled adulthood. On the contrary, the monkeys so reared eventually showed patterns that cannot fail to impress one as remarkably parallel to the picture Omwake's and Solnit's blind child presented in her first therapeutic contact.

The present case offers opportunity for a study that I think would have considerable importance for the psychology of blindness. It is related to my emphasis earlier on the essential autonomy of the synthetic function, and it involves the question of the extent to which blind behavior reflects this primary autonomy and what my co-workers and I have referred to elsewhere as cognitive style (Klein, 1958; Gardner et al., 1959). By cognitive style I mean the relatively autonomous organizational directions of a function that are not directly determined by instinctual pressures.

Blindness, I have said, is to be understood not in terms of the loss of visual function but in the manner or organization of the information provided by the residual modalities. In the same logic, personality and cognitive styles are not in the retina, nor in the cochlear nucleus, nor in the corresponding cortical centers of these modalities. This implies that the effects of blindness might be determined by structural properties of ego control that transcend channels of sensory input and impose their organizational rules on the information provided by the intact modalities. Would it be possible, therefore, to speak of field independence or field dependence (Witkin et al., 1954) or of leveling and sharpening, scanning and focusing (Gardner et al., 1959) in the blind? This is not to underestimate that this particular child's struggle with blindness cannot be divorced from the special conditions of her family setting. Blindness may, however, to an unknown degree take the behavioral course it does because of organizational propensities that existed from the first in this particular child. The question has to do with how personality tendencies themselves *determine* the manner of coping with blindness. Ordinarily the issue would be difficult to approach directly. In the usual instances of blindness one cannot know whether the personality tendencies observed are themselves secondary derivatives of the restrictions created by the sensory deficit.

Now in this respect, the present case offers an extraordinary opportunity arising from the fact that the case is a twin, reared in the same household. Not much is said of the twin's sighted sister. It would be most valuable to know in what respects, *despite* the blindness, there are overlappings of temperament and cognitive style between the two children. Offhand, we should expect vast differences. But would not the similarities, should we find them, be of equal interest, especially in evaluating the consequences of the sensory deficit? In terms of such overlappings, it would be enlightening to evaluate the significance of blindness in the child's life space.

One other facet of the blind child's symptomatology—the libidinization of sounds—deserves further comment. I have remarked that the intellectual deficits of the blind are not as dramatic as the seeing person's perspective toward his world would imply. Yet there is a major source of disadvantage that emerges vividly in the Omwake and Solnit report which the authors emphasize with sensitivity—a disadvantage for adjustment that arises not from the *loss* of information from the visual channel, but from the *maximizing* of informational possibilities in an overemphasized intact channel. Vision helps reduce the encroachments of drive tension upon other modalities that are less well suited than vision for representing environmental structures. In this sense, a normally functioning visual apparatus shrinks auditory stimulation by reducing its status to that of a supportive medium for visually given information, and is an important asset for dealing with auditory stimulation defensively.

Finally I should at least briefly spotlight another factor that gives blindness a special significance for this particular child. It is the peculiar dilemma of being a *blind* twin. We know from Arlow (1960), Burlingham (1952), and others that twins develop rebelliousness from each other out of the necessity to reaffirm and reassert *distinctions*. The situation in the present case is different; the blind twin must discover in what ways she is the *same* as her sister. From the urgency of her gropings to achieve a conceptualization of blindness, I suspect this to be a very critical consideration. She has the same birthday, yet she experienced unequal treatment, especially in respect to the nursemaid. Surely twinship *and* blindness create in this child the problem of coming to terms with the bases and significance of her *in*equality.

BIBLIOGRAPHY

Anokhin, P. K. (1961), Features of the Afferent Apparatus of the Conditioned Reflex and Their Importance for Psychology. In: *Recent Soviet Psychology*, ed. N. O'Connor. New York: Liveright.

Arlow, J. A. (1960), Fantasy Systems in Twins. *Psa. Quart.*, XXIX.

Blank, H. R. (1957), Psychoanalysis and Blindness. *Psa. Quart.*, XXVI.

Burlingham, D. T. (1952), *Twins: A Study of Three Pairs of Identical Twins*. New York: International Universities Press.

Erikson, E. H. (1959), *Identity and the Life Cycle* [*Psychological Issues*, Monogr. No. 1]. New York: International Universities Press.

Gardner, R., Holzman, P. S., Klein, G. S., Linton, H., & Spence, D. P. (1959), *Cognitive Control: A Study of Individual Consistencies in Cognitive Behavior* [*Psychological Issues*, Monogr. No. 4]. New York: International Universities Press.

Harlow, H. F. & Comstock, G. C. (1961), Development of Affectional Patterns in Primates. Presented at the New York State Divisional Meeting of the American Psychiatric Association.

—— & Harlow, M. K. (1961), A Study of Animal Affection. *Natural History*, LXX.

Hartmann, H. (1950), The Mutual Influences in the Development of Ego and Id. *This Annual*, V.

Klein, G. S. (1958), Cognitive Control and Motivation. In: *Assessment of Human Motives*, ed. G. Lindzey. New York: Rinehart.

Lifton, R. J. (1961), *Thought Reform and the Psychology of Totalism*. New York: Norton.

Omwake, E. & Solnit, A. S. (1961), "It Isn't Fair": The Treatment of a Blind Child. *This Annual*, XVI.

Rapaport, D. (1953), On the Psychoanalytic Theory of Affects. *Int. J. Psa.*, XXXIV.

—— (1960), On the Psychoanalytic Theory of Motivation. In: *Nebraska Symposium on Motivation*, ed. M. R. Jones. Lincoln: University of Nebraska Press.

Solomon, P., Kubzansky, P., Leiderman, P. H., Mendelson, J. H., Trumbull, R., & Wexler, D., eds. (1961), *Sensory Deprivation.* Cambridge: Harvard University Press.

Tyler, L. A. (1956), *The Psychology of Human Differences.* New York: Appleton-Century-Crofts.

Witkin, H. A., Loomis, H. B., Hertzman, M., Machover, K., Bretnall Meissner, P., & Wapner, S. (1954), *Personality Through Perception: An Experimental and Clinical Study.* New York: Harper.

EGO IDEAL AND SUPEREGO

JEANNE LAMPL-DE GROOT, M.D. (Amsterdam)

Originally the terms "ego ideal" and "superego" were used by Freud interchangeably. This fact can be explained historically. From the study of psychopathology, especially of melancholic disorders, Freud concluded that a part of the ego (a province within the ego) could oppose itself to the ego proper, making demands upon it and punishing it as formerly the parents had done. This means that through the process of identification the superego is formed as a substructure of the ego. In the course of development this process occurs at the end of the phallic phase (at the onset of latency) as a result of the solution of the oedipal object relationships. The superego is, according to Freud's formulation, the heir of the oedipus complex, and comprises the child's wish to be like the parents (ideal formation) and to comply with the parental restrictions and demands (superego in a narrower sense). These conceptualizations could account for and explain a variety of pathological phenomena in individuals (Freud, 1914, 1917, 1923, 1924a, 1924b, 1925, 1931) as well as in mankind (Freud, 1921, 1927b, 1930, 1939). In addition, they also explained normal psychological processes, e.g., humor (1927a).

Notwithstanding the gains in insight, there continued to exist a number of problems and inconsistencies which, according to Freud, were in need of further study and explanation. In recent years several authors have made contributions to the superego problems. For a more detailed review of the literature, I refer the reader to Sandler (1960).

From a structural point of view, I think we must adhere to Freud's conception of the superego as a special substructure in the

Read before the 22nd Congress of the International Psycho-Analytical Association in Edinburgh, August, 1961.

human mind, established at the onset of latency. Yet how are we to explain the difficulties and confusions around this concept which many authors have mentioned? Structuralization of the mind is a maturational and developmental process. The genetic point of view has brought about many clarifications of mental processes. I therefore propose to turn to the genesis of mental substructures of the ego in approximately normal development, and to examine separately the ideal formation and the self-criticizing punishing agency.

THE GENESIS OF EGO SUBSTRUCTURES

The Genesis of the Ego Ideal

The child is born with an unstructured mind. The inborn potentialities out of which a structured mind is developed during growth are called by Freud the id in a wider sense; Hartmann (1939, 1950) speaks of the "undifferentiated phase." The newborn has vital needs which have to be sufficiently satisfied in order to guarantee survival and to ensure the reign of the pleasure principle. As long as the infant-mother unity is need-satisfying there is no stimulation for accelerating the maturational process. However, birth itself already causes unpleasurable sensations, and soon afterwards the satisfaction of needs does not occur as immediately and as completely so as to avoid unpleasure. The experiences of alternate pleasure and pain stimulate development, and gradually a primitive structuralization of the mind comes into being. A number of functions begin to develop: sensual stimuli are laid down into memory traces (structuralization of the brain), outside and inside are distinguished (object and self), testing of reality, etc. I do not need to mention all of them, they are too well known as functions which later on will be organized. In the structured mind they build up that ego organization which must attempt to allow sufficient satisfaction of needs and wishes and at the same time to adjust to the necessities of life and to the demands of the environment.[1]

I will now turn to a special function of the very primitive ego, manifesting itself already in the first months of life, because I think

[1] Modern ego psychology is so far advanced as to give us a fairly good insight into the development of a number of functions of the ego organization (Hartmann, 1939, 1950; and many other authors).

it has a bearing on our topic, the genesis of the later-established ego ideal.

When the little baby becomes aware of unpleasurable stimuli and tensions he is still bodily too immature to take appropriate action. He cannot produce food or warmth or comfort when he is hungry or cold or nearly overwhelmed by inner tensions. When the mother is not instantly available the infant takes refuge in "hallucinatory wish fulfillment," as Freud called it in earlier times.

I think these hallucinations occur already at a time when the function of distinguishing between self and outside world is not yet established. They appear during the narcissistic stage, when the mother (or the breast) is still part of the internal narcissistic milieu and not yet an object (Hoffer, 1950). However, as "hallucinating" does not abolish unpleasure in the long run, whereas the mother does, we may consider these processes as the starting point for the development of distinction between inner and outer world.

As long as no object outside the self is recognized these hallucinations are not yet fantasies, centering around an object that provides pleasure or abolition of unpleasure. They are self-centered and, as far as they can temporarily alleviate discomfort, the gain is narcissistic satisfaction.

The reason why I dwelt so long on this early and primitive ego function is that, in my opinion, we meet here with the basis of the ego ideal. In terms of structuralization we could speak of a forerunner of the ego ideal. According to this assumption, the genesis of the ego ideal is to be found in an ego function, which serves to provide pleasure and to undo pain, caused by frustrations. This latter function has already been described by me in another paper (1949). The ego ideal is an *agency of wish fulfillment.* If we pursue the further development of these primitive hallucinatory wish fulfillments, I think we find confirmation of this assumption.

When the infant has learned to distinguish between self and outer world he makes an object attachment to the breast and the mother, and he expects the mother to provide satisfaction. This object attachment is still a narcissistic one; the mother is loved not for her own sake, but merely as a need-satisfying object.

During this period of differentiation between self and object new sources of unpleasure arise for the infant when the mother does not provide satisfaction and love as completely and as instantly as he wants them. Even the most loving and devoted mother is unable to fulfill every wish, to abolish every pain or discomfort in her child. There are always situations when the child feels disappointed, frustrated, and above all *powerless* because he is unable to bring about a change in this painful state of unpleasure. To deal with this condition, so dangerous for his self-esteem (his narcissistic equilibrium), the child develops alongside the primitive hallucinatory wish fulfillments his comforting fantasies of grandeur and omnipotence. Together with the formation of object relations (first need-satisfying attachments, and later on relations of object constancy), the fantasies of omnipotence and idealization of his self continue to exist. They can easily be observed in toddlers in the preoedipal phase.

I mention two examples, among many: little John, aged two years, ten months, told his mother his penis would grow to be as big as the garden hose; he would fill the ocean and a big steamer would take him overseas.

Little Ann (three years) said: "When my penis will be as big as Dick's [her elder brother]. . . ." When her mother remarked: "But you are a little girl, only boys have a penis, why do you think you will get one?" Ann replied: "When I want it, I'll get it!"

The fantasies of grandeur are a narcissistic gratification and they heighten self-esteem. But gradually they begin to fail to do so because the child has the painful experience that they have no influence upon the actual events, and he feels his total powerlessness vis-à-vis reality. He then takes refuge in a second edition of fantasies which provide narcissistic gratification. He idealizes his parents and attributes to them omnipotence, in which he himself partakes. These images of ideal and almighty parents persist much longer, because the parents are, in comparison with the child, really much stronger, and more powerful. These fantasies flourish especially during the oedipal phase in which the child identifies himself with the parent of the same sex in order to replace him (or her) with the other parent. In normal development the child at the end of the oedipal phase accepts reality more or less through recognizing his powerlessness and the impossibility of being the mother's (or the father's) lover. His attachment to the parents is desexualized (neutralized) and a similar change takes places in his ego ideal. The contents of the ego

ideal are no longer exclusively: "I am as potent in sexual life and
in other achievements as the parents." The ideals are partly transferred to attainable goals: learning, development of bodily and
mental skills, understanding of reality and life in general. We know
that even so-called "normal" adults sometimes take refuge in former
fantasies of omnipotence in narcissistically frustrating situations.
However, when they are able to live up to their own mature norms
and ethics, they experience a more lasting and much greater satisfaction. *The ego ideal,* even when developed into norms, ethics, and
social ideals, *remains essentially an agency of wish fulfillment,* and it
supports the ego in dealing with the inevitable disappointments and
frustrations inherent in human life. In a way, it is still an ego function. However, just because it has its own contents and because it
sometimes puts a distance between itself and the other organized
ego functions, we can speak of an established substructure (or province) within the ego.

I shall next discuss the self-criticizing, prohibiting, and punishing agency which we could term "superego in a narrower sense" or
"conscience."

The Genesis of the Superego

Before the infant distinguishes between self and outside world
there is no question of "prohibitions, demands, or punishment."
The infant merely experiences sensations of unpleasure. When the
distinction between self and environment has been established the
infant may experience restrictions of his needs and wishes from
outside as prohibitions or demands. It seems plausible to assume
that the earlier unpleasurable sensations form the basis of his experience of these restrictions. When he protests against complying with
them, anxiety may arise. In order to avoid anxiety and to preserve
the object (later on the love of the object), he will begin to try to
live up to the demands.

The toddler may, to a certain extent, internalize the parental
demands and even their punishments. The acceptance of the inevitable environmental claims leads to the establishment of an ego
function, which can be considered to be a forerunner of conscience
and which thus is an *agency of restriction* imposed upon the little
child from outside. The conflict is between child and environment

and is apt to arouse anxiety, but not yet guilt. Only at the end of the oedipal phase, when the child must give up his sexual wishes, do the environmental demands and restrictions become an inner property. The ego functions of renouncing certain wish fulfillments and of complying with parental demands now can be structuralized into the judging superego or conscience.

In normal development the superego and the ego ideal guide the ego in its double task, on the one hand of allowing the individual to have sufficient satisfaction of drives, needs, impulses, etc., and on the other hand of modifying and sublimating part of them in order to live up to the demands of the outside world and to cope with the inevitable restrictions.

Summary

The genesis of the ego ideal and of the restricting superego or conscience is different. The ego ideal is originally and essentially a *need-satisfying agency,* whereas the superego (or conscience) is originally and essentially *a restricting and prohibiting agency*.

In the development of the ego ideal four phases can be distinguished:

1. "Hallucinatory" wish fulfillment in the narcissistic phase (in which self and outer world are not yet distinguished)
2. Fantasies of grandeur and omnipotence of the self after the infant has become aware of a distinction between inside and outside
3. Fantasies of the parents being omnipotent, and sharing their omnipotence after experiencing his own powerlessness
4. Formation of ethics and ideals as attainable goals after disillusionment by the idealized parents.

In the development of the restricting superego, four phases can be distinguished:

1. Experience of sensations of unpleasure
2. Renunciation of wish fulfillment and compliance with parental demands in order to preserve the parents' love
3. Internalization of single demands through identification with some parental demands during the preoedipal phase
4. Inner conscience and internal acceptance of restrictions and

punishments imposed by the parents and the wider environment
in order to guarantee a social relationship within a certain class
or group or milieu.

Now the question arises: how was it that originally both ego
ideal and restricting superego were seen as one single agency and
one substructure within the ego? I believe it is because at the onset
of latency their establishment is centered around the same object
representations, the parental images, the purely narcissistic prestages
having been abandoned. The content of the ego ideal, once the third
phase of its development has been reached, could be expressed as
follows: "I am like my parents (that is, in fantasy: omnipotent)."
The content of the superego from an early stage of its development
onward could be described in the following way: "I will live up to
the parents' demands, and punish myself like they punished me when
I fail to do so (that is, in fantasy: I have to be obedient to avoid loss
of love of the parents)."

The ego ideal's content, "I am like the parents," implies taking
over parental ideals and ethics. The superego's content, "I have to
do what the parents require of me," implies taking over parental
restrictions and prohibitions. Both institutions are marked by identification with the parents and the parental images. From the structural point of view, we can describe them as substructures within
the ego, as a change of part of the ego through these identifications.

If we examine their functions, however, they serve opposite
ends. The ego ideal serves wish fulfillment and is a gratifying agency.
The conscience (superego in the narrower sense) is a restricting and
prohibiting agency. However, in this strictly schematic sense, this
statement is true only in a very harmonious development. Because
both agencies unite into one substructure, they may considerably
influence each other's functions. The ego ideal's content, "I am like
my parents," can acquire an imperative compulsive character: "I
must be like my parents." Later on high ideals in general may be
experienced as demands.

Even within the range of so-called "normality" there are many
individual differences which can be explained in two ways: (1) we
may assume a definite and rigid change of function after the establishment of the substructure superego in the wider sense; and (2) we

may see them as individual variations which already show a tendency toward inharmonious development. I myself am inclined toward the second explanation, because in a number of cases we clearly observe that living up to ethics, ideals, and norms is and remains a source of pleasure. It may provide real satisfaction through heightening self-esteem and self-assurance and so promote a number of gratifying ego activities. A strong compulsion to normative and ethical behavior (Kant's categorical imperative) points to an oversevere, judging superego, as is, for example, often found in persons with an obsessional-neurotic character. As in many other instances, the transitions between "normality" and "pathology" are fluent.

Be this as it may, the origins of both agencies can be traced back to infancy. Under certain circumstances (most clearly in pathology), a disintegration of the one or the other, sometimes of both at the same time, takes place and regression to primitive, infantile stages occurs. Identifications with the mother and with the father naturally differ from each other. These as well as identifications made on different levels of development may again come to the fore and may cause splits in the entity of both agencies.

The Visibility of Structure in the Mind

I now want to take up a problem which Freud mentioned on several occasions but to which other psychoanalysts have not paid sufficient attention. In the behavior of a "normal," well-integrated, harmoniously developed adult, we cannot always directly distinguish the different structures and substructures of the mind, because in this case the mind acts as a whole. When a person's ego has secured sufficient satisfaction of id needs and impulses and when the ego is able to master the id strivings which cannot be satisfied, using their (neutralized) energy for constructive purposes, it is no longer possible to distinguish clearly what share the ego and id have in a number of activities. The same applies to a distinction between shares of the (judging) superego and the ego ideal in these activities. A person capable of living up to his inner ethics and ideals *and* capable of sound self-criticism, who can provide himself with sufficient gratifications in accordance with his own environment, acts as a whole, as an entity. The fact that the provinces of the mind were originally distinct and separate entities becomes apparent only under special circumstances. In "normal" individuals this occurs in specific life situations which require a reorientation, e.g., in adolescence where the former balance between id and ego, ego ideal and superego has to be revised due to the maturing sexuality, love life, and object choices. I described some of the problems involved in my paper "On Adolescence" (1960). In the menopause and in old age other problems arise. In these phases of relative unbalance the different structures of the mind and the various identifications may become much more visible until a new harmony is again achieved. It then becomes very clear that a variety of new contents has been added to the original ones.

In disturbed, inharmonious development which leads to neuroses, ego distortions, delinquency, psychoses, etc., the structuralization of the mind becomes much more observable. Partial and unequal regressions to earlier developmental stages of id, ego, ego ideal, and superego provide a clearer picture of how the mind was structuralized in the course of maturation and development.

For practical purposes we try to assess the nature and gravity of given disturbances and of their accessibility to psychoanalytic (or other psychotherapeutic) treatment. Treatment aims at tracing back the disturbances to their origins in order to enable the mature ego to employ the mental energies in a different (and healthier) way. In this context, it is necessary to look for criteria enabling us to assess the extent to which different parts of the structured mind have contributed to the disturbance. In many instances, the differences in the development of the superego and ego ideal may play an important role in the final outcome of the disturbance.

SOME PRACTICAL CONSIDERATIONS IN REGARD TO PSYCHOPATHOLOGY

The Classical Psychoneuroses

In hysteria, phobia, and obsessional neurosis a regression of libido and aggression to earlier developmental stages takes place in consequence of severe guilt feelings and strong castration anxiety. This early statement of Freud's can still be confirmed in our daily analytic work. The primary regression of the drives is sometimes followed by a secondary regression of a number of ego functions in connection with defensive processes and of some rigid defense mechanisms.[2] We then speak of ego distortions. The ego functions laid down in the ego ideal and restricting superego may participate in these events. This is clearly observable in obsessional neurotics. Here the drives regress to the anal phase and this regression is followed by a restriction of ego activities, e.g., of sublimated actions, and by a regression of the restricting superego, which becomes a very sadistic agency through sexualization and turning of aggression toward the self. The ego ideal may secondarily regress to the phase of fantasies of grandeur and omnipotence, of magical thinking. These processes cause distortion of reality testing. Usually a part of the ego is still very well able to judge reality, while another part follows the regressed egoideal functions and adheres to a belief in the possibility of magically influencing the environment. Thus, splits in the ego and ego ideal have come into being, and the patient feels torn apart.

In hysterical patients, the ego disturbance observable as a consequence of the regression of libido to the phallic phase seems to be less severe. It limits itself to an inhibition of some functions, e.g., of memory. The function of memory is more or less impaired through the defense mechanism of repression, which causes gaps in the patient's life history and may have a bearing on his judgment of reality factors.

Narcissistic Neuroses, Borderline Cases, and Psychoses

A different process seems to have occurred in these disorders. Here we may assume a regression of ego functions together with the libidinal regression. Both could be called primary regression. An alternative could be a disturbance of ego activities in the prephallic stage, an arrest of ego maturation, or a severe retardation in development originating already in the preoedipal phase. In narcissistic neuroses, it is sometimes difficult to decide whether we are dealing with an early arrest or with regression. In psychoses and borderline cases, there seems to be a closer tie to an early level of ego development. Concerning large areas of the restricting superego and of the ego ideal we clearly observe a position of an infantile nature. In these patients we see that the restricting superego has only partly

2 The distinction between primary and secondary ego regression is used by Anna Freud in the assessment of childhood development.

reached the state of an inner voice, of a real conscience. These patients can submit only to the actual restrictions coming from outside, and then under the pressure of severe anxiety and primitive fears. The internalized part is limited mostly to self-punishment of a very sadistic, cruel, archaic nature. The contents of the ego ideal of borderline patients are still the primitive ideals of the little child, the fantasies of grandeur and omnipotence. A development toward adult morals and ethics is lacking or defective. Naturally, the interplay between the id and the defective ego and superego functions may cause further distortions of the ego ideal, and thus interfere with its normal functioning.

Delinquents

A special discordance of the superego and ego-ideal development is found in delinquents. In my paper, "Neurotics, Delinquents and Ideal-Formation" (1949), I described some vicissitudes of the defective development of ideals and conscience. It is well known that delinquents often suffer from a severe, punishing superego, and that they often commit antisocial acts in order to satisfy their need for punishment. In many of these offenders we find a poorly developed ego ideal clinging to very primitive fantasies of grandeur. These pleasurable fantasies are retained in order to compensate for the pain experienced in the clash with the environment. The ego ideal has in principle preserved its original character as a wish-fulfilling agency. The superego in its turn holds to its restricting and punishing function, though both are distorted and fail to function in an adequate way. The ego ideal's failure to provide real and adequate wish fulfillments creates new frustrations, which in their turn cause further regression to primitive fantasies of omnipotence.

These sketchy remarks on different developments, normal and abnormal, are necessarily oversimplified. We must never forget that the different stages of preoedipal development contribute to the genesis of the ego, the restricting superego, and the ego ideal. The archaic state of mind scarcely ever disappears completely. Even with minor disturbances an inharmonious growth of these agencies can come into being. I have already mentioned that in approximately "normal" adolescence, disharmonies between the different parts and functions of the mind can be observed (1949). Within the ego-ideal functions proper, there may be unbalance as well. A person can have highly developed norms and ethics in one area, together with defective ones in other areas. One example out of many can be found in delinquency. A group of delinquents can adjust to a severe code of norms within their own group while offending the norms of the larger community and society. The same is valid for the restricting superego. Very severe demands and self-punishment in one area can exist side by side with refusal of acceptance of inevitable restrictions in other fields, e.g., where property and interests of other people are concerned.

SUMMARY

The ego ideal and the restricting superego originate alongside each other in primitive forerunners in infancy. They may be considered as special ego areas with their own functions. At the onset of the latency period they are centered around the parental images.

In harmonious development, they act together as a substructure within the ego organization, guiding the ego in its achievements. Throughout life the ego ideal remains essentially an agency of wish fulfillment. The superego is a restricting agency, necessary for living in a given community.

In abnormal development, traces of the origins of both ego ideal and superego can be observed as a consequence of fixations on and regressions to primitive developmental stages. The different identifications may be used as defense mechanisms in a pathological way and so add to the disharmony of the individual.

BIBLIOGRAPHY

Freud, A. (1936), *The Ego and the Mechanisms of Defense.* New York: International Universities Press, 1946.
Freud, S. (1914), On Narcissism: an Introduction. *Standard Edition,* XIV. London: Hogarth Press, 1957.
—— (1917), Mourning and Melancholia. *Standard Edition,* XIV. London: Hogarth Press, 1957.
—— (1921), Group Psychology and the Analysis of the Ego. *Standard Edition,* XVIII. London: Hogarth Press, 1955.
—— (1923), *The Ego and the Id.* London: Hogarth Press, 1927.
—— (1924a), The Economic Problem in Masochism. *Collected Papers,* II. London: Hogarth Press, 1946.

—— (1924b), The Passing of the Oedipus Complex. *Collected Papers*, II. London: Hogarth Press, 1946.

—— (1925), Some Psychological Consequences of the Anatomical Distinction Between the Sexes. *Collected Papers*, II. London: Hogarth Press, 1946.

—— (1927a), Humor. *Collected Papers*, V. London: Hogarth Press, 1950.

—— (1927b), *The Future of an Illusion*. London: Hogarth Press, 1928.

—— (1930), *Civilization and Its Discontents*. London: Hogarth Press, 1946.

—— (1931), Female Sexuality. *Collected Papers*, V. London: Hogarth Press, 1950.

—— (1932), *New Introductory Lectures on Psychoanalysis*. New York: Norton, 1933.

—— (1938), *An Outline of Psychoanalysis*. New York: Norton, 1949.

—— (1939), *Moses and Monotheism*. New York: Vintage Books, 1955.

Hartmann, H. (1939), *Ego Psychology and the Problem of Adaptation*. New York: International Universities Press, 1958.

—— (1950), Comments on the Psychoanalytic Theory of the Ego. *This Annual*, V.

Hoffer, W. (1950), A Reconsideration of Freud's Concept "Primary Narcissism." Unpublished Manuscript.

Lampl-de Groot, J. (1947), On the Development of Ego and Superego. *Int. J. Psa.*, XXVIII.

—— (1949), Neurotics, Delinquents and Ideal-Formation. In: *Searchlights on Delinquency*, ed. K. R. Eissler. New York: International Universities Press.

—— (1960), On Adolescence. *This Annual*, XV.

Sandler, J. (1960), On the Concept of Superego. *This Annual*, XV.

Schafer, R. (1960), The Loving and Beloved Superego in Freud's Structural Theory. *This Annual*, XV.

THE CLASSIFICATION OF SUPEREGO MATERIAL IN THE HAMPSTEAD INDEX

JOSEPH SANDLER, Ph.D., MARIA KAWENOKA, M.A.,
LILY NEURATH, B.A., BERNARD ROSENBLATT, Ph.D.,
ANNELIESE SCHNURMANN, B.A., and JOHN SIGAL, Ph.D.
(London)

In an earlier paper (Sandler, 1960) a theoretical model of superego functioning was put forward in an attempt to resolve a number of practical problems which had arisen in the classification of clinical material derived from the analyses of child patients, and relating to the superego. A further statement of aspects of this model is to be found in this Volume (see pp. 128-145). Accounts of the Hampstead Index have been given elsewhere (Anna Freud, 1959; Sandler, 1960, 1961).

In the present report an attempt has been made to present a preliminary and tentative system of classification based on the superego model, together with illustrative clinical examples derived from material at present recorded in the Index. This classification is by no means a final or complete one, and the headings and definitions are continually being revised as new clinical material comes to our attention.[1] There is, for obvious reasons, considerable overlap of headings.

The superego can be conceived of as having two main aspects.

The investigation reported here has been aided by a joint grant from the Foundations' Fund for Research in Psychiatry, New Haven, Connecticut, and the Psychoanalytic Research and Development Fund, Inc., New York.

The material used has been collected at the Hampstead Child-Therapy Clinic, a therapeutic and research center financed by the following foundations: The Field Foundation, Inc., New York; The Ford Foundation, New York; The Foundations' Fund for Research in Psychiatry, New Haven, Connecticut; The Anna Freud Foundation, New York; The Grant Foundation, Inc., New York; The Estate of Flora Haas, New York; The Old Dominion Foundation, U.S.A.; The Psychoanalytic Research and Development Fund, Inc., New York; The Taconic Foundation, New York.

[1] Since this paper has been written a substantial number of revisions has been made.

First, it includes a system of authority figures (either real persons or introjects); second, it embraces certain ego responses to these authority figures.

The approach adopted is designed to take into account difficulties in assessing superego functions in the actual therapeutic situation. More specifically it has been found necessary to consider the reactions of the ego, not only to the introjects, but also to real authority figures in the environment, as well as to externalized representatives of introjected authority figures.

Introjection in this context is regarded as consisting essentially of a transfer of authority from the perceived real object to its internal representative. This is a special usage of the term introjection and does not include ordinary perceiving and "taking in," but rather a definite transferring of status from the external figure to the superego. Moreover, introjection as used here is quite different from identification, which will be defined below.

Externalization of the superego here means the process of investing an external figure with the qualities of the introject and reacting to it as if it were the introject.

Some of the headings listed refer to general statements about the superego as a structure, while others embrace the responses of the ego to both internal and external authority. It is not necessary for a child to have achieved a structured superego in order to index clinical material in this section. A child of two, for instance, who behaves in a particular way in order to take account of the moral precepts of the parents will be reacting on the basis of a model of the parents which may only later become structuralized in the superego (introjected) .[2]

The headings and definitions which follow have been taken from the first draft manual for indexing superego material. The examples given should be understood as fragments of entire case records, necessarily out of context, and are given here for purposes of illustration only. Normally the index cards upon which this material is recorded contain detailed references to the regular case reports from which the examples have been extracted, so that those undertaking research work using the Index may be able to locate fuller information.

[2] For a fuller account, see Sandler (1960).

The six main headings in the superego section of the Index given below will later be broken down further into many subheadings. Definitions and criteria for classification under these headings will be given, together with illustrative examples.

    I. Characteristics
   II. Sources
  III. Contents Activating the Superego System
  IV. Ego Responses
   V. Regulation of the Feeling of Well-Being
  VI. Extent of Organization and Structuralization

I. Characteristics

Cards in this section contain statements referring to characteristics of the superego organization functioning as a structure or as a preautonomous superego schema. Where the superego is still in its preautonomous state, its characteristics will merge with features of authority figures in the child's object world, but will not necessarily be identical with them.

Etiological factors should be indicated in the text (e.g., particularly severe conflict over habit training, feeding; conflicts over temporary regression or over aggression).

Some indication should be given of the degree to which the characteristics are present.

Cards should indicate the particular impulses and actions tolerated or not tolerated, as the case may be.

The subheadings in this section are as follows:

  A. Supportive and Adequate
  B. Severe
  C. Demanding
  D. Indulgent
  E. Unpredictable and Inconsistent
  F. Uneven
  G. Corruptible
  H. Other Subheadings

A. *Supportive and Adequate*

The superego provides a sufficient degree of security and well-being appropriate for age-adequate independence and adjustment to reality.

B. *Severe*

Intolerant, sadistic, hypercritical, etc.

Example: Girl, age 6 (treated by M. Kawenoka)

The severity of her superego is reflected in her highly critical and demanding attitude toward herself; in her intense guilt feelings (e.g., over masturbation or aggression); in her tendency to self-punishment and bodily self-damage. In the course of her analysis, conflict over her aggressive drives appeared to be most intense and persistent, being related to her first separation from her mother (witness the onset of eczema at about that time).

Apart from her strong aggressive and anal drives (possibly innate), the following factors contributed to the severity of her superego: (1) the introjection of a very strict, obsessional father (she showed an identification with this introject); (2) a taboo in her family on the expression of aggression, which led to an increase in the aggression felt to be residing in her introjects; (3) her identification with the religious precepts so important in her home; (4) her identification with her parents' (especially her father's) highly critical attitude toward her.

C. *Demanding*

High standards of conduct or performance.

Example: Boy, age 10 (treated by L. Folkart)

He has already internalized his parents' high expectations of him. He cannot live up to these and therefore has to give up many activities which he feels he will not be able to accomplish. This can best be seen in regard to learning; e.g., when making a helicopter he decided not to put on some rather intricate and difficult transfers, explaining that they were not really necessary.

D. *Indulgent*

Overtolerant.

E. *Unpredictable and Inconsistent*

Varying superego responses to the *same* impulses or behavior of the child. (Distinguish this characteristic from "uneven.")[3]

F. *Uneven*

The superego reacts differently to *different* impulses. For example, some component drives may be permitted direct expression, while others are not tolerated. This heading should be used when the unevenness does not correspond to that which is expected at the age level of the child.

Example: Boy, age 10 (treated by I. Elkan)

He is often tormented by a harsh superego. It is characteristic of him to deprive himself of pleasure and enjoyment because of guilt. He has given many examples of how critical he feels of himself.

He does not want anyone to look "inside" him because "it is all nasty"—"I do nasty things." He comes for treatment because he is "naughty." When playing a game he remarks, "Naughty little me—peepy little me." When he almost hit the analyst with a key he said, "Oh naughty," and was excessively remorseful. He thinks his father should make strict rules and that he does not "deserve" to be picked for the choir because he talks in class and forgets his homework. He thinks that he deserves to be short-sighted because he looked too much and too closely at TV, wanting "to see every little detail."

On the other hand, he is very rebellious against authority most of the time and obstinately refuses to accept rules or reasonable prohibitions of his parents and teachers. For instance, he planned to come to the Clinic on his bike after dark, talking as if his parents' explicit prohibition against this was not known to him. Also he is excessively demanding of money, sweets, and the fulfillment of any wish he may have, and reacts with screaming tempers to their frustration.

G. *Corruptible*

The ego successfully deals with tension with external or internal authority by measures such as "buying off," placating, bribing, etc.

---

[3] For an account of three cases showing this characteristic, see A.-M. Sandler, Daunton, and Schnurmann (1957).

Example: Girl, age 13 (treated by A.-M. Sandler)

She is often able to use certain tricks to isolate her feelings of guilt and thus be quite free to go ahead, for example, with her scoptophilic activities. Her general feelings of being found out, or being unworthy, or just guilty are then completely isolated from the actual action, source of anxiety and guilt. She is, for example, able to act without any inhibition due to guilt when she acts for someone else. For example, she wrote very free love letters for B.'s boy friend, G.

II. Sources

An attempt should be made in this subsection to differentiate between object sources and instinctual sources. It should be recognized, however, that the child's object representations are much influenced and often distorted by his drives, wishes, and fantasies.

Object Sources

The particular objects in the environment of the child whose perceived characteristics enter into the presuperego schema and into the superego. The child's perception of the objects may, of course, be influenced in a number of ways, e.g., by idealization.

Instinctual Sources

The way in which the child's own instinctual drives and their derivatives are deployed in the superego, e.g., the reinforcement of the child's superego by his own aggression.

Example: Girl, age 5 (treated by M. Wheeler)

Her mother has been the most important figure in her world. She appears to be the superego figure much more strongly than the father.

Her superego in general seemed strong as indicated by her use of compliance as a response resulting from introjection of the castrating mother.

She attempts to do what mother wishes even in the treatment room where she now knows many activities are permitted. She is very frightened that the therapist might tell her mother about "forbidden" or "important" activities and conversations so that before one of her mother's visits, she always behaves in a controlled fashion in treatment.

III. Contents Activating the Superego System

The instinctual impulse, fantasy, affect, and the activity which typically activate the superego system should be specified. Distinguish as far as possible the unconscious from the conscious content. Include contents leading to anticipation of a reaction by external authority figures, for example, scoptophilia, masturbation, oedipal strivings, competition, success, etc.

The variety of contents in this section is so great that separate subheadings are not listed in the manual.

Example: Boy, age 13 (treated by R. Oppenheimer)

Competition.—Whenever he has talked a lot about his father's weaknesses and has brought aggressive material against him, he then tells the therapist of some nice things his father does. Quite often these talks are followed by his talking about his fear of dentists and barbers, which are interpreted as his fear of retaliation due to his guilt feelings.

Example: Boy, age 5 (treated by C. Heinicke)

Oedipal Wishes.—He showed anxiety about having had the mother to himself all week (father was away and the boy was the only "man" around the house). The idea of such a situation plus the unknown consequences provoked considerable anxiety especially as the day of the father's return approached.

Example: Boy, age 8 (treated by K. W. Gilbert)

Sexual Knowledge.—He has two sets of morals. At home he is treated like a small boy and consequently does not come out with his "big boy" knowledge. However, in school and at the Clinic where he can show off his knowledge he finds himself in conflict over this. When the therapist told him she had permission to discuss his sexual knowledge with him he said: "But I don't approve of it."

Example: Girl, age 11 (treated by B. Carr)

Pleasure and Success.—She shows excessive guilt over enjoying pleasure and being successful. She is unable to tell the therapist of pleasant things that have happened to her, for example, that she was chosen as the lead in the school play or that she has been to a party. If she is anticipating a pleasant week end, she says she hopes the therapist will have a nice week end.

Her guilt over outdoing others is extreme. She does not want to be the top at school, for the other girls would be jealous.

IV. Ego Responses

This subsection should ideally include all aspects of the ego's reaction to tension with internal or external authority.[4]

Material in this section refers to the responses resulting from fear of or wish to please or control internal or external authority. It should be noted whether the response follows an irruption of forbidden impulse in act or in fantasy, whether the response is predominantly autoplastic or alloplastic. The degree of sexualization should be indicated. Cards indexed under headings other than "affective states" should indicate the underlying affect.

The subheadings in this section are as follows:

A. Affective States
B. Fear of Punishment
C. Compliance
D. Defiance
E. Self-punishment
F. Provocation of Punishment
G. Self-depreciation
H. Making Amends
I. Demand for Approval and Reassurance
J. Avoidance
K. Rationalization and Excuses
L. Concealment
M. Anticipation of Unjust Accusation
N. "Splitting of Self"
O. Use of External Persons
P. Compensation by Fantasy
Q. Ideal Formation
R. Identification
S. Other Subheadings

[4] The list given here is not complete, and is continuous with a number of headings relating to aspects of ego functioning which are to be found in the Ego Manual of the Index.

A. *Affective States*

This heading is used when the therapist wishes to highlight the affective state. The cards should contain the evidence[5] on which the inference of the affective response is based, i.e., verbalization, motor behavior, reactions to interpretation, etc. If ideational rather than affective content is to be stressed, the material is indexed elsewhere. Examples of affective states noted in the Index are: Anxiety and worry, elation (including hypomania), feelings of guilt, feelings of well-being (contentedness), remorse, sadness (including depressive affect), shame, self-loathing, etc.

Example: Boy, age 9 (treated by B. Rosenblatt)

Anxiety and Worry.—Worries were one of his main symptoms (shown as a sleeping disturbance) at the time of referral. He had "bad thoughts" which troubled him especially at night, and he feared burglars and murderers. These phobic reactions could be understood and were interpreted as being due to the projection of unacceptable impulses upon familial objects, followed by further displacement. By the talion principle he feared that he would be attacked and robbed in the same way as he wanted to attack and rob.

These fears were in consequence of his "bad thoughts," and often gave him what he called "bad nights," which he felt to be a form of punishment.

Example: Girl, age 6 (treated by M. Kawenoka)

Feelings of Guilt.—She often gave evidence of intense guilt feelings about her aggressive wishes, masturbation, and sex play. She did not verbalize her feelings as such, but they could be inferred from her accounts of her brothers' naughty acts. These accounts were frequently maneuvers aimed at diminishing her own sense of guilt. Her guilt feelings could also be inferred from her provocative behavior aimed at receiving punishment and from actually causing herself to fall on a number of occasions.

B. *Fear of Punishment*

This particular affective response merits a heading of its own. The child's fear of punishment may be reality-based or distorted in

---

5 Our recent experience with the Index disclosed that affective states are seldom verbalized by child patients, and must usually be inferred indirectly. As a consequence of this, a research project is planned to make more explicit the criteria for inferring the existence of particular affective states in children.

varying degrees by fantasies and by defense mechanisms such as pro-jection and displacement. The content of the child's fear should contain the notion of punishment and should be described as far as possible (e.g., fears of being deserted, of disease, of criticism, etc.).

C. *Compliance*

The material should show compliance in act or fantasy to the demands of internal or external reality. This heading should include instances of overcompliance following the break-through of forbid-den wishes in act or fantasy.

Example: Boy, age 7 (treated by V. Thompson)
He complied with his mother's wish that he should terminate his analysis, even though he did not wish to do so. He expressed this compliance in a frequently repeated phrase: "I don't matter." That this was compliance to an authority which had been introjected to some extent was shown by the fact that he knew that even though he could continue with his analysis and would in reality not be punished if he expressed this wish clearly, he was nevertheless unable to put up a fight for its continuance.

D. *Defiance*

Material is included here showing deliberate disregard, dis-obedience, rejection of, or rebellion against internal or external authority.

E. *Self-punishment*

This section contains cards referring to self-inflicted damage or punishment where this results from tension with inner or outer authority. Three categories are distinguished:
(a) *Bodily damage.*—We include here forms of bodily hurt or damage which have been brought about consciously or uncon-sciously, deliberately or "by accident." Also included is the develop-ment or exacerbation of bodily symptoms for purposes of self-punishment.

Example: Boy, age 5 (treated by R. Oppenheimer)
When his material showed curiosity about his parents' activities át night and the therapist told him in story form that she could talk

with him about it, he denied curiosity and became restless. He climbed about on the furniture and several times the therapist had to hold him to prevent him from falling. Finally, he wanted to sit on a chair and slipped down, cutting his head badly.

On another occasion he felt angry because their household helper had brought him to the Clinic instead of his mother. When the therapist wanted to discuss this with him he got angry and started throwing bricks at her. Doing this he fell backwards and bumped his head against the cupboard.

(b) *Failure.*—Indexed here is material relating to the destruction of achievements or "spoiling" the outcome of activities before their completion.

Example: Boy, age 15 (treated by R. Oppenheimer)

After taking money from the therapist's purse, he came to the next session punctually. When the therapist confronted him with the fact that she knew he had stolen, he sat very quietly, avoided looking at her, and wiped his penknife. He then chopped off pieces of his hair and cut bits out of his ruler. When he played card games in the following session, he did not cheat as he usually did, but lost every game. Interpretation of his guilt feelings brought confirmatory material.

(c) *Suffering in Other Ways.*—This includes forms of moral masochism, permitting oneself to be exploited, and other types of self-damage and self-punishment.

Example: Girl, age 7 (treated by M. Flummerfelt)

She was unable to use the treatment for her own benefit because she had bragged at home about being the only one in the family to have a nice Clinic lady. Her inability to talk in the session is related to her need for punishment.

F. *Provocation of Punishment*

Cards under this heading should state the way in which the provocation serves to reduce tension with inner or outer authority. Also included are attempts made to reduce tension with inner or outer authority through the substitution of lesser offenses (e.g., certain forms of delinquency). Forms of moral masochism which involve provocation are indexed here.

Example: Girl, age 16 (treated by A. Bene)

Her appearance and behavior were often geared to provoke interest and suspicion of her person and of her activities. This was acted out twice on the Underground when she failed to pay the exact amount of money for her fare and then behaved in such a conspicuous way that she got herself into trouble (Juvenile Court). Her frequent violent outbursts at home were also the expression of her wish to be punished for the sexual feelings she had toward her parents. On these occasions—according to her—she put herself artificially into a state of rage. This was repeated frequently in the transference when she wished to get a rebuff from the therapist for the erotic wishes she had toward her.

Her exhibitionistic way of walking and dressing were meant to call mother's and therapist's attention to her prostitution fantasies, and via punishment or prohibition from these authority figures she hoped to gain control over these wishes.

G. *Self-depreciation*

This includes devaluation of the self and of achievements (e.g., expressions of inferiority, inadequacy, and wickedness). Material should show clearly that the self-depreciation is a response to tension with inner or outer authority.

Example: Girl, age 6 (treated by A. Schnurmann)

She feels that she is damaged, dirty, and not worthy of love. Her superego functions quite independently of outside authority, whose reassurance she rejects.

While painting she referred to a dirty-looking green color in her paintbox and said, "We are going to use it because we never have before. It is a poor, neglected green. We tell it that it is nice, but it knows that it is not, but we pretend that it is, whispering all the time that it is really an ugly color."

H. *Making Amends*

This includes apologies, appeasement, atonement, reparation, etc. The essence of material indexed here is that it implies more than compliance with parental demands.

Example: Girl, age 12 (treated by B. Gordon)

She feels guilty when members of her family are ill and has to buy them presents. She insists on strict observance of silence on Remembrance Day. Her guilt feelings derive from her aggressive and oedipal fantasies and early sadistic desires toward mother and father, and her death wishes against sister.

Her guilt feelings and need to show her badness in symptoms were relieved through interpretation of and linking with: (1) her fantasies of sadistic acquisition of the mother's breast and father's penis; (2) her intense oedipal murderous wishes; and (3) her consequent fear of being mad.

I. *Demand for Approval and Reassurance*

Requests for expressions of approval or forgiveness from external authority in order to mitigate tension with inner or outer authority are indexed here.

Example: Boy, age 7 (treated by H. Kennedy)

He reacted to the slightest indication of disapproval (imagined or real) with great anxiety. He immediately wanted reassurance that he was liked, that the therapist will not leave him and will look after him.

Following the departure of his nanny, this anxiety became more pronounced and he would insist that the therapist should "look after him with her eyes," i.e., look at him approvingly.

J. *Avoidance*

Material indexed here should illustrate the avoidance of specific situations or acts which are consciously or unconsciously anticipated to evoke conflict with inner or outer authority. Included here are both the avoidance by the child of the scene of temptation and the removal of the source of temptation.

Example: Girl, age 6 (treated by A. Schnurmann)

Her treatment during the first two years of her analysis took place in the basement of the Clinic, and she felt very attracted by the water taps in the back kitchen and the sand tray in the garden. She often made use of these for aggressive messing. When the temptation and guilt threatened to overwhelm her she would run out of the kitchen or garden almost in a panic, either before or after the "forbidden" act.

K. *Rationalization and Excuses*

This includes both excuses to others and self-justification.

Example: Boy, age 10 (treated by B. Gordon)

He uses various methods to cope with his strong sense of guilt. Some outstanding ones are a kind of rationalization: "One must be mad to do it, so one does not know what one is doing." At the same time madness is punishment for forbidden wishes or actions. Another form of saving himself feeling guilty is "empty-headedness," similarly a compromise between exoneration from guilt by cutting out conscious thinking and self-punishment.

L. *Concealment*

The emphasis here is on conscious concealment, including denying and lying.

Example: Boy, age 8 (treated by B. Rosenblatt)

In order to evade the guilt feelings he might experience if he told the therapist of some of his activities, he often concealed them from the therapist or lied about them. For example, after analysis had shown that he and his brother played active sexual games together, the therapist asked him directly if they handled each other's genitals. He denied this, but his mother reported spontaneously that the two boys grabbed each other's genitals in the bath.

M. *Anticipation of Unjust Accusation*

This includes not only fantasies or anticipation of manifestly unjust criticism, but also the maneuvering of situations to evoke accusation. Here a feeling of righteousness replaces the guilt.

Example: Girl, age 12 (treated by E. Yeo)

She had many fantasies anticipating aggression from parents, teachers, therapist, etc., and her own consequent defiance. This was displaced to absurdly unimportant misdemeanors; e.g., she imagines the Club Crafts teacher will be angry because she has not done very good blanket stitch on a toy. "I don't care what she says: I'm not going to do it again," etc. Similarly in the transference; she fantasies the therapist's anger and her defiance if she discards one sheet of drawing paper and starts on a new one.

Example: Girl, age 7 (treated by A. Schnurmann)

She cheats in games. But she occasionally contrives to be "caught" by the therapist, when in fact she has played straight and can indignantly protest her innocence. She also often tells lies in which she represents her wishes as facts; e.g., that she is going on a school journey, that she will stay up till midnight, that the parents are buying a car, etc. But when she tells the therapist one reality event which is obviously true, e.g., that the grandparents are coming for dinner or that she is going to a party, she reproaches the therapist for not believing her, and repeats this accusation in front of the mother whom she asks to confirm that what she has said is true.

At the back of this is her guilt about her sexual activities which she kept secret and lied about to the therapist.

N. *"Splitting of Self"*

We include here the utilization of two or more simultaneous self-images, usually of the form of "good" and "bad" selves (so-called "splitting of the self"), enabling the child to disown and at times also to enjoy forbidden wishes, impulses or acts.

Example: Girl, age 12 (treated by B. Gordon)

In the first treatment phase Marian thought of herself as a wholly bad person, as she had already shown in the test situation. When able to tolerate good and bad feelings, Marian thought of herself as a dual personality, Mary and Ann, the bad and the good girl. This is based on the split in her object relationships. In discussing Marian's splitting her name into two, Mary and Ann, it was mentioned that Mary is also the name of the (paternal) grandmother who is very much hated by Marian's mother; therefore, "Mary" not only represents Marian's own bad half, but it also personifies the person whom the mother hates. To love the mother goes together with being loved by her, hence the rejection of this part of her name.

O. *Use of External Persons*

The text should indicate whether external persons or their representatives are merely perceived as authority figures or whether the child wishes, provokes, or seduces external objects to act like, replace, or supplement his superego figures, or uses them to lessen guilt. The text should indicate whether external objects are used to inhibit or to sanction instinctual expression.[6]

A number of subcategories are distinguished:

(a) *Shifting of Guilt and Responsibility* for forbidden acts, thoughts and wishes.

By blaming others: This includes the attribution of responsibility for the forbidden act or wish to another person.

[6] The whole topic of projection and externalization, in respect to ego and superego functioning, is at present being investigated as part of an index research project.

Example: Girl, age 11 (treated by R. Oppenheimer)

She complained that her parents never told her what to do and never made her do things such as homework. She feels that her mother does not give her enough guidance, and that the reason for this is that mother does not care sufficiently. She also complains sometimes about her teachers that they do not exactly tell her what to do.

By provocation: "Provocation" is used here to include all means, conscious or unconscious, whereby others are induced to gratify a forbidden wish and thus to bear responsibility for the forbidden gratification. An example of this would be the case of a child who, instead of masturbating, provokes others into handling his body in such a way as to give the child sexual pleasure, and thereby avoids masturbation guilt. We include here such phenomena as the instigation of others to commit acts "by proxy," or being the "mover behind the scene," etc.[7]

Example: Boy, age 9 (treated by B. Rosenblatt)

One of this child's gains from his sadomasochistic relationship with his brother was that it reduced his feeling of guilt and responsibility for erections and sexual pleasure. This was interpreted in one of his sessions when he brought the following material: his brother and he had a quarrel over some biscuits. The interpretation given was that he had provoked the quarrel to get his brother's attention. Later in the hour he called the therapist's attention to a bruise which he had received while playing football. He repeated several times that the bruise "is growing bigger." The interpretation was then given (based on his previous material) that his penis got bigger when he wrestled with his brother or provoked his brother to attack him physically. By provoking these attacks his penis could grow bigger and feel good without his having to touch it and without his therefore feeling guilty.

(b) *Sharing of Guilt and Responsibility.*—Here the child dilutes his guilt feelings through sharing the responsibility with others (e.g., "It wasn't only me").

Example: Boy, age 11 (treated by B. Gordon)

He organized a gang of friends with the avowed purpose of doing good deeds. The main purpose was to attack fathers and extort money

[7] The "Sabbath-goy" mechanism. (A Sabbath-goy is a gentile employed by orthodox Jews to perform acts forbidden to Jews on the Sabbath.)

from them. This took place as a consequence of his unsuccessful attempts to take his father's place. He sought strength and exculpation of guilt through numbers and the extrafamily group.

(c) *Finding Fault in Others.*—This includes the lessening of guilt feelings by finding fault in others. This "fault finding" need not necessarily be for the forbidden act or wish, but may be for other acts or faults as well (e.g., "picking on" others).

(d) *Substitution of Authority Figures.*—This includes the use of external figures or institutions (the Church, Boy Scouts, etc.) to replace or supplement the child's authority figures.

Example: Boy, age 6 (treated by V. Thompson)

He has used religious concepts as extensions of the parental moral demands, which he had not completely internalized, to prevent the expression of his instinctual wishes. At a time when he was much preoccupied with the effects of his aggression, he made the soldiers in his games carry a church round with them which they used both on land and sea, in order to "say their prayers." This was understood as a wish to protect himself in this way from his aggressive fantasies. Similarly, whenever a discussion of adult sexual activities, or castration fears, or masturbation came up, he asked the therapist: "And why do you never talk about the devil?" Or he made some reference to Hell.

(e) *Displacement of Authority Figures.*—This is the process by which external persons are perceived as, or made to act like, the child's internal or external authority figures as a means of reducing tension with inner or outer authority. This includes so-called "projection of the superego," e.g., investing a neutral stranger with the authority and quality of the introject. This is perhaps most commonly observed in the treatment situation.

Here the qualities of the authority figure, in addition to its authority, are transferred to the other person, whereas in "substitution of authority figures" only the authority and status of the authority figures are transferred.

Example: Boy, age 8 (treated by B. Rosenblatt)

He saw the therapist in the transference as someone who could be pleased with him and approve of him, in the same way as his father. He tried his best to be a good patient and sometimes asked at the end of his hour whether it had been a good one or not.

(f) *Other Uses of External Persons.*—This section contains all other uses of external persons or institutions for the purpose of reducing tension with inner or outer authority.

P. *Compensation by Fantasy*

This is planned to contain all the child's fantasies which are related to the child's creation of an imaginative situation directed toward reducing tension with internal or external authority. At present cards belonging here are classified in the Fantasy section of the Index, which is being revised.

Example: Boy, age 13 (treated by I. Paret)
According to his family, he habitually told exaggerated and untrue stories. His "tales" were an outcome of his need to deal with feelings of inadequacy which arise from a highly critical superego.

Q. *Ideal Formation*

The classification of the sources, functions, and characteristics of the self-ideal (ego ideal) is being prepared. At present material is placed under this heading at the therapist's discretion.

R. *Identification*

Identification is regarded as an ego activity, and no formal differentiation is made between so-called superego and ego identifications (Sandler, 1960, 1962; Sandler and Rosenblatt, 1962). However, identification can serve a number of functions, some of which relate to the regulation of tension with inner or outer authority; therefore, a scheme of classification of identification according to a number of criteria is being devised. At present all material relating to identification is being indexed in the Ego section of the Index.[8]

---

[8] The relevant section in the Ego manual reads: *Identification* (covering certain usages of the terms introjection and incorporation in the literature): The appropriation by the individual of a mental or physical attribute, real or fantasied, of the object world, becoming, or being treated as, part of the self-representation, or the ideal self, permanently or temporarily. Although this is a process serving ego development in general, it can be put to specific defensive use. The latter happens when such appropriations are made to avoid or mitigate external or internal threats or dangers. If this is the case, the text cards should be placed under the appropriate "Defenses" heading.

Included in this section for the time being will be cards illustrating such ego

V. Regulation of the Feeling of Well-being

This is at present under investigation. For the time being, cards should be place under this heading when they contain material referring to the influence, or lack of influence, of authority figures upon the child's feelings of well-being and self-esteem. Cards should show in this connection the motives for the child's authority-oriented behavior, and also the extent to which this behavior is effective in regard to the regulation of well-being. It is not sufficient here to speak of "guilt feelings," but an attempt should be made to break these down into specific components. A distinction should be made, for example, between such factors as: the gaining of a feeling of omnipotence through identification with admired objects, or its opposite, the feeling of worthlessness which can arise from a lack of such identification; the loss or gain of love from the object (we include here loss of the object); the experience or avoidance of physical hurt; retaliation or reward in kind; losing or gaining a penis or its equivalent; praising or condemnation; shaming or admiring; and other punishments or rewards (e.g., gifts versus deprivations).

The degree of reality or fantasy in the child's anticipations should be indicated.

Example: Girl,[9] age 9 (treated by C. Legg)

With entry into school her methods of increasing her feeling of well-being (narcissistic supplies) gradually became more appropriate to her age, and were no longer confined to simple dependence on her loved objects. Previously she had reinforced her need for physical contact by clutching people aggressively. Her very primitive attempt to control the object was now replaced by attempts to increase her self-esteem by winning praise from her parents for the successful performance of everyday tasks.

VI. Extent of Organization and Structuralization

Any illustrative material relevant to stages or processes of superego development should be indexed here. Cards should give a pic-

---

responses to superego figures as "the child feeling like, behaving like, or professing the standards of admired, respected or feared objects, or their internal representatives."

The Ego manual of the Index also further differentiates various subtypes of identification.

[9] A blind child.

ture of the state of superego development and also indicate changes during the course of treatment.

Where external persons are habitually used as authority figures an attempt should be made to differentiate between the tendencies to use persons and institutions as

(1) externalization of introjects (externalization of superego);
(2) replacements for introjects;
(3) as real figures of authority who are relatively independent of the introjects.

It may be found convenient to use the following two subheadings:

Organization of the superego. The extent to which aspects of the authority figures and ego responses and functions are coordinated and integrated (irrespective of whether introjection of authority and consequent establishment of the superego as an autonomous structure has taken place).

Structuralization of the superego. The extent to which the superego functions autonomously, i.e., the extent to which external authority has been introjected.

Example: Girl, age 7 (treated by A. Bene)

In the first year of treatment her uncontrolled aggressive outbursts and the damaging way she treated her own self and body showed the conflict between instinctual forces and her ego's attempt to deal with them in the service of the punitive forces of her superego. In the course of the analysis she was able to work through her oedipal rivalry and establish identification with her mother.

Mother's intellectual ambitions became her ideals. She drove herself with unusual harshness to learn and read, which she had previously refused to do, and which she did now with the same intensity as her previous aggressive activities. This intensity and strictness loosened toward the end of analysis and in the subsequent year. Intellectual ambitions became her own, and she was able to be successful in her studies, where previously she could not learn at all.

Example: Boy, age 13 (treated by R. Oppenheimer)

He does not show much superego conflict. He is afraid of punishment and retaliation, and of loss of love if found out. If he can do so safely, he will follow his impulses. This can be particularly well seen in his stealing, which he keeps a secret from his parents but talks about to his therapist. His dependence on his mother for decisions also shows that he has not yet been able to internalize fully the parents' standards, a fact which is understood to be due to his fixation to the oedipal level.

During the second half of the second year of treatment he has shown a little more superego conflict, but he still would rather depend on external objects to advise him whether he should do a thing or not. This is largely due to the fact that he reacts with guilt when he takes a decision upon himself feeling that his mother will not like it when he acts in an independent way. She makes him feel that he can only be loved by her if he does what she says. He then rebels when this is not in accordance with his own wishes, but is unable to internalize her standards.

Example: Girl, age 7 (treated by I. Paret)

She is an autistic child arrested at a very primitive level of libidinal and ego development and there is no evidence of a structured superego. However, after eighteen months of treatment she was able to internalize a prohibition. She wanted to enter another therapist's treatment room and the therapist had to prevent this by holding the door shut. The patient shouted. The next day when passing the same room she grunted loudly while the therapist still had to hold the door closed. Afterwards the therapist did not need to hold the door, and she simply grunted and did not attempt to go in. On the following day and from then on she passed this door with or without the therapist, gave a tiny grunt to herself, and did not try to enter.

It cannot be emphasized too strongly that the headings given above are provisional and tentative, and are designed to demonstrate a mode of approach to the recording of superego material rather than to provide a completed system of classification.

BIBLIOGRAPHY

Freud, A. (1959), Clinical Studies in Psychoanalysis: Research Project of the Hampstead Child-Therapy Clinic. *This Annual,* XIV.

Sandler, A.-M., Daunton, E., & Schnurmann, A. (1957), Inconsistency in the Mother As a Factor in Character Development: A Comparative Study. *This Annual,* XII.

Sandler, J. (1960), On the Concept of Superego. *This Annual,* XV.

—— (1961), The Hampstead Index As an Instrument of Psycho-Analytic Research (read to the 22nd International Psycho-Analytical Congress, Edinburgh). *Int. J. Psa.* (in press).

—— (1962), Psychology and Psychoanalysis. *Brit. J. Med. Psychol.,* XXXV.

—— & Rosenblatt, B. (1962), The Concept of the Representational World. *This Annual,* XVII.

THE CONCEPT OF THE REPRESENTATIONAL WORLD

JOSEPH SANDLER, PH.D. and

BERNARD ROSENBLATT, PH.D. (London)

It may seem strange at first sight that such a formal and routine procedure as constructing an index to psychoanalytic case material could be the focus of active, and at times exciting, research. However, this is indeed the case, and the present paper aims at giving some of the work which has been going on in the research committees of the Index.

Those of us who work on the Index have been impressed by the way in which the need to categorize and classify psychoanalytic material derived from the analyses of child patients forces us to think about our theoretical models, to go into these models in more detail, occasionally to supplement or modify them, and finally to define exactly what we mean by the terms we use. There is a constant interaction between our clinical material and our theoretical formulations, an interaction which seems to us to be an essential constituent of all scientific procedures (Sandler, 1961).

Based on a paper presented to a meeting (prior to the International Psycho-Analytical Congress, Edinburgh) at the Hampstead Child-Therapy Clinic, July, 1961. The work reported here has been aided by a joint grant from the Foundations' Fund for Research in Psychiatry, New Haven, Connecticut, and the Psychoanalytic Research and Development Fund, Inc., New York.

The material used has been taken from the Hampstead Child-Therapy Clinic, a therapeutic and research center financed by the following foundations: The Field Foundation, Inc., New York; The Ford Foundation, New York; The Foundations' Fund for Research in Psychiatry, New Haven, Connecticut; The Anna Freud Foundation, New York; The Grant Foundation, Inc., New York; The Estate of Flora Haas, New York; The Old Dominion Foundation, U.S.A.; The Psychoanalytic Research and Development Fund, Inc., New York; The Taconic Foundation, New York.

Grateful acknowledgment is due to Miss Anna Freud, Professor Irving Janis, Mrs. L. Neurath, Mrs. A.-M. Sandler, Mrs. M. Kawenoka, Miss A. Bene, Mrs. H. Kennedy, Mrs. S. Rosenfeld, and Miss A. Schnurmann, who have all contributed to the formulations in this paper. Special thanks are also due to Dr. K. R. Eissler for valuable and stimulating comments on an earlier formulation of these ideas.

The material which follows has been selected from some of the work of three research groups (Superego, Fantasy, and Self-Esteem groups) of the Index. All this work is cooperative, a number of therapists and analysts being involved. The present account deals with a conceptual thread which has run through much of our research work, beginning with our work on the superego, and continuing into problems of self-esteem regulation and the function of fantasy.[1]

Although the notion of the *superego* plays an important part in clinical work and in psychoanalytic theory, it was noticed a little while ago that therapists tended, when indexing their cases, to avoid conceptualizing their material in terms of the participation of the superego. They turned instead to other sections of the Index and preferred to classify their material there, in sections such as "Treatment Situation and Technique," "Object Relationships," and so on. (This can occur because therapists are permitted, when indexing their material, to choose the avenue of approach which they prefer, and which appears to them to encompass the analytic material most satisfactorily.) A study of this phenomenon[2] showed that at least two factors were operating to produce it. The first was that what may have been internalized as the superego in a child patient often tended to be externalized as a transference relationship in the treatment situation. This led to an apparent "dissolution" of the superego. For example, if a child's superego had been largely influenced by the child's object relationship to his father, this might tend to re-establish itself as a relationship to the therapist in the course of treat-

[1] The research groups are primarily discussion groups dealing with various theoretical issues in their relation to actual indexed clinical material, and the membership of the different groups overlaps considerably. One of the techniques used in the work of such groups is for one or more of the members to present, in rather dogmatic form, formulations as they stand at any one moment. These are then critically discussed by the other members. The paper shows the influence of this method, and it should be stressed that the theoretical propositions included in it are to some extent still tentative, and discussion of them is proceeding. Some of the terms used—for instance, "representation" and "representational world"—are provisional, and it is possible, in the light of recent correspondence with Mr. James Strachey, that these will be altered.

Essentially, this presentation is in the nature of a scaffolding, which raises in turn further interesting theoretical problems.

[2] A full discussion of the indexing problems leading to the formation of the Superego research group, and the findings and formulations which arose from the work of the group, may be found elsewhere (Sandler, 1960).

ment. The therapist might then be inclined to see the material produced by the child more clearly in terms of the externalized conflictual relationship rather than the internal structural one, and would index the material accordingly.

This observation has opened up a number of research problems. Do we see in this phenomenon a general tendency in all children (or adults, for that matter) to re-externalize internal conflicts, or, as seems more likely, is this tendency greater in some children than in others? If such differences exist, what determines them?

Apart from the so-called dissolution or regression of the superego in the analytic situation, it became clear to us that one of the difficulties that the therapists had in indexing their material in superego terms was the unclarities and contradictions which exist in psychoanalytic theory about such concepts as identification and introjection, the difference between "superego" and "ego" identifications, and so on.[3]

It was remarkable that as long as we did not have to categorize the actual analytic observations, we could set down definitions which appeared to be suitable and adequate. However, their relative lack of exactitude often emerged when we had to apply these definitions to the clinical observations; or conversely, when we had to fit the clinical observations to the categories which we had defined in theoretical terms. At this point we were forced to sit down and produce a theoretical construction which would be, at one and the same time, strictly psychoanalytic, and yet would prove serviceable enough to encompass our clinical observations. As a consequence of this, the Superego group produced a theoretical model which appeared to contain our material satisfactorily, and which we believe did no violence to Freud's statements on the ego ideal and superego. In this we found ourselves leaning particularly on the formulations in his paper on "Narcissism" (1914). We also felt that we had to take into account recent developments in psychoanalytic ego psychology and in the related theory of perception—a field of study which has become an increasingly important part of psychoanalytic psychology.

In all our considerations we have made use of a notion which seems to us to be a central one in psychoanalysis, that of the child's

[3] When the Superego group turned to the Ego research group for guidance, it was found that they had been encountering exactly the same difficulties.

subjective *world*, a world which is only gradually differentiated in the course of development as a consequence of processes of biological and psychological adaptation. As we have used it, it includes Freud's *internal world* (1938) and Hartmann's *inner world* (1939) (both *innere Welt* in the original German), and is related to the concepts of the child's world described by Piaget (1937) and Werner (1940) as well as to the work of Head (1926) and Schilder (1935) on the body schema or image.

In the last chapter of the *Outline of Psychoanalysis* (1938), a chapter called "The Internal World," Freud differentiates between the *external* and *internal* worlds of the child. The child's objects are initially located in the external world, but by the age of about five, an important change has taken place. "A portion of the external world has, at least partially, been given up as an object and instead, by means of identification, taken into the ego—that is, has become an integral part of the internal world. This new mental agency continues to carry on the functions which have hitherto been performed by the corresponding people in the external world. . . ." (In this account of superego formation Freud did not find it necessary to differentiate between identification and introjection.)

Freud's use of the terms "internal" and "external" is meant to be purely descriptive. Before the formation of the superego proper, the child's objects exist in the external world, and with superego formation they acquire an autonomous existence in the mind of the child in the form of a new mental agency, and are thus, descriptively, internal.

However, if we take into account our knowledge that perception of objects in the external world cannot take place without the development, within the ego of the child, of an increasingly organized and complex set of representations of external reality, then we have to go further than a purely descriptive differentiation between "internal" and "external," and for our present theoretical purpose, we will have to approach the metapsychological problem of the child's "world" from a rather different point of view.

The representations which the child constructs enable him to perceive sensations arising from various sources, to organize, and structure them in a meaningful way. We know that perception is an *active* process (Sandler, 1959) by means of which the ego transforms raw sensory data into meaningful percepts. From this it follows that the child creates, within its perceptual or *representational* world, images and organizations of his internal as well as external environment. It is well known that the infant constantly confuses aspects of what we as *observers* would describe as "internal" and external" reality within its representational world.[4]

All this means that in order to know what is "outside," the child has to create a representation of that "outside" as part of his representational world, and this process is quite distinct from the internalization of aspects of the parents which accompanies the resolution of the oedipus complex.

We know that in the course of development, the child creates stable images of objects existing in the external world. These images are located within the representational world of the child, but refer to what the child learns to experience as the "external" world. The process of superego formation, of transferring the authority and status of the love objects to the "inner" world, can only take place after the child has learned to perceive his objects, i.e., after he has created stable object representations in his representational world.

It is evident that if we take such a view, it is extremely difficult to talk of introjection or identification as simply "taking in" the parents. The parents must first be perceived in order later to be introjected[5] and in order to be perceived they must have been built up within the representational world as object representations of one sort or another. In order to avoid confusion, it is necessary to relate the terms used here to those employed in an earlier published formulation in "On the Concept of Superego" (Sandler, 1960).

From this it seemed to us that the notions of introjection and identification can be conceptualized in terms of changes of cathexis within the representational world. In order to do this, we have found it necessary to distinguish between the ego as a structure or organized

[4] The problem of consciousness is not discussed here. We take for granted the existence of unconscious perception, of unconscious representations. If a percept is to have the quality of consciousness, we may assume that it receives an additional cathexis (whether this is simply a hypercathexis or a special "attention" cathexis is a further problem).

[5] The term "introjection" is used here in a restricted sense to refer only to the processes of transfer of authority and status from objects in the "external" world to the superego in the "internal" world, as described by Freud in the *Outline*, referred to earlier in this paper.

set of functions on the one hand, and the representational world on the other. The construction of a representational world is one of the functions of the ego, which has, however, many additional functions—never sensed and thus never perceived, consciously or unconsciously. A specialized part of the representational world consists of symbols for things, activities, and relationships, and provides the furniture for the ego function of thinking.

The representational world contains more than object or thing representations. Sensations arising from the child's own body in its interaction with its environment result in the formation of a body representation (body schema), and the psychic representations of instinctual drives find form as need and affect representations.

At this point it is useful to introduce a distinction between representations and images. A representation can be considered to have a more or less enduring existence as an organization or schema which is constructed out of a multitude of impressions. A child experiences many images of his mother—mother feeding, mother talking, mother sitting down, mother standing up, mother preparing food, etc.— and on the basis of these gradually creates a mother representation which encompasses a whole range of mother images, all of which bear the label "mother."

The development of these representations has been studied in detail by Piaget, who has shown that an enduring representation (as distinct from image) cannot be said to be well established before about the sixteenth month of life. This would be "perceptual" object constancy as opposed to the "instinctual" object constancy of psychoanalysis. (Needless to say, these images are at first extremely rudimentary and are initially indistinguishable from experiences of need satisfaction.) Similarly we can distinguish a body representation which endures in time once maturity is reached, and which encompasses the whole range of experienced body states and activities, from a body image[6] which would be the temporary image of a particular body state or activity.

The notion of body representation can be extended to that of self-representation. Indeed, we can paraphrase Freud to say that the

[6] "Body image" in the sense in which it is used here is thus not the same as Schilder's use of the term. For Schilder, "body image" corresponds to Head's "body schema" and our "body representation."

self-representation (one of the meanings of "ego" in Freud's writings) is first and foremost a body representation. The self-representation is, however, much more than a body representation. It includes
all those aspects of the child's experience and activities which he
later feels (consciously or unconsciously) to be his own. It has a
status which parallels that of object representations, except that it
refers to the child himself.[7]

By the self-representation we mean that organization which represents the person as he has consciously and unconsciously perceived
himself, and which forms an integral part of the representational
world. This self-organization is a perceptual and conceptual organization within the representational world. The construction of the
representational world is a product of ego functions, and the self-
and object representations are part of the representational world.

The representational world might be compared to a stage set
within a theater. The characters on the stage represent the child's
various objects, as well as the child himself. Needless to say, the child
is usually the hero of the piece. The theater, which contains the stage,
would correspond to aspects of the ego, and the various functions
such as scene shifting, raising or lowering the curtain, and all the
machinery auxiliary to the actual stage production would correspond
to those ego functions of which we are not normally aware.

Whereas the characters on this stage correspond, in this model, to
self- and object *representations*, their particular form and expression
at any one point in the play correspond to self- and object *images*.
(Although this distinction has not been fully maintained for the
purposes of this paper, it is an important one.)

Clearly the delineation of discrete self- and object representations
in the representational world can only come about gradually, with
maturation and experience. We assume that initially the child's
representational world contains only the crudest representations of
pleasure and unpleasure, of need-satisfying experiences and activities, and it is only gradually that the infant learns to distinguish self
from not-self, and self from object in his representational world.

---

[7] The ontogenetic development of representations of body and self from an undifferentiated sensorium is a fascinating study in itself, and much remains to be
explored in this area. See Edith Jacobson's valuable contribution (1954).

The use of the term "self" by Spiegel (1959) appears to be identical with the
present use of the term "self-representation."

The gradual establishment of self-boundaries (at first body boundaries) is a part of normal development, and their absence at a time when we would expect them to have been established, or their disappearance once they have been established, would lead us to suspect a pathological affection of one or more important ego functions.

It is convenient at this juncture to introduce the idea of the *shape* of a self- or object representation or image to denote the particular form and character assumed by that representation or image in the representational world at any one moment. The notion of "shape" is particularly useful as a sort of shorthand, and we have made extensive use of it in simple diagrams in our discussions of the various changes which take place, during the course of development and under the influence of various defensive activities of the ego, in the child's representational world. The child who feels angry at one moment, and the subject of attack at another, shows a change in the shape of his self-representation—or alternatively, his self-image (be it conscious or unconscious) has changed. Moreover, the shape of an unconscious self-representation may be different from that shape which is permitted access to consciousness or motility. Thus we could speak of a child who has an unconscious aggressive wish to attack an object as having a particular shape of his self-representation —the unconscious image of himself attacking the object—which is not ego syntonic and which is only permitted to proceed to consciousness or motility once its shape has been changed by means of defensive activity on the part of the ego.

The self-representation can assume a wide variety of shapes and forms, depending on the pressures of the id, the requirements of the external world, and the demands and standards of the introjects. Some shapes of the self-representation would, as has been said, evoke conflicts within the ego if they were allowed discharge to motility or consciousness, and the defense mechanisms are directed against their emergence.

This refers, of course, to the expression of id impulses. It is perfectly consistent with psychoanalytic metapsychology to link the expression of an instinctual need with a shape of the self-representation, or, for that matter, with the shape of an object representation. Needs soon become transformed into *wishes* of one sort or another in the course of development, and these wishes involve self- and object representations. Thus an unconscious wish, let us say, to exhibit one's body to another, involves the unconscious perception by the ego of an image of the object reacting in some way. These self- and object images must, it seems to us, be unconsciously appreciated by the ego and be dealt with in some way by it, e.g., by repression (or some other form of defense) or by permitting an acceptable derivative to gain access to consciousness or motility. The distortion of the unconscious wish involves changes in the shape of the self- and object representations.

Other shapes of the self-representation are versions which would provide the child with the greatest narcissistic gain, and represent ideal selves for the child (as in the "superman" daydreams of latency). Clearly such ideal selves begin to be formed in pregenital times, and their exploration has thrown some light on a number of aspects of what has been broadly conceptualized as the ego ideal. More will be said of these ideal selves later.

It is important to delineate the relation between the representational world and the ego. It is a function of the ego to construct a representational world from the original undifferentiated sensorium of the infant. This goes hand in hand with ego development, for the building up of representations is a *sine qua non* for ego development, and is itself a prerequisite for progressive adaptation. In this the ego is and remains the active agency. The representational world is never an active agent—it is rather a set of indications which guides the ego to appropriate adaptive or defensive activity. It may be compared to a radar or television screen providing meaningful information upon which action can be based. The ego makes use of self-, object or affect representations, and of the symbols derived from them, in its effort to maintain equilibrium. It can permit them in an undistorted way, or modify them according to its needs.

The representational world provides the material for the ego's perceptual structuring of sensory impulses, for imagination and fantasy, for direct and modified action, for language, symbols, and for trial action in thought.

Using the concept of the representational world, it has been possible to avoid certain theoretical difficulties which have been met with in the course of our work, and to define such mechanisms as identification and introjection in a relatively simple way. These definitions have been tested out in the course of indexing psycho-analytic case material, and have so far proved serviceable.

Identification becomes for us a modification of the self-representation on the basis of another (usually an object) representation as a model. Temporary identification and imitation would be a change in the shape of the self-image which would not show itself as an enduring change in the self-representation. More enduring identifications would be manifested as organized changes in the self-representation. The representation used as a model in identification may, of course, be largely based on fantasy.

While it is perfectly correct to say that identification is a modification of the ego, it would appear to be more specific and helpful to define it as a modification of the self-representation, a modification which can, nevertheless, result in far-reaching changes in the ego, for the representational world is intimately involved in the child's psychological experience and behavior.

Within the representational world of the child, identification with an object would be the coalescence or fusion of a self-representation and an object representation, or a change in the self-representation, so that the object representation is duplicated.

A child may also identify with an ideal self. In this case we would speak of "identification with the ideal." This is particularly important in superego formation. Thus, for example, a child may construct an "ideal self" based on parental example or precept before it is capable of changing the shape of the self to conform with the ideal. Then, perhaps at a much later date, circumstances (such as physical and psychological maturation) make it possible for the child to identify with the ideal (as in a child's later identification with the professional activities of a lost parent).

Identification which is the result of momentary *fusion* of self- and object representations is, under certain circumstances, a normal process, and the basis for such phenomena as empathy. Where such fusion is of longer duration, and self-boundaries are not intact, a psychotic process may be present.

Identification which is the outcome of *duplicating* the object representation is normally seen as part of the process of loosening of the object tie; the object is then no longer as important as before, but still exists as an object representation apart from the self-representation. The boundaries of the self remain intact.

Introjection, as we have defined it (we refer here to the introjections which normally accompany the resolution of the oedipus complex, and which result in the formation of a structured superego), would be a completely different process. It can be regarded as the vesting of certain object representations with a special status, so that these are felt to have all the authority and power of the real parents. As Freud (1938) puts it: "This new mental agency continues to carry on the functions which have hitherto been performed by the corresponding people in the external world."

We know, however, that distortions in the object representation accompany the process of introjection. In particular, the child may transfer much of his own aggression to the parental representations, so that they can appear to him to be far more severe and punitive than his parents ever were in reality.

Introjection in this sense means that the child reacts, in the absence of the parents, as if they were present. It does not mean that the child copies the parents—this would be identification. It is as if the child says to himself, "I shall be what my parents wanted me to be, as if they were now here," rather than "I shall be like my parents." An example would be the child who obeys a parental injunction (in the absence of the parents) not to stay up late, even though the parents habitually do so themselves. If he identified with the parents, he would stay up late.

One could say, loosely, that the child identifies with the parents' demands. Probably, in introjection, there is always an accompanying identification with an *ideal self-representation* communicated to the child by the parents, or based on the child's distortions of the parents' wishes or reactions.

Identification can be observed to occur long before the onset of the oedipal phase, and continues, in one form or another, throughout life. Those identifications which have a special relation to the resolution of the oedipus complex can be considered to differ from somewhat earlier identifications in their content rather than in their mechanism. The child who identifies with the moral attitudes and behavior of his parents may do so either as an identification with parental representations at the same time as introjection takes place, or may do so following introjection of his parental object representations (or aspects of these). In the latter case we may have the phenomenon of *identification with the introject*. This is an extremely common occurrence, seen particularly when the child has, in his turn, become a parent, and for the first time identifies with his (introjected) parental attitudes in his attitudes to his own children. Such identification with an introject probably plays an important part in a girl's normal transformation into a mother.

Identification with the introject can also be seen in children's play. For example, it can be detected in the child who, feeling guilty (anticipating the disapproval of his superego), turns on another child and criticizes him in exactly the same way as he feels criticized (or feels about to be criticized) by an introject. We all know those patients who bring their guilt feelings to an analytic session in the shape of self-righteous criticism of others.

On the basis of the theory of superego functioning which we constructed, it was possible in our Index work to attempt a classification of clinical observations which would resolve some of the difficulties we had previously met in indexing superego material. We did not now call upon therapists to distinguish between "ego" and "superego" identifications,[8] for in practice it is not possible to make any such distinction; nor did we ask them to decide in every case whether the superego conflict they saw was conflict with inner or outer authority, for the distinction between the two often fades when a patient externalizes an introject, re-creating an inner conflict in the transference.[9] What we did do was to devise a multiple ap-

[8] This theoretical differentiation, based in the main upon the observed differences between identifications made before the resolution of the oedipus complex and those made as a consequence of it, represents an attempt to make a distinction between oedipal *introjections* and both preoedipal and oedipal *identifications*. If introjection and identification are distinguished as suggested earlier in this paper, the need for separating these two types of "identification" disappears. Indeed, it is impossible in practice to make such a separation except on the often arbitrary basis of the content of the identification.

[9] This has been referred to before as the apparent "dissolution" of the superego in the analytic situation. It is, of course, not confined to the analytic hour, for there are many people who have to keep their introjects more or less constantly externalized. It is often extremely difficult to decide in such cases whether introjection has in fact occurred or not, and the theoretical distinction between an internalized object relationship which is compulsively re-created and the externalization of an introject is one which needs further exploration.

proach under a number of different headings (Sandler et al., 1962).[10]

One of these Index headings refers to statements which the therapist can make on the basis of his clinical material about the extent of organization and structuralization of the superego, a second heading to its characteristics. This is followed by a section referring to its object and instinctual sources, and a section concerned with contents activating the superego system. It would not be appropriate to go into these here, but two further sections are perhaps of special interest. The first of these we have called the *Ego Response.*

The ego has to deal with tension arising within itself in its desire to satisfy the instincts, to cope with reality and to serve authority. It will use essentially the same techniques for dealing with inner authority as it has developed for coping with the real parents, and the way in which the ego attempts to resolve tension with inner or outer authority we have called the "ego response." Examination of our indexed material has shown us that there is an almost unlimited range of ego responses for coping with such tension with authority. These range from compliance and defiance to self-punishment of various sorts, to demands for approval and reassurance, to rationalization and concealment, and so on. Identification is one of the most important of the ego responses—the ego deals with tension with inner or outer authority by altering its self-representation to duplicate the object, and the child's feelings and behavior change accordingly.

Of special research interest for us has been the variety of methods used by the child for the reduction of tension with authority which involve the voluntary or involuntary cooperation of external persons. The Superego research group has prepared a tentative classification of those guilt-reducing techniques which involve the manipulation or provocation of others (for example, the ways in which others can be seduced into bearing responsibility for a forbidden act). This is particularly important in the study of delinquents.

A further part of the Superego section has been called *The Regulation of the Feeling of Well-Being.* A central part of our theory of the superego is that the parental introjects serve not only to criticize and punish but also to encourage and support—as the

10 See this Volume, pp. 107-127.

parents do, although a gross difference may exist between the parent representations and introjects. We have taken the view that the ego creates and maintains the superego because the introjects in turn provide the child with positive libidinal and aggressive gains.

Reference has been made both to tension with authority and to guilt, and the terms have been used more or less synonymously. When we came to consider guilt feelings, it was found that these could arise from a number of *different* anxieties. We found, when confronted with index cards which related to tension between the ego on the one hand and authority on the other, that we had to ask questions such as these: Is the relationship between the child and parent or introject characterized by the expectation of loss or gain of affection from the object, or by the expectation of the loss or restoration of the object? Does the child anticipate the experiencing or avoidance of physical hurt or danger? Does it expect to lose or gain a penis or its equivalent? Does it expect retaliation in kind, or reward in kind, praise or condemnation? Does the child expect to be shamed or admired, to receive gifts or to suffer deprivations? And what is the degree of fantasy or historical reality in these expectations? It seems to be not enough, when we have to categorize our material, to use the broad categories of guilt feeling or castration anxiety.[11]

Linked with the problem of the regulation of well-being, and partly arising from our consideration of it in the Superego research group, has been the observation that the child directs much of his activity toward maintaining the narcissistic integrity of his self-representation. This involves us in the problem of the role and conceptual status of the ego ideal; in order to look at some of the problems which have arisen in this connection, the Self-Esteem research group was formed.

This group has been concerned with further exploring and elaborating our conceptualization of the representational world, with special reference to the development of a differentiated self-representation in the child, and to the methods which the child uses, at

11 A number of interesting theoretical problems arise in this area. Is there, for instance, a general affective component in all these anxieties? How do the specific threats or rewards relate to various phases in the child's development? To what extent is there a fusion of all the different components, and so on?

different ages, to maintain an optimal level of narcissistic cathexis of the self-representation. Our theoretical formulations have constantly been referred back to the indexed material.

The notion of the representational world as described earlier has made it easier to illustrate such concepts as primary and secondary narcissism. *Primary narcissim* would be the libidinal cathexis of the self-representation as it is formed from an initially undifferentiated sensory matrix. Even with the differentiation of objects in the representational world (which follows the differentiation of self-representation from "not-self"), object representations do not necessarily receive a libidinal cathexis except in so far as they serve a need-satisfying function.[12] When, however, the stage of object love is reached, part of the libidinal cathexis of the self-representation is transferred to the object representation, and we get a differentiation of primary narcissism into (a) residual libidinal (narcissistic) cathexis of the self-representation, and (b) object cathexis.

If libidinal cathexis is withdrawn from an object representation and secondarily directed toward the self-representation, it would correspond to what we understand by *secondary narcissism*. It is clear that identification is one of the ego mechanisms which greatly facilitates the transposition of object cathexis into secondary narcissism.

In the same way as we can conceive of the libidinal cathexis of the growing child as being initially directed toward pleasurable experiences, so we can postulate an *aggressive* cathexis of unpleasurable experiences. Parallel with the development from the initial undifferentiated autoerotic phase, through a stage of primary narcissism to object love and secondary narcissism, we can assume a corresponding development with regard to aggression.[13]

[12] This does not exactly correspond to the formulations presented in the paper on the superego (Sandler, 1960), in which primary narcissism was regarded as existing before the differentiation of a self-representation. The present formulation is more consistent with Freud's statement that a phase of autoerotism precedes primary narcissism. The initial autoerotic phase can be considered to be one in which there is libidinal cathexis of pleasurable need-satisfying experiences only, before the existence of organized self- and object representations. The development of primary narcissism from autoerotism can be linked with the emergence of the self-representation. A paper on this topic is in preparation in collaboration with Dr. H. Nagera.

[13] This complicated subject will be dealt with elsewhere. It may be that the differentiation between impressions which receive a libidinal cathexis and those which are cathected with aggression is the vehicle for the differentiation of the self-representa-

We can regard the transfer of aggressive cathexis from the object representation to the self-representation as being the counterpart of secondary narcissism, and being an important component of masochism.

One of the exercises undertaken by the Self-Esteem research group has been to examine a number of indexed cases from the point of view of constructing what might be called cathectic balance sheets. The narcissistic cathexis of the self-representation has to maintain minimum reserves, and a number of factors are always operating to reduce what might be called the child's narcissistic credit. Of course, owing to unfortunate occurrences in the early years, this narcissistic credit may have been low to start with, or there might be something operating to cause a constant drain on the reserves.

Credit may be restored by a variety of measures, and these vary enormously from child to child. Some of the measures are, like the similar operations of the bank, short term, while others may be long term and manifest themselves as excellent adaptations and ego qualities, as symptoms or character traits of one sort or another, or as behavior problems and delinquencies. Such a narcissistic "balance sheet" is, as may be expected, a perfectly normal phenomenon, although healthy persons have substantial internal reserves and are not pathologically dependent on, for example, constant expressions of approval from others. The study of the various techniques used by different people to regulate the level of narcissistic cathexis of the self-representation is a fascinating and rewarding one, and reaches far into the domain of social psychology—into the study of the functions of the social group, of status symbols, etc. We do not want to push the analogy of the bank balance too far, in spite of the temptation to draw a parallel between economic and psychic depressions.

Mention has been made of the notion of ideal self-images. It has become clear to us that the sources of these ideal selves are manifold, and that they represent more than mere copies of idealized parental figures in the representational world of the child. It may even be that they have been transmitted as ideals by parents who have never behaved in the ways concerned at all—much of what

---

tion from "not-self" and later from object representations. The first self-representation may be, as has often been suggested, a "pleasure self," everything unpleasant (and therefore cathected with aggression rather than libido) being relegated to the "not-self."

goes into the ideal self-image is second or even third hand, and it is obviously of clinical importance whether the ideal which the child has gained from his parents is capable of realization or not.

The self-ideal is an ideal shape of the self-image which is capable of (conscious or unconscious) visualization by the child. It is a desired shape of the self—the "self-I-would-like-to-be," and when the child becomes capable of actually changing the shape of his self-representation to conform with one of the "ideal" shapes, we can speak of *identification with the ideal* having taken place.

In the course of looking at the various methods which children use to restore narcissistic cathexis, we have been struck by the enormous extent to which recourse is had to what we have called *compensation in fantasy*. If we regard fantasy as the purposive manipulation in imagination of the representational world, it is easy to see how the narcissistic cathexis of the self-representation (the hero in such fantasies) is restored through the assumption in fantasy of one of the ideal shapes—that is, a self-image which will yield the greatest degree of narcissistic gratification and well-being.

Other techniques of narcissistic regulation are at present being explored by the Self-Esteem group, but the theoretical problems relating to the conceptualization of compensation in fantasy are of such interest that we have recently formed a Fantasy research group. This group is concerned not only with the metapsychology of fantasy, with special reference to the representational world, but also with the large task of providing a meaningful classification of the material contained in the fantasy section of the Index.[14]

Indexed material relating to the employment of the various defense mechanisms and defensive measures are being examined from the point of view of the correlated changes in the representational world.

In this paper an attempt has been made to take up a single theme, namely, the possibilities for our psychoanalytic theory of the concept of the representational world. Although much of this must appear, as it has been presented here, as speculative and tentative, it should be stressed that it is not idle speculation. We have been guided

---

[14] The need to classify this material has thrown up a number of further problems, and it appears that the Fantasy group will have to assume the functions of a play, dream, and drama group as well!

throughout by our need to conceptualize and categorize the material recorded by therapists about their analytic cases according to psychoanalytic theory; and this theory is far from being a static one. The ultimate test of our theories must be their applicability to clinical observations, even though these observations must themselves inevitably be affected by the theoretical orientation of the observer. It seems that we have here a spiral of development, in which there is a progressive interaction of theory and observation. It is in this area of the testing out of theoretical ideas that the Index may be making one of its contributions to psychoanalysis.

BIBLIOGRAPHY

Freud, S. (1914), On Narcissism: an Introduction. *Standard Edition,* XIV. London: Hogarth Press, 1957.
—— (1938), *An Outline of Psychoanalysis.* New York: Norton, 1949.
Hartmann, H. (1939), *Ego Psychology and the Problem of Adaptation.* New York: International Universities Press, 1958.
Head, H. (1926), *Aphasia and Kindred Disorders of Speech.* New York: Macmillan.
Jacobson, E. (1954), The Self and the Object World: Vicissitudes of Their Infantile Cathexes and Their Influence on Ideational and Affective Development. *This Annual,* IX.
Piaget, J. (1937), *The Construction of Reality in the Child.* New York: Basic Books, 1954.
Sandler, J. (1959), The Background of Safety. Paper read to the 21st International Psycho-Analytical Congress, Copenhagen.
—— (1960), On the Concept of Superego. *This Annual,* XV.
—— (1961), The Hampstead Index As an Instrument of Psycho-Analytic Research (read to the 22nd International Psycho-Analytical Congress, Edinburgh). *Int. J. Psa.* (in press).
—— Kawenoka, M., Neurath, L., Rosenblatt, B., Schnurmann, A., & Sigal, J. (1962), The Classification of Superego Material in the Hampstead Index. *This Annual,* XVII.
Schilder, P. (1935), *The Image and Appearance of the Human Body.* New York: International Universities Press, 1950.
Spiegel, L. A. (1959), The Self, the Sense of Self, and Perception. *This Annual,* XIV.
Werner, H. (1940), *Comparative Psychology of Mental Development.* New York: International Universities Press, 1957.

ASPECTS OF NORMAL AND PATHOLOGICAL DEVELOPMENT

ASSESSMENT OF CHILDHOOD DISTURBANCES

ANNA FREUD, LL.D. (London)

When diagnosing the mental disturbances of children, the child analyst is confronted with difficulties which are due to the shifting internal scene in a developing individual and which are not met with in adult psychiatry.

One of these difficulties concerns the fact that, during development, symptoms, inhibitions, and anxieties do not necessarily carry the same significance which they assume at a later date. Although in some cases they may be lasting, and thus the first signs of permanent pathology, in other cases they need be no more than transient appearances of stress which emerge whenever a particular phase of development makes specially high demands on a child's personality. After adaptation to that particular phase has been achieved, or when its peak has passed, these seemingly pathological appearances either may disappear again without leaving much trace, or make way for others. In either case, what is left behind may be no more than an area of heightened vulnerability. These semblances of "spontaneous cures" are the equivalent of what used to be called "outgrowing" of difficulties, a phrase which, though outmoded, is in reality still quite appropriate.

Another difficulty for the diagnostician is bound up with the

This short article is a preliminary communication, extracted from an extensive study of normal and abnormal child development, the publication of which is in preparation by the author. The "Diagnostic Profile" contained in it has to be considered as a tentative draft, open to amendment and revision of all its parts, after their usefulness has been tested against clinical material over a prolonged period.

The case material on which the considerations are based is that of the Hampstead Child-Therapy Clinic, an institution maintained by The Field Foundation, Inc., New York; The Ford Foundation, New York; The Foundations' Fund for Research in Psychiatry, New Haven, Connecticut; The Anna Freud Foundation, New York; The Grant Foundation, Inc., New York; The Estate of Flora Haas, New York; The Old Dominion Foundation, U.S.A.; The Psychoanalytic Research and Development Fund, Inc., New York; The Taconic Foundation, Inc., New York.

well-known fact that there are no childhood alternatives to the adult's efficiency or failure in sex and work, vital factors which are used in adult psychiatry as indications of intactness or disturbance. Although in what follows efforts will be made to outline some "age-adequate tasks" for children, these are by no means of similar diagnostic significance.

Since, thus, neither symptomatology nor life tasks can be taken as reliable guides to the assessment of mental health or illness in childhood, we are left with the alternative idea[1] that the capacity to develop progressively, or respectively the damage to that capacity, are the most significant factors in determining a child's mental future. Accordingly, it becomes the diagnostician's task to ascertain where a given child stands on the developmental scale, whether his position is age adequate, retarded or precocious, and in what respect; and to what extent the observable internal and external circumstances and existent symptoms are interfering with the possibilities of future growth.

But even this more circumscribed task, namely, to place the case of a given child in the correct position on the scale of normal or pathological development, is admittedly difficult, all the more so since, besides psychoanalysis, several other disciplines such as descriptive and dynamic psychiatry, psychology, and the social sciences have a stake in it. For the child analyst the appraisal of the child serves not only practical but also theoretical aims. To the first category belong the decision for and against treatment and the choice of therapeutic method; to the second, the attempts to formulate clearer pictures of the initial phases of those mental disorders which are known now principally in their later stages; to distinguish transitory from permanent pathology; and in general to increase insight into the developmental processes themselves.

The analyst's requirement for the latter purposes is a comprehensive metapsychological picture of the child (i.e., one containing structural, dynamic, economic, genetic, and adaptive data). This order cannot be filled with the comparatively meager facts elicited from the children or their parents at their first contact with the Clinic. Therefore, the task of assessment, which begins with the

---

[1] Suggested by me in "Indications for Child Analysis." *This Annual,* I, 1946.

diagnostic team, is continued by the child analyst, i.e., it passes from the stage of initial diagnostic procedure into the stage of therapy. Since in analysis the method of therapy coincides with the method of exploration, the whole bulk of analytic material can be utilized for the latter purpose or, as happens in analytic teamwork in the Clinic, be handed back to the diagnostician to confirm, correct, and expand his first impressions of the case.

In what follows we attempt to outline the setting up of a meta-psychological framework of this kind, i.e., of a *"developmental profile"* in which the result of the analyst's diagnostic thinking is broken up into its component parts. Profiles of this kind can be drawn up at various junctures, namely, after the first contact between child and Clinic (preliminary diagnostic stage), during analysis (treatment stage), and after the end of analysis or follow-up (terminal stage). If this is done, the profile serves not only as a tool for the completion and verification of diagnosis but also as an instrument to measure treatment results, i.e., as a check on the efficacy of psychoanalytic treatment.

At the diagnostic stage the profile for each case should be initiated by the referral symptoms of the child, his description, his family background and history, and an enumeration of the possibly significant environmental influences. From these it proceeds to the internal picture of the child which contains information about the *structure* of his personality; the *dynamic* interplay within the structure; some *economic* factors concerning drive activity and the relative strength of id and ego forces; his adaptation to reality; and some genetic assumptions (to be verified during and after treatment). Thus, broken up into items, an individual profile may look as follows:

Draft of Diagnostic Profile

I. REASON FOR REFERRAL (Arrests in Development, Behavior Problems, Anxieties, Inhibitions, Symptoms, etc.)

II. DESCRIPTION OF CHILD (Personal appearance, Moods, Manner, etc.)

III. FAMILY BACKGROUND AND PERSONAL HISTORY

IV. Possibly Significant Environmental Influences

V. Assessments of Development

A. *Drive Development*

    1. Libido.—Examine and state

       (a) with regard to *phase development:*

          whether in the sequence of libidinal phases (oral, anal, phallic; latency; preadolescence, adolescence) the child has ever proceeded to his age-adequate stage, and especially beyond the anal to the phallic level;

          whether he has achieved phase dominance on it;

          whether, at the time of assessment, this highest level is being maintained or has been abandoned regressively for an earlier one;

       (b) with regard to *libido distribution:*

          whether the self is cathected as well as the object world, and whether there is sufficient narcissism (primary and secondary, invested in the body, the ego, or the superego) to ensure self-regard, self-esteem, a sense of well-being, without leading to overestimation of the self, undue independence of the objects, etc.; state degree of dependence of self-regard on object relations;

       (c) with regard to *object libido:*

          whether in the level and quality of object relationships (narcissistic, anaclitic, object constancy, preoedipal, oedipal, postoedipal, adolescent) the child has proceeded according to age;

          whether, at the time of assessment, the highest level reached is being maintained or has been abandoned regressively;

          whether or not the existent object relationships correspond with the maintained or regressed level of phase development.

    2. Aggression.—Examine the aggressive expressions at the disposal of the child:

       (a) according to their quantity, i.e., presence or absence in the manifest picture;

   (b) according to their quality, i.e., correspondence with the
       level of libido development;
   (c) according to their direction toward either the object world
       or the self.

B. *Ego and Superego Development*
   (a) Examine and state the intactness or defects of ego apparatus,
       serving perception, memory, motility, etc.;
   (b) Examine and state in detail the intactness or otherwise of
       ego *functions* (memory, reality testing, synthesis, control of
       motility, speech, secondary thought processes. Look out for
       primary deficiencies. Note unevennesses in the levels reached.
       Include results of Intelligence Tests);
   (c) Examine in detail the status of the *defense organization* and
       consider:
       whether defense is employed specifically against *individual
           drives* (to be identified here) or, more generally, against
           drive activity and instinctual pleasure as such;
       whether defenses are *age adequate,* too primitive, or too pre-
           cocious;
       whether defense is *balanced,* i.e., whether the ego has at its
           disposal the use of many of the important mechanisms or
           is restricted to the excessive use of single ones;
       whether defense is *effective,* especially in its dealing with
           anxiety, whether it results in equilibrium or disequilib-
           rium, lability, mobility or deadlock within the structure;
       whether and how far the child's defense against the drives
           is dependent on the object world or independent of it
           (superego development);
   (d) Note any secondary interference of defense activity with ego
       achievements, i.e., the price paid by the individual for the
       upkeep of the defense organization.

C. *Development of the Total Personality*
   (Lines of Development and Mastery of Tasks)
   While drive and ego development are viewed separately for purposes of dissection, their action is seen as combined in the *lines of
development* which lead from the individual's state of infantile

immaturity and dependence to the gradual mastery of his own body and its functions, to adaptation to the object world, reality and the social community, as well as to the building up of an inner structure. Whatever level has been reached by a given child in any of these respects represents the end point of a historical sequence which can be traced, reconstructed, scrutinized for defects (this to be done during and after treatment), and in which ego, superego, as well as drive development have played their part. Under the influence of external and internal factors these lines of development may proceed at a fairly equal rate, i.e., harmoniously, or with wide divergences of speed, which lead to the many existent imbalances, variations, and incongruities in personality development. (See, for example, excessive speech and thought development combined with infantilism of needs, fantasies and wishes; good achievement of object constancy combined with low frustration tolerance and primitive defense system; or complete dependence for feeding, defecation, etc., combined with fairly mature intellectual and moral standards.)

At the time of diagnosis, the status of these developmental lines can be investigated by using for the purpose of examination any one of the many situations in life which pose for the child an immediate problem of mastery. Although such tasks may seem simple and harmless when viewed from the outside, the demands made by them on the personality show up clearly when they are translated into terms of psychic reality. Such translations are the indispensable prerequisites for assessing the meaning of successful mastery as well as for understanding failure and for alloting it correctly to the right sources in either the drives or the ego agencies.

Examples of such situations as they may occur in the life of every child are the following:

separation from the mother;
birth of sibling;
illness and surgical intervention;
hospitalization;
entry into nursery school;
school entry;
the step from the triangular oedipal situation into a community of peers;
the step from play to work;

the arousal of new genital strivings in adolescence;

the step from the infantile objects within the family to new love
     objects outside the family;

(For one particular situation of this kind, namely, "Entry into
Nursery School," the psychological significance of the event has been
traced in detail, taking into account the demands made on all parts
of the personality.)

VI. Genetic Assessments (Regression and Fixation Points)

Since we assume that all infantile neuroses (and some psychotic
disturbances of children) are initiated by libido regressions to fixation points at various early levels, the location of these trouble spots
in the history of the child is one of the vital concerns of the diagnostician. At the time of initial diagnosis such areas are betrayed:

(a) by certain forms of manifest *behavior* which are character-
     istic for the given child and allow conclusions as to the
     underlying id processes which have undergone repression
     and modification but have left an unmistakable imprint. The
     best example is the overt obsessional character where clean-
     liness, orderliness, punctuality, hoarding, doubt, indecision,
     slowing up, etc., betray the special difficulty experienced by
     the child when coping with the impulses of the anal-sadistic
     phase, i.e., a fixation to that phase. Similarly, other character
     formations or attitudes betray fixation points at other levels,
     or in other areas. (Concern for health, safety of parents and
     siblings show a special difficulty of coping with the death
     wishes of infancy; fear of medicines, food fads, etc., point to
     defense against oral fantasies; shyness to that against exhibi-
     tionism; homesickness to unsolved ambivalence, etc.):

(b) by the child's fantasy activity, sometimes betrayed accident-
     ally in the diagnostic procedure, usually only available
     through personality tests. (During analysis, the child's con-
     scious and unconscious fantasies provide, of course, the fullest
     information about the pathogenically important parts of his
     developmental history);

(c) by those items in the symptomatology where the relations be-
     tween surface and depth are firmly established, not open to
     variation, and well known to the diagnostician as are the

symptoms of the obsessional neurosis with their known fixation points. In contrast, symptoms such as lying, stealing, bed wetting, etc., with their multiple causation, convey no genetic information at the diagnostic stage.

For the diagnostician trained in the assessment of adult disturbances, it is important to note that infantile regression differs in various respects from regression in the adult; it does not always require fixation points and it does not need to be permanent. As "temporary regression" it takes place along the developmental lines mentioned before, and forms part of normal development as an attempt at adaptation and response to frustration. Such temporary regression may give rise to pathology, but the latter will be short-lived and reversible. For purposes of assessment the two types of regression (temporary or permanent, spontaneously reversible or irreversible) have to be distinguished from each other, only the former type justifying therapy.

VII. Dynamic and Structural Assessments (Conflicts)

Behavior is governed by the interplay of internal with external forces, or of internal forces (conscious or unconscious) with each other, i.e., by the outcome of conflicts. Examine the conflicts in the given case and classify them as:

(a) external conflicts between the id-ego agencies and the object world (arousing fear of the object world);

(b) internalized conflicts between ego-superego and id after the ego agencies have taken over and represent to the id the demands of the object world (arousing guilt);

(c) internal conflicts between insufficiently fused or incompatible drive representatives (such as unsolved ambivalence, activity versus passivity, masculinity versus femininity, etc.).

According to the predominance of any one of the three types it may be possible to arrive at assessments of:

(1) the level of maturity, i.e., the relative independence of the child's personality structure;

(2) the severity of his disturbance;

(3) the intensity of therapy needed for alleviation or removal of the disturbance.

VIII. Assessment of Some General Characteristics

The whole personality of the child should be scrutinized also for certain general characteristics which are of possible significance for predicting the chances for spontaneous recovery and reaction to treatment. Examine in this connection the following areas:

(a) the child's frustration tolerance. Where (in respect of developmental age) the tolerance for tension and frustration is unusually low, more anxiety will be generated than can be coped with, and the pathological sequence of regression, defense activity, and symptom formation will be more easily set in motion. Where frustration tolerance is high, equilibrium will be maintained, or regained, more successfully;

(b) the child's sublimation potential. Individuals differ widely in the degree to which displaced, aim-inhibited, and neutralized gratification can recompense them for frustrated drive fulfillment. Acceptance of these former types of gratification (or freeing of the sublimation potential in treatment) may reduce the need for pathological solutions;

(c) the child's over-all attitude to anxiety. Examine how far the child's defense against fear of the external world and anxiety caused by the internal world is based exclusively on phobic measures and countercathexes which are in themselves closely related to pathology; and how far there is a tendency actively to master external and internal danger situations, the latter being a sign of a basically healthy, well-balanced ego structure;

(d) progressive developmental forces versus regressive tendencies. Both are, normally, present in the immature personality. Where the former outweigh the latter, the chances for normality and spontaneous recoveries are increased; symptom formation is more transitory since strong forward moves to the next developmental level alter the inner balance of forces. Where the latter, i.e., regression, predominate, the resistances against treatment and the stubbornness of pathological solutions will be more formidable. The economic relations between the two tendencies can be deduced from watching the child's struggle between the active wish to grow up and his reluctance to renounce the passive pleasures of infancy.

IX. Diagnosis

Finally, it is the diagnostician's task to reassemble the items mentioned above and to combine them in a clinically meaningful assessment. He will have to decide between a number of categorizations such as the following:

(1) that, in spite of current manifest behavior disturbances, the personality growth of the child is essentially healthy and falls within the wide range of "variations of normality";

(2) that existent pathological formations (symptoms) are of a transitory nature and can be classed as by-products of developmental strain;

(3) that there are permanent regressions which, on the one hand, cause more permanent symptom formation and, on the other hand, have impoverishing effects on libido progression and crippling effects on ego growth. According to the location of the fixation points and the amount of ego-superego damage, the character structure or symptoms produced will be of a neurotic, psychotic, or delinquent nature;

(4) that there are primary deficiencies of an organic nature or early deprivations which distort development and structuralization and produce retarded, defective, and nontypical personalities;

(5) that there are destructive processes at work (of organic, toxic, or psychic, known or unknown origin) which have effected, or are on the point of effecting, a disruption of mental growth.

HAMPSTEAD NURSERY FOLLOW-UP STUDIES

1. Sudden Separation and Its Effect Followed Over Twenty Years

ILSE HELLMAN, PH.D. (London)

Observational data recorded during war work with young children in the Hampstead Nurseries can now, twenty years later, serve as a basis for a small number of follow-up studies. Where follow-up contacts in later childhood and adolescence revealed problems for which psychoanalytic treatment seemed indicated, the children and their parents were informed of the opportunity for treatment at the Hampstead Child-Therapy Clinic. Only a few, however, have fully recognized their need and undertaken psychoanalysis. In these cases, the observations recorded in the Nursery and the subsequent analytic data provide rich material for comparison and verification of the assumptions made earlier. Studies based on this material are now in their final stages, and papers dealing with the details of the findings are in preparation.

The Hampstead Follow-up Study has been concerned also with children whose development has proceeded satisfactorily and who have been able to deal with inner problems and external circumstances in ways which did not call for therapeutic intervention. The analytic material of these cases would have been of great interest for research, but the fact that these children were not in need of treatment has made it impossible to study their development by this method.

Without insight into unconscious processes, a long-term study of development is severely limited. Nevertheless, we have found that observations recorded over a period of years can lead to valuable

This paper forms part of a Research Project entitled "Hampstead Nurseries Follow-up Study" which is conducted at the Hampstead Child-Therapy Clinic, London. It has been financed by the Ford Foundation, New York.

conclusions if certain items found in early observations are followed and compared with subsequent observations made in direct contact with the children and their parents. The selection of trends that can be followed under these conditions needs careful consideration.

The following study of a girl, Jane, is based on such material. Jane was two years eight months when she entered the Hampstead Nursery and is now twenty-three years old.

Nature of Observational Data

The material used for this study differs in some important respects from material used in long-term studies elsewhere. In most other studies, the observations are planned with regard to frequency, time, place, and circumstances under which they are made. While this procedure has the advantage of facilitating the systematic selection and comparison of data, it has the disadvantage that the data obtainable in planned situations contain only very limited aspects of the child's personality.

Our observations have not been collected according to a set plan. The common aim of observers in the Hampstead Nurseries was to record any item that seemed worth noting when it appeared to contribute to our knowledge of development, either confirming or contradicting expected reactions, bringing new points to our attention, or helping toward a clearer understanding of an individual child. In our view, observations made in real life situations and by observers with whom the child has a relationship have a greater value than systematically collected data gained in set situations by neutral observers.

The child's spontaneous communications to people with whom he has a relationship permit insight into his emotional life as well as into fantasies related to the elaboration of past external experiences. His capacity to maintain object relationships over a long period and the nature of these object relationships can also be assessed.

In my role as "substitute mother" during the years 1941-1945, I was able to observe Jane in the context of daily life. My observations were supplemented by other members of the Nursery staff who were well known to the child. Observations deriving from follow-up contacts through later childhood and adolescence into adult life were mainly made by me. One other observer who had also been on the Nursery staff and whom Jane had spontaneously contacted at the age of eleven, when she heard that the former Nursery worker was in the same town where she went to school, has contributed reports on her observations. While contacts during latency and adolescence were infrequent, they have become very frequent again during the last year.

While a variety of problems of child development can be followed up in this material, I have here centered my attention on the traumatic experience which this child went through in our presence and on the traces which her sudden separation from her mother left on her personality. For this reason, I have focused on the relationship of her present personality to the very traumatic separation experience in her third year of life.

THE NURSERY SETTING

The Hampstead Nurseries were residential war nurseries organized by Anna Freud and Dorothy Burlingham and financed by the Foster Parents Plan, Inc., New York. Their aim was to provide comparative safety for young children whose mothers had decided against being evacuated with their children and who had to work in order to provide for themselves and their children. A large number of the children were fatherless. The Nurseries were planned in a way to reduce as far as possible the ill effects of separation. Parents had free access to their children and each child was provided with a "substitute mother" among the nursery staff. Each staff member had a "family" of up to four children to look after. Although the children were in constant touch with all other children and staff in the house, they turned to their "substitute mother" whenever they needed special attention.

JANE'S DEVELOPMENT

Separation from Mother

Jane entered the Hampstead Nursery under unusual and specially traumatic circumstances. She had not been prepared for the separation. She had come with her mother to accompany a friend who had arranged to bring her small boy, Bob, to the Nursery. Jane's mother decided on the spur of the moment, when she saw the Nursery, to ask if she could leave Jane there too. This was agreed to because war conditions had become very dangerous and it was considered wise to accept Jane even though no preparation for this new situation had been possible. Jane had been born on the same day as Bob, in the same hospital ward, and it was hoped that the close friendship which existed between these mothers and children, who had met almost daily throughout their life, would be a help in Jane's adjustment to the new place. However, her reaction to the sudden separation was overwhelming. It has been described in the Monthly Report of the Hampstead Nurseries (August 1941) by Anna Freud and Dorothy Burlingham as follows: "Jane was a gay and beautiful girl, well developed for her age. She was at first delighted with the new experience. When after several hours she understood that this meant separation from her mother, she broke down completely, cried incessantly and was hard to quiet. Frequent visits from the mother only seemed to aggravate this state. She formed apparently violent attachments with surprising quickness, but it took her a very long time to deal with the shock of separation."

Jane presented the picture of a child who had withdrawn her interest from the happenings around her. She spent much time sucking intensively with a far-away look on her face.

She would often turn toward the wall and show little response to being talked to. During the first weeks while her need to be close to one of the nurses was constant and still indiscriminate, she insisted on holding on and clinging to the nearest person. One of the nurses tied a skipping rope around her waist which permitted her to use both hands for work. Jane was content when she could hold on to the handle of this rope.

In the Annual Report of the Hampstead Nurseries (1942) the authors described Jane's progress as follows: "Jane was the child who took the longest time to adapt herself to nursery life. Her development was arrested through her concentration on her longing, her disappointments and her varying moods of stubbornness and depression. She entered in July and began at last to show signs of settling down about Christmas time. She began to transfer her affections, to be gay and to start all sorts of interests."

The observers who witnessed Jane's distress during the first days and weeks and her slow recovery during the first half year were much concerned with the long-term effect of this traumatic experience on the child. In order to mitigate the unfavorable consequences and to help the child back to normal functioning, Jane was provided with continuous substitute mothering by the adults of her own choice, and her mother was encouraged to visit whenever she was able to do so. She made ample use of this opportunity, and Jane was not in fact separated from her mother for more than two consecutive days during this stage. Bob remained Jane's close friend during their stay at the Nursery. His presence provided continuity, but Jane was always the leading partner in their relationship.

Research into the effects of separation shows that a great variety of inner and outer conditions must be taken into account in each individual case in order to evaluate the nature and degree of the ill effect on a child's further development: the age of the child; the nature of the mother-child relationship preceding the separation; the level of maturity reached by the child in the important aspects of his personality, i.e., his libidinal and aggressive development, his object relationships, and the nature of his defenses. There are additional factors which have great influence on the child's potential recovery from the separation trauma: the substitute mothering which is offered and the way it is used by the child; the mother's reaction to the child's various manifestations of distress and anger, and the mother's reaction to the child's attachment to the substitute mother. As far as they were open to direct observation, we have data on all these aspects of Jane's experiences which followed the shock of being left in the Nursery.

Jane's History Preceding Entry into the Hampstead Nursery

The main facts about Jane's life and her development during the first two and a half years were gradually pieced together from her mother's accounts and confirmed by the mother's friend who had known Jane from birth.

Jane was an illegitimate child. The mother was twenty-nine years old when Jane was born. The father was a married man with whom Jane's mother had had a relationship for some time and of whom she was very fond. He took considerable interest in the baby, as his marriage had remained childless, and he continued to visit the mother and Jane and to support them financially until Jane was seven years old. Mother and child lived in a home for unmarried mothers during the first six weeks after leaving the hospital. They moved to a family where Jane's mother worked as domestic help. The mother said that she had never considered parting with her baby, and the absence of ambivalence was remarkable also in her subsequent relationship.

Jane was weaned at eight weeks, as the mother found that she could not go on with breast feeding when she started work. She was much concerned about this early weaning and later often talked about it with signs of guilt, once she knew that early weaning could have an unfavorable effect on children. From our later knowledge of the mother and her way of dealing with the child it was obvious that she had tried to compensate for breast feeding by much emphasis on food, sweets, the freedom to suck, and a great deal of kissing. She derived much pleasure from making Jane look attractive and spent much time and thought on Jane's appearance.

It was also evident that the mother's determination to keep the baby with her at all cost and the fact that she was a very competent domestic worker had made it possible for her to find posts where she was allowed to have her baby with her, to look after her during her work, and to have her sleep in her room. It is not known how many times the mother changed her employment during this phase; it appears that she changed posts at least twice, but that she never parted with Jane.

Physical Development

According to the mother, Jane had been a large, well-developed, and attractive baby at birth and was much admired by nurses and other mothers. Her feeding was satisfactory, she had no illnesses, and she was described as well advanced and active compared with other babies.

Libidinal Development

Jane's oral fixation was marked and her intense need to suck and eat sweets was an important feature. She had also a great struggle to gain control over her bowel and bladder.

Ego Development

Jane was described as alert and active, taking notice early, able to imitate movements and sounds and to say her first words early. All these memories about Jane's babyhood were reported by the mother on occasions when she compared her with babies whom she saw at the Hampstead Nursery. Her pride in Jane's good endowment was evident throughout and it seems clear that Jane had been much stimulated by her. Stimulation had also come from the members of the families by whom Jane's mother was employed and whose household they shared. When Jane was admitted to the Nursery her speech was well advanced, and so was her motor control.

The Mother's Personality

Jane's mother had herself been an illegitimate child and had been brought up in an institution. She sometimes spoke about her childhood in the convent, comparing the strict rules and deprivations with the free and satisfying nursery life at Hampstead. She was, however, very attached to the nuns who had brought her up, especially to the Mother Superior whom she still visited, and she expressed much gratitude for what they had done for her. This was later expressed also in her choice of school for Jane whom she wanted to be taught by nuns.

The mother's personality features which became known to us and which are likely to have had a favorable effect were the following. She had an excellent capacity to make and maintain relationships over a long time. Her friendship with Bob's mother has continued now for twenty-three years, she visits some of her former employers, has remained attached to the organizers of the Hampstead Nurseries, and has always kept contact with me, turning to me for advice whenever she felt in need of it.

She is intelligent and very adaptable and showed a great capacity to learn. She was eager to understand the background of the educational methods used at the Nursery and has for many years consistently read the pages on child psychology which I wrote in a weekly paper for parents. She has attempted to modify her own approach to Jane accordingly, and has later been very successful in dealing with the problems of a stepson who was a disturbed institution child when she married his father.

Some unfavorable aspects of the mother's personality also became known to us. While the mother's capacity for forming and keeping relationships was remarkable, closer contact revealed antisocial character traits and delinquent tendencies. These manifested themselves in a number of situations in which "outwitting other people in order to break rules" and especially to get more than her share played a part. Such "successes" were related with obvious pride. All these incidents were connected with the wish to give Jane more than rationing would permit, especially where sweets and clothes were concerned.

During the second half of Jane's first year in the Nursery it became possible for the mother to join the household staff. This allowed her and Jane free access to each other as the mother worked in the house where Jane spent the greatest part of the day and where she slept. Both made ample use of this opportunity, but Jane's interest in activities in the Nursery School which was in another house was by then greater than the wish to stay with her mother and she decided of her own accord to go out for the mornings. Her growing skills and her enjoyment of the nursery school were very marked, and the mother's encouragement and pride played a great part in this progress.

The Vicissitudes of Jane's Separation Anxiety

From the second year of her stay in the Nursery onward, i.e., after she was four years old, Jane did not show extreme reactions to separations from her mother. She admitted that she missed her, was longing for her, and was angry when the mother stayed away longer than Jane had expected her to do. Jane's relationship to her substitute mother and other members of the staff were by then so well established that she felt free to talk about her feelings. She was one of the children best able to verbalize her thoughts and feelings, and it was clear that her capacity to express herself and to deal with ambivalent feelings against her mother in an open way were of the greatest help to her. This came to play an even greater part when, in her sixth year, war conditions made it necessary for the children to leave London and move to the country. This meant that Jane was for the first time separated from her mother for periods of one month, as visiting could not be arranged more frequently owing to distance and transport conditions. During the same period she was also separated from her substitute mother for a great part of each week.

During this phase Jane's thumb sucking at bedtime became intensified and she regressed to bed wetting, from which she had not been consistently free for long. She nevertheless remained active and made great strides in sublimatory activities. She started school and learned eagerly and well. She took part in many country activities which were new to the child who had grown up in town.

Separation Anxiety Manifested in Relation to Lost Objects

During the second year of her stay in the Nursery Jane went through a phase of distress following the loss of her favorite toy animal. She had become very attached to a toy cat which had been her constant companion. This was lost at the cleaner's after Jane had had an infectious disease. When it became clear that the cat could not be traced, Jane was inconsolable, cried for it nightly, and talked about it a great deal in the daytime. It was obvious that this loss had revived her distress at the time of the other separations. She did not react to this loss by expressing her wish to be reunited, because *she* felt the need for the comfort the cat had given her; rather all her feelings were expressed in terms of identification with it, sharing in fantasy the cat's feeling of being lost. "I keep thinking of the poor lost pussy, it looks at me with its sad green eyes! It's far away from me and from all the people who love it."

The cat and its loss have remained fresh in Jane's memory, while she cannot recall her arrival at the Nursery or her distress about being left. She referred to the cat during each of the follow-up visits. The facts themselves have remained unaltered in her mind: "Do you remember when my dear pussy cat went to the cleaners and never came back?" But gradually the theme of the lost animal became elaborated in her fantasy in the following way: during a visit at the age of nine years when Jane had again mentioned the incident, she told me later that she had decided on her future career; she wanted to open and run a home for lost cats. This was an elaborate plan and her arguments ended with the words: "There should be no lost pussies in the world." When the subject of her future career came up again a year later Jane had decided to become a veterinary surgeon. This became even more realistic in the following year when she won a scholarship to grammar school which would allow her to go on to study at a university.

Throughout the years when the fantasy about the home for lost cats and later the wish to become a veterinary surgeon were in the foreground, Jane spent much of her free time looking after cats and other pets with much kindness and the competence that is typical of her and her mother.

A year later Jane had changed her mind about her future career. She said to me: "I have changed my mind—it must be an orphanage that I will be running. Little children are so sad without their mummies and I will let them have a pussy each." In this fantasy the lost kitten and the lost child have merged, and Jane sees her role in providing for them all the mothering that she herself lost when she was suddenly separated from her mother.

During this time Jane started looking after babies, especially one who, like herself, had no father. Jane proudly pointed out each of the baby's achievements as if she were talking about her own child. In this she seemed fully identified with her mother who had welcomed every new step in Jane's development with so much pride.

For a long time Jane's plans for the future had been entirely centered around the wish to become someone who could make lost animals or orphan children happy. Reality gave her the opportunity when she was eleven years old. Her mother then married a man who had lost his wife. He had a son who had been in an institution since his mother's death. When her mother hesitatingly approached Jane about her stepfather's son and his wish to have him at home, Jane insisted that he must not be left in the institution any longer and asked to be allowed to fetch him herself. It was decided that the little boy who was five years old should come home. Jane, aged twelve by then, took over the greatest part of his care, mothered him, and, according to her mother, showed such real understanding of his needs and difficulties that she was able to help him adapt to family life, which he had hardly known before.

A year later, a former Nursery worker who visited the family reported: "Jane is crazy about pets. In their small house at present live father, mother, the stepbrother, grandfather, uncle, aunt, and a boy cousin, but still they have room for a cat with two kittens, a dog and a puppy, and in the garden are rabbits and chickens. Jane adores looking after them and loves puppies and chickens alike. She calls all these animals by name and wishes she could have more."

Reaction to Mother's Marriage

On the surface Jane seemed to adjust very well to the complete change from being her mother's only concern to having to share her not only with her husband but with the stepbrother who needed so much of her attention. During the same year, however, signs of withdrawal, dreaminess, and a succession of fainting attacks made their appearance. Jane continued at first to be on friendly terms with her mother, and she made a good relationship with the stepfather. At the same time her teachers observed the symptoms mentioned above which appeared mainly at school. It was not possible at the time to get insight into the conflicts aroused by the mother's marriage; and only recently, twelve years later, has Jane been able to give an account of some of her angry and disturbed feelings. She felt that her mother had let her down, not because she had married, but because she had changed in her behavior toward her. She had become aggressive and short-tempered when Jane seemed to be interfering between her and her husband. In Jane's own words: "It was as if I'd lost the mother I knew and had to get to know a new one; she was so different." She felt that it was through the stepfather's kindness and understanding that she later regained her good relationship with her mother. The stepfather was fond of Jane and said spontaneously: "No man could wish for a kinder, better daughter; she makes us all happy."

Jane's Active Moves toward Independence

In following Jane's reaction to separation through puberty and adolescence, it becomes quite clear that she has actively arranged to be away from home more and more. At the same time, she is obviously happy to return there. Already from the age of eleven onward she went by train to a nearby town and spent all day at school, returning home in the evening. Soon after, she began to spend week ends and part of her holidays with friends. Throughout these years her interest in new people and places became an outstanding feature, and there are no signs that her increasing removal from the family circle is based on an angry wish to separate from her mother, as is often found in adolescents. On the contrary, according to both her mother's and her stepfather's accounts, her kindness and gaiety contribute greatly to the family's happiness. It appears, also, that the ever-growing difference between her own education and interests and those of her family does not form an obstacle. Jane, on the contrary, contributes by her new interests and does not hesitate to introduce her friends to the family.

After leaving school, Jane decided on a teacher's training college in London which meant that she could live at home only during her holidays. At that time, when she was eighteen, she met questions about any anxious reaction to being away from her mother with astonishment and showed that she was totally unaware of the experience she had gone through when she was in her third year. She said that she had never felt anxious when away from home and developed plans to travel to foreign countries as soon as possible. These she carried out with much pleasure.

In her choice of career, Jane had moved away from the earlier fantasies of having to care for lost animals or children. What had remained was her wish to work with children. She felt that she was not the sort of person who could live in an institution, as would have been necessary if she had stuck to her earlier plan. She chose biology and physical education as her two subjects, because these had been her best subjects in the last years at school. Her love of nature and the wish that children should be taught about animals and plants in a way that would make them really interested in rather than be bored by the lessons were topics which she discussed with enthusiasm. Her pleasure in her bodily skill and her talent for organization were directed toward planning games and competitions. At present she is in charge of all arrangements for outdoor activities of a large London grammar school, and she gets great satisfaction from planning both the physical and intellectual activities outside school such as visits to sports events, museums, etc. She has won the cup in last year's yachting race of the seaside town where she lives and greatly enjoyed all the publicity and popularity among young people after this event.

Adult Life in London

As an adult with a self-chosen satisfying career, Jane has organized her life to provide her with rich opportunities for both work and pleasure.

When I asked her to stay with me until she had found a flat, she did so with great pleasure, but her active search and her clear idea about what she was looking for made it possible for her to find what she wanted within a week. When asked what had determined her choice, she said: "It has to be a place that is comfortable and attractive, where it is homey and I am independent at the same time." This sentence characterizes her present relationship to her home and to me.

Further discussion of her choice of a flat has opened up the whole question of the role which I as her "substitute mother" played in her development. Initially I had emerged from the number of nurses in the Hampstead Nursery to whom Jane had held on indiscriminately as the one she wanted in her mother's absence. Gradually she became closely attached to me. She first used me entirely as a substitute for her mother, to fulfill her needs as they made themselves felt. But I became to mean more than the person who provided her with what she really wanted from her mother. Later Jane was able to have a relationship with me as a person who was separate from her mother and to take and enjoy the new and different things she could get from me.

In Jane's personality, in her tastes and choice of career, it is possible to trace aspects of her identification with me. Jane has herself traced back some of these links and is conscious of them. In discussing her choice of flat, for instance, Jane said that as soon as she had seen the one which was furnished with period furniture, she no longer considered any one of the others. Thinking about her preference for this led her at first to my present house which contains much antique furniture. She then remembered my room in the Hampstead Nursery which had contained some of the same furniture and where Jane had spent much time. Jane also believes that her

interest in foreign countries and especially foreign food is related
to me who came from the Continent. Her earlier need for oral satisfaction is now largely satisfied through her pleasure in cooking and
eating unusual dishes.

Conclusion

The knowledge of Jane's development and of her present personality is confined to those areas into which insight has been
possible through direct observation by an analytically trained observer with whom she has maintained a warm and lasting relationship.

Insight into other aspects has not been possible. This is due partly
to the fact that unconscious material was inaccessible, and partly to
my gradually becoming aware that one large area of Jane's thinking
and feeling cannot be approached, because it is blocked by far-
reaching repression as well as by conscious reluctance to discuss this
subject. It concerns all memories and feelings connected with her
father whom she knew up to the age of six and who visited her at
the Nursery whenever he was on leave from the army. Jane maintains that she has no memory of him and has never mentioned a wish
to contact him. She has formed a warm relationship with her stepfather and has at present a close relationship to a young man who
shares her interests and whom she hopes to marry. In this she differs
greatly from the many other illegitimate girls whom we have had
the opportunity to study by direct observation or in analysis. It is so
far impossible to say, however, whether her heterosexual relationship
will be a well-adjusted one.

An assessment of Jane's present personality on the basis of the
material available shows her to be a well-adjusted young woman who
has been able to solve her conflicts without a far-reaching use of
pathological mechanisms.

In her instinctual development, in her ego and superego, and in
her object relationships, Jane functions on an adult level with
apparently little interference from inner conflicts. The only symptom
which Jane occasionally shows in moments of tension is a brief and
repeated sigh which intersperses her speech. It is not impossible that

analytic investigation would disclose the compression of a great deal of complex emotional material in this symptom.

The question poses itself which factors in the inner and outer conditions of her life have made it possible for this fatherless, homeless girl, who was severely traumatized through separation from her mother in the third year, to reach adulthood with as little apparent damage. Among the most important factors probably are the nature of Jane's personality, the developmental levels she had reached, and the good relationship with her mother before the separation. Although she regressed severely in both her libidinal and ego development, her innate capacities enabled her to make a forward move again within a comparatively short time.

It seems of great importance to me that at the time of separation Jane's development had been well advanced with regard to her object relationship and had undoubtedly reached the stage of object constancy. This enabled her to maintain the relationship with her mother in spite of the frequent interruptions during the first months of separation. This factor also made it possible for Jane to form a close and longlasting relationship with me after the first weeks of indiscriminate clinging. Although this relationship to me was at first characterized by features of need fulfillment and of the anaclitic stage, she was able to regain and later move forward to more advanced forms of object relationship.

The innate ego capacities, namely, her good intelligence and the unimpaired use of her capacity to verbalize, have played a large part in Jane's recovery. She emerged from the initial helplessly confused feeling about her mother's disappearances and reappearances by making use of the available clues that could lead to orientation in time and place. The trust in her mother which had existed before the shock of being left gradually reappeared, as the mother kept to the promises she made about her visits.

Furthermore, Jane's freedom to put her anger into words whenever her mother had disappointed her helped to reduce anxiety, especially as the mother responded freely with expressions of love and was able to tolerate Jane's anger without arousing undue guilt.

The interest in this long-term study lies in the fact that the observers who had seen the child during her traumatic experience in which she reacted with greatest distress had felt that this could not pass without interfering with Jane's further development and personality. Nevertheless, the observations of her development and the assessment of her present personality show that the trauma had neither stopped ongoing development nor left a disturbing mark on her adult life.

DECLINE AND RECOVERY IN THE LIFE
OF A THREE-YEAR-OLD

or

DATA IN PSYCHOANALYTIC PERSPECTIVE ON
THE MOTHER-CHILD RELATIONSHIP

(Alternately subtitle as major title.)

ERNST KRIS, Ph.D.

Editor's Note.—Ernst Kris started writing this essay in 1956. It was unfinished at the time of his sudden death in February of the following year. The first part had been once revised by him from the first draft; the second part is a first draft; the chapter on "Anxiety and Despair" is clearly incomplete. Kris left no notes which would indicate where he wanted to place this chapter; nor do there exist any notes concerning what parts of the paper he considered in need of reformulations or additions, or concerning which of the rich variety of subjects this paper touches upon he would have liked to present in greater detail.

We find in this paper all the essential elements of Ernst Kris's style of thinking and presentation, all those characteristics of the man and his work that have made him one of the truly creative and inspiring psychoanalysts of our time. We find in it his broad capacity for empathy, his vivid and acute observation, his incisive and at the same time flexible thinking, his mastery in developing the interactions of clinical and theoretical work, and his superior gift for communicating his thoughts. I do not think that we ought to apologize for publishing his unfinished essay. A point could even be made for the thesis that in this case, as in others, it is in "unfinished works" that certain characteristics of the creative individual manifest themselves with particular clarity.

Beyond this, we want to mention that some of the theoretical and methodological statements in this paper have been made here for the first time. Some of them have been used by others as their points of departure for further research. I am thinking, among others, of

175

articles by Marianne Kris (1957), Ritvo and Solnit (1958, 1960), and of a book by Provence and Lipton [Coleman] that will soon be published. And I want to emphasize the relevance of this paper by Ernst Kris for the "Family Study" conducted at the Yale Child Study Center. One of the suggestive hypotheses contained in this essay has recently been dealt with by Provence and Ritvo (1961). Some others, equally important today as they were when Ernst Kris first formulated them, have so far not found the general interest they unquestionably deserve.

It has been decided to print this paper by and large as written by the author. Only minor changes have been made by Dr. Marianne Kris and Dr. Sally Provence. Additions by the Editors have been inserted in brackets. The Bibliography was also added by the Editors.

HEINZ HARTMANN, M.D.

[Part 1]

I. Introduction

A. *The Problem*

It is late in Spring, close to the end of the school year, and the nursery school group is playing in the yard. The morning is well advanced, and the first of the parents come to take their children home. They have been expected. The ten three-year-olds who form the group have been together since September, twice a week for three morning hours, which seemed long at first and have become shorter as the months progressed. The children have formed something more than fleeting attachments among each other and distinct relationships to the teachers, and to the psychiatrists acting as helpers in the group, each of whom had devoted special attention to one of the children throughout the school year. And yet leaving the group comes easily. The call of the home has not lost its unique power. There are few who display their pleasure; most seem proud to have been found in the midst of some activity, which the parent is supposed to watch for a moment or two before the child surrenders the world (of his own) in which he had been living for the past few hours. This is the average picture that mirrors the conflict of the age between growing independence and old attachment. Even in this clearly structured situation variations are infinite. The intensity with which the parent is welcomed, the speed with which the activity is abandoned, the way of parting depend on a large number of obvious factors: what sort of a morning it has been; how successful it was in terms of social experience; whether or not the preferred teacher or playmate and the preferred toy have been readily available; whether it is one of the rare mornings when father comes, or whether the mother comes alone or with the baby on her arm; what had happened earlier that morning at home, before they left for school. But these circumstances or experiences do not account for the full extent of the variations that strike observers who have learned to perceive individual demeanor within the typical behavior patterns of three-year-olds. The attempt to contribute to an understanding of the nature, extent, and sources of such individual differences stands as an impressive, and in a sense intimidating problem in the background of this report and of some others, more detailed and richer ones, which are to deal with other children of this group of ten.

Anne's reaction to the going-home situation differs in a few elements from that of others. She seems pleasantly surprised at her mother's arrival, but there is no stormy welcome. Is it that the mother, a woman with clear green eyes and a friendly though somewhat stereotyped smile, has taught her to avoid intensive bodily contacts, since she is well advanced in her pregnancy—or is it a more general trait of Anne's behavior? The latter it must be, since even with teachers and playmates the short good-by procedure is more like that of an adult than that of a young child. There is also the clear and well-enunciated speech, appropriately used, with noticeable pride in achievement. Anne's graceful small body moves once more down the slide; she was one in a row of three who had been waiting for their turn, and she wanted to take her turn once more before she leaves. She is fully alert to the pleasure, but her hands grasp the edge of the slide perhaps somewhat more firmly than those of other children; her sharp, almost shrieking laughter may also be somewhat more excited. But after this interlude she easily adapts to the mother's request, straightens her hair with a furtive gesture—a gesture obviously borrowed from the mother—and is ready to leave. Hand in hand the two walk through the gate of the yard, a contented pair.

No description of Anne's behavior during a short time span, however subtle, can convey satisfactorily the multitude of impressions which constitute the "individual traits of behavior." Only if we extend the time span do our chances of capturing the specific in the general increase. But it is not this pathway which we here intend to follow: we shall try to present Anne's life history and to trace a number of factors which, through their interaction, have presumably contributed to make her what she is. This life history has been a particularly dramatic one; Anne has gone through experiences of most pronounced and shaking deprivations during her first year. When we meet her at three she has recovered from physical retardation and developmental arrest, is a friendly and mostly smiling child, and her physical status is satisfactory.

The central question with which this study deals is thus laid out: How have decline and recovery come about, and how lasting does the recovery promise to be? While the second of these questions will be left to inference and speculation, we hope to be able to specify in some detail that decline and recovery can both be viewed as related to the interplay of parents and child.[1]

B. *The Nature of the Data*

The data which we shall use in this presentation differ from those usually available to psychoanalysts. The observations of this child were not gleaned in psychoanalytic or psychiatric treatment situations. They were gathered in interviews with the mother centered around development and care of the child, in numerous observations of home life, and of the child in a variety of settings, which a longitudinal study conducted at the Child Study Center of Yale University offered.[2]

Families participating in the study had been referred to the Child Study Center by the Obstetrical Clinic of the Grace-New Haven Community Hospital. In the mind of the patients the institu-

[1] A preliminary and partial presentation of some of these questions was offered by M. Kris in a paper delivered at Arden House (1954). The report has not been published. For some remarks of A. Freud on this report, see *The Psychoanalytic Study of the Child*, Vol. IX [pp. 70-71, 1954].

[2] The Study was in part supported by a grant from the Commonwealth Fund in New York City.

tions were closely affiliated as part of the Yale University Medical Center.

Three criteria crystallized and guided our selections: (1) The mothers had to be "normal" primiparas. (2) There should be some reasonable prospect that the families would remain in New Haven for the subsequent five years. (3) The parents had to be ready to cooperate with the staff in a study "of the development of the child's personality in his family setting." They had to agree to regular interviews with the social worker, starting during pregnancy";[3] to regular and, during the first year, frequent well-baby clinics and developmental examinations. In exchange the study offered complete well- and sick-baby care, and later the prospect of free school attendance at the nursery school of the Child Study Center.

The influence of these facilities on the readiness of young couples to participate is difficult to evaluate. It stands to reason that parents feeling a need of institutional support for economic or psychological reasons were more likely to be attracted by the plan than others.[4] In the case of Anne's mother, these and other incentives seem to have been at work. The contact with "the University," i.e., with the staff of specialists of considerable educational status, satisfied some of her own intellectual aspirations; the participation gave her a special position among the expectant mothers of the community; it promised to alleviate economic pressure and be of some help in the bewilderment and conflict into which her pregnancy had thrown her, and of which she seemed to have been aware without initially fully admitting it to herself.

Compared to other longitudinal studies on which reports are available in the literature, this one was different in various respects. The contacts were strictly "service-centered." Participants were not seen without a direct relation to the current situation in which they lived, and the focus of contact was always derived from one aspect or another of child care in the broadest sense of the word. This included much of the family interaction, the life and problems of parents and siblings; the latter were given comparable though not as extensive attention as the original study child itself.

[3] In Anne's case, the professional status of the interviewer was characterized in terms of her special interest in problems of pregnant women and young mothers.

[4] See also K. Wolf, 1950? p. ? [1952].

While the character of the contact imposed, at least initially, had certain limitations, it proved beneficial as time progressed since the information we gained appeared in a dynamically structured context. Thus the "history" of the childhood of Anne's mother was not elicited in a structured interview by systematic questioning; all we know came to light during the vicissitudes of her relation with Anne.[5] Moreover, the length of the contact itself proved fruitful: the attitude of the mother to her first infant appeared in a much clearer profile when certain of its peculiarities could be studied when her second and third child were born. By the same token, the strict relation to the service purpose allowed for intimate observations of the parent-child relationship which otherwise would not have been available: the mother was seen not only with the child in well-baby clinic during medical and developmental examinations, during the social worker's home visit, but also during day and night home calls of the pediatrician when the child had an illness. As the child grew up and joined the nursery school, the opportunities for observation multiplied, and the number of observers reporting on mother and child (or contributing accidental observations) grew.

From the beginning of our work a considerable number of individuals had occasion to observe the child in one situation or another. During the well-baby clinics opportunities for observation were provided through a one-way vision screen; and later the nursery school was regularly visited by some, and intermittently visited by others, of those who attended the numerous research meetings in which the material was currently discussed. When mother and child visited the Child Study Center, Mrs. Adams was casually seen by many staff members, and some of the "nodding acquaintances" soon developed into more familiar contacts.

In addition to its assets, the multiplicity of observers might have contained certain dangers had we not succeeded in combining it with a continuity of observing personnel. A number of the observers, particularly the pediatrician who combined the function of physician and developmental examiner (in addition to other more complex functions about which a word will be said later), have remained the same throughout the course of the study and have in their under-

---

[5] See on this point below p. [???]. In our conferences much care was taken to assess in which context any information was gained.

standing grown with the child. However, even those, who for external reasons had to be added to the team and to replace members who dropped out, profited from the total duration of the study contact: a "transference to the institution" (Reider, 19 [53]) had developed. A familiarity with its staff, reciprocated in varying degrees by the individual workers, could comparatively easily be extended to new staff members. This became particularly clear in the contact of this family with the social worker. In Anne's case over the years of the study it happened that three social workers had to be assigned to the family. In others there was no change. It was the length of contact and the increase of trust in the venture of which the family was a part that seemed to be mainly responsible for the fact that information tended to become more personal and relevant as time proceeded. Much that concerned the earliest reactions of the mother to the child gained its meaning in the light of information which she volunteered years later, when under the pressure of some family crisis the social worker could offer help and guidance (McCollum, 1956). Those who joined the staff at a later date had the opportunity to study the record which contained not only the observational material itself, but also the large set of prognostications, ruminations, and hunches, some apt, some far afield, which seem to present themselves when a multidisciplinary team and a vast variety of data are constantly brought in relation to new clinical impressions and theoretical expectations.[6] However, the specificity of the study rests in the fact that these expectations were based on psychoanalysis. All members of the staff had for some time been familiar with psychoanalysis and all who had direct contact with the family had been analyzed.

There is no doubt that the hypotheses of psychoanalysis have infiltrated into the observations themselves. No observer, we believe, can or should be seen as being a blank screen. A wisely moderated and continuously checked relation of observation to expectation seemed to us on the whole to guarantee satisfactory procedures. The fact that the team was a multidisciplinary one, that many participants came from long and independent training in their special area of work seemed to provide for checks and balances in each instance

---

[6] For details of the personnel participating in the Study and in the research conferences, and for a description of the record, see Appendix I; for "prognostications," see p. [?].

when the reported observations were discussed and their meaning tentatively evaluated. The effect of this cooperative venture was highly stimulating. To the psychoanalysts of the team in particular it was full of challenge. While there will be opportunities to give instances of this in the course of the paper, it may be appropriate to mention here some aspects on which this challenge became focused. The absence of the kind of material with which the analysts were familiar imposed upon them the need to translate what they had learned from the study data into the context of their analytic experience. Analysts are used to discover the past in the present. The discussions of the current experiences of mother and child were geared to the future. Wherever advice or guidance—medical or educational—is offered, the future has our attention. This then implies that on many occasions the possibility existed to compare views held and recorded at one time with "the outcome"—an experience stimulating or humiliating depending on one's personal reaction when faced with clear-cut limitations of our knowledge.

The task of the analyst during the work of the study and the report on some of the material direct our attention to the nature of these limitations.[7] Much of the data here used, e.g., those on the development of the child during its first year not only have little resemblance to what analysts learn from their patients, they have also only a limited resemblance to the striking and fundamental work of analysts who observed large groups of children during shorter time periods in different settings (Spitz, Bowlby) or with less intensive observations over many years (Fries).

Our interest is focused on the individual child in his family surrounding. Our material on Anne is presented with an avowed intent: to draw attention to one of the ways in which a critical and traumatic earliest childhood may come about, and how it appears when studied while it develops. We hope by this report to stimulate interest in further similar studies which might add materials to psychoanalytic work in reconstruction by detailed and, as it were, naturalistic recording. However, in selecting the way in which data are to be presented, we once more follow the lead of experience that psychoanalytic work supplies: the starting point of our thinking was

---

[7] See also below (Conclusions).

Anne at age three. In order to keep the two time perspectives apart
—the one we had followed when the data were collected, i.e., the
perspective of the future, and the other from which we are working
while reporting on these data, i.e., scrutiny of the past—we shall
endeavor at crucial points to indicate divergences which their comparison reveals.

The presentation of a biographical picture based on data supplied by multiple observations affords an opportunity of contributing to psychoanalysis in another sense. Though we cannot aim at
validating or invalidating propositions, a survey of those propositions
which prove useful in the present context is suggestive: they form a
unit, in the sense of an implied hierarchical organization, and more
than once will it be possible to select preferred alternative propositions within this unit.

II. The Parents: Some Biographical Information

Though in our research project contacts with mothers are infinitely more frequent and more intensive than those with fathers,
in hardly any case has it proved so difficult to draw the image of the
father as in the case of Mr. Adams. He is by nature a retiring young
man, with a rare but friendly smile which may blossom into laughter
when Anne, the three-year-old, greets him enthusiastically. His
precise New England manner covers a somewhat diffident deport-
ment. He always seems hard pressed for time and working against
odds. During most of the period of our contacts he was working in a
law firm and concerned with completing work for an advanced
degree at an early date in order to achieve full financial independence.

He had come successfully through a hard life, as far as we know
without severe psychological impairment. He had lost his father at
six or seven, and had been sent to an Episcopalian boarding school
whose headmaster had apparently become a friendly mentor and an
important ideal in the secular, though not in the religious, conduct
of life. Anne's brother was later to be named after this man and
Mr. Adams's father. Drafted shortly after the completion of school,
Mr. Adams was a prisoner of war for part of his military service. He
started studies after the war in Boston where he met his wife.

Mr. Adams describes his mother as severe and determined; when she appeared on the scene of Anne's life, her interventions seemed to confirm this impression. Stern, resolute, with Victorian standards, presumably frozen by a hard life, she had supported her four children after her husband's death by independent business activities. She remarried late in life and moved with her second husband to another country. Little is known about Mr. Adams's relation to his siblings with whom, at the time of our study, he maintained contact by correspondence only.

Mrs. Adams's appearance stands in marked contrast to her husband. Somewhat full in build, of medium height, she has a ready and outgoing smile at her command which enlivens the attractive features of a roundish face. Simply but tastefully dressed, neat without obvious effort, there is also frequently a tinge of artificiality about her. Most noticeable is the precision in speech and accent of the foreign-born girl whose speech has to come up to the standards of her well-educated husband. Her attempts to cast her own behavior into the mold of the rigid New England pattern in which her husband grew up are generally noticeable. At times when she is preoccupied or involved in conflict those slightly forced adaptations seem to disintegrate and it is as if her behavior became somewhat amorphous. In good times, however, her determined, well-organized demeanor and her purposeful attempts at empathy tend to impress favorably those with whom she is about to establish contact.

The only child of her parents' marriage, she grew up in her South American homeland under favorable economic conditions. Her father held an important administrative position in industry and the family lived in considerable comfort. During the summer they went to the maternal grandmother's house in a mountainous and forested area nostalgically recalled by Mrs. Adams. When she was nine years old the financial decline of the family started. The industry in which her father was active closed down and within five years both parents died. After a short stay with an aunt, to whom she had been sent before her father's death, Mrs. Adams, in early adolescence, was made to follow a ten-year-older half brother who had emigrated to the United States and held at the time a position in Boston. He fully accepted parental authority and obligation which he later shared with his wife. They have remained dominant figures in Mrs. Adams's life, and observers who have seen the two families living together confirm the impression that Mrs. Adams conveys. Throughout the years of our acquaintance with her, contact with the half brother and his wife seemed to restore her confidence, and yet there is some evidence that closeness to and separation from the brother play a more complex role. It seems that she could gain independence better if she were on her own; and yet she would be driven back to him with great force. She herself, however, is barely aware of her attachment. Under the half brother's guidance she completed her schooling in Boston which led her away from intellectual pursuits and toward artistic pursuits. This was apparently in opposition to what her parents might have expected but in fact was unconsciously tied to the memory of her father who had dabbled in the arts though he considered art an "unmanly" occupation. Mrs. Adams made her father's hobby into her profession in which she achieved some success early in adult life. In the years of her professional training she experienced some platonic infatuations, but after a short while the interest died down. She met her husband through the boy friend of a roommate, was astonished when she discovered that he was interested in her. She was initially hesitant about marriage, but decided to accept, possibly influenced by the fact that her half brother had moved away from Boston. Mrs. Adams continued with her work and her husband with his studies. Life was happy and gay, with much chance for travel and relaxation. They had no intention of settling down when they moved to New Haven. Shortly after they had moved Mrs. Adams discovered that she was pregnant.[8]

While information about Mrs. Adams's life during her adolescent and later years was comparatively difficult to obtain and had here and there to be implemented by direct questions, information concerning the years of Mrs. Adams's childhood and her relation to her parents appeared spontaneously and in manifold variations. It was in these childhood years that the stage was set for her later life, and for Anne's earliest experiences.

We put at the beginning a tale about her parents' marriage. The

[8] Three months after Anne's birth the fact that Anne's birth had not been planned is already vigorously disclaimed; later there is evidence that the memory of it is actually repressed.

first husband of Mrs. Adams's mother had died when their little boy was six years of age. Mrs. Adams's father saw the widow playing with the boy and fell in love with her. Shortly thereafter they married. Tales of this kind are of a peculiar impact which makes them worth remembering, quite apart from the possibility that the tradition itself may have been molded into shape by the teller of the tale. To Mrs. Adams, the story is part of the evidence that her father, who at the time of his marriage was a man in his middle thirties, wanted a boy child. Whatever she reports on her early experiences with her father—and in a contact of four years' duration there were many occasions when one item or another appeared—were elaborations on this theme. She is at times aware of the connection in which she presents the material; and often seems to heap evidence upon evidence as if trying to prove the case.

Stocky, muscular, and vigorous, a mountain climber and horseman, her father was interested in sports and physical exercise. When a physical handicap of the stepson thwarted attempts to make him into an athlete, his interest focused upon the little girl. She was made to wear boys' clothes and haircut, and at five years of age she was started on a course of weight lifting and systematic exercise. She was to be "brave" and a "big" girl and was to overcome her fear of animals. In her schoolwork, if things did not come easily enough, she was tutored in order to shine. The demand for perfection was both unrelenting and insistent. When the report card was less good than expected the father would refuse to speak to her. There are early recollections about some strong reactions to this: she longed to be the little girl that could hide behind her mother's skirt. Her feeling of being physically inferior is linked to the father's training which her mother seemed to have viewed as "foolish." As a baby she had been beautiful, but later she felt she had become unattractive. There is no doubt that the way in which she views her body is derived in part from the way in which she views these early experiences. She dislikes her stocky, overweight figure, her short fingers, her varicose veins, her enormous breasts—a derogatory self-image which contrasts sharply with her present appearance. Similarly she thinks of herself as "nonintellectual" with a mind "like a sieve," at times as stupid, and believes that she is a "down-to-earth" person.

And yet she enjoys at times impressing people with her intellectual gifts, attempts somewhat marred by even higher aspirations.[9]

The self-derogatory picture clusters obviously around her role as a woman and is supplemented by a variety of psychosomatic symptoms. She has conflicts about being a wife and mother, and at least throughout the first years of Anne's life she repeatedly thinks about returning to work. In this she consciously follows the example of her own mother who as a widow had supported herself and her son and relinquished work only under the pressure of sickness.

Mrs. Adams has the impression that her mother led an unhappy and frustrated life. She was "terrifically in love with her husband, but they were not compatible." She was idle and dissatisfied. Housework was done by servants, and care of the child was entrusted to various hands, e.g., even to the maternal grandmother. She breast-fed the baby, but she obviously did not know how to bring up a daughter. In later years this relationship was not a close one, and not one that we might expect between mother and daughter; rather they were close to each other primarily as friends. The mother was not able to relate the facts of life to the child. However, already as a child she was made to share in many important decisions concerning the family.

There is ample evidence of Mrs. Adams's deep resentment of her parents, but whenever this resentment appears she will deny its existence in the same breath. Thus, when she expresses her resentment of her father's training, she will add how delighted the father was with her, how they adored each other, how he brought her candy and cakes.[10]

When she refers to her mother's lack of interest in her and recalls times when she felt lonely as a child, she counters this with the idea that "we were friends after all." When on rare occasions she criticizes her husband, the criticism is soon balanced and smoothed out. The reproaches she levels against him are in many ways similar to those that she levels against her father: too many demands, too little under-

---

[9] Mrs. Adams rates on intelligence tests as superior.

[10] One of the most marked patterns of Mrs. Adams's behavior during the years of our contact seems directly related to this experience. Whenever threatened by disappointment in herself and others, whenever she merges into a depressed mood, she turns to sweets. Her weight curve becomes a reliable indicator of her mood; in peace she is not overweight, but burdened she grows heavier.

standing. In almost the same breath she observes that Mr. Adams is often absorbed in his thoughts and that she must help organize his life. While Mr. Adams shares his wife's interest in art and literature —the "higher things in life"—he is unbendingly, though not always optimistically, independent where his work and his career are concerned. Mrs. Adams seems to resent this attitude.

The conflict of which we gained some glimpses on the surface reaches deep into her personal life. While the apprehension about libidinal manifestations, the turning away from too much instinctual gratification, and an attempt at control are conscious, the conflict with the instinctual life concerns aggression. We have mentioned how the defense against ambivalent feelings characterizes Mrs. Adams's utterances. These instances render only a feeble impression of her constant and hard struggle against her own aggressive impulses. While she mentions only an occasional obsessional-compulsive symptom (for instance, the urge to recheck on the gas jets when leaving her home), the dynamics of an obsessional-compulsive pattern permeate her behavior. When she appears dissatisfied or depressed one gains the impression that she had devaluated herself instead of devaluating or attacking an outside person.

Independently from our clinical evaluation of Mrs. Adams's personality, a diagnostic study of her Rorschach record supplied a similar impression.[11]

While the information which Mrs. Adams supplies is scanty compared to the set of data with which analysts are wont to work, in evaluating this information one particular feature has to be taken into account; we are not dealing with a set of anamnestic data or with a life chronicle. Our information concerning Mrs. Adams's early years has appeared spontaneously in a dynamic context in which the present in which she has been living led her mind back to the past. Her recollections were stimulated by the experience of pregnancy and delivery and by the care of the child with all its traumatic vicissitudes. In addition, the general setup of the study (more than any specific inquiries by interviewer or pediatrician) may have encouraged her reminiscing. The relation between past and

[11 E.K. placed a ? in the margin of the following paragraph. He probably wondered whether this material should be placed elsewhere since it seems more related to earlier pages.]

present is in some instances particularly dramatic: Mrs. Adams's recollections of her parents in childhood seem item by item related to her own experiences with Anne. During her pregnancy only a boy is expected; her disappointment at the birth of a girl was evident; she feels unable to handle a small child, but when she can become a teacher and the procedures of developmental testing supply a yard-stick for the measure of performance the relationship to the child changes: a teacher-pupil pattern and a "companionable" relation-ship in which mother and child appear as "equals" give her some chance to establish closer contact. We shall in various places of the paper advance tentative subsidiary hypotheses on the dynamics of this relationship. At this point it must suffice to stress that Mrs. Adams, largely identified with her parents, re-enacts actively what she recalls of her own experiences. While she consciously disapproves of the way she has been raised, she is driven to repeat what she views as her own experience, thus illustrating one of the ways in which the cycle of generations affects parent-child relationship.

III. Pregnancy, Delivery, and Early Child Care

The course of Mrs. Adams's pregnancy was uneventful in every clinical sense of the word. Physical discomfort was slight during the first few weeks and returned only toward the end, when Mrs. Adams felt tense and sleepless in part due to some mild urinary-tract involvement.

Except for this last period she felt cheerful and determined. Her apprehensions and anxieties seemed not particularly intense; they were well focused, centered on definite problems, and by this very fact revealing of the intensity with which denial operated: the baby was expected to be a boy, and only for a boy a name had been provided.[12]

When she heard that a relative had had a stillborn child, she did not show any undue anxiety, but when she saw a mongolian child and read about the frequency of cerebral palsy, her apprehension

[12] A few weeks before delivery, in a conversation with the pediatrician, who explained that part of her role would be to help Mrs. Adams to enjoy being a mother, Mrs. Adams, who had previously stated that she was not "one of these women who just have to have children around, just for the sake of having children" added: "I don't know why I want a boy, but I just do."

became manifest: the thought of being pitied because of a defect
in the child seemed unbearable. The impending delivery itself
seemed to her a fearful experience; she was definitely afraid of the
pain involved and described in detail her low tolerance for physical
stress, particularly in relation to experiences with dentists. Her most
definite and articulate apprehension concerned the handling of the
infant. In order to illustrate the dynamics of this apprehension we
here present the gist of an interview during the seventh month of
pregnancy, in our third contact with Mrs. Adams.

> Mrs. Adams feels that once the baby is born everything will be
> different and that it is a very final kind of change. She believes
> that they will always be responsible for this youngster, even
> when it gets to be quite a bit older. Granted that she wants the
> responsibility, she realizes that they will never be free again. Mrs.
> Adams believes that part of her fear and apprehension at taking
> care of the baby comes from the fact that she was babied for so
> long and that this has something to do with her feeling now. She
> thinks her husband would be better with the baby than she. She
> said that she has a terrifically quick temper, that she flares up
> suddenly and then it's past, but that she is extremely impatient.

This sequence of thoughts, which starts at the conscious level,
with the fear of the disruptions of the plans for her life, leads from
unfamiliarity with infants and the competition with the baby[13] to
the fear of her attacks against the baby, stimulated by her "im-
patience."

At a time when we were still unfamiliar with Mrs. Adams's conflict, the pediatrician who saw her during her eighth month of
pregnancy was impressed that she was eager to be instructed about
the baby's care so that she would feel better equipped to manage,
but that she did not seem to anticipate pleasure or enjoyment of
the baby. The thought of this burden seems to have grown during
the last weeks of pregnancy. Mrs. Adams found it difficult to relax
"if your mind is going a mile a minute, then you can't really relax,
and how does one go about thinking about nothing?"

The delivery was easy, and its last phase proceeded rapidly. The

13 When Anne was two months old and was admired by the interviewer Mrs.
Adams produced a photograph of herself at age one year which had always been
admired.

obstetrician had not anticipated that she would do so well during labor and the postpartum period. At the same time another physician was impressed by the many questions Mrs. Adams had about her physical condition, indicating an underlying anxiety that over-shadowed her interest in the baby at that time.

She seemed rather detached from the baby during the lying-in period and was not perceptive of the infant's attractiveness or of the discomfort expressed by the crying. She was happy to be supported in her wish to give up breast feeding after a disappointing attempt. She felt that her breasts might smother the infant.

During the first months of Anne's life Mrs. Adams's handling of the child was repeatedly observed: she did not seem tense, had a good control of the situation, and handled the baby's body without dif-ficulty, but she had a way of holding the infant, at quite a distance from her, rarely cuddling Anne. There was annoyance about the fact that after four weeks Anne, who took only twenty or thirty minutes for a feeding during the daytime wanted to spend an hour and a half at night taking the bottle. A month later Mrs. Adams told us she did not pick up Anne very much as the baby did not seem to need it and she did not want to spoil her. The child, the mother thought, seemed to like to be talked to best of all and to be talked to in her crib without being handled. While Mrs. Adams seemed initially mainly concerned with her own performance as mother, soon the baby's developmental progress became important to her. Later, when she became aware of the fact that other—even younger infants—had developed more rapidly, she started to be depressed; she feared that the child was abnormal and she asked for reassurance from the pediatrician, which was offered in a carefully guarded way in order to impress upon the mother the necessity for changes in the handling of the child.

The interest in the child's performance was clearly linked to her fear of being pitied as the mother of a defective child. At the same time it was linked to another trend of thought. Mrs. Adams found the baby not so attractive long before the child showed symptoms of developmental retardation and at a time when others felt that the child had great appeal. Mrs. Adams expressed the hope that Anne would be clever since in her eyes she was not so pretty. She felt that the infant resembled her husband's family and not so much her own.

In this way she expressed some feeling of strangeness toward the baby. Feeding and care were a duty, and at seven months the feeding problem was aggravated by the child's unmistakably growing interest in her environment which deprived Mrs. Adams of the possibility to read while feeding her.

Of the data which might illustrate the environment in which Anne grew up, those which concern the lack of contact between the mother and her child are numerous and impressive. There was a disability of the mother to understand the baby's needs, and a problem in perceiving cues which came from the child. Some examples concern the feeding situation. Mrs. Adams would start to prepare the bottle not when the child woke up but only at the moment when the child began to cry. She often felt upset and helpless when the intensity of the baby's crying mounted; then she was apt to react strongly and in ways that did not alleviate the situation. The mother, especially when depressed, was often unaware of the time that had elapsed between feedings. At other times there was an insistence upon rationed quantities of food which were unrelated to the infant's needs of the moment. When the child was almost one year of age the mother expressed concern about her decrease in appetite. At the same time a feeding was observed in which Mrs. Adams was unable, for inner reasons, to permit the child to have more milk when she obviously wanted it. Our observer added that Anne, who had been happy until the moment of refusal, became very quiet and subdued.

The impression that both the absence of physical contact and the difficulty in understanding the child's needs are only part and parcel of deeper ambivalent feelings which have become centered upon the infant is well substantiated. Especially when the child was fussy or crying the mother's inner aggressive excitement increased. While this fluctuated in intensity, it seemed to have been mounting when Anne was around six months of age. In such states when attempts to calm the child by feeding or picking her up had failed, Mrs. Adams was prone to adopt punitive measures. These measures ranged from leaving the infant to her own resources, to shouting and even to spanking the child. The more excited the child's crying grew the stronger grew the mother's urge to hit. When reporting about her actions Mrs. Adams expressed feelings of guilt, but at the same time she would add, perhaps in an attempt to justify herself, that though she hits hard she also loves hard.[14]

Mrs. Adams's attitude to Anne as neonate and small infant could be enlarged considerably without enriching the picture. There is a consistency about this material, and our records do not contain any observation which would deepen the impression conveyed by those here reported or referred to.

Conjectures on the dynamics of this attitude can start from Mrs. Adams's own statement. The infant is experienced without awareness as a rival in appearance, a competitor for attention, and as an intruder into her life. She is disappointed at having given birth to a girl. Three years later, when her son is born and a dense layer of repression will cover all reminiscences of her experiences with Anne, she will still remember this initial disappointment.[15] And yet this disappointment—presumably related to Mrs. Adams's own masculine wishes—which may have set the tone for the subsequent experiences between Mrs. Adams and her infant daughter cannot explain the extent and nature of the difficulties in perception to which we have referred. Three years later in the care of her boy some of the attitudes here noted will reappear. The setting then is different: Mrs. Adams has found a new balance in life, motherhood, and marriage, and yet she will express a certain lack of understanding for her second newborn.[16] There is no doubt that a small infant's helplessness and total demandingness stimulate in her responses of which distraction and casualness are the most moderate expressions. The assumption that her own repressed wishes of a passive and infantile nature and her envy of the infant play a decisive role seems well supported. We are reminded of the facts that the complaints against

[14] The intensity and nature of the conflict which beset Mrs. Adams during the early months of Anne's life was illustrated by a number of episodes in which she called the pediatrician to determine whether some aspect of her care of the infant had done irreparable harm.

[15] At this point a distortion of memory occurs apparently to ward off guilt feelings; she believes she remembers that when the obstetrician, to whom she remained attached, first spoke to her, he said in his excitement, "It is a boy."

[16] See below p. [?] for speculations about the reasons for the infinitely greater intensity of Mrs. Adams's ambivalent feelings toward her small daughter, compared to those toward her son as an infant; one might assume that in her disappointment she also feels identified with her father's disappointment at having "only" a daughter.

her mother describe a feeling of deep dissatisfaction possibly surviving from, but very surely projected into, her own infancy.[17]

We have up to this point referred to two unconscious themes
which seem powerfully to determine Mrs. Adams's behavior to her
infant daughter. The one, presumably more deeply buried, concerns
the reproachfully harbored longing for a true mother, the wish to be
and not to have the infant. It reverberates throughout the history of
our observation in Mrs. Adams's struggle for an adequate diet for
herself and may have supplied important components to the feeding
struggle between mother and daughter. Interconnected with it is the
wish for a male child with whom to identify—the wish for the penis.
Derivatives of this wish color Mrs. Adams's ambition for Anne who
remains as it were "part of herself." The interest in her progress
and intellectual achievement, the emphasis on appearance and manners impress us more when we meet Anne at age two and three. And
yet to point to these plausibly interconnected wishes in the make-up
of Mrs. Adams seems far from satisfactory. In naming deeply rooted
impulses active in every woman we have not reached anything which
seems specific. However, we cannot be satisfied to utilize in a general way our knowledge of psychological dynamics but are forced to
attempt a more detailed reconstruction of unconscious impulses and
fantasies.

Rivalry with the infant can only be one of the themes in Mrs.
Adams's conflict. There are deeper conflicts at work which we can
only tentatively reconstruct. Such reconstructions naturally lack the
richness and the precision of its models in analytic work where they
are gradually developed in constant interaction with the patient's
response. Yet we find no way of avoiding these reconstructions since
these or similar assumptions give us a chance to connect various
apparently unconnected data of behavior. Moreover, without such
assumptions we would be left with a cliché: the rejecting or hostile
mother who damages her child because she cannot control her own
selfishness or hostility.[18]

[17] For the role of the rivalrous attitude in mothers after delivery and during early
infancy of their children, see Escalona, 1950? (Macy Foundation) [Escalona, 1949] and
Benedek, 1950? [Benedek, 1949].
[18] For the variety of these clichés see reports of the first International Congress of
Child Psychiatry by E. Kris.

Mrs. Adams's conflict is infinitely more complex: it is fraught with many vicissitudes. To put in outline form what will later be reported in detail: when the harmful effects of her attitude became apparent and the baby developed crying spells, a mounting rage became soon uncontrollable and she hit the infant. We infer that she has perhaps become aware of some guilt feeling and, in turning against the "naughty" child, she tried to shift the responsibility away from herself, but the balance is precarious and Anne's condition deteriorates further and serious developmental arrest appears. At the time of the severe crying spells and the retardation of the child Mrs. Adams shows unmistakable signs of an increase in her depressive reaction. Later when she can become a teacher to the child the relationship to Anne changes: the teacher-pupil pattern and a companionable relationship in which the mother and child appear as equal give her some chance to establish closer contact.

It seems obvious that in the second of these phases when she becomes Anne's teacher she re-enacts her own recollections about her father's relationship to her. It is our impression that next to this repetition of what persists in her memory as a possibly idealized, screened image of her own childhood, another unconscious version of this relationship exists in a fantasy. This fantasy would contain a struggle between a little girl and her father, a "battle of wills" in which the girl is beaten by the father. These assumptions are derived from many items of observation spread over the years of our contact with Mrs. Adams.

We suggest that her lack of understanding of the infant is due to the fact that in her mind the infant daughter is overshadowed by the image of an older child; the nursing situation is devalued in favor of a fantasy relation (the beating fantasy). The feeding relation, for instance, is not only characterized by deficits: there is also a clearly provocative element in it, an attempt to heighten the child's tension and to build up a scene which may lead to spanking.

A similarly set scene is observed one year later when mother and child glare at each other furiously with "tigerlike" looks. But now the situation is eased by the fact that Anne can respond, that she is no longer the "helpless" infant; and we will have occasion to report in detail how the interaction of mother and child in these later scenes has its impact on both. Even Anne, the four-year-old, and her mother are interlocked in a peculiarly poignant battle of wills—complicated by the fact that the fantasy of the mother has molded the child, and that the child repeats in her relation to the mother some of the experiences which the mother inflicted upon her much earlier. The choice of Anne's mechanisms of defense seems determined by these experiences. It is a process that illustrates how in the cycle of generations unconscious determinants of the parent-child relationship are transmitted.

The content analysis of the mother's attitudes through the first three years of life compiled by the social worker shows that it is possible to distinguish between types of the child's behavior which aroused sharply negative reactions in the mother and stimulate anxiety and/or aggression from those types of behavior which she tolerates or appreciates.

During the first year the crying and other insistent demands for attention stimulate outbursts in the mother; messiness is borne with suppressed anger; poor food intake or evidence of the child's retardation in the motor area are connected with the thought of later intellectual deficit and seem mainly anxiety provoking. Positively valued are the opposite attitudes: the child's lack of demand, quietness, and progress as manifested mainly during the first two months. There is not enough, or not conclusive enough, evidence concerning autoerotic behavior. It seems that rocking and thumb sucking were tolerated, but that mouthing of other objects tended to be prohibited.

During the second year messiness, particularly in eating, and resistance to bowel training seemed intolerable; the child's opposition to and aggression against the mother, the latter frequently manifested in wild, tigerlike looks, are equally intolerable. The child's demand for the mother through crying is less disturbing since the bottle is offered as a substitute. The mother appreciates compliance in all areas, particularly in bowel training (accomplished toward the end of the second year) and the progress the child makes under her instruction.

During the third year the mother tends to be intensely angered by messiness with food or water, by the child's clinging to the bottle, which the mother had earlier promoted, and by demands for the mother's attention as they particularly recur during weaning.

She is made anxious through the insufficient food intake and through what she experienced as Anne's physical defects, each of them matched by defects which she recalls from her own childhood (see page [???]). She reacts to the child's attachment to a transitional object and to the father with jealousy and denial. Anne's masturbatory activity makes the mother anxious and she denies it at the same time. She appreciates the child's independence when it gives her time for herself, but later shows growing annoyance when in the four-year-old the independence becomes assertive and aggressive. She values highly the well-mannered little girl's social compliance and cooperativeness. Most striking, however, is one difference: she can now use physical contact to comfort Anne, and hence the child's crying tends to arouse her anger only when the crying becomes uncontrollable.

[Part 2]

I. Anne's History

A. THE PERIOD OF DECLINE

1. *The First Nine Months*

As a newborn, Anne was characterized as a very attractive, small, and beautifully proportioned infant. She was alert looking when awake and fully normal with a suggestion of slight immaturity. She was easy to hold, in no way stiff or hypertonic, and settled down easily in one's arms. She moved vigorously. The holding had a marked comforting effect and so had the changing of positions. When held she looked around without crying for several minutes.

This description presents a composite picture of the pediatrician's experience with Anne during her first days of life when the child was seen daily in the hospital. During the first two months of Anne's life, our contact with the family was less close than at any later time. The Adams's left town immediately after the return from the hospital, and Mrs. Adams and the baby stayed for several weeks with her half brother, a period during which contact with the pediatrician was continued by mail. After their return, the baby was seen at home for a checkup. She seemed to develop well, and the pediatrician's attention was at that time focused on understanding the mother's attitude and on establishing effective contact with her in dealing with the immediate problems of child care. On this occasion Mrs. Adams complained about the length of the feeding period at night compared with the period during the daytime. When the pediatrician expressed the expectation that night feeding could be discontinued sometime in the near future, the mother seemed relieved.[19] Later, during the second month of Anne's life, the parents took a week's vacation, leaving the baby with the half brother's family. Shortly thereafter, when Anne was nine weeks old, she was seen in her first well-baby clinic. The physical and developmental examinations did not reveal any striking features. The baby seemed to get along well; the tests were interpreted as indicating that the slight immaturity in motor development was still noticeable. Moreover, the baby's "language," i.e., the vocalizations which constitute the most characteristic part of the infant's social responsiveness, was considerably in advance of her chronological age. The profile was viewed as typical of a well-endowed, but slightly immature infant.[20]

And yet, already at this well-baby clinic the pediatrician felt uneasy about the mother's approach and about the adequacy of the stimulation offered. When Mrs. Adams reported that she did not pick up the baby frequently, that she was afraid of spoiling Anne, and when she revealed her reluctance for close physical contact offering various rationalizations, the pediatrician pointed out that Anne might be asking more in the way of attention from the adult now that she was two months of age and beginning to be quite responsive socially.

The mother reacted immediately: she expected that this was true and that giving Anne more attention would make her develop faster. We do not intend in the further course of this presentation to reproduce the exchange between mother and pediatrician or social worker in any detail. It seems worth reporting that at that

[19] Shortly thereafter Anne developed into an excellent sleeper.

[20] These impressions founded on the Gesell tests were corroborated by those of the Hetzer-Wolf test, evaluated by K. Wolf two years later in the following way: The evaluation speaks of a "very advanced child," with "an excellent balance of receptivity and reactivity," and "unusual facility to discriminate," of an infant with the potentiality "to develop into a gifted child."

time the pediatrician was in no position fully to appreciate the bearing of Mrs. Adams's remarks. The pediatrician saw that Mrs. Adams would consider it now "legitimate" to play with Anne more or to handle her more because this would make her develop faster. The pediatrician noted that the idea that this might also be fun for the mother did not come up. It was later easy to reinterpret this in a different light, but at the time we were not yet familiar with Mrs. Adams and though some of the prognostications which were made had already pointed in the right direction, we were not ready to follow consistently the lead of our own interpretations. The child was well and in speaking of her future demands, the pediatrician had only drawn the mother's attention to the problems she might normally expect to encounter. A number of factors contributed to strengthen denial among the observers and among the research group. There was the mother's "interest" in speaking about her child, and it was for some time not evident that this interest was centered exclusively on her own and on the child's performance. There was the efficiency of her management which concealed its more damaging features. Thus, in all observations of the feeding situation it was stressed how firmly the baby was held, and only gradually was it noted how little physical and emotional contact there was between mother and child. In one of the descriptions of the feeding situation at home when Anne was two months old, it was mentioned that Mrs. Adams held the baby at quite a distance from her, not cuddling her. The pediatrician who observed this feeding felt that it looked uncomfortable for mother and child but the mother did not appear tense. It was particularly emphasized that the lower limbs, for instance, were left dangling or stiffly stretched without ever touching the mother's body. The same strange postural configurations were seen again when three years later Mrs. Adams was observed feeding her boy.[21] When it was brought to Mrs. Adams's attention how well she seemed able to perform all her duties in spite of the apprehen-

---

21 Three years later, observers in the well-baby clinic noted that the mother overlooked the growing restlessness of the infant boy and when the pediatrician brought it to her attention, the mother offered the baby a pacifier, pensively adding that she would not have done this with Anne. When the pediatrician suggested that she feed the baby, she put him across her knee and once more there was minimal contact between her own and the child's body. As the child fed the mother continued to talk to the pediatrician.

sions she had felt during pregnancy, her reply indicated that she never doubted herself but wondered about Anne's ability to manage.

A further factor which may have delayed the realization of the specific qualities of the environment in which Anne developed was that after the first well-baby clinic a new pediatrician, who had just joined the group, was assigned to the case. In retrospect, the earliest signs of the later, more extensive disturbance in Anne's development was perceivable in her second well-baby clinic when Anne was fifteen weeks old.

At fifteen weeks, her neuromuscular maturation was fully age-adequate, and the immaturity of the motor system in the neuro-physiological sense was no longer present. The continued acuteness of visual perception and discrimination was reflected in her visual recognition of the bottle and her early awareness of strangers (eight weeks in advance of the usual age). Inanimate objects were of little interest to her. They had not become invested for her to the extent that one usually sees in babies of this age, and it was almost impossible to induce her to accept them. She was more visually preoccupied with the adult than most infants of her age who have had adequate social stimulation. Language as revealed in cooing, babbling, and socially linked vocalizing at which she had been advanced on the nine-week examination was now slightly below normal for her age.

Anne's performance reflects certain deficiencies of stimulation in the environment. Low investment in the toys and the depressed language and intense visual preoccupation with the adult are common findings in the institutional infants at this age. One way in which Anne differs from the institutional infant of this age is in her discrimination of strangers.

Two months later, at twenty-six weeks of age, the signs of insufficient social and physical stimulation were clearly evident. Her neuromuscular maturation as reflected in the character of the grasping patterns was slightly above age, but this equipment was put to minimal use. Gross motor development was below age with no evidence of organic disorder—either physical or neurological. Interest in toys was still low, although the toys were of slightly more interest than on the fifteen-week examination. She showed no displeasure when they were removed. There was less preoccupation

with the examiner although Anne did initiate social contact by
smiling and more interest in play with her own body (mouthing
of hands and feet, looking at hands). Language was delayed both in
output and in level of development. She preferred the handling of
a single toy rather than one in each hand although she was quite
capable of holding two. It was suggested that she found two stimuli
too intense, but there was no way to confirm this. Language and
gross motor development were her lowest areas.

When Anne was thirty-four weeks old, her general developmental
quotient had dropped below 100 for the first time. Gross motor
skills and language were now six weeks behind. There was brief
interest in the toys which she picked up and dropped often as though
they were hot. There was wide scatter in her adaptive performance,
with some successes as high as forty weeks. An interesting observation will illustrate some of the discrepancies between her basic equipment for functioning and the way she looked in relation to her
contact with people. She was able to "match" two cubes holding one
in each hand and approximating them in the midline. This activity
with the toy reflects the maturation of a particular pattern of adaptation which is also demonstrated in the average infant by the ability
at the same age to play pat-a-cake. The pat-a-cake game, however,
is much more dependent upon social stimulation. Anne matches
cubes and does not play pat-a-cake. An interesting observation was
the negative reaction to the mother's approach as contrasted with the
positive reaction to the examiner's approach. At fifteen weeks there
had been fearfulness of the examiner's approach which was alleviated
by the mother; at twenty-six weeks there was no differential reaction
between the two; at thirty-four weeks there was negative response
to the mother and positive response to the examiner. Five weeks
later, at thirty-nine weeks, some anxiety to the stranger was present
which was minimized by being on the mother's lap. Fine motor
development was the only age-adequate sector. Adaptive functions
which had previously shown wide scatter but had averaged at age
now showed even wider scatter. There were a few adaptive successes
at forty weeks described as being of poor quality. Some attempts to
crawl on her belly were noted, but she could not yet creep. Language
was her lowest performance, seven weeks below her age.

She would retrieve a toy she had dropped within reach but would not change position to get it if the toy was out of reach, nor could she solve the problem of uncovering it if it were hidden within reach. Thus both interest in the toy and ability to remember the disappeared object were below age.

By this time Anne's condition gave rise to intense concern from the study staff. Her crying spells, her extreme fearfulness, her poor nutritional condition, and some similarities of her developmental profile to that of children in institutions suggested the need for immediate measures. Before we proceed with our account, we have to supplement the developmental picture of the first nine months by further observations which we prefer to present in the context of some more general considerations.

2. *Discussion and Further Observation*

a. Deficit and provocation in Mother-Child Contact

The state of retardation and distress in which we find Anne at nine and a half months invites some further comment. We mentioned that her developmental status as measured by test performance reminds us of that of children brought up in institutions; and yet the conditions under which Anne grew up show in a superficial sense no similarity with those in orphanages or children's homes.[22] The deprivation suffered by infants in institutions has often been related to two factors: it has been thought to be due to the multiplicity of individuals who shared in the care of these infants in the absence of *one* mother with all that this entails, and to the shortness of the time spent in the care of these children. Neither of these factors applies to the case of Anne; her mother was the only person who took care of her (at least apart from the parents' vacation trip) and did not call upon a baby sitter until Anne was . . . [in her second year]. We have no measure of the time devoted to the child's care,

[22] Quote literature on children's homes from Rheingold and the bibliography she gives [1956].

In the following we utilized data, observations, and inferences from a longitudinal study of individual cases of children living in an institution since early infancy by R. W. Coleman Lipton and S. A. Provence, which is being prepared for publication [see Provence and Lipton, 1962]. (On some preliminary comparisons of these children with Anne, see Coleman and Provence, *Pediatrics* . . . [1957]. The interpretation of these findings was the subject of many consultations and discussions between Lipton, Provence, and the senior author who has elsewhere offered some preliminary comments on this material. See Kris, 1954 [1955].

but it seems unlikely that Anne and her mother were less in each other's company "together in one room" than other infants and their mothers. Nor was Mrs. Adams's handling of the child in any gross sense negligent. There was, as we indicated, a dry competence about the care Anne received, and before the decline started to become manifest, during the earliest months of her life, the mother occasionally noticed, for instance, some of Anne's enjoyments during her daily bath. Moreover, there was always the father's interest in Anne; though he is rarely mentioned in our observations, he is described as adoring toward the one-month-old baby by an observer, and we hear from the mother that he likes to "rough house" with the infant. But such contact must have been rare. When he came home from work, the infant was mostly asleep and since he had the feeling of working against time, he seems to have felt that this was unavoidable. Later, when the child was disturbed and retarded in many functions, he was the one who refused to show concern, not out of lack of attachment to Anne, but, according to his statements, the baby seemed to him to be at all times fully satisfactory.

The environmental deficit, then, to which we may attribute the similarity of Anne's developmental profile to that of children in institutions cannot be explained by the similarity of general conditions. Anne was reared as a family child in the ordinary sense of the word. The deficit to which we attribute her retardation can be traced to a specific set of elements in the care she received: both physical and play contacts between mother and child were kept at a limit. There was little or no free interaction or emotional interplay between the two. In this specific sense we may speak of a marked lack of stimulation.

But it is only Anne's developmental profile that reminds us of children in institutions. Her behavior differs from them in several essential respects. Her bad nutritional status, the frantic crying spells, and the marked, at times hardly controllable, fear of the stranger are not part of the syndrome of children in the institutions mentioned before (Provence and Lipton). Though at times a normal tendency toward crying or tearfulness will appear, we see features in Anne's behavior which reach an intensity that forces us to consider them as symptoms. These symptoms are, we suggest, not due to lack of stimulation, but rather to a specific kind of provocative overstimulation which was bound to produce mounting tension in the child without offering appropriate avenues of discharge. The distinction between lack of interactional stimulation and an abundance of provocative, irritating stimulation in the child's care may at first seem artificial. In the unconscious motivation of the mother those tendencies must have been closely interrelated. The "reason" why she avoids handling and cuddling of her baby can hardly be isolated from the other reasons that lead her to postpone feeding until the baby was crying, and to approach the crib but not to comfort the infant by lifting her out. In both these instances the double attitude leads to or is expressed in the same action. What starts as avoidance of physical contact leads to the infant's desperate crying and the crying in turn to mounting excitement in the mother.[23] At least in the feeding situation, the mounting tension can be clearly followed in the sequence of our data. In Anne as a newborn the pressure of physiological need seems to be moderate.[24] She could easily wait for feeding and was promptly comforted by holding. As if in response to remarks of the pediatrician who has earlier stressed Anne's capacities in this direction, we hear the mother saying of the three-month-old that her capacity to wait does not "impress" her. Somewhat later, when under the impact of frustration and irritation Anne tends to cry for long periods and the mother tries to wait until the crying stops, Mrs. Adams compares the crying to that of a cat, but, she adds, with a cat one knows what to do. . . . And finally, at the time before she can admit to the fact that she is spanking the

[23] The assumption that the handling of the baby has an intensely stimulating effect on the mother, as the pediatrician had sensed, suggests a tentative expansion of our reconstruction of an unconscious fantasy of Mrs. Adams; the child, one might postulate, represents also a female phallus and it is the phallus which is being beaten. It is claimed (Bonaparte, 1954 [1953]), that this fantasy in which the phallus replaces the clitoris not only occurs frequently in female patients but represents a regular phase of normal female development. Be this as it may, even without the assumption that the unconscious drive derivative should be crystallized in and derived from this fantasy, the dovetailing and interlocking of each, of the lack of physical contact and the provocation of the infant's irritation, are, psychologically speaking, plausible. Some members of the research staff suggest that some influence from the superego might prompt the mother to keep a distance: namely, a protective attitude of the mother to shield the child from damage from the aggressive impulses.

[24] At the present stage of our knowledge, such comparative estimates of individual characteristics existing at birth seems unavoidable as long as exact measurements are not available. It is our experience that such estimates can be validated by judges with comparable professional experience.

infant, she describes Anne's crying and indicates that it makes her feel wild inside.[25] Though no curve of the mounting crying spells can be charted, their increase after two months and their gradually rising intensity after three months are apparent. This trend which is duplicated in several other areas of Anne's period of decline is in full agreement with the findings of other investigators who date an important change in the mental functioning of the infant between two and three months.[26] Up to this point growth was, as it were, relatively independent of the personal nature of infant care. From this moment on, the human contact becomes essential. A further discussion of these findings seems aided by the use of two terminological distinctions. We distinguish development from maturation (Hartmann and Kris, 1946 [1945]) and distinguish between the ego and the apparatus it uses (Hartmann, 1939). Maturation here designates growth processes relatively independent from environmental influence, from "learning" in the broadest sense; development designates those growth processes which are characterized by this dependence. Psychic structure in the individual arises in a process of differentiation. During the neonatal period, when differentiation plays little part, the distinction between the ego as a however rudimentary central organization and the physiological apparatus it uses will be of little help in organizing data of infant observation. Later that distinction will seem to be essential. The two terminological distinctions we here adopt are obviously interlocking. Maturation would be largely concerned with the growth in apparatus function, the ego with the growth of processes in which experiences of the

25 It should be kept in mind that we do not know exactly how frequently the child was spanked. Our data stem from the mother, and her confessions are always proffered with deep guilt, though they rarely go into great detail.

26 Quote Gesell, Spitz, particularly Spitz's paper in French [1954], and Hoffer. What those observers of growth processes describe as a growing capacity of the child to perceive and react to humans around him fits into the setting of psychoanalytic theory as a highly invested function that serves important meanings. The fact that the developmental status of children in institutions tends to show the beginning of dysfunction and retardation sometime shortly after three months is impressive evidence of the nature of these meanings. It should, however, be stressed that usually developmental decline becomes fully noticeable only after five months. A certain lack of precision of these date lines is due to the large number of factors; for instance, to the variation in the length of the preceding institutional life of the child and to the completeness of the tests and observational data, and also apparently to differences in individual "vulnerability."

nature of learning and contact with the environment play an essential part.

The observation on Anne, as far as it is parallel to that of children in institutions, suggests that up to two or three months maturation proceeded, as it were, on its own accord. After that period in some instances the effects of maturation on Anne's growth can be clearly discerned and differentiated from the normal development of which they are an essential part. In our description of Anne's development we spoke of the fact that a function had matured but was not being used. The grasping pattern was available to her, but the two cues are not being coordinated. She can clap her hands, but she does not succeed in a pat-a-cake. This latest instance is clearly of a special order since it concerns communication between child and mother, the developmental area where retardation is most related to the restricted interaction of mother and child. The developmental examinations permit us to follow the retardation in Anne particularly clearly. From active babbling at two months, the decline leads to clear retardation after four months of age. As in many instances of institutionalized children, the relation between maturation and development can in this area be indicated clearly: the child is able to pronounce consonants, but they do not merge with vowels to form first syllables and later designations with multiple meanings (Provence and Lipton [1962]).

However, these are the simple instances. Other more complex ones remind us of the fact of how much detailed investigation will be required in order to clarify even fundamental issues. At the present stage of our knowledge, the simple formula of growth of the neuromuscular apparatus vs. its use, of maturation vs. development does not satisfactorily describe the bulk of observations pertaining to the first half year of life. Moreover, in later months this distinction becomes more and more difficult to handle since soon the environmental deficit may lead to some impairment of the maturation pattern itself.

One of the test findings in which Anne's case fully resembles that of children in institutions concerns the discrepancy between the normal functioning of hands and arms compared to the poorer functioning of lower limbs: when held in a standing position at . . . [six to eight] months, Anne would not extend her legs to support her weight while her hands and arms functioned well. As we shall see in the further progress of our report, the development of her fine motor functions (i.e., the fingers and their interaction) will remain more advanced than other (gross) motor functions. Since no physiological data seem to account for this difference, psycho-analytic considerations gain a more than subsidiary function. They concern the specific position of the infant's hands through their capacity to release oral tension or to regulate its discharge. Hoffer (1949) who has advanced this view and surveyed his own observations in the light of the general knowledge on early phases of growth (Gesell and Ilg, 1937, 1943) suggests that throughout the first year of life the child is building up through the help of the hands-mouth contact "an oral-tactile concept of his own body and the world around him and regulates to a certain extent by this means his erotic and aggressive (active) drives." Early stages of this sequence can be observed during the third and fourth months: "from inter-uterine life onward" the hand is "closely allied to the mouth for the sake of relieving tension and within this alliance leads to the first achievement of the primitive ego . . . [the hand] becomes the most useful and versatile servant of the ego . . . [through its] function of relieving tension." In the terminology we have adopted, we would stress the advance of the apparatus which in Hoffer's presentation seems to be enhanced by the finger play of the child. This finger play, typical for the age of sixteen weeks, was reported of Anne by her mother, but was less than that of other infants. When the child's fingers finger his fingers, a simultaneous experience of touching and being touched is carried out in the one act, sometimes in an experimental sense or with an experimental zest, as one might imagine, a study of the limits of the self.

The intimate connection of hands, and secondarily of arms, with the mouth and with the self-gratification during the sucking activities might then in part account for the fact that the growth of the function is relatively more independent of stimulation by the mother than that of other parts of the body. These other parts, we might say, purposefully introducing a metaphor, are "energized" only by the mother's handling of the infant.

Since the exposition of M. Ribble (1943), it is generally accepted as an empirical fact that the mother of the infant fulfills important functions through the stimulations normally connected with infant care. For example, there is constant interaction between mother and child during the feeding situation; the ministrations of the mother supply a wide range of sensory experiences, tactile, visual, and kinesthetic, without which satisfactory development would be difficult to achieve. Little is known about the effect of specific deficits in child care though attempts to delineate their effects in one area or another are not missing. None of the numerous studies, neither those dealing with the difference between breast-fed and bottle-fed infants nor with the advantages of cradling, to mention only extremes, seem at this stage of our knowledge to offer convincing insight.[27] The prevailing impression indicates that any specific deficit in child care is frequently or mostly no more than the expression of the general attitude of the mother which may have affected other areas of experience in the child besides the one on which the specific investigation has focused. Nor have anthropological studies on the effect of specific child-care methods in certain cultures thrown light on problems here under discussion.

From clinical experience with more severely disturbed, somewhat older children who sometimes become accessible to therapy only if the therapeutic contact is introduced by substitute mothering, one gains once more the impression that the total experience of closeness in a physical and emotional sense between mother and child can only in exceptional cases be viewed in terms of specific partial gratifications and deprivations. This then suggests the assumption as adequate to our present transient stage of knowledge that a state of general comfort, a certain level of comfort, is of essential importance. According to the infant's equipment and his specific needs, this level can be achieved by varying intensities of actual maternal attention, understanding, and ministrations.

In applying the conceptual model of psychoanalytic thinking to the balance between comfort and discomfort in the infant's experience, *we formulate the following hypothesis: comfort serves to build object relationships, discomfort stimulates the differentiation, i.e., structure formation in the psychic apparatus.* No comfort situation can be permanent. Few are likely to be fully satisfactory. The mem-

---

[27] Quote Goldmann-Eisler and the paper in French on cradling. More promising material in the clinical studies seem to stem from longitudinal observations.

ory of food satisfaction derived from the model of satiation substitutes for the missing elements in actual satisfaction in any concrete situation. We assume that when the actual satisfaction originally was regularly "too low" the imprint of the memory image related to satiation would not be of the kind to serve as an adequate supplement to the actual experience.

This formula, compressed as it is, concerns a wide range of processes. The investment of the maternal object promotes a sharp distinction between the self and the outer world; its correlate is the capacity of the at first hallucinatory recall of the missed object or part object from which satisfaction was derived. These first steps in formation of structure are, we assume, coincidental with change in the child's processes. To remain in the area of our example: the memory trace of the object is now permanently invested, psychic energy now exists, and from now on continues to exist in two kinds, mobile and bound. The gradual enrichment of memory traces of the object and of the self proceeds through an interchange between object and self which one may assume follows a functional pattern which only gradually unfolds. At this point, however, our assumptions have to be left in considerable vagueness since any precision would distort the complexity of simultaneous and interacting processes. Moreover, the specific danger of adultomorphic connotation is great. When we speak of the fact that the child acquires the ability to use his own motor apparatus from the mother, we have no learning by imitation in mind though such learning may in selected areas play a subsidiary part from the early months of life.[28] It is subsidiary to processes in which perception and memory of the need-gratifying object are merged with the first notions of the self. We may assume that at an early age any contact with the mother is experienced by the child as the reinforcement of merging, particularly of the feeding situation itself, and only gradually the differentiation between self and nonself comes about in a close interaction of maturational and developmental processes. One might, furthermore, assume that

---

28 One notion as to the ways in which the child acquires abilities, of the ways in which the child learns, may be usefully compared with those of Hebb [1949] and his theory of behavior with the sharp distinction between early (fundamental) and later phases of learning. It must suffice here to point in a general way to the possibility that we may gain advantages in utilizing Hebb's model.

as far as motor development is concerned, the maturational spurts act as sharp incentives to progress, possibly as a sharper incentive than in other areas of development.

The division of the child's person from that of the mother proceeds with various speeds in various areas of function. Our observations seem to indicate that all the areas are affected, and that tension between comfort and discomfort has originally, in the newborn, been extraordinarily great and cannot be reached by the hallucinatory imagination of the child. Normally, already at three months, this hallucinatory imagination is in certain situations clearly structured by the experience. Perception and memory interact to produce an anticipation of the future when the child learns to wait for its feeding and registers in the mother's preparation the cues for the forthcoming satisfaction. Benedek [1949], who was the first to stress the prospective importance of this stage of development speaks here of the stage of confidence.[29] We believe that concomitant with the more structured experience in the interaction between mother and child, the capacity to accept and invest substitutes for the maternal figure develops. The interest of the child in experiences with toys is derived from here.

In Anne's development the low investment of the comfort situation, the inadequate structure of the experience with the mother, seems to be paralleled by her inability to take interest in toys or to play with other inanimate objects which might substitute for the human object,[30] a retardation which will last for a long time. It will persist in the inability to perform independent problem solving. The test situation in which this problem solving is first studied is one in which a toy is hidden by a cloth or screen (in the last quarter of the first year). The child is to retrieve the toy. The observations of Anne and of institutional children give the impression that at first the hidden toy is not important enough to be recovered. Soon, however, it appears that initiative to evaluate the situation, the activity necessary to retrieve the toy, is blocked: a deficit in thinking seems to be operating.

[29] See also Erikson [1950] on Trust.
[30] The idea of the investment of the inanimate object is derived from the mother-child relationship as it was first expressed by K. Wolf (1948).

Anxiety and Despair

The decline of Anne's nutritional status can be traced to the period between six and seven months. She had always been a small baby. Her birth weight (5½ lbs.) put her in the 25 percentile of normal infant girls. At three months she had dropped to the 10 percentile, but in view of her appearance and other physical findings this seemed not alarming. She still maintained an adequate nutritional status at six months. Then the weight curve dropped below the 3 percentile.[31] At this point she looked very thin. It was not the thinness of a bony baby but rather a thinness of a limp unmuscular kind. The unhappiness of her facial expression was described by all those who saw her at this time; though the observers vary in the words they choose, all were impressed by both lack of vitality and sadness in her appearance. The impressions gained at well-baby clinics were undoubtedly more marked than those found in the home environment. The child seemed to react to her mother's tension, which had been steadily growing since Anne's mother had become aware of the fact that younger babies were further advanced in their development than Anne. But this mortification fitted in with a desolate mood, evidenced by the mother's increase in weight and a growing discontent. When later this mood was discussed with her, she spoke of her loneliness during the day, her lack of occupation, as contributory factors, but was herself aware of the fact that she could not fully understand the nature of her mood. The care of the infant imposed upon Mrs. Adams a very great strain. One gains the impression that the previously mentioned scenes between mother and baby have played a decisive, and possibly a trigger role in her depressive reaction. The lack of precision of our information at this point is part of the limitations which the setup of the study imposed.

The interaction between the mood of the child and that of the mother could thus be traced only in a general way. The clearest specific instance was the crying of the infant, and this crying soon grew into spells of tantrumlike violence, first reported when the

---

[31] The lowest point was reached at nine months, she passed above the 3 percentile at one year, dropped again between twelve and fifteen months, reached the 3 percentile once more at fifteen months. From then on it continued to rise. Her weight in her second year of life continued on the 10 percentile of the curve. During her third year her weight was somewhat lower.

child was nine months of age. On this occasion the mother described in a diary she had been asked to keep that the child cried to exhaustion, was inconsolable until she fell asleep, and though she had cried in a similar fashion before, she had never cried to such a degree. The few reported occasions on which such spells occurred seemed related to two factors: the strangeness of the environment and physical exhaustion. One of these conditions was observed by the staff during a well-baby clinic, when Anne was one year of age, when the mother and child had come from a vacation resort after a bus ride of an hour and a half, the first in the child's life.[32] The effect of the child's crying on all observers was lasting, as if they had witnessed a tragic experience. They found themselves watching a child that could not be reached or comforted, but was left to her own uncontrollable despair. On this occasion all observers professed that they had never seen a condition of the same character. It might well be that the regularity of the impressions was due to one crucial circumstance: while the crying was of the greatest intensity, all observers agreed that Anne looked considerably younger than her age.

Neither the nutritional deficiency nor the role of crying and despair in Anne's life between three and twelve months are in line with the behavior of children in institutions. We relate them to the special conditions of her upbringing, to the at first overstimulating and provocative understimulating attitude of the mother, to the situation which possibly with some extravagance might be described as tantalizing: there was the human object, there was some contact, but not the comfort which was expected of it.

In order to attempt an understanding of this conflict we turn to the most significant symptom in which Anne's behavior differs from that of children in institutions, to her excessive fear of the stranger:

The fear of stranger as normal phenomenon.
> Rheingold.

The antecedents in Anne.
The smile at the neighbor.
The reversal of the fear.

---

[32] The mother had refused help that had been offered in bringing the child to the well-baby clinic. She did not want to "impose" on the study staff.

The relation to the father:

The good object can't reach her (highly speculative).

The sole position of the mother. *She, only she, can comfort. Assumption of two images sharply divided from each other.*

Frustration brings the negative image up.

The normal character of this.

Psychoanalytic speculation on the relation between self-love and object love.

Grief and depression, love (?) duress as leading to the extreme condition.

Appendix I

LIST OF PARTICIPANTS

This list should be so organized that each participant and his function is indicated with the length of time which he has worked with the study. I suggest that we start with those who have been with the study longest and arrange the group in a sequence.

After those immediately involved with the study of Anne the list should include those who were present at the research meetings, and contributed to some extent, for instance, to the nursery conferences.

I have drafted here some notes regarding the record which seem not very good to me. The record of the case comprises more than 1000 type-written pages. It contains extensive reports on 23 home visits and 6 office contacts with social workers, on 20 well-baby clinics, 13 pediatric home visits, 11 pediatric office visits, 23 pediatric phone consultations, and several letters exchanged between the mother and the pediatrician during vacation time. The developmental tests were administered by the pediatrician, and the test during a follow-up study at the age of four, by a psychologist who was previously not familiar with Anne. During well-baby clinics the medical examination and the tests were observed by one of two observers whose observations are recorded on 18 occasions; 6 of the tests were observed and especially evaluated by Dr. K. M. Wolf. During the nursery school year Anne's behavior was separately described by the nursery school staff and by 10 special observations by other staff members. During the year listed the case was discussed in 29 conferences of the full staff after nursery school sessions. The total number of individuals participating in the recording of the material, not including various assistant teachers in the nursery school, reaches well over 20. Among them are such occasional observers not listed above as: the obstetrical nursing staff in the hospital and the driver who repeatedly brought mother and child from her home to the well-baby clinic.

BIBLIOGRAPHY*

Benedek, T. (1949), The Psychosomatic Implications of the Primary Unit: Mother-Child. *Amer. J. Orthopsychiat.*, XIX. Reprinted as Chapter 12 in *Psychosexual Functions in Women*. New York: Ronald Press, 1952.

Bonaparte, M. (1953), *Female Sexuality*. New York: International Universities Press.

Coleman [Lipton], R. W. & Provence, S. (1957), Environmental Retardation (Hospitalism) in Infants Living in Families. *Pediatrics*, XIX.

Erikson, E. H. (1950). *Childhood and Society*. New York: Norton.

Escalona, S. K. (1949), The Psychological Situation of Mother and Child upon Return from the Hospital. In: *Problems of Infancy and Childhood* [Transactions of the Third Conference], ed. M. J. E. Senn. New York: Josiah Macy, Jr. Foundation.

Gesell, A. & Armatruda, C. S. (1947), *Developmental Diagnosis*. New York: Hoeber.

—— & Ilg, F. L. (1937), *Feeding Behavior of Infants*. Philadelphia: Lippincott.

—— & —— (1943), *Infant and Child in the Culture of Today*. New York: Harper.

Hartmann, H. (1939), *Ego Psychology and the Problem of Adaptation*. New York: International Universities Press, 1958.

—— & Kris, E. (1945), The Genetic Approach in Psychoanalysis. *This Annual*, I.

Hebb, D. O. (1949), *Organization of Behavior*. New York: Wiley.

Hoffer, W. (1949), Mouth, Hand, and Ego-Integration. *This Annual*, III/IV.

—— (1950), Development of the Body Ego. *This Annual*, V.

Kris, E. (1955), Neutralization and Sublimation: Observations on Young Children. *This Annual*, X.

—— et al. (1954), Problems of Infantile Neurosis: A Discussion. *This Annual*, IX.

Kris, M. (1957), The Use of Prediction in a Longitudinal Study. *This Annual*, XII.

McCollum, A. T. (1956), A Clinical Caseworker in Interdisciplinary Research. *Social Work*, pp. 88-102.

Provence, S. & Lipton [Coleman], R. W. (1962), *The Development of Institutionalized Infants: A Comparison with Family-Reared Infants*. New York: International Universities Press (in Press).

—— & Ritvo, S. (1961), Effects of Deprivation on Institutionalized Infants: Disturbances in Development of Relationship to Inanimate Objects. *This Annual*, XVI.

Reider, N. (1953), A Type of Transference to Institutions. *Bull. Menninger Clin.*, XVII.

Rheingold, H. L. (1956), *The Modification of Social Responsiveness in Institutional Babies*. Lafayette, Ind.: Society for Research in Child Development Monographs.

Ribble, M. (1943), *The Rights of Infants*. New York: Columbia University Press.

Ritvo, S. & Solnit, A. J. (1958), Influences of Early Mother-Child Interaction on Identification Processes. *This Annual*, XIII.

* Some of the works to which Ernst Kris referred in the text could not be verified and are therefore omitted from the Bibliography.

—— & —— (1960), The Relationship of Early Ego Identifications to Superego Formation. *Int. J. Psa.*, XLI.

Spitz, R. A. (1945), Hospitalism: An Inquiry into the Genesis of Psychiatric Conditions in Early Childhood. *This Annual,* I.

—— (1954), Genèse des premières relations objectales. *Rev. Franç. Psa.*, XXVIII.

Wolf, K. M. (1948), Unpublished seminar notes.

—— (1952), Observation of Individual Tendencies in the First Year of Life. In: *Problems of Infancy and Childhood* [Transactions of the Sixth Conference], ed. M. J. E. Senn. New York: Josiah Macy, Jr. Foundation, 1953.

DEFENSE, SYMPTOM, AND CHARACTER

SEYMOUR L. LUSTMAN, Ph.D., M.D. (New Haven)

This paper will attempt to use the phenomenological data of child analysis to examine the genetic interrelationships between defense, symptom, and character formation. To do this, I will focus primarily on the similarities and differences between two rather sharply delineated behavioral patterns, and attempt to trace some of their vicissitudes as they emerged in the analysis of a child. One pattern, cleansing, at the apex of its frequency gave the appearance of a compulsive symptomatic act. With the passage of time, further maturation, and the progress of the analysis, its frequency sharply diminished, but aspects of it remained which approached a character trait. The "symptomatic" aspects of this behavior will then be contrasted with another behavioral pattern, "bravery," which assumed a more clearly defined characterological basis. It is my thesis that a developmental approach to the emergence of these behavioral configurations affords opportunities to bring relevant empirical data into closer relationships with psychoanalytic theory.

METHODOLOGY

Since this problem can be approached with a variety of investigatory techniques, I would like to preface my material with some general methodological concerns. One major problem of psychoanalytic research lies in the area of defining the "sample" which is under study. Such definitions have very direct implications for

From the Yale University Child Study Center and Department of Psychiatry.

This study was supported by grants from The Foundations' Fund for Research in Psychiatry, United States Public Health Service—National Institute of Mental Health, and The Psychoanalytic Research and Development Fund.

I would like to express my appreciation to Drs. S. Ritvo, M. Kris, W. Pious, and M. J. E. Senn for their aid and interest.

research design and particularly for the nature and size of the population to be studied. For example, one way to approach this particular problem of character and symptom development would be within a nosological framework. One would then quite likely set up two groups of patients, one with character disorders and the other with symptom neuroses, and compare them. While at first glance this seems to have the advantage of a greater number of "cases," upon closer examination this advantage may prove spurious. The validity of any noted differences or similarities in such a study would depend explicitly upon the matching of variables within the two groups. Psychoanalysis has demonstrated that formative forces are so incredibly intricate, subtle, and complex, that it becomes virtually impossible to match even two people for other than the most superficial actuarial factors such as age, sex, social class, etc. (elements of this difficulty exist even in twin studies). While it could be argued that there are sampling techniques to minimize this problem, they are of such a nature as to preclude the use of psychoanalysis as a research tool. This is not to say that such research approaches are not valuable; my remarks merely refer to their relative merits in psychoanalytic research on a problem such as this.

On the other hand, by definition, the problem can be explicitly stated in terms of the investigation of patterns of behavior, rather than of groups of patients, or nosological entities. If one uses this investigatory framework, the single case method (Hartmann, 1959; Pious, 1961; Frank, 1959) or stochastic case (Chassan, 1961) becomes relatively more advantageous. Remaining cognizant of the burden of criticism of "uniqueness," need for "reduplicatability," etc., it may still prove to be the relatively more fruitful approach by virtue of its self-matching characteristics. Not only are all actuarial characteristics matched, but all significant hereditary characteristics, all significant object relations, all significant drive characteristics, all historical events, and even the therapeutic experience are as close to identical as is humanly possible. With this greater certainty of identity of variables, the investigator is freer to search for significant factors. By this I mean that the probability that any noted differences or similarities will not prove to be due to unmatched (and possibly, unknown) variables or combinations of variables is minimized.

In this study, the sample becomes a large number of specific incidents belonging to one behavioral pattern which can then be compared to a large number of specific incidents belonging to another pattern of behavior. With such a methodological approach, since the number of incidents is great, one could even apply statistical measures if so inclined.

However, if one studies behavior, the behavior itself must not be inferred but must be available to observation as well as to psychoanalytic understanding. It is precisely this accessibility to direct observation of very specific behavioral patterns which makes the research potential of child analysis so great. Historically, child analysis has always been very close to research interests. It arose as much out of concern for corroboration of the developmental theory derived from Freud's reconstructions of adult analyses as it did from therapeutic intent. Prior to the establishment of techniques of child analysis, Freud (1905) pointed to both the need and the dangers of supplementary direct work with children as follows, "The direct observation of children has the disadvantages of working upon data which are easily misunderstandable; psycho-analysis is made difficult by the fact that it can only reach its data, as well as its conclusions, after long détours. But by co-operation the two methods can attain a satisfactory degree of certainty in their findings" (p. 201).

With the technical and theoretical development of child analysis as a field, the danger of "easily misunderstood material" has sharply diminished. Hartmann and Kris have repeatedly stated that the field of direct observation of children has become an ever-increasing source of live data of increasing import. This has been misunderstood by some to mean that with children observational techniques can replace psychoanalysis. Hartmann and Kris had reference to the child prior to the age at which child analysis could be used. From then on, the techniques of child analysis differ considerably from those of experiment and observation—even when the latter are carried out by psychoanalytically trained or sophisticated experimenters and observers. It is precisely the inextricability of the *threefold* function of psychoanalysis as a theory, therapy, and research "instrument" which makes child analysis the richer source of research data.

As stated above, the greatest advantage which accrues to the child analyst lies in the nature of the data which are available to him.

By virtue of the child's use of play as communication and particularly because it is the natural mode of behavior for the child, the child analyst is in a position of using a research tool which is actually a combination of direct, participant observation of "natural behavior" (play) and verbal communication in a setting of (psychoanalytic) therapeutic continuity in time, space, and interaction. The latter brings with it the depth of knowledge of the child stemming not only from contact with him, but from contact with his environment, which makes his play maximally understandable (Anna Freud, Bornstein, M. Kris).

Although there are differences of opinion within the field concerning the analyst's contact with outside sources, it is generally felt that with the preoedipal, oedipal, and latency child the regular contact of the child analyst with the parents and others (teachers, social workers, etc.) is useful for therapy and vital for research. It yields a degree of corroborative material not usually available to research workers. Furthermore, the meaningfulness of this "yield" is in direct proportion to the degree that the motivations of the clinical situation replace the superficiality which plagues constructed experiment and observation.

The above is no attempt to minimize the contributions from adult analysis and from research which uses analytic theory but not analytic method. As a matter of fact, there is every reason to believe that combinations of techniques—such as are used in simultaneous analyses of parent and child—appear to be the ideal research methods for developmental investigations, even though the problem of how to deal with large masses of disparate data remains.

The phenomenological data of child analysis are very frequently the play of the child. For this reason I shall briefly review the psychoanalytic theory of play as derived from the work of Sigmund Freud, Anna Freud and her followers, Waelder, E. Kris, and Peller. The usefulness of child's play to the analytic investigator lies in the fact that through it the child breaks up both internal and external experiences into smaller segments of experience with the purpose of mastery. In essence, this uses the mechanism of the repetition compulsion.

This is accomplished via a transformation from passivity to activity which enables the analyst to observe and understand the impact of both external events and internal forces upon the child. Of particular import to the analytic investigator are the opportunities to follow the child's developing modes of coping with such forces in terms of their metapsychological components. Through play, wish fulfillment becomes apparent and is made all the more palpable by a leave of absence from both reality and superego. This makes accessible to the analyst the child's fantasies about himself and objects.

In the course of the analysis of any child, one becomes aware of certain play patterns which are repetitive and which serve certain ego functions. Of concern to my topic is one particular manifestation of the internal state as revealed in the play pattern which Erikson (1937, 1940) has classically described as "play disruption." He defines this as the sudden and complete, or the diffused and slowly spreading inability to play, and contrasts it to the more natural turning from a particular play activity as a result of play satiation. Peller (1954), speaking to the same point, states that "small quantities of anxiety are mastered in play, but anxiety of a high intensity disrupts play."

She further points out that "play ceases to be play when the child loses his ability to stop when he wants to, when he becomes glued to one phase, to one episode." Then play may become a "phobic defense." The essential point is that the obsessive rituals of childhood are not play in the sense of the psychoanalytic theory of play reviewed above, but rather are closer to those ego structures involved in mastery, particularly the defensive structures. As a matter of fact, all play has within it varying degrees of defensive function in the sense of Kris's (1934) statement that "play wards off unpleasure."

Since this study will be concerned with play behavior, I shall now briefly describe the two classes of behavior. The cleansing behavior was very close to the play disruption delineated by Erikson and Peller, but might better be classified as a very abrupt *play substitution*. It did not characterize the child when she was so anxiety ridden that play was impossible; it rather represented, in my opinion, play in the core of which was imbedded her defensive operations against the anxiety mobilized at that particular period. When a given direction in play was attended by an excessive mounting of anxiety, an abrupt disruption of *that* avenue of play occurred but without a paralysis of the play function. Instead of becoming immobilized, the "cleansing" substitution occurred, which at its most severe or intense level approached what Peller called an obsessive ritual—no longer play. In contrast to this, there were incidents of more classic play disruption during which the child was unable to play.

On the other hand, the bravery as a character trait was ubiquitous in this child's behavior. However, even though it remained indigenous to the child's usual mode of functioning, there were many discreet episodes which were dramatic in their boldness and audacity —and which could be categorized as "brave acts."

One final word about the collection and recording of the data. Wendy was seen four times a week over a period of four years. Each psychoanalytic hour was dictated immediately following its termination and every attempt was made to be phenomenologically complete, using more the descriptive methods of observational research. The effort was to establish an ongoing phenomenological record of the behavior of the child, in addition to the psychoanalytic formulations about that behavior. While the formulations changed from time to time, reflecting more complete understanding, the basic data of this paper remain the dictated descriptions of the hours. One must note in passing that there is by now a large literature on recording interviews. No attempt was made to make such recordings in this analysis, because for child analysis one would obviously require sound motion picture techniques and I have not the certainty that these afford that much greater research advantage—particularly in view of the difficulties of dealing with such large masses of data. In any event, it is my conviction that while much was undoubtedly lost, the over-all goal of phenomenological descriptiveness and the method of immediacy of dictation yield an extraordinarily complete ongoing record.

CLINICAL DATA

The child to be described was the older of two sisters and was brought to analysis at the age of four and a half. By parental description, Wendy was motorically hyperactive from birth. This single fact was consistently put forth by the mother as the core reason for Wendy's problems. From infancy on the mother unremittingly experienced Wendy as a perpetually squirming, writhing, red-faced, angry child who was insatiable in her demands. This both permitted and evoked a particularly physical, persistently intimate pattern of mothering and surveillance—a pattern which can best be described as omnipresent, apprehensive, sexually and aggressively seductive, tempestuous, and characterized by extreme ambivalence and intense mutual excitement.

The father experienced an undisguised delight in this hyperactivity, although from the .beginning he recognized that there was a private and inviolable relationship between mother and daughter. In spite of this, he was able to establish a close bond with the child which, for both, centered around her vigor. His pleasure in Wendy increased as her energies were channeled into frank boyishness. This came about in large part as a direct response to his wish. Thus, prior to the birth of the sister she was reared as a boy, even to the extent of being called a boy's name by the father.

The birth of the younger sister wreaked havoc with these intense parental-child interactions and modes of relating. It was mutual in the sense of its impact on the parents as well as the child. The father transferred his allegiance and wishes to the new child. He did this so abruptly and so completely, that Wendy's reaction had many qualities of a bereavement. Wendy was left with a sense of incomprehensible abandonment which had as its sequelae depression, anger, an increase of masculine wishes, a deepening sense of defect, and heightened sibling rivalry. A major consequence was that in her loneliness she turned, once again almost exclusively, to the mother which further intensified an already tumultuous relationship.

At the time she was brought to treatment the infant precursors had "blossomed" to the point where both parents complained that she was a moody, depressed, irritable, and totally exasperating child. When first seen, although obviously depressed, Wendy was nimble, graceful, fair of face and form. She was a study in contrasts, presenting a constant clash of femininity versus masculinity. In the twinkling of an eye she could move from the graceful pirouette of the ballerina to the heavy-footed parody of a "Western gunfighter." She was alternately skillful, nymphlike, with a practiced feminine propriety, then lumberingly inept, unwieldy, even ponderous, for one so small.

Nevertheless, fundamentally I experienced a quality of winsome amiability, an artless charm, which was in sharp contrast to the "malevolence" described by the mother. These different reactions were, in fact, related to one of the mother's complaints. She felt that all who saw Wendy reacted to her as if she was a "charming child." The mother could consciously perceive *only* her disruptiveness, while she experienced this charming quality as a deception which the child was practicing. In reality, the charm was present and seemed quite clearly related to the major underlying theme of the analysis during this period—the conflict between masculinity and femininity and her attempts to master her masculine strivings. As a slight digression, I would like to advance the hypothesis that the essence of Wendy's charm was rooted in the unexpected and the very incongruity of her bisexuality. She was, by appearance, very pretty and quite feminine, and I think this was precisely what made her masculine behavior acceptable and even captivating to most who saw her. It had all the qualities of an amusing masquerade, a façade under which one could readily see the blond delicacy of a pretty little girl with a radiant, though rare, smile.

Neither space nor the purpose of this paper will permit any further discussion of the family into which this child was born and by which she was reared, nor the therapeutic aspects of the analysis into which she was placed. The major focus will be on her play behavior in analysis. This was flamboyant and expressive, accompanied by mercurial moods ranging from deep immobilized depression to the most volatile eruptions of ebullient hyperactivity. Her favorite game in the early period of the analysis was gunfighter, in which she portrayed either Wyatt Earp or Roy Rogers. Developmentally, it is interesting to note that as the analysis progressed, this favorite game was modified in significant ways. The direction of the change progressed from being a boy (Wyatt Earp or Roy Rogers) to being a "tomboy," wherein the underlying theme was now portrayed with the child in the role of Dale Evans or Annie Oakley. Gradually these heroines were given up, and a much greater preponderance of the play became quite feminine in character such as mother games, nurse, etc.

I shall now focus on the behavioral pattern of "cleansing," which first appeared in the treatment situation as a sharp departure from her earlier and habitual sloppiness. Over the period of four years during which Wendy was seen, a total of seventy-four "cleansing episodes" occurred. In every instance of this, the child was involved in some sort of play or direct communication which became a source of increasing excitement and anxiety. There would then be an attempt at mastery via the abrupt play substitution of cleaning.

The degree to which these episodes approached compulsive rituals or uncontrollable reactions varied and will be discussed more fully later. Although I have elected to focus upon the symptomatic, defensive, and characterological interrelationships of this child's play, it is well to remember the caution of Anna Freud (1946) to the effect that just as there is not a one-to-one equation between play and free association, there is not a corresponding equation between play interruption and resistance or defense. The play substitution which I will describe in greater detail was a quite complicated piece of behavior—sometimes assuming the form of a symptom and sometimes that of a character trait—but it invariably included identifiable defensive and synthetic functions. In trying to evaluate any behavioral unit, one can take cognizance of the complexity only by trying to discern the various components which contributed to this behavior and how they were synthesized within it. Recent analyses of behavior by Brenman (1952) and Pious (1961) are excellent examples of this. At any rate, it would be the grossest sort of oversimplification to regard these play disruptions and play substitutions as simple "resistances" occurring in the analysis.

Taking the period of the analysis as a whole, the cleansing behavior broadened in the sense of its being used by the child to help her cope with a greater variety of anxiety-producing situations. However, as it emerged in the analysis, it seemed most clearly to be involved with the child's conflict over masturbation, which in itself was imbedded in the related context of messiness versus cleanliness, femininity versus masculinity, and courage versus fear and shame. I knew from the mother that there was mutual masturbation between the sisters in the home and that this occurred most frequently in the bathroom and in the bathtub around bathing. Masturbation itself first appeared quite early in the analysis when there were several incidents of blatant, provocative masturbation, usually occurring at the very end of the hour. The first intimation of mutual masturbation occurred around the very excited and exciting game of little dolls playing in a swimming pool. This game was repeatedly abruptly replaced by excessive cleaning, sometimes of her hands, sometimes of the dolls, and sometimes of the swimming pool itself. I will not reproduce all such hours, but will select some representative samples to show their thematic continuity.

At the age of five, much preoccupied with the differences between boys and girls, Wendy told me about how she had been born a boy. While doing this, she proceeded to strip all the clothing off a large number of dolls. When I asked what she was looking for, she told me she was separating the boys from the girls. In response to my question how she was able to tell them apart, she pointed to the genital area, saying that girls have "wee-wee holes" and the boys have "penises." Using water in a little toy nursing bottle, Wendy began to feed the "doll children," finally focusing on one little doll which she called the "little girl." After feeding her, Wendy squirted water in her "wee-wee hole" and then very abruptly gave her a bath and washed her hair.

Several months later, under the impact of much sexual curiosity, a great deal of primal-scene material in the play, and considerable penis envy, she focused on a boy doll named Bobby who was different from girls because he sat down to defecate but stood to urinate. Wendy very realistically demonstrated her knowledge of this by placing the doll's hands in front of him as if he were holding a penis. This led back to her having observed her father while urinating and more discussion about differences between boys and girls. The high point of the hour occurred when, in the play, the father got chicken pox and had to be put to bed. As Wendy played this out, Bobby was in the bed before the father arrived and when the two were in bed together, Wendy became very anxious. She started to punish Bobby and at this point went back to bathroom play involving the washing of all the dolls, cleaning them very scrupulously with water and paper towels, all the while chiding them and insisting that they keep themselves clean. It should be stated that sexualized visits to the parents' bed and sharing of the sister's bed were a current concern at her home.

About a year later, these themes continued in the play as follows: Wendy was telling me that she had terrible secrets which she did not want her mother to find out. One was that she liked to eat play dough, another was she liked to pick her nose and eat the pickings, and mostly that her mother would get very angry with her if she knew any of these secrets. She then told me that she and her sister played games and Mommy and Daddy would get very angry if they knew about that. She refused to tell me what the games were, but constructed a dollhouse so that the open back side of it faced us and then repeatedly went through putting figures in the house, coming around to the other side and inviting me to peek in the window at what they were doing. Her description was that the little dolls were preparing for baths and playing very exciting games. At this point, Wendy very abruptly took the dolls out of the dollhouse play and vigorously scrubbed them in the bathroom of the playroom.

The same mutual masturbatory theme recurred about a year later in a more clearly defined fashion. The play took the form of two little girl children (portrayed by dolls) who played very frenzied games together and then had to be scrubbed because they both had "diaper rashes."

At the age of seven and a half, Wendy instituted a doctor game which consisted of taking care of several dolls. These were large rubber dolls with two holes in them, one a mouth, and the other in the region of the buttocks equivalent to an anus. As the doctor, Wendy decided it was time to take the dolls' temperatures and stuck a thermometer in one doll's mouth. She quickly took this out, stuck it in the rear end of the doll. She seemed very puzzled, took it out again, and once more stuck it in the mouth. I could not get her to respond to her air of puzzlement. I then asked her how the baby felt while she was doing that. With this too direct question, Wendy became anxious, abruptly went to the bathroom, shut the door, and after some time I once again found her with the mop, engaged in vigorous cleansing of the room.

The predominant mode of behavior of this child throughout the analysis was phallic. Her sexual confusion and masculine strivings resulted in a markedly intrusive mode of behavior. As Wendy herself put it, ". . . a girl can have thirty more gallons of boy in her than girl." While there was a progression in play themes—for example, the cowboy-gunfighter games yielding to more feminine play—on the whole, the child's behavior never clearly went into what could be called a latency period. There was an ever-present "ease of regression" to anal preoccupations and modes of behavior.

Some of the more prominent "characterological behavior" of this period seemed to be related to this regression to anal preoccupations, and particularly to the issue of retention and cleanliness. In addition to the many episodes of cleansing behavior listed above, there was a great deal of hoarding and hiding of material in the playroom so that other patients could not get at them; there were many attempts to lock the doors to keep other patients out; and the bathroom itself was quite prominent as a locus of play.

There was a great deal of "spying" in relation to bathroom activity, and periodic preoccupation with "smells." Much of her sibling rivalry was reactivated and played out with me around her extreme jealousy of another patient of mine—a little boy. In relation to this boy she unleashed a whole variety of "tricks," most of which had to do with locking him out of the bathroom. The primary trick involved was that Wendy would go into the bathroom, lock the door from the inside and crawl through the small space underneath the door—thus leaving the bathroom door locked to "surprise" the little boy when he could not get in.

Thus, trickiness, sneakiness, spying, were all character traits which occupied a good deal of the analysis. However, for my present purposes I will focus on a brief description of her character trait of "bravery." The family myth shared by mother, father, and both children was that Wendy was absolutely fearless. Many instances were related (as complaints) by the parents—and occurred within the treatment—wherein the child seemingly placed herself in great danger, heedless of the consequences. This daring but reckless "courageousness" was apparent from the very beginning in the bold way she separated from her mother and in the way she explored the treatment room. Not only was bravery a frequent characteristic of the games she played, but it was also quite apparent in the amount of boisterous climbing, jumping, and explorations of the building. It was particularly prominent in her reaction to injuries, of which there were many, during the hours. In all of this she could only be described as "brave." The underlying terror and sometimes counterphobic behavior were never acknowledged by the parents, in spite of numerous attempts to point the child's fears out to them. Although such acts evoked consciously expressed exasperation and complaint, there was an unspoken element of pride, appreciation, and even envy within both parents. Actually, in most instances, unless the

underlying terror was excessive (and this was rare), Wendy did evolve
the character trait of excessive and aggressive bravery. She was unusually and characteristically bold, decisive, and never hesitant to act.
For Wendy, this was one aspect of masculinity which could survive
relatively unchanged in a girl.

Discussion

The data indicate that in the early part of the analysis any veiled
reference to masturbation, or mutual masturbation, made Wendy
very anxious and would result in her washing her hands and subsequently washing the dolls. However, between the ages of six and
seven, incidents where exciting sexualized games were hinted at
resulted in an abrupt and out-of-context scrubbing or cleansing of
some part of the room. A cursory examination of whether the scrubbing behavior was restricted to the body, or the toys, or the room
itself[1] suggests that the most archaic regression involves the body
itself—i.e., in all instances here, washing rather compulsively her
hands. From the body there is an orderly progression to toys and
then to the room itself. This sequence implies that the regressive
elements in a hand-washing compulsion of an adult are greater than
the regressive elements of, for example, a house-cleaning compulsion.
Another way of stating this is that one aspect of development as
revealed by this kind of play is an ever-broadening sphere of skills
and materials with consequently increasingly distant displacements.

The astonishing specificity and plastic quality of the symptom
of cleansing and the behavior surrounding it beg comment. It is as
if the child took precisely the location, and precisely the activity, and
reproduced it in the symptomatic act. Bathing, masturbation, anal
play, spying, exhibitionism, all occur very specifically in Wendy's
life around the bathroom. This was precisely where she played them
out in treatment; moreover, she incorporated them into the symptomatic act itself. It was as if the bathroom and the "dirty, exciting,
frightening" play (representative, in part, of the strength of the
impulse) brought about the danger and fear of getting caught and

---

[1] Erikson (1940, 1950) described this succinctly as the autosphere, the microsphere,
or the macrosphere.

were controlled by secrecy and by washing, cleaning, and making
it all right. However, this was done without ever relinquishing the
impulse aspect of the behavior, for mutual masturbation occurred
around washing. One gets the impression that some of the intensity
of the symptomatic cleansing behavior was derived from the toilet as
the scene, the washing as a masturbatory activity, and anal components of the masturbatory play.

Under the sway of a passionate sibling rivalry and an unremitting
penis envy, there emerged the aforementioned characteristic pattern
of tricks and secrets, all for the purpose of preventing other children
from "getting at her things." Sneakiness, hoarding, trickery, as character traits were related, in part, to the masturbatory activity and
showed a possible reciprocal relation to the symptomatic act. For
example, the mother reported that whereas the child continued to
show the isolated cleansing behavior at home and was not quite as
sloppy as she had been, she had developed a hoarding habit. Many
things that were thrown out, as well as other items, would somehow
find their way into the drawers of her cabinet where they were preserved. In the treatment, compulsive washing was, for a time, replaced
by hoarding.

In view of these manifestations of anality, it is of interest to
go back to the mother's account of Wendy's toilet training. She
described it as an extremely turbulent, difficult period in which the
child would hide behind the chairs to have her bowel movements.
The mother began by training Wendy to have her bowel movements
on paper (she placed paper behind the chairs) and only after a protracted struggle succeeded in getting Wendy to have her bowel
movements in the toilet. Toilet training, in addition, coincided with
the birth and infancy of the younger sister, and may well have carried with it the connotation of pregnancy fantasies. At any rate, via
the "surveillance" aspects of the mothering, one can derive quite
clearly some of the genetic elements of being sneaky, tricky, and
stubborn throughout this struggle with the mother for autonomy
and mastery. Actually, the struggle with the mother itself continued
unabated but used a variety of different "arenas."

In this regard, I might refer briefly to the episodes of "messing"
that occurred during the analysis. These were less frequent than the
cleansing episodes and in many instances were either warded off or

immediately followed by cleansing episodes, thus clearly establishing the component of reaction formation, reversal, and undoing. This was indicated, for example, in play around making a fecal mess out of clay and then washing. It was also demonstrated by Wendy's need to wash her hands following an incorrect perception of some powdered material on the floor of the playroom as being "bird bowel movement." It was further demonstrated by the frequent excessive amount of hand washing which followed actual bowel movements occurring during treatment hours. During the course of the analysis, her struggle with messiness was somewhat resolved and achieved a degree of secondary ego autonomy. Both the mother and I observed that she had gradually become a much neater child, and was able to function as such with no apparent effort or conflict.

In discussing the defensive aspects of the cleansing behavior, I am aware of the fact that some workers prefer to limit the concept of defense to pathogenic conflicts, whereas others also use it in the sense of "normal defenses." Certainly some aspects of what I have been describing occur in all children as they struggle with similar conflicts. However, the behavior described in this paper very frequently bordered on a pathological symptom in which the defensive component of the "compromise" could be discerned.

The motives for defense emerging from a survey of the immediate antecedent themes which "triggered off" this cleansing behavior show an increasing amount of superego anxiety, particularly related to masturbatory guilt and the destructive impulses directed toward the mother and the sister. This anxiety further shows a progressive degree of internalization, which at first seemed to be objective anxiety in the sense of the child definitively fearing that her mother would "find out." In the early part of the analysis this was expressed as a great fear that I would reveal the secrets to the mother, or that the mother would peek at us, or in some other way "find out," and then injure her. This fear seemed to underlie Wendy's frequent statement, "You know no such thing." In addition, there was more dramatic evidence in the child's feeling that she had incontrovertible evidence that mothers were crazy and did kill or injure children.

One finds a hierarchy of defensive maneuvers characterized by a regression from a phallic to an anal mode of behavior with elements of reaction formation, of undoing, displacements, etc. There is, furthermore, externalization or projection in the act itself. Most prominent are identifications, particularly with the aggressor.

The hierarchical layering of defense must then be placed within a hierarchical layering of defense and impulse. While a more direct instinctual expression was avoided, discharge still occurred. In my experience, the energetic discharge quality of the cleansing behavior (and the "bravery") was outstanding. Rereading my notes I find that I was frequently moved to describe the behavior as an "orgy" of cleaning or as having an orgiastic quality. At any rate, it is quite clear that some discharge occurred from which a much lower level of tension emerged. Furthermore, it would be safe to describe many, if not most, of the cleansing episodes as an "attack" on whatever was being cleansed. Two outstanding examples of this had to do with the child's cleaning of the blackboard with such energy that she finally completely effaced the board, which had to be replaced. For this reason I would speculatively suggest that much of the energy which was bound into this defensive structure was of an aggressive source and was made available in this form via the defusion attendant upon regression (Hartmann, 1950b). Indeed, the qualitatively most energetic and vehement episodes quite clearly seemed to be related to Wendy's attempt to master some of her own aggressive impulses—primarily directed against the sister and the mother.

Before contrasting the symptomatic aspects of the cleansing behavior with the bravery, the complexity of the cleansing behavior must be especially noted. The fact that at times it would look like a symptomatic act and at others like a character trait is in great part due to the process of development and the fact that "solidification" or more rigidly enduring structuralization had not yet occurred. In a child of this age, ego and superego development are still fluctuant processes. Moreover, I maintain that all symptomatic acts have intimately related characterological structures.

Bearing this in mind and assuming the intricate, the sometimes parallel and sometimes reciprocal, relationship described above, there is some value in examining more closely the relationship between the character trait and the symptom. If one conceptualizes an important aspect of what occurred throughout this analysis as a progressive internalization and structure building—not only of sexually and aggressively suggestive danger situations, but of controls as well—what, then, are the factors which influence or predispose this developmental process toward one or the other direction?

As an overview, one can approach the problem in terms of the similarities between character and symptom. In both, regressive elements appear with a discernible defusion of libidinal and aggressive components as a concomitant of such regression. Both afford the child a striking degree of discharge, although in both the directness and perhaps the degree of the discharge are altered. Both are greatly influenced by the defensive functions of the ego. One could certainly say that character trait *and* symptom arise out of the interplay of impulse, anxiety, conflict, and defense. In addition, one finds that the synthetic function of the ego has produced a more or less adaptive mode of functioning and resultant state of adaptation.

However, herein lies one crucial difference. The adaptive value of the character trait is consistently related to reality. One can agree, as does Beres (1961), with the definition of Glover (1925) that character is "a set of organized behaviour reactions founded on and tending to preserve a stable equilibrium between Id-tendencies and submission to Reality: they are characterized by more or less satisfactory adaptation along lines of displacement" (p. 63). This stability and the relationship to external reality make the character trait more adaptive in a reality sense than the symptomatic act. This is at least true for the individual, though not necessarily true for the society. The behavioral pattern of the character trait left this child much less frequently immobilized, better integrated, and generally functioning in a more adaptive way. This may have been more apparent in connection with character traits other than bravery. I say this because it may be argued that the adaptive value of the bravery must be questioned because of the self-destructive elements in it. For example, it is conceivable that some other workers would consider this bravery as maladaptive because in play with boys it led to fighting and the possibility of injury. But even here the bravery was geared to external reality and permitted this child's intelligence, imagination, and initiative to crystallize the role of a leader which was quite adaptive. On the other hand, the cleansing behavior was geared only to an *inner* reality and had no relationship to the external reality, i.e., it mattered not at all whether what was being cleaned was clean or dirty, or whether the activity had any contextual relationship to a particular play sequence.

It may well be true that certain defenses lend themselves more readily to symptom formation and others more readily to characterological development. In this child, reaction formation, reversal, undoing, seem to be equally involved in either symptom formation or character trait. However, rationalization as a defense seems much more clearly related to the possible development of a character trait. In Wendy, there may be a predisposing factor in her brightness, but if so, this would seem to operate selectively, based on other factors. Thus, if one examines her bravery, one finds that around all instances of brave acts, not only were the components of reversals, reaction formation, and undoing identifiable, but in addition, it was around external intervention in all such episodes where this child rationalized so well that she became, in the words of the mother, a "guard house lawyer."

It is then quite striking to note that this very impressive, logical, verbal ability to rationalize in a "guard house lawyer" manner was never prominent and rarely even present when masturbatory material was prevalent, as in the cleansing behavior.

Thus, using these two "excited" behavioral patterns as examples, while both were interpreted to the child, it was only the fearlessness and bravery which was defended by extensive "argument." The consistent absence of such argument about interpretations relevant to the cleansing behavior was all the more impressive because of the obvious ease with which this child could have rationalized it in terms of the dolls being dirty, etc.

The essence of whether the developmental process goes predominantly in the direction of a symptom or a character trait has most to do with the issue of ego syntonicity. The ability of the ego to preserve interstructural and intrastructural harmony depends not only on its synthetic and defensive functions but also on the strength and character of the drives and particularly on the development of the ego ideal and superego.

Approached from the side of the impulse, it is difficult to discern, in this particular material, wherein lies the difference regarding the developmental direction. For example, it has been stated by numerous analysts that character traits have less of the drive characteristic than are apparent in symptoms. I do not think this is true in the case of Wendy. This may be an individual difference in terms of drive intensity of this particular child, or it may be a more general developmental difference. By that I mean that the intensity of the drive characteristic of the child (either in symptom or character trait) may appear differently from those in the adult because the growing, developing child is generally closer to the primary process than is the adult. This is a matter for further research. However, in Wendy, I could not help but be impressed with the striking degree of discharge and impulse gratification present in both symptom and character trait. Yet, as stated above, the discharge via characterological behavior was geared to elements of external reality and, in general, more adaptive.

It seems to me that by examination of these data, the most essential element in terms of the aforementioned developmental direction has to do with ego-ideal and superego formation, their impact upon the synthetic and defensive functions of the ego, and the means by which they enter into the syntonic alliance which characterizes the character trait.

Conceptually, the problem has been approached in many ways (Freud, 1908; Hartmann, 1960; Reich, 1958, 1960).[2] Novey (1955) approaches the issue of ego syntonicity by carefully defined differentiations between the ego ideal and the superego. He is of the opinion that "the ego ideal" as a concept should not be used to describe "the punishing or loving superego" which is based on the resolution of the oedipal struggle. Although he relates the ego ideal to the superego, he conceives of the ego ideal as having its roots in early pregenital, narcissistic operations against anxiety, but as being acquired later than the oedipal superego. In this way, while the superego may be ego alien, by definition the ego ideal is always ego syntonic.

A recent conceptualization proposed by Loewald (1962) seems to me to have great explanatory potential. Here the ego ideal takes on more the quality of a developmental process which stands genetically between the "ideal ego" and the "superego." It represents a

[2] In a recent, stimulating paper, Schafer (1962), emphasizing the confusion surrounding the concept "ego ideal," has suggested that it be abandoned and replaced with carefully defined concepts of ego interest, superego interests, and ideal self.

longed-for state of narcissistic perfection—a wished-for oneness with the all-powerful parent—and is shaped by mutually projected idealizations stemming from both the parent and the child.

Loewald introduces and stresses such concepts as degrees of internalization and externalization, and a concept of distance from the "ego-core."[3] Such concepts are useful for a theory of character formation, since implicit in them are definitions of modes of character formation and of ego syntonicity. Conceptually, ego-ideal or superego elements may, through a process of progressive degrees of internalization, become elements of the ego proper. As Loewald states it, "internalization of aspects of a lost love object, if observed over long periods of time, . . . may be progressive so that eventually what was an ego-ideal or superego element becomes an element of the ego proper, becomes realized as an ego trait rather than being an internal demand. . . ." This movement and integration of more peripheral elements into the "ego-core" depend on a postulate of distance and a corollary postulate of related tension. To quote Loewald again, "Underlying the concept of superego as a differentiated grade in the ego is the idea of distance from an ego-core. Unless there is a degree of tension between this ego-core and the superego, they are not distinguishable." This could be one useful way of defining degrees of ego syntonicity, which is so central to character formation.

Accordingly, Loewald's conception of the superego is that of an enduring structure, whose constituent elements may change. For my purpose I would conceptualize that a continuum of parental elements exists for the child, ranging from external authority through superego and ego ideal to the "ego-core." Along this continuum, through complex, relatively reversible processes of internalization and externalization, one can account for the inter- and intrastructural shifts of these elements.[4] This is conceived of as an ongoing, dynamic, and economic process, dependent upon a synchronization of structural elements and object relationships, and involving neutralization and deneutralization of psychic energy accompanying the internalization and externalization processes.

---

[3] Internalization is here used as a generic term to cover such mechanisms as incorporation, introjection, identification, "internal object," etc.

[4] Although present in normal development, it is less apparent than the dramatic shifts seen in psychotic states.

Returning to the two behavioral patterns described, there was continued conscious parental disapproval of both. In both behavioral patterns there were strong evidences of compliance with unconscious parental wishes. Over a period of time, varying degrees of internalization became apparent in both. However, in one pattern the internalization went to an ego element and character trait, and in the other, to a superego conflict and a symptom formation. The main difference between the two seems to lie in the ego-alien or ego-syntonic quality (or tension) between the child's ego and the unconscious needs and demands of the parental ego ideal, and particularly, conflicts of the parental superego.

The child's "bravery" was completely congruent with the unconscious needs of both parents. Evidence of this was implied in the mother's complete inability to recognize fear in Wendy and in her surreptitious pride in Wendy's early boldness. Moreover, it permitted the kind of "mothering" so crucial to this mother. The father was more openly proud of this seeming "independence" and endowed it with a masculine cast. Thus, this compliance was part of an internalization or identification process with elements of the parental ego ideal and superego. Actually, it demonstrated the kind of mutual idealization of parent and child which, as a superego element, is much closer to the concept of an ego ideal, one shaped by mutually projected idealizations.

On the other hand, the masturbatory behavior of the child was reacted to with great ambivalence—particularly on the part of the mother. The child was placed in a complex state of conflict which was a reflection of the superego conflict of the mother. Not only were prohibitions internalized as threats, but a much more complicated state of parental seduction and prohibition was involved. But within this constellation, unconscious punitive elements were much more clearly defined than in the bravery, and also showed more clearly the structuralization as superego elements in the child.

Thus, the child felt no guilt and little inhibition about her feats of bravery, in spite of the consciously expressed disapproval of the parents. At the same time, she manifested considerable confusion and a degree of developing superego guilt about masturbation.

If we leave aside such matters as equipmental givens, it follows that the first ego syntonicity is not exclusively an intrapsychic ego syntonicity but rather primarily a syntonicity with the parental ego. If the structural development of the child—molding and being molded by the parental relationships—produces behavior which is consonant with the unconscious needs of the parents, the likelihood of a character trait is enhanced. The internalizations of such aspects of the love object have a greater likelihood of becoming integrated, without tension, in the developing ego core. On the other hand, when behavior is alien to the superego demands of the parent, the likelihood is greater for crystallization as superego elements with corresponding tension and the possibility of symptom formation. This is particularly so if a parental superego conflict is internalized.

It seems to me that the relationship of ego-ideal and superego functioning to the aforementioned processes is of crucial research import. This might be stated in genetic terms: for a character trait to develop it must first be syntonic with the ego ideal and superego of the parent. Although theoretically any superego element may become internalized as an element of the ego, it is particularly in those areas usually conceptualized as ego ideal where the possibility of character trait seems to be enhanced. The bravery is an example of such a mutually projected and idealized ego-ideal element. Its premature internalization as a character trait in the child may have been enhanced by the mourning process caused by the early abandonment which the child experienced as her father turned from her. The bravery is an element of the idealized lost object which becomes reinstated in the character trait as an element of the ego. It corresponds to the period of near-narcissistic perfection in Wendy's life—referred to nostalgically by the child as the time she was a "boy" and called so by her daddy.

Clinically, one can wonder why this child did not develop an obsessive-compulsive disorder. There is every reason to expect that she could have done this. There were formative forces within the family constellation which would foster this; there was precocious ego development, pronounced ambivalence, regression to anal modes of behavior, and the obsessional turning into the opposite with much preoccupation of both sides of any issue. One can say the predisposition to such a development was certainly there, and it may yet occur.

There was a slow, but decided, decline in the number of cleansing episodes as the analysis progressed. Much of the therapeutic effort

was directed precisely at the defenses described above and undoubtedly had some impact on their not solidifying into a symptomatic
neurosis. In general, interpretations were of the order that whenever
Wendy became anxious it made her feel better to clean something
up. At the same time, attempts were made to focus on what it was
that had made her feel so anxious, and to introduce her unconscious
motives into the analytic work. In addition, there was age, and with
it some progression in the developmental phase, with diminution
in the pre-emptory quality of the instinctual manifestations and more
effective methods of displacement and reorganization of defenses
in warding off anxiety.

As I have stated earlier, the most prominent themes in the
analysis—especially during the height of these play substitutions—
had to do with the child's struggle to master her masculine strivings,
her sexual confusion, her castrated sense of defect, her extreme penis
envy, her passionate sibling rivalry, and the actual seduction in the
form of mutual masturbatory experiences. The reduction in the
frequency of the cleaning episodes may be due, in part, to resolution
of some of the problems by virtue of treatment and further maturation. For example, it is possible to correlate this directly with the
aforementioned developmental sequence of masculine play where
this child went from playing as if she were a boy through playing like
a tomboy through the emergence of more feminine play. Although
it is by no means a closed issue, she is now closer to a resolution of
her conflict over masculinity versus femininity.

The bravery, on the other hand, showed a great stability and
was relatively refractory to change. In spite of a great deal of analytic
work, particularly around the maladaptive aspects of injury, it proved
more resistant to modification. In fact, it became a more stable mode
of functioning.

In conclusion, I would like to cite two hours of Wendy's treatment in some detail. They demonstrate her courage, her symptom,
some of the nature of the analytic interventions, but also the resilient
and restitutive quality of her ego. She had an unusual ability to
reconstitute herself after what seemed to be devastating bouts of
anxiety.

The hours reproduced occurred on a Monday and a Tuesday.
During the previous week she had been preoccupied with her anger

with me and jealousy of the little boy patient who had the hour before hers. In addition, there had been the much more chronic concern with distrust of mothers and masturbatory secrets.

At the beginning of the Monday hour Wendy was quite subdued, seemed almost sleepy, and played as if in a trance. She wanted to play "War," a card game, which was done in a very smooth, quiet fashion. I was just wondering to myself why Wendy was so subdued, when suddenly she flung the entire deck of cards full in my face.

I recovered from the shock to see Wendy looking fleetingly frightened and pacing nervously around the room. I pointed out how frightened she was, which she stoutly denied. I described to her her way of being "brave" when she felt just the opposite, which met with further denials of any fear. I then asked her why she had hit me, why she was so angry. She turned her back, regained her composure, and then said she did not know why she was angry. In response to my pressing her, she told me she would tell me "tomorrow." I then told her I thought she was angry because she had seen me with the little boy patient. At this point she got up and went through her usual defensive activities against the awareness of her underlying anxiety. First she picked up a rifle and flung it over her shoulder, and then she noticed a broom which a cleaning lady had left in the corner of the room.

Wendy took the broom and began a frenzied sweeping of the floor. Once again I wondered out loud why she was so anxious, to which she replied that she was angry with me because I had looked at the floor and smiled. For this I was to be punished by a "million and nine smacks" on the head with the broom. She then turned the tables by demanding to know why I had looked at the floor and smiled, saying she wasn't going to leave the room until I explained it to her. I interpreted this reversal of roles, trying to show her that it was a little bit like my trying to find out why she had hit me. She became very noisy at this point, telling me not to say anything. At the end of the hour she was very reluctant to leave, still insisting that I tell her why I had smiled. I told her that I was probably thinking about how clean the floor was going to get because I knew Wendy always felt better after she cleaned something when she was upset.

The next hour was complicated by the fact that I had feared I would not be able to reach the office in time to see Wendy and had phoned to cancel. When I found I could reach the office in time, I phoned and asked the mother to bring the child.

Wendy shouted, "There he is," when she saw me and came bounding up the stairs, taking my arm. In the playroom I commented on how "mixed up" all this canceling business must have been to Wendy. She said that her mother had told her first I wasn't coming, and then that I was, and that she was very glad to see me.

I tried to find out what she had thought when I first canceled and got no response from her. I then made the comment that I bet she thought it had something to do with her hitting me in the face because she was so angry and jealous of the little boy, to which she said, "You know no such thing."

She then wanted to play "War" again (the same card game which initiated the aggressive outburst the day before), and during the course of this card game I reminded her that today was the day we had decided to tell each other why she was angry with me and had hit me in the face and why I had looked at the floor and smiled. She agreed and told me to tell first. I told her again that I probably smiled because I knew that every time Wendy had a "funny kind of feeling" (Wendy's description of the internal experience of anxiety) it made her feel so much better if she washed something or cleaned something or tidied up—and I know that she was feeling very upset about having hit me because she felt jealous of the little boy. Wendy again said, "You know no such thing," and refused to tell me why she was so angry, saying that I had lied and insisting she didn't know why she had gotten so angry. She then had to have a bowel movement and when I heard her washing her hands for an excessive amount of time, I went to the bathroom where I found Wendy busily engaged with Ajax and sponges scouring the wash basin and scouring the floor.

I made the same interpretation about her cleansing activity and wondered why she felt so "funny" at this time, to which she responded, "I hope I don't have to say this again—you know no such thing." It should be stated again that the repetition of this phrase had a long history of being a direct statement of her dread of my discovery of her masturbatory secrets about herself and about her sister, and her consuming jealousy of the sister.

She then brought out a broom, wanted to play house, and ordered me to participate in the cleaning up activity. In the course of this, Wendy arranged to hit me with the broom handle, which made her genuinely distressed. She ran to me, patted my head, told me how terribly sorry she was. Within the play I accepted her apology and then told her I thought she was also telling me she was sorry that she had hit me on the head with the cards, to which she responded, with a smile, "Sometimes those things happen."

CONCLUSIONS

In closing, I should like to add a speculation about what equipmental contribution could be involved in the defensive aspects of her cleaning behavior and bravery. First of all, she was a doer; secondly, whatever she did she did with singular vigor. Her way of coping with anxiety had within it the inextricable qualities of a motoric discharge. From the mother's vivid description of this child we can assume that Wendy was, from infancy, a hyperactive[5] youngster, who perhaps by endowment had available to her readily accessible channels for motoric discharge, or higher drive components, or lower thresholds. In addition, this propensity met with the expectation and encouragement of both mother and father (albeit in very different ways), who dealt with this child as if she were a boy—more than just a boy, a very aggressive, active boy. The situation then evolved in which certain congenital equipmental characteristics, being buttressed and encouraged by parental interaction, led into the direction of inevitable conflict.

In speaking of the defensive processes involved in these behavioral patterns, I have deliberately avoided addressing myself to the point of the processes of identification. This is not because they did not have crucial import—quite the contrary. I have avoided it because the entire area of parental interchange in the life of this child is so complicated that it deserves separate and detailed treatment, which is planned in the near future.

[5] I use "hyperactive" in a descriptive sense and not in that introduced by Fries & Woolf (1953), who designate "hyperactivity" as a pathological feature.

I would also like to make one more comment about my having, for the purposes of this paper, so oversimplified these most complex behavioral patterns. The remarks made in this paper do not cover all aspects of the behavior. This was most clearly brought home to me in terms of the predictability of the behavioral patterns. As her analyst, I was always able to predict her bravery—and I was able to predict to myself (with fair degree of success) many instances when either cleansing or regression to gunplay would occur. But there were other incidents when it was quite reasonable to expect that this behavior would occur and when it did not materialize. Further research plans include the analysis of those incidents where the expected did not materialize and a comparison with the incidents where it did.

In summary, material from the analysis of a child was cited to demonstrate the intimate relationship between defense, symptomatic act, and character formation. The data suggest that the difference between character and symptom may be a quantitative rather than a qualitative one, and that underlying all symptom formation is a basic character structure which is consonant with it. However, a developmental direction is apparent which may determine the predominance of either a character pattern or a symptomatic act. In this material, the differences seem most directly related to the degree of developmental internalization of parental ego-ideal and superego demands and conflicts. It is my belief that mutually projected and idealized elements of the ego ideal are more likely to become elements of the ego, whereas parental superego conflicts are more likely to be internalized as superego elements which are more peripheral to the ego core.

BIBLIOGRAPHY

Beres, D. (1961), Character Formation. In: *Adolescents*, ed. S. Lorand & H. I. Schneer. New York: Harper.

Bornstein, B. (1948), Emotional Barriers in the Understanding and Treatment of Young Children. *Amer. J. Orthopsychiat.*, XVIII.

Brenman, M. (1952), On Teasing and Being Teased. *This Annual*, VII.

Buxbaum, E. (1954), Technique of Child Therapy. *This Annual*, IX.

Chassan, J. B. (1961), Stochastic Models of the Single Case As the Basis of Clinical Research Design. *Behav. Sci.*, VI.

Erikson, E. (1937), Configurations in Play—Clinical Notes. *Psa. Quart.*, VI.

—— (1940), Studies in the Interpretation of Play: I. Clinical Observations of Play Disruption in Young Children. *Genet. Psychol. Monogr.*, XXII.

—— (1950), *Childhood and Society*. New York: Norton.

Frank, J. D. (1959), Psychotherapy Research Project: Phipps Clinic. In: *Research in Psychotherapy*. Washington: American Psychological Association.

Freud, A. (1936), *The Ego and the Mechanisms of Defense*. New York: International Universities Press, 1946.

—— (1946), *The Psychoanalytic Treatment of Children*. New York: International Universities Press, 1959.

Freud, S. (1905), Three Essays on the Theory of Sexuality. *Standard Edition*, VII. London: Hogarth Press, 1953.

—— (1908), Character and Anal Eroticism. *Collected Papers*, II. London: Hogarth Press, 1924.

—— (1913), The Claims of Psycho-Analysis to Scientific Interest. *Standard Edition*, XIII. London: Hogarth Press, 1955.

—— (1920), Beyond the Pleasure Principle. *Standard Edition*, XVIII. London: Hogarth Press, 1950.

Fries, M. E. & Woolf, P. J. (1953), Some Hypotheses on the Role of the Congenital Activity Type in Personality Development. *This Annual*, VIII.

Glover, E. (1925), The Neurotic Character. In: *On the Early Development of the Mind*. New York: International Universities Press, 1956.

Hartmann, H. (1950a), Psychoanalysis and Developmental Psychology. *This Annual*, V.

—— (1950b), Comments on the Psychoanalytic Theory of the Ego. *This Annual*, V.

—— (1958), Comments on the Scientific Aspects of Psychoanalysis. *This Annual*, XIII.

—— (1959), Psychoanalysis As a Scientific Theory. In: *Psychoanalysis, Scientific Method, and Philosophy*, ed. S. Hook. New York: New York University Press.

—— (1960), *Psychoanalysis and Moral Values*. New York: International Universities Press.

—— & Kris, E. (1945), The Genetic Approach in Psychoanalysis. *This Annual*, I.

—— —— & Loewenstein, R. M. (1946), Comments on the Formation of Psychic Structure. *This Annual*, II.

Kris, E. (1934), The Psychology of Caricature. In: *Psychoanalytic Explorations in Art*. New York: International Universities Press, 1952.

—— (1950), Notes on the Development and on Some Current Problems of Psychoanalytic Child Psychology. *This Annual*, V.

—— (1951), Opening Remarks on Psychoanalytic Child Psychology. *This Annual*, VI.

—— (1955), Neutralization and Sublimation: Observations on Young Children. *This Annual*, X.

Loewald, H. (1962), Internalization, Separation, Mourning and the Superego. *Psa. Quart.*, in press.

Novey, S. (1955), The Role of the Superego and Ego Ideal in Character Formation. *Int. J. Psa.*, XXXVI.

Nunberg, H. (1932), *Principles of Psychoanalysis*. New York: International Universities Press, 1955.

Peller, L. (1954), Libidinal Phases, Ego Development, and Play. *This Annual*, IX.

Pious, W. (1961), A Provisional Hypothesis about the Nature of Schizophrenic Behavior. In: *Psychotherapy of Psychoses*, ed. A. Burton. New York: Basic Books.

Rank, B. (1942), Where Child-analysis Stands Today. *Amer. Imago*, III.

Rapaport, D. & Gill, M. (1959), The Points of View and Assumptions of Metapsychology. *Int. J. Psa.*, XL.

Reich, A. (1958), A Character Formation Representing the Integration of Unusual Conflict Solutions into the Ego Structure. *This Annual*, XIII.

—— (1960), Pathologic Forms of Self-Esteem Regulation. *This Annual*, XV.

Schafer, R. (1962), Ego Ideal, Ego Standards, and the Ideal Self. Read before the
    Western New England Psychoanalytic Association.
Spitz, R. A. (1950), Relevancy of Direct Infant Observation. *This Annual*, V.
—— (1959), *A Genetic Field Theory of Ego Formation*. New York: International
    Universities Press.
Waelder, R. (1933), The Psychoanalytic Theory of Play. *Psa. Quart.*, II.

MOTHERING AS AN INFLUENCE ON EARLY DEVELOPMENT

A Study of Well-Baby Clinic Records

JOYCE ROBERTSON (London)

Variations in Development in the First Year

When a mother swells with pride as she recounts her baby's achievements, or complains that he is not as accomplished as another, we tend to listen indulgently. We know that despite variations en route all normal babies will eventually smile, sit up, crawl, walk, and talk. The fact that babies develop at varying rates during the first year is commonly regarded as unimportant in itself.

It is well known that babies reared in institutions develop unfavorably and slowly in the first year as compared to family babies, even where the institution has made the best possible efforts to provide substitute mothering. Thus Anna Freud and Dorothy Burlingham (1944) say in *Infants Without Families*:

> Whenever we have an opportunity to compare our five to twelve-months-old babies with family babies out of average homes we are struck by the greater liveliness and better social response of the family child. The latter is usually more advanced in reaching out for objects and in active play. He is more active in watching the movements of people in the room and more responsive to their leaving or entering, since whoever comes and goes is known to him and concerns him in some way. A child of that age is, of course, unable to take in and differentiate between all the changing personalities in a baby ward or big nursery. For the same reason the baby's emotional response to changing expression, face or voice, of the grown-up person may be slower to develop. His ability to imitate which he develops from the eighth month

The Well-Baby Clinic, as part of the Hampstead Child-Therapy Clinic, is directed by Dr. Josefine Stross and is maintained by the Grant Foundation, Inc., New York.

onward is stimulated in a lesser degree where contact with the grown-up is less frequent, or less close, or has to be divided between several grown-ups as is inevitable in a nursery. Even where our residential babies are stronger and healthier, these differences in intellectual and emotional development are suffi- cient to make the private baby appear more "advanced" and therefore more satisfactory. The comparative backwardness of the residential baby at this stage is due to the comparative unfulfill- ment of his emotional needs which at this age equal in impor- tance the various needs of the body [p. 13f.].

It is now common knowledge that the failure of institutions to meet the emotional needs of a young child arises mainly from the number of people participating in his care. But it is not possible to make a simple antithesis between multiple care and the care of a mother. In this paper I wish to show:

1. Even when the child is in the sole care of a devoted mother, defects in the quality of her mothering can result in emotional needs being unfulfilled.

2. Deficient mothering in the first year causes poor general development which can look similar to, but is not to be confused with, retardation due to organic defect.[1]

3. The impairment resulting from the experience of deficient mothering will persist after the first year, but may become partially obscured by neurotic features.

The importance of this concept is that since subtle deficiencies inimical to the good development of the infant may exist in women who otherwise function adequately, these defects may easily go unnoticed; and since they are particularly difficult to detect in retro- spective case histories, their contribution to faulty development may be overlooked.

A Study of Well-Baby Clinic Records

The Well-Baby Clinic of the Hampstead Child-Therapy Clinic has been in existence since 1957. Children who were then in the first year of life are now between three and five years of age. In addition to continuing under the care of the Well-Baby Clinic, many of them attend our nursery school where they can be seen as a group.

1 Points 1 and 2 have been stressed by Coleman and Provence (1957).

Watching these children play together I became interested in the differences in muscular tone—the strong sturdiness of some as contrasted to the flabby limpness of others, the directed and skillful movements of some and the clumsy uncoordination of others. I noticed that the clumsy ones were those whose mothering during the first year had been recorded as unsatisfactory, and formed the hypothesis that there is a connection between deficient mothering and disturbed motor development.

To test this hypothesis I have studied the observations on these children and their mothers which I had recorded during the previous four years of the Clinic's existence. These records describe the physical and emotional development of these children, and the observable features of the mothers' handling, but the records were not designed to throw light on any specific aspect.

Areas of Development Observed

Although my intention was to study muscular development, it soon became clear that this could not be isolated from the rest of development. In observing and assessing the normality of development in the first year, I have therefore considered the following areas:

1. Bodily tonus
2. Muscular activity and achievements
3. Quality and quantity of responsiveness
   (a) to the mother
   (b) to the wider environment
4. Communication
5. Expression of feeling

For the purpose of this study little notice is taken of fluctuations which occur during illness or holidays, or of isolated areas of late development.

Correlation of Mothering Quality and Infant Development

There are twenty-five mother-infant pairs whom I observed from the babies' first months of life.[2] A simple analysis of the children's status at twelve months of age shows the following:

---

[2] There are in fact twenty-three mothers with twenty-five children. For purposes of this communication these are dealt with as twenty-five separate mother-infant pairs.

1. There was a group of five babies whose development, in comparison with the other twenty, was poor in the following areas: bodily tonus, muscular development, responsiveness both to the mother and to the wider environment, ability to communicate, expression of feeling. Paradoxically, alongside the general dullness and the lower developmental levels, there was in four of the five babies a heightened visual perception (James, 1960).

2. Very early in the lives of these five babies, the maternal responses had been recorded as unsatisfactory because they were lacking in meaningful affect. Some of the mothers made a normal impression in social situations. The deficiency of their mothering responses could be detected only when they and their infants were seen together. Furthermore, a mother who was deficient in relation to the infant under observation might be completely adequate in relation to another of her children, or to this infant at a later stage of development.

3. Some of the mothers of the remaining twenty babies had personality and character traits which by common standards would be regarded as unsatisfactory, but each of them was able to answer adequately to the emotional needs of her baby.

4. None of the twenty adequately mothered babies was poorly developed at twelve months.

5. None of the five inadequately mothered babies was satisfactorily developed at twelve months.

INADEQUATE MOTHERING

Interrelation Between Deficient Mothering and Disturbed Infant Development

From Clinic records I will now describe the nature of the defective response in the mothers of the five babies, and the interrelationship between the quality of the mothering and disturbed infant development. At the end of the first year the babies were behind their peers on every level, but there was no doubt as to their potential normality. From the early months our concern was directed toward bringing about a change in the way the mothers responded toward them. But though in some minor ways improvements were effected, these did not alter the main trend of development.

Peter.—When first seen at a few weeks old Peter was a picture-book baby, contented and round, delicately colored, and presenting no problems. His mother handled him competently but appeared harassed and depressed. She was conscientious, devoted to her son, and pleased with his development. But she was an unhappy woman, seriously inhibited in her ability to express feeling or to witness it in others.

Peter first smiled at about six weeks, but did not progress to the free smiling which is typical of babies between two and three months. When talked to he would listen and look, move his limbs and head and lips, but only rarely would the expected smile appear. His mother did not try to elicit smiles from him, and she became uneasy when I tried to do so. When he wriggled in response to my talking to him, she said, "He is embarrassed," and thereby gave the first clue to her inhibition. We were to become very familiar with this inability to elicit or to answer to an emotional response.

She did not talk to her baby or play with him. In the waiting room mother and child would sit silent and still like two wooden figures. By the time Peter was seven months old his lack of facial expression, lack of bodily movement, and lack of expression of feeling were conspicuous.

When he cried she would hold his shoulder as one might do to a strange school child found crying in the street. Inadequate comforting led in his case to the gradual development of an exceptional ability to control his tears when in pain. He would tremble, flush, screw up his eyes, and swallow his tears. By the time he was a year old this meager response had gone; even injections did not make him cry.

He was slow in attaining the usual developmental steps: he sat up, crawled, and pulled himself into a standing position just before his first birthday. He walked at sixteen months, and said his first words at two years.

It became clear that subdued unresponsiveness was what his mother wanted. The attention and stimulation that came his way during illness, or on one of the frequent family holidays spent in hotels, brought about more demanding behavior. In our judgment, this behavior was more normal, but it invariably caused his mother to complain.

Peter always looked healthy, but there was no animation or pleasure in his body movements or in his facial expression. In the consulting room he sat silently on his mother's knee, intently watching whatever was going on but rarely responding. His watching sometimes had a self-protective quality, like that of a petrified animal—eyes staring, body tense and stiff—waiting and watching for danger. When a therapist first observed him at eighteen months of age his unwillingness to respond to stimuli made her ask: "Is he psychotic?"

At three years he sucks his thumb a great deal, and his play is hindered by it. He is passive—watching rather than doing or responding. When he is excited he has a disturbing habit of standing rigid, trembling, and making unusual hand and finger movements.

He is now in the nursery group, where the following was recorded after his first week:

> He takes little notice of the other children and his teachers, tending to ignore grownups who speak to him. He makes no spontaneous move to amuse himself, but stands rather near his mother looking about in a dazed, inhibited way, not really watching anything, not looking for anything to play with.
> Peter makes a queer impression with his rapid alternations of joyous excitement and inhibition. Even his expressions of joy seem somehow unnatural and inappropriate to his age or to the occasion, for instance, when he names objects. He does not seem to know how to communicate with his mother, to express his wishes verbally, or to be aware of what to expect from her, the way one would expect at his age. His closeness to his mother is not simply like that of a younger child.

Beatrice.—Her mother was conscientious but lacking in intuition, warmth, and identification with her baby. The work with her consisted largely in trying to make her aware of the baby's needs. In a limited and unintuitive way she did much of what was suggested to her, but it was impossible to invest her care with feeling.

At three months mother and baby made a curious impression of dullness. They would look at each other silently, with expressionless faces, and there was little evidence of contact between them. Beatrice had less bodily movement, less expression, and was less responsive than is normal for babies of her age.

At six months she was serious and her looking had a staring, intense, and apprehensive quality. She looked with interest at toys and was aware of the person offering them, but she showed no pleasure and rarely any movement toward them. A glimmer of a smile appeared very occasionally.

At seven and a half months she had not attempted to turn over. Mrs. A. reported that as Beatrice was happiest when left alone in her cot or pram, she never took her shopping or for walks. She left the child unsupervised in the garden for long periods, even while she went to the hairdresser or the dentist.

This mother did not fulfill the role of comforter. When her child cried, for instance, after an injection, it called out no response. She would look away from Beatrice and continue talking. When Beatrice wanted attention—wanted to be lifted from the floor, for instance— she would again look away to avoid responding. It was painful to witness a baby trying to get protection and response from a mother who defended herself by being blind to these demands.

The reason for this mother's looking away was not difficult to understand, but it was one which reassurances were unable to touch, and it held the key to the original inhibition and to the improvement which we saw later. Her own mother had for many years suffered from disseminated sclerosis and Mrs. A. had been much affected by her erratic movements. She remembered as a school child being ashamed and afraid that her mother would behave badly in front of her friends. When she was faced with the jerky, uncoordinated movements characteristic of babies, all her old feelings were revived—hence, the need to look away.

But when toward the end of the first year the baby's movements became more coordinated, the mother was able to respond more adequately. Beatrice showed some improvement too, though she was still tense and lacking in animation. A tight-lipped little smile was the only sign of pleasure.[3]

Maurice and Gordon.—These two boys were siblings. Both showed the effects of deficient mothering—with due allowance for other factors.

Maurice was a baby who cried from birth. Breast feeding was

[3] Observation ceased at one year because the family left the country.

never established. At three months he was in a hospital for twenty-four hours, accompanied by his mother, to have a hernia repaired. It may be that bodily discomfort added its weight to the usual run of difficulties experienced in the early weeks. By five months he was overwhelmed by anxiety, screaming at everything and everybody, and this typified his behavior for the rest of the first year.

It was difficult to assess his normality at this time because of the all-pervading apprehension. Much of his energy seemed to go into being alert for danger or into crying in fear. He did not make contact. To offer a toy or even to look at him was to risk provoking the most excruciating screams.

At nine months he could grasp and put things to his mouth, but was flabby and moved his limbs very little. He did not attempt to sit or crawl. To strengthen his flabby muscles and to encourage movements, exercises were suggested; but his mother did not do them. When he eventually walked and talked there was a noticeable peculiarity about both activities. His movements were slow, stiff, and overcautious, and he held his head and shoulders in an abnormally tense way. His movements lacked pleasure and spontaneity. Though his vocabulary was good, he spoke in a high-pitched staccato manner which never failed to draw comment. Over his whole being there was an air of diffuse anxiety.

The behavior which characterized this mother was her imperturbability and the detached way in which she could discuss Maurice's difficulties. Initially her control of anxiety and the calm way in which she handled this very difficult first child appeared to be positive features, though it was puzzling that she could not give him the comfort he so badly needed. It seemed reasonable that she expressed no pleasure in a child who did nothing to elicit it.

Gordon was born when Maurice was twenty-one months old, and though small he thrived. The mother's imperturbability, which had seemed an admirable quality in relation to a screaming and apprehensive baby, was now recognized as remoteness and excessive control of feeling when directed to a more normal baby.[4]

After four months this baby began to show a lack of bodily movement, a dulled responsiveness, and a deceptive state of content-

[4] See Marianne Kris's description of a similar case (1957).

ment. He could be left alone for long periods without demanding attention. At nine months of age he was still and quiet and showed little animation. He smiled in response to attention, but made no attempt to reach out to people or to things. Again, exercises were suggested to stimulate the baby; but again the mother did not do them. When talking about it, she was well aware of her resistance to doing exercises with her babies. It was noticeable that she did not fondle or kiss them. Bodily contact did not come easily to her and was kept at a minimum. Maurice, who had the hernia, may well have been in special need of body contact—one of the things his mother could not give.

Remoteness and lack of empathy affected her ability to answer even the physical needs of her babies. On one occasion she was waiting with her two children for a car lift home. The younger child, then six months old, began to cry and the cry soon mounted to a scream—enough to cause comment from the rest of the Clinic. The mother was less concerned than everyone else and, explaining that he was tired, put the baby into his carry-cot in the corner of the room. But the baby did not sleep, he went on screaming. Since in principle we try to adhere to "Mother knows best," no comment was made. But when the screaming went on and became more desperate, I eventually intervened and suggested I get a drink of milk because he might be hungry. The mother counted up the hours and came to the conclusion that he was due for a feeding. She thereupon opened her blouse and fed the baby.

Her aloofness, her rigid control of feeling, her avoidance of body contact, and lack of empathy meant that she was unable to meet the needs of her children on many levels. To know why this was so one would have to know the nature of the feeling which she was so rigidly controlling.

Remoteness and lack of empathy were reported by the nursery observers when Maurice was two and one half years old:

> Maurice is quiet and subdued, even sad, but is quite trusting. He often asks his mother questions: "What's that for, Mummy?" but his mother tends to give replies like: "I must tell you honestly I don't know"—conscientious replies that are a bit too grown up or intellectual for Maurice. After which she returns to her knitting and must seem rather distant to Maurice. Though

kindly, she does not seem much inclined to leave the adult world and enter into his childish enjoyments. One day Maurice played with the balls and slide with wonder and delight. But every time he tried to call his mother's attention to his game saying, "Look, look," she replied without grasping what Maurice was showing her.

[When Maurice was three years two months, they said:] Maurice speaks in a monotonous, affectless way, and says inappropriate things as though repeating what he has heard an adult say. His movements are stiff and tense and lack spontaneity and he walks with his knees rubbing together. Maurice does not initiate any activity for himself. It is very pronounced that he never takes the active role in play, e.g., never initiates a new step, develops any fantasy, or starts any conversation. When the teachers do not engage him in play he just walks around seemingly quiet and interested.

Mary and Norman.—These two siblings developed in completely different ways. Mary, the first child, was breast-fed for two and a half months, but it was not a success. The mother reported that she disliked feeding the baby, and the baby did not enjoy it either. Toward the end of the third month Mary refused the breast and the bottle that was offered in its stead. A period of chaos followed during which Mary was fed entirely on solids, until at four and a half months satisfactory bottle feeding was established.

Mary was a beautiful baby, but at seven months her large watchful eyes were expressionless and her mouth drooped unhappily; she showed no pleasure in anything. Her development was slow and dull, but she seemed more sensitive and perceptive than a baby should be, too aware of the changing mood and expression of the adult. She sat at eleven months, crawled at thirteen months, walked at seventeen months, and said her first words at eighteen months. She was undemanding, and was left alone for long periods of time.

From the very beginning the mother was aware that she was dissatisfied and unhappy with Mary and got no pleasure from her. Though there were times when the closeness of their relationship was obvious, this closeness came in flashes and was not maintained.

By the time Mary was a year old the mother was comparing her unfavorably with every other baby she saw, and rejecting her by word and gesture. Our efforts to help her to stimulate and cathect the baby she sabotaged by the way she carried out the advice. For instance, when it was suggested that Mary needed company, the mother put her for long periods in the front garden where she could see passers-by; and later when Mary needed scope for free movement the mother emptied a room of furniture and left her there by herself. Thus she succeeded in protecting herself from entering into a closer relationship with the child.

When Mary was two and a half years of age the mother complained of Mary's lack of pleasure, her inability to concentrate or to bear frustration, and her greedy demandingness. She was sucking, masturbating, and rocking a lot. The relationship between mother and child was so bad and the child's misery so acute that early entry into nursery school seemed the only solution.

A colleague seeing Mary for the first time at three years of age described her as a "not very bright little girl of a little below-average in intelligence." The nursery staff consistently recorded a similar impression:

> Mary is appealing and evokes a protective attitude in the adults. She makes affectionate relationships. She does not speak a great deal and has poor coordination, and in all other areas she lags behind. She is inclined to be greedy and has no idea of sharing with other children. She masturbates in an uninhibited way. She has a short concentration span.

They asked: "Is this a case of organic mental retardation?" But when at four and a half years school entrance had to be arranged, an intelligence test revealed an above-average I.Q. of 116.

When Mary was three years old a second child was born, and in contrast to her he developed well. He was communicative and full of life and movement. The mother was aware of a difference between her feelings for this child and the first. She said, "This time I feel like a real mother."

It is to be noted that soon after Mary's birth the mother went into analysis. Perhaps because of this she could respond with positive affect by the time Norman was born three years later, and could enjoy motherhood. Perhaps also because this second child was a boy she could give him what she could not give to a girl. Some of this improved mothering ability overflowed onto Mary, but it was still not consistently available to her and was perhaps too late.

This mother maintains a satisfactory marriage and has good social relationships. It is therefore not surprising that some colleagues, impressed by Mary's general demeanor, were of the opinion that the defect lay in the child's inheritance. But to those of us who witnessed the interplay between mother and daughter in the first year it seemed clear that inadequate mothering played the primary part in bringing about Mary's unsatisfactory development.

There are no set rules to mothering. To decipher and adequately meet the needs of her baby a mother must be able to have empathy with him. If she cannot empathize, then she must fail as these mothers failed.

In each of the instances described, the mother was conscientious and concerned. The object tie was, at the manifest level, intact; but its quality was in question. The babies showed a heightened perception—a special quality of looking, as though taking over part of the mother's proper role of protector. This activity of looking took precedence over doing or responding.

At first glance it might appear that development was retarded, but a closer look reveals that the behavior would not be normal even in a younger child. Development was not retarded but faulty.

In the first year, subtle faults in development may be mistakenly regarded as slight and transient deviations from the norm. It may seem unimportant whether a child focuses his eyes at three weeks or six weeks, smiles at four weeks or at seven weeks, grasps at twenty weeks or at twenty-eight weeks, crawls at nine months or at twelve months, walks at twelve months or at seventeen months. Yet our material shows that these first ego activities are helped on, or not helped on, according to the quality of the emotional interplay between mother and child; and that delayed achievement appears to correlate with poor quality performance. When crawling and walking are eventually achieved the increased activity may conceal temporarily the lack of integrated development. It was the poor performance still evident in the third and fourth year which prompted this study.

Early Clues to Inadequate Mothering

It will be asked on what grounds assessments are made on mothers who are seen for only half an hour each week, and even then only in a limited situation. My answer is that although mothers differ greatly in the degree to which in the presence of a third party they openly demonstrate their attitude to their babies, *any* mother who on a clinic visit sits for half an hour or more with her newborn baby reveals a great deal to the trained observer.

There are the changing expressions on the face of a mother who is in contact with the baby, her body movements in response to the baby's stirrings, her hands as they steady the stretching limbs, the moments when in answer to a whimper she withdraws from the conversation, the way in which she strokes and kisses the top of the baby's head, or curls and uncurls his fingers and toes are evidence enough. Similarly revealing is the behavior of the mother who puts her baby in the far corner of the room out of sight and reach, who shows neither pleasure nor anxiety.

One such mother walked into the consulting room, put her five-week-old baby on the couch as if he was a parcel, and then sat some yards away to discuss him. The baby was as though still *in utero*, unmoving and with eyes closed. During the medical examination of her baby she stood aside from him, described him as "ghastly" because he had spots on his face, and was offended by the color of his hair. She was nauseated by the sight of his dirty napkin and grumbled at him for spitting on his nightie. There was no point of positive contact between them.

When the baby was nine weeks old the lack of closeness between them could be seen in the way she handled him. When she lifted him she did it awkwardly and jerkily, without supporting his head. She sat with the baby on her knee, but held at arms length in a sitting position. He was a crumpled bundle, with head and eyes rolling about alarmingly. He was held in such a way that the mother could not see his face, and when at one time she caught sight of his rolling eyes she put her hand over his whole face and told him to "find your eyes." With his eyes as crossed as ever, and his head lolling about drunkenly, he smiled and gurgled—not at his mother's face and voice, because these were not available to him—but at a brightly colored scarf at her neck.

She had no idea how to make contact with him and her efforts were sometimes incongruous; for example, she lifted his foot and squashed his nose with his big toe, and though this amused her it startled the baby and made him wince.

Confirmation of this mother's attitudes came from her accounts of happenings elsewhere. For instance, she told how during week ends spent at the family country house he had from birth been handed over to a nanny who put him to sleep in a room out of everyone's hearing, explaining that if it was not intended to answer the night cries of a baby then he should not be heard. He was fed at 10 P.M. then put back into his cot until 6 A.M. The mother knew from his behavior during the week that he awoke at 5 A.M. and cried until he was fed. But she voiced no anxiety that during the week end his night cries would not be heard, no sadness or concern that he would certainly cry with hunger for one hour in the morning, and no wish to take action to relieve the situation for him.

Another clue is a mother's readiness to separate from her young infant. One mother weaned her baby at two weeks of age, because "it is such a nuisance if one wants to go out," and went on a skiing holiday when the baby was seven weeks old. She showed neither anxiety nor regret at parting from the baby. On return her only comment was that "everything was fine, just fine. Nobody missed anybody."

I suggest that although it may be appropriate that a mother can separate from an older child without anxiety, this is biologically inappropriate in the mother of a young infant and may be a bad prognosis for the relationship.

A baby mothered in this way, without warmth or empathy, will develop broadly along the same lines as other babies. He will focus his eyes, smile, babble, find his limbs; but he will do it largely alone. There will be no fusion between the baby's achievements and the mother's pleasure and support; and for lack of mother as intermediary there will be less reaching out to the environment. His pleasures will be those he can find for himself, and they will most easily be found in his own body. The balance between sufficient stimulation and potentially overwhelming experiences will not be maintained, and the baby may attempt to take over part of his own protection.

As early as eight to ten weeks the consequences are low quality and quantity of body movement, slow responses, serious facial expression, with eyes incongruously alert and watchful. The mother will say, "But he is so contented," meaning that he is undemanding; or "He is happiest when alone in his cot," unaware that her baby may be withdrawing. With the passage of time these deficiencies become more gross. The uncomforted baby who swallows his tears at seven months may not cry at twelve months.

Criteria for Assessing Mothering

The postnatal period from birth to eight weeks is one of adaptation. The mother adjusts to the new demands made upon her, to the reality of this baby, and there is a reshuffle of relationships within the family to permit the integration of the new member.

The baby has been created out of a complicated marriage relationship. Will the father's reaction to the baby be the kind wanted and expected by the mother? What kind of baby did each of them hope for in size, sex, and appearance? How did the mother experience her pregnancy and confinement? Was the baby planned? If not, did she come to terms during pregnancy with the idea of motherhood?

The baby himself will be adjusting to life outside the womb, initially demanding little more than that his physical comforts be maintained. He sleeps or feeds or cries, his awareness stretching no further than to feel discomfort or lack of discomfort.

Sometimes mother and baby come to terms quickly and easily, and before the first month is out their response to each other contains positive and pleasurable elements; but physical difficulties common to the postnatal period may hinder adaptation. It remains an open question to what extent the degree of difficulty experienced in these first weeks influences the eventual quality of the relationship (Bibring, 1959). The records of the Well-Baby Clinic are not sufficiently detailed to give a definite answer, but indications are that a warm relationship is often established despite considerable early difficulties; conversely, a beginning free of physical difficulty does not necessarily signify a satisfactory first year.

The outcome of the adaptive period is successful when, on balance, the mother:

1. feels and expresses pleasure not only in owning her baby but in the activities of mothering;

2. is aware of her baby's affective states and able to respond to them;
3. uses the heightened anxiety which is normal during this period in the service of her baby. (Lack of anxiety at this time may be an ominous sign.)

When by the end of the second month a mother is still not fulfilling these three criteria, there appear to be four possible reasons for her failure:

1. it may be caused by a prolonged postnatal state that will pass;
2. it may be caused by current stress in the mother's personal life, for example, the death of a near relation;
3. it may indicate a neurotic response to this particular child or to this phase in his development;
4. it may reflect a feature of the mother's basic personality which will be similarly evident in her other relationships, including to her other children.

In the weeks that follow birth a baby's needs are not always easy to understand. His crying can be dealt with in various ways. It can be stopped by food, by body contact, by cuddling and rocking; or he can be left to cry until he exhausts himself and sleeps. Already in the first weeks the personality and the background of the mother will determine which method she chooses and which balance she achieves. If, for instance, she is a woman to whom body contact does not come easily, she may stop the crying by giving extra food. To some extent the baby will accept this. Another mother, following the older methods of child rearing, may leave the baby to cry. A baby will adjust to almost any condition and survive—but at a cost.

During the first few weeks of life the experiences of babies will therefore differ greatly. In bodily discomfort they may be soothed by being nursed or fed. When restless they may be sung to or fondled, or they may be left to cry. Their needs may be understood correctly and answered appropriately, or not. They may get food when they are restless, and fondling when they are hungry. They may be handled lovingly or impersonally, or even with hostility.

This early time is like the beginning of a children's spelling game, when the letters are dealt. From then on the play of each partner answers and in turn affects the play of the other, with neither wholly responsible for the outcome—the final word.

THE NATURE AND FUNCTION OF ADEQUATE MOTHERING

Although in the few days after birth the baby shows only discomfort or lack of discomfort, gradually a third state is added in which the baby responds in a minute way to the human voice and tries to focus on the human face. The way in which the environment, mainly the mother, responds to these minute responses and those which follow, appears to set the tone for the first year's development.

Although Gesell (1946) says that a baby stares vacantly until the twelve tiny eye muscles begin to coordinate at about six weeks, it is common experience that a well-mothered baby responds and smiles much earlier.

One mother demonstrated how she evoked a response very near to smiling when her baby was two and a half weeks old. She held the baby's foot, sat very still in such a way that her face was in the baby's line of vision, and spoke quietly to her. After a minute or so of lip, eye, and nostril movements the baby looked directly at the mother and dimples appeared in her cheeks. At two and a half weeks it was not a smile, but it was a response. When she was a month old this baby was focusing and unmistakably smiling.

Another mother sat with her third baby, then nearly six weeks old. As she spoke the baby turned, looked at the mother's face, and smiled with rich facial expression and accompanying limb movements. When the richness of the baby's response was commented on, the mother said, "We play and talk to our babies, but some mothers don't."

A baby can hear earlier than he can focus. Anyone who has talked to a very young infant of about ten days knows that in response his lips, eyes, and nostrils move, and then his head swivels. It is not inconceivable that the making of these early movements promotes early focusing and smiling, and that the lack of such stimulation delays the mastering of them.

By two and a half to three months the well-mothered baby has a repertoire of accomplishments. He will have mastered them with his mother's participation. In the early weeks most babies have difficulty in getting and keeping their thumbs in their mouths. Mothers often lend assistance by steadying the jerking hand, gradually withdrawing help as the baby becomes more proficient.

A very young infant conveys awareness to the mother by eye movements when she talks to him. She gives him the opportunity to focus by putting her face in his line of vision while she talks or sings to him. She steadies the rolling head until he can hold it himself. She gives him her fingers to play with until such time as he can play with his own fingers and hands.

The mother values and encourages these minute responses. By her own libidinal involvement she libidinizes the various areas in the child where the early achievements take place. Although his early achievements will culminate during the third month in a general responsiveness to anyone who smiles or talks to him, this is usually short-lived. By the fourth month the well-mothered baby differentiates between the mother and all other people, and withdraws to some extent even from other members of the family. It is therefore again in the close relationship to the mother that the development of the next few months proceeds.

The communication already begun in eliciting and answering the first minute responses is gradually added to. Once the baby can clasp and unclasp his fingers he will be given the opportunity to grasp his mother's fingers and then a toy. Babbling and laughing is accompanied by stronger and more varied body movements. He will be assisted in his first fumblings; and the play, the learning to manipulate, the communication, his mother's pleasure and affection will be fused into one experience. Each new function that appears will be used by them in their moments of play. The baby of four or five months pushes when he feels a surface under his feet. His mother holds him in such a way that his feet wedge against her body, and together they will play with this latest muscular movement.

A mother reported that her baby had pulled on the cot bars, lifted head and shoulders off the pillow. She added, "Now he loves it if I give him two fingers so that he can pull himself into a sitting position." This movement was mastered, and with the increase of muscular strength which it gave the next followed—that of pulling himself into a kneeling position.

In brief:

1. New movements, initiated by the baby or elicited by the mother, are perfected with her support and encouragement.

2. Because the acquisition of new skills is all part of his play with his mother, he gets special pleasure and satisfaction from them.

3. The skills are directed outward, and become at first part of his communication with his mother and then via her to the environment.

Alongside this handling of his bodily activities runs the mother's empathic response to his emotional states. She keeps a balance between adequate stimulation and potentially overwhelming new experiences, giving and withdrawing support as necessary.

The baby whose responses are answered, who is helped from the very beginning to get pleasure from his early strivings and eventually to master them, progresses smoothly from one achievement to the next. He is not content to babble to himself or to play for very long with his own fingers and feet. The baby who has been given attention, whose responses have been answered, continues to demand these responses. He cries when hurt or unhappy and expects comfort: he expresses his happiness too and wants to share it.

Not all the Well-Baby Clinic mothers are able to have such an intimate life with their infants. Those who have done so have produced babies who are alert, active, communicative, and expressive, on tip-toe for new experiences. Being mothered adequately does not guarantee development free of neurosis, but it promotes a sturdy ego with which to meet conflicts (Winnicott, 1960).

Conclusion

I have tried to show in this paper that indications of deficient mothering which seriously threaten the over-all development of an infant can be detected early in the first year. Three out of the four inadequately mothered children with whom contact was maintained were so disturbed in their fourth year that they needed psychoanalytic treatment. Well-Baby Clinic guidance had proved insufficient to prevent the onset of disturbance (Robertson, 1960).

One's spontaneous wish is to provide adequate substitute mothering for infants endangered in this way. But the mothers reported here would not have understood any reason for handing them over to anyone else. They wanted their babies and loved them. Psychoanalysis for the mother would not bring results quickly enough, even if she had the insight and were willing to be analyzed.

Therefore the question remains: Is there any form of intervention that would be effective?

I offer this paper in an attempt to subtract a little from the unknown boundaries of endowment, believing as I do that the factors I have described are important influences in the development of all normal infants, and to draw attention to a serious problem in preventive mental health.

BIBLIOGRAPHY

Bibring, G. (1959), Psychological Processes in Pregnancy. *This Annual,* XIV.

Coleman, R. W. & Provence, S. (1957), Environmental Retardation (Hospitalism) in Infants Living in Families. *Pediatrics,* XIX.

Freud, A. & Burlingham, D. (1944), *Infants Without Families.* New York: International Universities Press.

Gesell, A. (1946), *How a Baby Grows.* London: Hamish Hamilton Medical Books.

James, M. (1960), Premature Ego Development: Some Observations upon Disturbances in the First Three Months of Life. *Int. J. Psa.,* XLI.

Kris, M. (1957), The Use of Prediction in a Longitudinal Study. *This Annual,* XII.

Robertson, J. (1960), Three Devoted Mothers: Some Limits Set by the Personality of the Mother. *Annual Report of the Well-Baby Clinic.* London: Hampstead Child-Therapy Course and Clinic.

Winnicott, D. W. (1960), The Theory of the Parent-Infant Relationship. *Int. J. Psa.,* XLI.

MATERNAL STIMULATION, PSYCHIC STRUCTURE, AND EARLY OBJECT RELATIONS

With Special Reference to Aggression and Denial

DAVID L. RUBINFINE, M.D. (New York)

In recent years, following Hartmann, Kris, and Loewenstein (1946), we have come to assume a developmentally undifferentiated phase in which ego and id are not yet distinguished. As a derivative of this position, it seems inherently probable that instinctual drive energies are also initially in an undifferentiated state from which, through maturation and via the impact of experience with the environment (conflict), libidinal and aggressive drive energies will develop *pari passu* with mental structure.[1] We take it for granted that the infant at first makes no distinction between self and nonself. When the ego apparatus of perception, memory, reality testing, etc., have achieved a certain degree of maturation, then, through experiences of frustration (postponement of gratification), the infant becomes aware that the need-satisfying object exists as an entity separate from himself and not under his control. This in turn suggests the possibility that the infant forms representations of both need satisfaction and frustration which later structuralize further into inner representations of need-satisfying (good) objects and frustrating (bad) objects. In this paper I shall be concerned with the structural and economic consequences of frustration and need satisfaction.

Presented at the American Psychoanalytic Association, May 1961, Chicago, Ill.; and the scientific meeting of the New York Psychoanalytic Society, October 17, 1961.

1 What is the heuristic advantage of assuming an undifferentiated instinctual reservoir? First and foremost it does not leave us with the uncomfortable problem of primary masochism, i.e., the need to postulate and account for vicissitudes of free aggression in an infant organism prior to such complex processes as fusion, neutralization, and externalization which require a significant differentiation of the ego and distinction of self from nonself.

We must assume that the newborn infant already has an inherent mental organization, much of it in Anlage form. He thus experiences his environment within the limitations of this existing organization. All experiences of drive tension and tension reduction are molded into that existing organization or schema and in turn alter the schema. In Piaget's terms, the ⸱aliment or nutriment is that behavior which characterizes the object which can be assimilated to the pre-existing schema (Wolff, 1960). Assimilation refers to the tendency of the organism to incorporate sensory and motor aspects of experience into the schema which is thereby altered so as to facilitate accommodation of the organism to the object. In analytic terms, both increase and decrease of tension are essential for structure formation.

Within very broad limits the infant organism is able to adapt to a wide variety of objects. This constantly changing schema constitutes the sensorimotor precursor of what later will be the object representation—the structural basis for subsequent object relations. The nuclear dynamism in its formation is the need-tension-gratification-tension-reduction sequence.

But what about experiences with the earliest object where there is no sensorimotor organization capable of assimilating the experience to make accommodation possible? Since Piaget is concerned only with what we might call conflict-free phenomena, he states that such experiences produce no change, i.e., are ignored (Wolff, 1960). We are, however, concerned with experience which cannot be ignored; for example, severe chronic tension states due to prolonged absence of the object, disease, intractable pain, or massive overstimulation.

In what follows I shall attempt to demonstrate that the mechanism of denial and its precursors play a most significant role in promoting assimilation and accommodation.[2] In other words, denial functions to make objects assimilable. Its operation can compensate, within broad limits, for intrusiveness or neglect on the part of the mothering object. Its operation can be detected in the hallucinatory wish fulfillment and in the transitional object—tiding the infant over disillusionment. We know from Freud's (1900) primary model of thought, and Rapaport's (1951) elaboration of it, that the cathexis of memory

[2] For purposes of economical exposition, the following statements are made in an apparently dogmatic fashion. In actuality they are advanced in a tentative attempt to apply a hypothesis systematically to a wide variety of data.

traces of the experience of need satisfaction and gratification is important for structure formation. It seems equally important for the infant organism that means exist whereby the experience of nongratification can be avoided or warded off.[3] However, according to the hypothesis, if the level of tension remains extremely high and is prolonged in time, this may lay the groundwork for later fixation to an ego state in which primitive mechanisms such as denial, introjection, and projection remain the major mechanisms of defense—endlessly operating in an attempt to repair the object and make it assimilable. In such instances object loss always seems to threaten.

On the other hand, where need satisfaction is always and imme-

[3] *First Primary Model of Thought:* Mounting drive tension—absence of drive object—hallucinatory image of it (positive hallucination).

Second Primary Model of Thought: Mounting drive tension—absence of drive object—hallucinating away tension (negative hallucination); (later: hallucinating away bad object).

The primary model of thought according to this hypothesis must be broken down into two parts: (1) the positive hallucination and (2) the negative hallucination. I believe Freud hints at this in the following passage from *The Interpretation of Dreams* (1900, p. 600):

"Let us examine the antithesis to the primary experience of satisfaction—namely, the experience of an external fright. Let us suppose that the primitive apparatus is impinged upon by a perceptual stimulus which is a source of painful excitation. Unco-ordinated motor manifestations will follow until one of them withdraws the apparatus from the perception and at the same time from the pain. If the perception re-appears, the movement will at once be repeated . . . till the perception has disappeared once more. In this case, no inclination will remain to recathect the perception of the source of pain, either hallucinatorily or in any other way. On the contrary, there will be an inclination in the primitive apparatus to drop the distressing memory-picture immediately, if anything happens to revive it, for the very reason that if its excitation were to overflow into perception it would provoke unpleasure. . . . It is a familiar fact that much of this avoidance of what is distressing—this ostrich policy—is still to be seen in the normal mental life of adults."

The biopsychologist Schneirla (1961) has classified biological responses as falling into two basic categories, i.e., approach and withdrawal. These subsequently develop and mature into the psychological responses or behaviors of seeking and avoidance. Both approach and withdrawal operate through certain executive apparatus already present at birth. Thus approach is linked with rooting, sucking, and grasping. The spitting out of the nipple, turning away of the head (Spitz, 1957), and reflex flexion reactions are apparatus of withdrawal which form the prototypes for later avoidance behavior ("No" of Spitz). We might also consider the "stimulus barrier" as a significant structure subserving withdrawal behavior.

As an answer to a criticism raised by Dr. Max Schur in discussing this paper, I wish to stress here that the infant organism is as capable of withdrawal behavior in a primitive, poorly organized sense as it is of approach. Hence it seems eminently reasonable to assume that such prototypes of denial as the negative hallucination are as central a part of the conceptual model of psychoanalysis as the "wish" typified by the positive hallucination.

diately available (i.e., deanimated), there should be a relative absence of tension. Without appropriately timed experiences of frustration and delay, there may result retardation in the development of various ego functions, among them the capacity to distinguish between self and nonself. Such failure of differentiation of self from object, and the consequent failure of defusion of self- and object representations, leads to interference with the development of the capacity to discharge aggressive drives toward an external object, and results in the turning of aggression against the self. I shall later mention some animal experiments (Harlow, 1959; Schneirla, 1961) which illustrate these themes and also suggest that serious impairment of ego development may occur when there is an absence of an active mothering object with whom identification can take place.

Finally, in the event of relative absence of mothering we might assume a failure to cathect the perceptual periphery. Here we might expect a picture like that seen in infants raised in an institution without mother or substitutes (Spitz, 1945; see also Schneirla's cats, 1961).

As a logical outcome of concern with the primitive defenses which the organism normally utilizes to preserve the object as good, and to ward off premature perception of the object as a separate entity, I shall advance the hypothesis that the primary cause of disturbance in object relations (that is, the earliest cause), is the premature differentiation of aggression out of the undifferentiated energetic reservoir.[4]

If during fetal or earliest infantile development enteroceptive or proprioceptive stimuli (disease, pain, etc.) are so intense and continuous as to render ineffective the buffering role of the maternal organism, this "pain" finds representation as failure of need satis-

---

[4] In discussing this paper, Dr. Rudolph M. Loewenstein raised the question: "What are the signs permitting an observer to infer the presence of aggressive drive prematurely differentiated from an undifferentiated energetic reservoir?" In general I would say that a predominance of withdrawal (later avoidance) behavior over approach and seeking might offer a significant clue. It is for this reason that I was attracted to the data collected by observers of autistic children (see below), for here we seem to have a confirmation of these hypotheses. Certainly all observers dealing with psychotic children attest to the preponderance of aggression in these children's behavior toward objects. This includes also a great deal of autoaggressive activity such as head banging. The relative absence of seeking behavior in infants might be inferred from failure of appearance of a smiling response or its extinction after appearing briefly.

faction (frustration).[5] Under these circumstances it seems possible that the aggressive drive differentiates first. This in turn could bring about a hypercathexis of the perceptual apparatus with aggression resulting in premature awareness of the object as separate from the self.[6] The object thus achieves representation as a frustrating or primarily "bad" object. I would suggest that to insure survival, there results in such infants a proliferation of what might be called the precursor of denial, i.e., a maintenance and intensification of the stimulus barrier, to the point of negative hallucination. It seems reasonable to assume that for this to result there must first have been some primordial perceptual registration of the object.[7]

To illustrate these themes, I shall present material dealing with (1) direct observations of normal infants; (2) atypical, autistic children; (3) excerpts from the treatment of a psychotic patient; (4) some data from animal experimentation.

OBSERVATIONS OF NORMAL INFANTS

A vivid three-dimensional portrait of two normal mother-child pairs by Escalona (1952)[8] will serve to establish a base line for the assessment of the role of variations of maternal stimulation and

[5] It seems necessary to assume that prior to the establishment of the distinction of self from nonself, such chronic and intense stimulation—whether it originates from within or without—is represented in the psyche as an experience of frustration, and later as due to a frustrating object.

[6] I am indebted to Dr. P. Glauber for calling to my attention the fact that in obsessive-compulsive neurosis, Freud inferred from reconstructive evidence a precocious development of the ego vis-à-vis the libido. Since at that time aggression was considered an "ego instinct," an interesting parallel to the hypothesis presented in this communication emerges.

[7] Implicit in this point of view is the idea that it is essential for the normal development of object relations that libido differentiate first out of the energic matrix and aggression later. This is ordinarily insured by the fact that maternal care serves as an adequate buffer against too intense external or internal stimulation. However, if the maternal partner adds to the excessive external stimulation, or if internal stimuli are too intense or prolonged, the result is that aggression differentiates first. In this connection, it seems to me that such a failure of mothering is responsible for the reduction in the effectiveness of the stimulus barrier; see, for example, the report of Bergman and Escalona (1949) on "Unusual Sensitivities in Very Young Children" and a premature cathexis of the boundaries of the self, especially in those instances where a constitutional inadequacy in this barrier is present.

[8] I choose this particular material because it is brilliantly phenomenological and innocent of what some critics would label analytic bias.

"buffering" in the genesis of psychic structure. Space unfortunately precludes reproduction of Escalona's description of the thirty-two-week-old baby boys (Jerry and Peter) and their mothers, and what follows must be limited to inferences based on her data. This will also serve to highlight, by contrast, certain aspects of the behavior of atypical children.

Escalona's data indicate that Jerry's mother responds intuitively to him; she reads his needs and Jerry himself is "easy to read"; and she confines her intrusions to times of need tension. These factors, it seems likely, have preserved a relatively undifferentiated state. He makes no sharp distinction between himself and his mother. She is an extension of him, primarily invested with narcissistic libido. Hence, there is no sharp distinction of mother from strangers, and no "stranger" anxiety. His experiences of frustration, and hence his aggressive discharges, occur in relation to inanimate objects. It is noteworthy too that the development of communication as contrasted to "contagion" is less differentiated in Jerry. In other words, we have a situation in which the mother has been able to keep the baby's experience of drive tension at a relatively low level. This mother can also be seen as relatively deanimated, and thus fostering a prolongation of the symbiotic phase. It is quite possible that Jerry's mother did not provide an optimum degree of positive stimulation for him.

On the other hand, Peter's mother, also a good mother, has a strong need to be differentiated by her baby from other objects, both human and inanimate, in the environment. Her intrusions, therefore, have not been approximated to occasions of relatively great need tension. Consequently, they have stimulated the development of ego functions. Peter has a clearly differentiated object relationship with her. He does distinguish self from mother and mother from strangers, and his interest in inanimate objects is not autonomous but is linked to his mother and is an integral part of his relationship with her. Because the mother is less intuitive and more complex in the sense that she is greatly preoccupied with her own feelings and needs (particularly for love, recognition, and to be seen as special and distinct from others) and because Peter himself is difficult "to read," there are occasions when need is not recognized and gratified for some time and the baby is forced to become aware of mother's separateness. It is important to note that these babies show variations in the timetable of development of object relations within the broad boundaries of what is normal. Both show clearly at least the beginning of object relations, although one already has specific object hunger (Peter), a hunger that has been fostered and encouraged by his mother's needs.[9] The greater discrimination in Peter's reaction to mother, strangers, inanimate objects, and the finer differentiation in his vocalization and expressive affective repertoire suggest that his perceptual apparatus has been more intensely cathected; i.e., that he perceives pleasure and pain more distinctly, particularly in relationship to human objects, than is true of Jerry.

AUTISTIC, ATYPICAL CHILDREN

These data can fruitfully be contrasted with certain phenomena characteristic of autistic or atypical children. Their behavior is well known from the vivid description by Bender, Bettelheim, Kanner, Mahler, Rank, etc. However, to emphasize my theme, I want to highlight a few of the data found by Ritvo and Provence (1953) in a study entitled "Form Perception and Imitation in Some Autistic Children." The children described ranged in age from twenty-two to thirty-nine months. All showed disturbances in object relations, interaction with toys, language, and motility. I shall focus on the difficulties in object relations. The authors report that these children showed "indifference to the presence or absence of a familiar person or human object in general," and this is interpreted as indicative of a failure of distinction of self from nonself. However, one cannot avoid the almost eerie impression that these children are truly and very skillfully avoiding human objects. As an example, the authors describe such a child who developed an extremely intense interest in the phonograph and in records which were played over and over again, always avoiding those portions of the record which had the human voice. This is subjectively borne out by reactions of the examiners and parents of these children. The authors report such comments as, "He shuts me out," "He doesn't look at me the way my other children did," and so forth. Another observation of extreme importance is that such children avoid imitating the behavior

---

[9] Mahler (1952) has pointed out that longing for an object can only occur after the object is cathected as separate from the self.

or voice of human objects in favor of adventitious sounds from outside.

(A related observation is that psychotic adolescents regularly are more afraid of little children than of adults or larger children. This seems to have to do with the suddenness and unpredictability of the motor behavior of younger children.) It is in this context, I believe, that we must understand the relation of the autistic child to toys and other inanimate objects. First, the objects are inanimate, with clear-cut and stable boundaries; they are unable to initiate action and are thus under the control of the child. One is reminded here of the role of the transitional object. My point here is that the pathology need not be, as Mahler (1952) has formulated it, a matter of failure of distinction of self and nonself; the pathology may rather consist in a much too early perception of the separateness of the object, due to a high level of need tension, pain, etc., from which the maternal organism cannot or does not protect and shield the child. This hypothesized premature awareness of the object may be associated with the premature differentiation of aggression with which such primordial object percepts are then invested. It is my argument that the negative hallucinatory quality of behavior of such atypical children in relation to human objects serves as a defense against awareness of these objects, thereby protecting both child and object from aggression. Mahler (1952) attributes the ego defect of such children to "excitation preventing the movement of instinctual energy from the internal organs to the perceptual periphery." I would suggest, rather, that the perceptual periphery is prematurely cathected with aggressive drive energy.[10] The work of Bergman and

[10] It is true that such children behave as though there is a loss of distinction of self from object. Objects are not recognized as separate and are often used as extensions of the self. It seems inherently probable to me that such phenomena represent a regressive "refusion"—an attempt to ward off the painful awareness of separateness and consequent cathexis of object and self with aggression (i.e., to ward off perception of the object as "bad" or primarily frustrating). It is thus my thesis that a cathexis of the mother-child unity with aggression threatens to disrupt this unity.

Using this thesis as a jumping-off point, I will later try to demonstrate how my young schizophrenic patient's major ego defect was not failure of differentiation of self from object, as it is usually conceptualized, but rather that the defect lay precisely in the fact that he could not tolerate the differentiation and resulting separateness from the object. At least one of the reasons for this was that then both self and object were cathected with dangerously destructive amounts of free aggression.

I think it is wrong to speak of differentiation of self from object as an end state

Escalona (1949) on "Unusual Sensitivities in Very Young Children" as well as the report by Ritvo and Provence (1953) of high form perception in such children are pertinent in this context. According to this point of view, cathexis is defensively withdrawn from human objects, although there is some evidence that these objects still find representation outside of awareness. If my point of view is correct, then the natural history of such children would look as follows:

If spontaneously, or through treatment, the ego is enabled to recathect external objects, it signifies that the imago of the bad object has succumbed to repression and we might then expect a picture like that seen in Mahler's (1952) symbiotic children. Later, under conditions of stress, this image may threaten to return from repression and the defenses then may range from catatonic withdrawal (again a variety of negative hallucinatory activity) to paranoid psychosis, including all the phenomena of introjects, influencing machines, and so forth.[11] An intermediate type of adjustment might be called a schizoid obsessive type in which adaptation to reality is maintained at the cost of maximum distance from objects.

EXCERPTS FROM THE TREATMENT OF A PSYCHOTIC PATIENT

Ted is now twenty-six years of age, and a very talented jazz musician who is, after six years of treatment, able to sustain disciplined work in his field without frequent, overwhelming experiences of rage and anxiety culminating in feelings of depersonalization, derealization, and peculiar hallucinatory bodily sensations. However, even now, a trivial incident, for example, a change in appointment time

---

and to limit this concept to such crystallized and stable structures. This would necessarily imply that such differentiation only occurred with the establishment of object constancy—i.e., when the child is able to keep a positively invested mental representation of the object when there is prolonged absence of the object. I prefer to see this as a process involving many progressively more differentiated percepts, memory traces, and affective experiences of both positive and negative character. Experiencing the mother as frustrating is indeed ubiquitous, but in the earliest phases of development gratification rather than frustration must predominate if normal object relations and structure formation are to occur.

[11] It is noteworthy that when such denial fails, the inanimate objects with which such children are preoccupied are reanimated and turn into persecutors (Mahler, 1960; Elkisch and Mahler, 1959). It seems to me that in these instances there is a last effort to defend against aggressive drive investment of the human object. Such phenomena are reminiscent of the phobic mechanisms of a later stage of development and may be confused with phobias as in the writings of Fairbairn, M. Klein, etc.

or my unscheduled and unplanned absence due to illness, touches off a chain of events in attenuated form that we have lived through repeatedly since I first knew him. After such an event, while he continues to keep his appointments, he seems to be doing so in a robotlike manner. His usually lively and friendly face is then dull and masklike. He sits cramped up and does not look at me; while he answers questions in gruntlike monosyllables, his perceptual apparatus is clearly occupied with inner events, mostly of a bodily character. He sniffs, clears his throat, coughs, and bends over with agonizing abdominal cramps. When he leaves, he locks himself in the washroom and one can hear him blowing his nose, painfully, tearingly, for fifteen or twenty minutes. At his home he avoids human contact and spends hours at the piano playing the same phrase repeatedly until it becomes annoying and then unbearable to a listener. He loses his sexual desires for his girl friend and instead masturbates many times daily. His interaction is largely with objects, connected one way or another with sound, but not human sound. Recently during such a period he became preoccupied with electronic music, i.e., sounds produced by a machine. During the initial years of his treatment, this picture was deeply complicated by the ingestion of huge quantities of alcohol and barbiturates. Often this was accompanied by dangerously self-destructive behavior.

Ted and I have gradually come to understand how desperately he needs to preserve a homeostatic state with me, in which I am an extension of him—a magical extension, always available and ready and able to protect him from any danger, internal or external. It is very surprising now to realize how carefully he protects himself and me against disappointment in me and against awareness that I am a separate person. As I stated before, our crisis-laden periods now occur only when some unavoidable event forces him to become aware that his life and experience are separate from mine. When such incidents do occur, he is flooded with aggressive impulses directed toward me and then for a time approximates the behavior of an autistic child, denying in an almost negative hallucination my existence and that of all human objects. During such episodes his aggressive impulses are turned inward, and due to prevalence of primary process there is full resomatization of all his affects, creating the above-described behavior. His libido is also turned into his body and onto inanimate objects over which he has control, like tape recorders or his piano, both of which he can animate or deanimate at will. Yet his tie to me is seen in his terrible struggle over whether to eject me and the obvious strong need to retain me (e.g., nose blowing, alternating constipation and diarrhea, respiratory irregularities, etc.).

Then ensues a brief period of depression. He stops playing with his toys, feels empty, useless, and without energy. It is a state of apathy. During this phase it is as though he had lost the most important part of himself. Gradually he begins to see me, but the atmosphere, the climate, is ominous and heavy. His attitude is one of extreme negativism, in which he oversleeps, arrives late, and expresses a strong conviction that treatment is meaningless and that my interpretations are ludicrous. At such times he is clearly angry at me, but also clearly, I exist. He sees me and does not like what he sees. He may cram the patients' toilet bowl with toilet tissue so that he can flush it and depart as it overflows, leaving a mess for me to clean up. When all seems lost and he has made it quite evident that he will not see me again, he turns up for his next hour on time bringing me his latest recording and as he smiles warmly at me, requests a Coke or some other refreshment.

No one, I am sure, will be surprised to learn that this young man had a mother who at all stages of his development was unable to allow him to regulate her intrusions autonomously. She began his toilet training at seven weeks of age by putting him on the pot periodically. She was always hypercritical, controlling, and at times physically abusive, beating the patient with a leather belt during his childhood. In late childhood and adolescence, her lever for achieving discipline had been the threat of sending him back to the orphanage from which he was adopted at the age of six weeks. While intensely intrusive, she was seldom experienced as "being there" in connection with need satisfaction and tension reduction. She was always deeply involved in social activities, charitable, and club work. She entertained a great deal, and she and the father attended innumerable cocktail parties at which she drank to excess and became coyly seductive. On her return from such parties, she would be irritable, hostile, and ready to criticize, berate and physically punish the patient. A succession of governesses took care of him throughout his early years, during the parents' absences on trips, etc. The family moved so often that he had to change schools six times from his seventh to his tenth year, and never had the opportunity of making friends. As soon as possible he was sent away to pre-prep and prep schools. He began to rebel passively against his mother in prepuberty, refusing to study, lying around in his room listening to music. His choice of musical idiom also had a strong rebellious component since his parents disapproved both of the music and the people with whom his work brought him into contact. His teen-age drinking and use of drugs such as marijuana were also designed to upset and infuriate his mother. His overt illness began during his first year in college. The first real awareness of intense sexual feeling toward a girl was coupled with a negativistic refusal to court her (that is, to take the initiative). He wanted her to make the advances and when this failed to materialize, he withdrew into hour after hour of work at the piano, drinking and taking benzedrine and barbiturates. He began to experience feelings of depersonalization, derealization, and shocklike bodily hallucinatory experiences of an orgastic character. These were accompanied by panicky feelings that he was going to die. This had been preceded by nightly wet dreams without content. He was hospitalized for a time at a psychiatric hospital where skillful protective care enabled him to reconstitute his previous schizoid, obsessive defenses.

I want to emphasize that this young man, confronted by intense drive needs and mounting rage toward the frustrating object, regressed to a state of hallucinatory wish fulfillment (by this, I refer to the shocklike erotic and orgastic bodily sensations). Evidence has mounted during his treatment that one of the governesses who took care of him must have stimulated his genitals and exposed herself to him. The hallucinatory shocks may have represented a cathexis of these early, buried memories to the point of sensory vividness. An identity of perception was thereby achieved, which protected him from his destructive wishes which would otherwise have resulted in loss of both object and self since object and self were not defused. In other words, the hallucinated bodily sensations constituted a denying fantasy. In the same way his bodily preoccupations and rituals helped him deny my separate existence in the transference and protected both of us against his rage.

Strong confirmatory evidence for this point of view can be found in a beautiful clinical vignette presented by Jacob Arlow (1952) in a symposium on *Psychotherapy with Schizophrenics* held at Yale University in 1950. I quote it in its entirety:

> During a quarrel with his wife, the patient had an impulse to kill her. At that moment, he looked at her face and had the following hallucination. His wife's face seemed to be sectioned radially, like a pie. Successively in clockwise fashion, the segments of her face were obliterated until her face appeared completely blank and contentless. At this moment, he became aware of intense hunger and went to the icebox for some milk. His anger was gone.

Here in bold relief, a negative hallucination, an extreme form of denial, operates to conserve the object and self against aggression. We can also infer the appearance of a denying fantasy, a hallucinatory wish fulfillment, in which the bad object is transformed into the good, need-satisfying object. The resemblance of the phenomena described to Lewin's dream screen suggests the possibility that the dream screen may also represent a denying fantasy.

Animal Experiments

By way of contrast, I shall cite a striking experimental demonstration of the immense significance of an optimum degree of maternal stimulation (including delay and frustration), which provides for (1) the turning outward of aggression, and (2) the energizing of the perceptual apparatus leading to the establishment of the distinction between self and nonself and of object relations. I refer to the recently publicized outcome of Harlow's (1959) work with rhesus infant monkeys raised with inanimate surrogate mothers (see also Schneirla and Rosenblatt, 1961). I will not review the details of this work other than to observe that in essence these monkeys began life with transitional objects, always available, never frustrating or rejecting, and never intrusive. These "mothers" were entirely under the autonomous control of the infant monkeys. Harlow (an investigator innocent of and unburdened by considerations relating to the formation of psychic structure) concluded at one point that these cloth surrogate mothers might even be superior to real mothers. However, observed at ages two to six years, these monkey children "are among the queerest monkeys ever." They are almost entirely asocial. A minority of them rage at passers-by from their cages. A larger proportion constantly bite and claw themselves (compare head banging), while the majority present "an unnerving picture of apathy." Hour after hour they sit in strangely contorted positions or huddle in the corners of their cages, seemingly seeing and hearing nothing. They do not clean or groom themselves as do normal monkeys. They do not play. Encounters between such individuals are random and accidental, resulting in no play or interaction or any kind of social responsiveness. Truly, these occurrences are not different from their responses to inanimate objects. Finally, they do not mate.

The scope of this paper precludes my elaborating on such questions as maternal activity and the role of identification in the development of object relations. It is clear, however, that the process of differentiation of self from nonself, and therefore the genesis of object relations, leans heavily on active maternal stimulation which gradually and progressively departs from perfect meshing with the infant's need tensions.

Denial and Object Relations

I shall conclude with some comments on the prototypes, genesis, and major function of the mechanism of denial which I feel plays so fateful a role in the development of object relations. These ideas were germinated in the fecund atmosphere of a section of the Ernst Kris Study Group which will report on its in-depth study of denial separately. I owe much of what follows to the enormous stimulation provided by this group. However, the ideas expressed in what follows are my own and I take full responsibility for them.

Considerations alluded to in this paper and other clinical experiences have suggested that the mechanism of denial is intimately related to the earliest attempts of the organism to achieve relative autonomy from thralldom to painful stimuli originating in the external world—or, more accurately, autonomy from painful affects generated by such stimuli. It seems consistent with our theory to assume that the earliest operation of denial is a function of apparatus, i.e., the organism has a screening apparatus which is capable of reducing a percept to a signal. This signal, if it evokes "pain and anxiety," or rather "unpleasure," is not allowed to achieve conscious registration, i.e., to reach awareness.[12] On the basis of clinical data I tentatively advance the hypothesis that denial is originally directed against painful percepts of the earliest object which might evoke aggression, and hence threaten object loss. Thus, this mechanism plays a special role in conserving object relations.

I believe that hallucinatory wish fulfillment constitutes the earliest psychological model of a denying fantasy. In a situation of mounting drive tension, in the absence of the need-satisfying object, a constellation of memory traces of previous gratifying experience is cathected to the point of perceptual vividness. Tension is thereby reduced temporarily, and momentary postponement of gratification is made possible. Thus, the hallucination defends the organism against awareness of failure of the need-satisfying object. Such awareness, as we know, is ultimately the pathway of crystallization of the distinction between self and nonself, the origin of awareness of separateness. Hence, this hallucinatory experience defends also against premature painful awareness of the object as a separate entity. Such premature awareness, as stated before, prior to the establishment of relative libidinal constancy may arouse a preponderance of free aggression and hence threaten object loss. Perhaps, to borrow a term from Melanie Klein, without subscribing to her timetable, denial protects the infant against the "paranoid position." It also follows that early and severe disturbances in object relationships constitute the most significant factor in the choice of denial as a preferred mechanism of defense. Parenthetically, it has occurred to me that the transitional object at a later stage of infantile development serves in the same capacity as does the hallucinatory wish fulfillment, that is, to bolster the denial of painful attributes of the object. As Winnicott (1953), puts it, it serves to tide the infant over his disillusion-

12 I am indebted to Dr. Max Schur for calling my attention to the work of Granit which demonstrated the presence of efferent nerve fibers in sensory end organs. This situation suggests an early physiological model of the screening apparatus alluded to above as well as a possible early stage in the evolution of the psychic apparatus in general and the stimulus barrier in particular. I am also grateful to Dr. Schur for pointing out to me the explicit formulation by Freud (1900) of the same hypothesis in his well-known "ostrich policy" statement in Chapter VII of *The Interpretation of Dreams.*

ment in the object, permitting him to deanimate the object and to control it. This particular function of denial, i.e., the conservation of the object against aggression, eventually falls, in the process of structural differentiation, to the superego (Rubinfine, 1952).

Finally, there is some evidence to support the idea that a differentiating grade within the superego—the benign, supportive aspect which perhaps represents the structural precipitate of the relationship with the loving maternal object—is able to instigate the use of denial of narcissistic threats in such phenomena as humor, mystical conversion experiences under extreme stress, and so forth. This is reminiscent of how the good fairy's wish undid or neutralized the bad fairy's death wish for Sleeping Beauty.

On the other hand, it must be recognized that the utilization of denial is restricted by superego formation and the appearance of the need for punishment in the psychic economy (Rubinfine, 1952).[13]

SUMMARY

In this paper I have endeavored to demonstrate that certain chronically prolonged, intense inner experiences which are registered and finally structuralized in the psyche as the "bad" or "frustrating" object result in structural, dynamic, and economic consequences for development. Chief among these are:

1. *Structural*
    (a) Distinction of the self from nonself occurs prematurely
    (b) Denial becomes prominent as a compensatory mechanism

2. *Economic*
    (a) There is premature differentiation of aggression out of the undifferentiated energic reservoir
    (b) There results a primary cathexis of the object with aggression

3. *Dynamic*

Object relations originate, in these instances, in an atmosphere of conflict rather than in one of need satisfaction and tension dis-

---

13 Whatever confusion exists about the role of the superego in denial might be resolved by a careful study of the intrasystemic relationships of the superego. Recently Schafer (1960) made a brilliant systematizing attempt in this direction. Also pertinent in this connection are studies by Milton Wexler (1951) on the role of the internal object in schizophrenia.

charge, producing a disturbance in object relations which is difficult to overcome at that time and in the future.

These events are assumed to occur during the first half of the first year of life, thus preceding the ordinary or normal sequence of differentiation of self from mother and mother from others (five- to eight-month anxiety).

I am in agreement with those observers who believe that the relationship with the mother begins at birth, but expresses itself in different ways as the sensory-cognitive-motor ego apparatus mature, differentiate, and mediate between instinct (drive) tension systems and external reality in ever more complex ways. This refers especially to the maturation and development of the capacity for symbol formation, anticipation, delay, and defense, leading among other results to the progressive refinement and differentiation of affects. I have attempted to underscore the adaptive significance of denial as well as its defensive aspects. A possible inference here is that defenses are not just special cognitive tools invoked only by experiences of conflict.

I also want to emphasize that I am not suggesting that object relations generally or normally arise primarily out of conflict, but only that the pathology of object relations is so linked. I am aware that object relations arise as an expression of drive patterns, and that their forms vary with the type and quality of the objects available in the environment. In this connection Lorenz's concept of imprinting (1935) and Harlow's monkeys are relevant.

Yet, in the course of normal development there *is* a drive-need-environment conflict. The environment does indeed inhibit and frustrate impulse. But it also offers objects to the drives, and opportunities (Erikson) for the unfolding of object attachments.

BIBLIOGRAPHY

Arlow, J. A. (1952), Discussion of Dr. Fromm-Reichmann's Paper. In: *Psychotherapy with Schizophrenics*, ed. E. Brody & F. C. Redlich. New York: International Universities Press, p. 118.

Bergman, P. & Escalona, S. (1949), Unusual Sensitivities in Very Young Children. *This Annual*, III/IV.

Elkisch, P. & Mahler, M. S. (1959), On Infantile Precursors of the Influencing Machine (Tausk). *This Annual*, XIV.

Engel, L. (1961), The Troubled Monkeys of Madison. *New York Times Supplement*, January 29, 1961.

Erikson, E. H. (1950), *Childhood and Society*. New York: Norton.

Escalona, S. (1952), Emotional Development in the First Year of Life. In: *Problems of Infancy and Childhood* [Transactions of the Sixth Conference], ed. M. J. E. Senn. New York: Josiah Macy, Jr. Foundation, 1953.

Freud, S. (1900), The Interpretation of Dreams. *Standard Edition*, V. London: Hogarth Press, 1953.

Granit, R. (1955), *Receptors and Sensory Perception*. New Haven: Yale University Press.

Harlow, H. F. (1959), Love in Infant Monkeys. *Sci. American*, CC.

Hartmann, H., Kris, E., & Loewenstein, R. M. (1946), Comments on the Formation of Psychic Structure. *This Annual*, II.

Lorenz, K. (1935), Companionship in Bird Life. In: *Instinctive Behavior*, ed. & tr. C. H. Schiller. New York: International Universities Press, 1957.

Mahler, M. S. (1952), On Child Psychosis and Schizophrenia: Autistic and Symbiotic Infantile Psychoses. *This Annual*, VII.

—— (1960), Perceptual De-differentiation and Psychotic 'Object Relationship.' *Int. J. Psa.*, XLI.

Rapaport, D., ed. (1951), *The Organization and Pathology of Thought*. New York: Columbia University Press.

Ritvo, S. & Provence, S. (1953), Form Perception and Imitation in Some Autistic Children: Diagnostic Findings and Their Contextual Interpretation. *This Annual*, VIII.

Rubinfine, D. L. (1952). On Denial of Objective Sources of Anxiety and 'Pain.' *Psa. Quart.*, XXI.

Schafer, R. (1960), The Loving and Beloved Superego in Freud's Structural Theory. *This Annual*, XV.

Schneirla, T. C. & Rosenblatt, J. S. (1961), Behavioral Organization and Genesis of the Social Bond in Insects and Mammals. *Amer. J. Orthopsychiat.*, XXI.

Spitz, R. A. (1945), Hospitalism: An Inquiry into the Genesis of Psychiatric Conditions in Earliest Childhood. *This Annual*, I.

—— (1957), *No and Yes: On the Beginnings of Human Communication*. New York: International Universities Press.

Wexler, M. (1951), The Structural Problem in Schizophrenia: Therapeutic Implications. *Int. J. Psa.*, XXXII.

Winnicott, D. W. (1953), Transitional Objects and Transitional Phenomena. *Int. J. Psa.*, XXXIV.

Wolff, P. H. (1960), *The Developmental Psychologies of Jean Piaget and Psychoanalysis* [*Psychological Issues*, Monogr. No. 5]. New York: International Universities Press.

AUTOEROTISM RE-EXAMINED

The Role of Early Sexual Behavior Patterns in Personality Formation

RENÉ A. SPITZ, M.D. (Denver)

There are few reports in the literature on direct observations of manifest sexual behavior in early infancy. There are two reasons for this, one is psychoanalytic, the other experimental psychological.

1. *The psychoanalytic reason:* Ordinarily it is not the masturbatory activity as such which engages the psychoanalyst's attention, but rather the problems which it raises for the patient's psychic economy, such as guilt, anxiety, conflict (both intrapsychic and with the surround) and a variety of symptoms. In infancy these problems do not exist. At this age the psychic structure on which they are predicated, the division of the psyche into superego, ego, and id, has not yet taken place. Accordingly, intrapsychic conflict does not arise and neither do guilt, anxiety, or defense.

2. *The experimental-psychological reason:* Little has been reported on infantile masturbation in experimental psychological literature, for the experimental psychologist is accustomed to examine behavior in organized, coherent units, which form a pattern.

Infants in the first year of life, however, mostly are not yet capable of the directed, volitional behavior required for the pattern we call the masturbatory act. At this age a more or less random play with various parts of the body, of which the genital is one, can be observed. This is a nonspecific activity; therefore I speak of this behavior as

Presented at the Panel on Masturbation at the Annual Meeting of the American Psychoanalytic Association in Chicago, Illinois, May, 1961.

From the University of Colorado Medical Center, Department of Psychiatry.

I am indebted to W. Godfrey Cobliner, Ph.D. for his critical assistance in the formulation of concepts, definitions, and propositions elaborated here as well as for his editorial work.

"genital play" and not as masturbation (Spitz and Wolf, 1949). I investigated this behavior on a total of 248 infants[1] who were observed through the first year of their life; we continued to observe a certain number of them during their second and third year. Of these subjects 170 were housed in a penal nursery with their mothers; 61 were observed in a foundling home, and 17 in their parents' home.

In the course of our investigation we were struck by the fact that in the first year of life the presence of genital play is covariant with the subject's developmental quotient on the one hand, with the quality of the existing mother-child relations on the other. The latter was to be expected, as we found in some of our other investigations that the developmental quotient is decisively influenced by and dependent on the nature of mother-child relations. Genital play, however, is not one of the items used in determining the developmental quotient in any of the infant tests known to me. Its covariance with the developmental quotient therefore was unanticipated.

GENITAL PLAY AND MOTHER-CHILD RELATIONS[2]

In view of the evidence of the decisive role of mother-child relations in autoerotic activities, we compared the three above-mentioned groups—the children in the penal nursery, those in the foundling home, and the children raised in their own families. We

[1] The infants were observed in three different environments, of which two were institutional. In the latter we observed the unselected total of the population with the exception of manifestly congenitally defective or sick infants. In other words, the infants who constitute our sample represent the average infants seen in well-baby clinics.

[2] In a paper written some fifteen years ago, the late Ernst Simmel (1948) adumbrated some of the ideas which I am developing in the present paper. He wrote: "In the stage of developing its object relationships, masturbation may be regarded as the infant's first social activity. For through this activity the child withdraws from the disappointing object which rejects its love and stimulates aggressive destructive reactions. In its own body, the child finds a substitutive gratification for the narcissistic trauma, replacing the object by its own genital as an object, and finding in itself a way of discharging object-directed erotic and aggressive tendencies. It has thus renounced direct instinctual gratifications from the real objects, but keeps an ideational relationship with them in masturbatory fantasies. Through masturbating the child begins to resolve its instinctual conflicts within itself without, I might say, bothering the objects; but it is forced again secondarily into conflict with them if the parents interfere with this masturbation which is the child's struggle for a pleasurable release of instinctual tension."

used the mother-child relations as the independent variable, the children's autoerotic activities as the dependent variable.

We found that (1) where the relation between mother and child was optimal, development in the first year of life surpassed the average in all respects, and genital play was present in all cases. (2) In the case of the infants where the relation between mother and child was a *problematic* one, genital play was much rarer and other autoerotic activities tended to replace it, while development, satisfactory on the average, was rather erratic. (3) Where the relation between mother and child was absent, general development dropped below the average, and genital play was completely missing.

These data confirm that during the first year of life autoerotic activities vary as a function of the prevailing object relations. This was indeed an unexpected finding. It has been somewhat surprising to me that it was not challenged in the course of the twelve or so intervening years. The single statement on the subject which came to my attention was that of Jeanne Lampl-de Groot (1950) who in a critique stated that this was not the whole story. I agree; indeed, in the introductory remarks we stated that our study was more in the nature of a description than that of classification; that it was an attempt at illustration; that our interpretations were tentative, and that the regularities found by us were to be considered in the nature of approximations; an orientation, as it were, within the map of the ontogenesis of sexuality and of its phenomenology.

That is my opinion to this day. I believe that longitudinal studies should enable future observers to connect the form which infantile autoerotism takes from its beginning, not only with the relationship between mother and child, but also with the behavioral patterns which will develop later; and in particular, with the patterns of defenses developed subsequently by the individual child.

Indications on this subsequent development are contained in observations made by me during the follow-up of the 61 infants housed in a foundling home. These children were studied intensively for four to six hours per day up to the end of their second year (Spitz, 1945). In the following two years we visited them at half-yearly intervals in order to record their further development, on which I shall report further on. As usual in longitudinal studies, the follow-up years brought a drastic reduction of this population. But

21 subjects, one third of the original population, could be followed for somewhat more than two additional years, bringing the older of these children into their fourth year. Regrettably enough, we were unable to follow our subjects further, so that we lack information on their development in latency and puberty.

Still, our follow-up visits yielded some data on the development of these children's autoerotic activities in the first four years of life. For reasons to be discussed later, I have not published these in my original report (Spitz, 1946). Recent experimentation on infant monkeys has yielded results which are strikingly parallel to these unpublished findings.

However, the direct application of conclusions drawn from animal experimentation to human psychology is not permissible. Caution must be exercised to avoid explaining the psychological processes of one species (e.g., man) with the help of insights achieved from experimentation with another species, particularly when the latter is on a level of minor complexity of organization. Therefore, when in what follows some animal experimentation is reported, it will not be for the sake of *explaining* conclusions I have drawn from my own findings in man. It will rather be as an illustration of a principle which I have always maintained, namely, that the convergence of findings in two or more different lines of research reinforces and validates conclusions reached independently in each of them.

In the present study I will avail myself of experiments performed by Harry Harlow (1959, 1960a, b, c, d, e) on rhesus monkeys and of the striking parallels between his findings and those which I have published on infants deprived of emotional supplies.[3]

Here the convergence of the findings sheds additional light on the problems surrounding masturbation and on its role in the development of man. This convergence of the findings in two independent lines of research permits us to draw further conclusions from them. These conclusions may throw additional light on the problems surrounding masturbation and its role in the development of man.

[3] In the following, a few data on the research, observations, and experiments made by Dr. Harry Harlow on laboratory-raised rhesus monkeys will be reported. I wish to thank Dr. Harlow for his generous courtesy in putting at my disposal not only the already published texts but also some mimeographed manuscripts with the reports on his more recent findings.

Sexual Behavior in Surrogate-Raised Rhesus Monkeys

Six years ago, Harlow began an intensive investigation to determine what factors are significant in initiating and maintaining mother-child relations, or, in his terms, "love." He based this investigation on a total of over 100 rhesus monkey infants, who were "raised" from birth by a dummy-mother, or rather by two. One of the dummies was a vaguely monkey-shaped wire model, bare, from which the nipple of a nursing bottle containing food protruded. The other was an identically shaped wire model, minus bottle, but covered with terrycloth. Through this ingenious but simple design Harlow was able to separate the rhesus babies' need for food, the nursing urge, from their need to cling (Hermann, 1936) and to observe the manifestations of each of the two urges independently from those of the other.

In the course of these experiments it turned out that the rhesus babies, though taking their food from the wire surrogate, did not stay with it, but after nursing went to the terrycloth surrogate and clung to that. They stayed seventeen hours a day with the foodless cloth-surrogate, and only one to two hours with the food-dispensing wire-surrogate.

Furthermore, whenever subjected to any stimulus causing fear, they would seek security with the terrycloth-surrogate and not with the food-dispensing wire-surrogate. Extensive conclusions regarding the nature of orality and "contact-comfort" (Bowlby, 1958) were drawn from this behavior; these, however, are not relevant to this discussion.

Of great interest, however, is the following: although rhesus monkeys are sexually mature at *three* years of age, not one of the surrogate-raised rhesus monkeys had copulated in the course of the first *six* years—this notwithstanding the fact that sexually mature rhesus females from the experiment were brought together with the following partners: (1) "sexually particularly experienced, kindly and patient breeding males," who had been raised normally by living rhesus mothers; (2) males raised on surrogate mothers in the same experimental setting as the females, but separately from them; (3) males raised together with the females on surrogate mothers.

From Harlow's mimeographed reports it is evident that the sur-rogate-raised females simply were completely bewildered by the advances of the breeding males, and did not know how to respond. In a number of cases they became hostile and bit the males. As for the males, neither those raised alone on surrogates nor those who had been raised together with a female on the same surrogate achieved copulation when brought together with oestrous females.

Recently I learned that success finally crowned Harlow's efforts:[4] one of the five- to six-year-old surrogate-raised females was success-fully brought to copulation with a male; and two of the younger, three- to four-year-old females have been successfully bred, I believe, after several months of what Harlow calls "monkey group psycho-therapy."

Obviously, it should now be of the greatest interest to find out how such surrogate-raised mothers will raise *their* offspring. Harlow's further observations will show how much of maternal behavior in rhesus monkeys is to be considered innate or hormonally deter-mined, and how much of it can be considered acquired in the course of object relations—in other terms, how much of it is experiential (Benjamin, 1961).

Furthermore, the sexual behavior of these second-generation rhesus monkeys, after they achieve their maturity, will also be of interest. We would like to know whether the Biblical pronounce-ment, "The fathers have eaten sour grapes, and the children's teeth are set on edge," applies also in the realm of the psyche, as we were wont to see it apply in the realm of hereditarily transmittable venereal disease.

THE MISSING FACTOR

It is gratifying to see my own findings so strikingly paralleled by Harlow's experiments. Like his surrogate-raised rhesus babies, the infants in the foundling home were deprived almost completely of maternal affection, of normal object relations. In these infants, geni-tal play and other autoerotic activities were absent. Conversely, in the children with good mother-child relations, observed in their fam-ilies, genital play was generally present. Accordingly, I advanced at

4 Personal communication.

the time (Spitz and Wolf, 1949) the hypothesis that in human infants the presence or absence of genital play in the first year of life depends on the nature of mother-child relations.

When I published these findings, I purposely refrained from voicing any speculation on the subsequent development of the sexual drive and its observable behavioral patterns in the affect-deprived infants. Nor did I formulate any hypothesis on the question whether the absence of sexual and autoerotic behavior patterns in infancy might influence the formation of defenses. Yet I have, of course, been fully aware of the powerful influence which sexual behavior exerts on the normal development of psychic structure, particularly in childhood.

However, there are limits to experimentation in infants. Therefore I could not create conditions permitting experimental proof of what I suspected; nor could I follow my subjects to sexual maturity, though I did follow them to their fourth year and found some of my tentative assumptions supported. And so I wondered how the absence of autoerotic activities in infancy and early childhood would affect psychic economy and dynamics at a later stage; and whether this absence would affect the formation of psychic structure. Thanks to Harlow's experiments, I do not have to continue with my reserve.

For Harlow, with the help of his ingenious experimental design, was able to perform experiments on the nonhuman animal which supported my assumptions on human development, for he could follow his subjects to sexual maturity and beyond. Accordingly, his findings prove in effect that the deprivation of affective relations with the mother has a number of highly significant consequences for the offspring of rhesus monkeys.

From my own observations on the one hand, from Harlow's more recent findings on the sexuality of surrogate-raised monkeys on the other, it is evident that something takes place in normal object relations between mother and infant which permits the implementation of the libidinal drive in the form of sexual behavior. Family-raised infants with good object relations play with their genitals toward the end of the first year. Foundling home infants deprived of object relations do not, even in their fourth year.

In the case of Harlow's monkeys, where the longitudinal study was continued to the animals' maturity, it was proved that the capacity for sexual functioning was *permanently* and irreversibly damaged. The object relations were damaged, not the gonads. Or, if one would put it in the language of the social psychologist, the relation to the "other" and to the "generalized other" (Mead, 1934) was damaged.

The essential point is that the damage in the surrogate-raised rhesus babies is permanent, for they achieve no sexual activity, even three years after they have reached maturity. This finding throws new light on observations we made during the follow-up of the foundling home infants. In the course of our semi-yearly visits we witnessed no autoerotic activity in these 21 infants. This was also confirmed by the reports of the personnel. At the time the meagerness of the data made this information appear inconclusive and therefore we did not include it in our publication. But now that it is paralleled by Harlow's findings, it appears to take on a new meaning.

It is perhaps licit to speculate how these object-relation-deprived children observed by me would have shaped up in this respect when they reached sexual maturity. If the parallels between Harlow's observations on surrogate-raised rhesus babies and my observations on affect-deprived infants should extend beyond the foundling home children's infancy to preschool age, latency, and puberty, then we have here a finding of major importance from a number of viewpoints.

Up to the present, Harlow did not include in his reports any information on the masturbatory activity of the rhesus monkey, be he feral, laboratory-reared, or surrogate-raised. However, it appears from Ford and Beach (1951) as well as from Yerkes and Eider (1936) that feral rhesus and other monkey males masturbate freely to ejaculation, although the data do not disclose at what age of the animal this can be first observed.[5]

The fact that Harlow does not speak of masturbation in the surrogate-raised rhesus monkeys permits us to assume that it cannot be

[5] In contrast to the male, it appears that masturbation is very infrequent in females. This observation is not paralleled in our study of human infants and their genital play during the first year of life. We would, however, not consider our findings conclusive in this respect, because of the relatively small number of children in whom we did observe genital play (a total of 38 cases). This difference between the sexes, if it does exist in the human also, is not relevant to the subject of our present investigation; though, as Ford and Beach (1951) remark, it is of considerable evolutionary significance. If confirmed in the human, it would also be of considerable significance for psychoanalytic theory, particularly in regard to the male-female, active-passive question.

very conspicuous. We may then ask ourselves what the nature of the disturbance of these animals could be. Actually, their behavior is reminiscent of psychiatric disorders in man: incapacity of contact, of expressing appropriate emotion; anxiety when confronted with specific emotion (sexual); heterotope[6] sexual attempts; and anxiety, hostile aggression, and destruction in response to sexual advances.

This, however, is not the problem which Harlow is investigating. The question he sought to answer was: what has the mother to offer the infant besides food and physical comfort; and what, if anything, is missing in the surrogate mother?

The best answer I can give to this question (and Harlow may not agree with me) is that food and comfort are needs which *must* be gratified. However, they provide only the immediate elements for barest survival. But if survival is understood beyond the immediate, beyond even the life of the individual and includes the survival of the species, then the indispensable element which is so paramount in the real mother and is missing in the surrogate is *reciprocity:* the circular exchange of affectively charged actions between mother and child.[7]

Any observation of the interaction between a mother and her baby makes this self-evident. Take a film I have of a mother putting the nipple of the milk bottle into the mouth of her seven-month-old. He reciprocates by putting his fingers into her mouth; she answers by moving her lips on his fingers, whereupon he twiddles his fingers, and she responds with a smile; all the while he stares at her face with rapt attention. Such little scenes can be observed in endless variations in any mother-child couple. They are the paradigm of what is missing in the surrogate mother.

Harlow in effect introduced the factor of reciprocity in an experiment in which two baby monkeys of the same age were raised together in a cage on a cloth-mother. As a result, these monkeys closely clutched each other all the time and were unable to form any

---

[6] *Heterotope* and *orthotope* are terms introduced by Sandor Rado in a paper given before the Berlin Psychoanalytic Society in 1930. Rado designated "orthotope" sexual activity which takes place between male and female sexual organs in a manner suitable to lead to impregnation. He called "heterotope" sexual activity in which organs other than the genital of one or both of the partners were involved.

[7] Reciprocity is a major sector of object relations. Some of its aspects will be discussed in several of my forthcoming papers.

other relations, to engage in any play, sexual or otherwise, with monkeys on their age level or older. Harlow calls them the *"together-together"* monkeys. What is missing here? Surely not reciprocity—if anything, there is too much of it.

Aspects of Anaclitic and Diatrophic Relations

It is this "too much" which offers the key to our problem. The difference between the same-age monkey and the mother is that two same-age monkeys have identical needs and reciprocally fulfill these completely. Thus they form a closed system, an isomorphic equation in which one side completely offsets the other. The result is stasis, complete paralysis.

The relation between child and mother is not like this at all. The two sides of the equation—the needs of the child versus the needs of the mother—are completely dissimilar, though in certain respects complementary. To express it in my own conceptual framework, that is in terms of object relations: from the dynamic point of view the baby's attitude and behavior are anaclitic. The mother's complementary response is what I called the diatrophic[8] attitude (Spitz, 1956). Due to the infant's helplessness, the anaclitic relationship encompasses the totality of the infant's commerce with the surround. Initially the anaclitic relation is an offshoot toward the periphery of the infant's primary narcissistic cathexis of his own person. Quanta of primary narcissistic cathexis attached to the gratification of the infant's needs are centered through the mediation of the oral zone on the mother to the exclusion of all the rest. This is a restatement, using different terms, of the proposition that in the first months of life the infant experiences the mother, and in particular her breast, as part of himself.

Not so the diatrophic attitude and relation. The mother's relation to her baby, while paramount, is only *primus inter pares*. In the nature of things the mother's relations to her husband, to her other children, her duties and responsibilities claim their share. Her relation to her baby comes first, of course, but share it must. And the mother, being a responsible adult, will also have to devote thought, attention, and time to a multitude of other activities.

---

[8] *Diatrophic* = to maintain, to support.

Actually this does not work to the detriment of the infant, for the diatrophic attitude is a need-gratifying one and, though ever-present, it is *implemented* only in response to the infant's anaclitic needs. In the first weeks of life these arise intermittently in a circadian rhythm,[9] and mesh with the widely spaced, relatively short waking periods. Indeed, one might think of the first weeks of life as an alternation of modes of being in the circadian rhythm—relatively more narcissistic periods of sleep alternating with relatively clear-cut anaclitic waking periods. In the human mother the implementation of the diatrophic attitude can therefore be discontinuous and can be compared to the operation of a circular feedback process.

In the rhesus baby the picture is quite different. While the human neonate expresses anaclitic *demands* during very few hours of the day only, we find Harlow's surrogate-raised rhesus babies (as a consequence of their incomparably longer wakefulness periods) clinging anaclitically to the surrogate mother seventeen to nineteen hours daily. They interrupt their clinging only for one or two hours to suckle at the feeding place—there remain few hours of the day when they are not behaving anaclitically.

Accordingly, two rhesus babies of equal age and raised together will have identical needs, namely, to cling to a warm, furry, living being. Therefore, they will cling to each other day and night, the anaclitic need of the one satisfying the anaclitic demand of the other and vice versa.

In contrast to the surrogate mother, a living rhesus mother has many other needs besides the implementation of the diatrophic attitude. These range from food seeking to playing, from grooming her baby to grooming other monkeys; and all the other business, social calls, and whatever else occupies a grown rhesus monkey. Therefore she offers her baby, besides food and the opportunity to cling, a wealth of action, shifting over a wide scale from approach to retreat, from embracing to rejecting, from gratification to frustration. The rhesus baby partner does nothing of the kind, for he has exactly the same needs as his age-equal counterpart. In the overwhelming majority these consist in clinging. In contrast, the rhesus mother inces-

[9] Circadian is derived from *circa diem*, and could perhaps best be translated as "around the clock," to be distinguished from diurnal, meaning occurring each day in the daytime, not at night.

santly provokes through her activities and initiatives adaptive responses to constantly varying situations from her infant.

Moreover, she is also constantly responding to the baby's initiatives with a whole gamut of different actions, which in their turn require a variety of appropriate responses. Partly through other-directed activities, and partly through activities aimed at her baby, the rhesus mother frustrates and often disciplines her baby, cuffing, scratching, and even biting him.

The circular social interactions which develop in the normal course of these mother-child relations are numberless and infinitely varied. Each requires a different adaptive response from the baby. To these responses the rhesus mother in turn will respond in a novel and, for the baby, unpredictable manner. Each of her reponses represents a push in the direction of the developmental unfolding of the infant's personality—each of them bringing him nearer to autonomy from the mother and to seeking contact not only with the "other" but also with the "generalized other."

Where in this picture the implementation of the sexual drive starts, is something which we can only guess; a great deal of further observation and experimentation will be needed to provide specific data. But we can guess that licking in the vertebrate, grooming in the monkey, fondling, cuddling, handling, primping, fussing, bathing and washing in the human child may well have *something* to do with it.

However, I am *not* ready to believe that bathing or washing, for example, becomes effective for the human child as an isolated action-interaction sequence. It becomes effective only as an action sequence imbedded in the whole variegated pattern of the individual mother-child relations. A good example for the wide-ranging interconnections of such an action sequence is to be found in nonprimate mammals. Rat babies will die if the mother does not lick their genitals for a number of days after birth; otherwise they are unable to urinate. How little we still know of the interdependence of the various systems, somatic and otherwise!

Coming back to Harlow's monkeys, I submit that the surrogate-raised rhesus babies are arrested on what in man we would call the primary narcissistic level; they clasp their own bodies; they clasp their mother. When older, they carry the cloth-mother with them in all activities, and she becomes an obstacle to initiating social activities with other monkeys.

If it is permissible to reverse Mahler's (1952) felicitous concept of the symbiotic-parasitic relationship, we might say that these rhesus babies have transformed the cloth-mother into a symbiotic host. This relation is strongly reminiscent of Winnicott's (1953) transitional object relation; but in effect it falls far short of it. For the transitional object really serves as a mediator, as a bridge leading to object relationship. The reason for this is that the transitional object is used only as a temporary substitute when the real object is unavailable. Not so the cloth-mother symbiote; she has become exclusive, she really *dis*places and *re*places the libidinal object—and this bars the road to all other relations.

The same applies to the "together-together" monkeys, where each partner becomes an obstacle to the true object relations of the other, as a result of the anaclitic gratification offered in the together-together relationship. If object relations proper are to become effective, anaclitic gratifications of a narcissistic nature must be abandoned. This is the kind of narcissistic relation which monkeys raised on the same surrogate mother with an age-equal partner establish and maintain; there is no frustration and therefore neither incentive nor push to form different relations.

The surrogate-raised monkeys who, when grown, carry the cloth-mother around, obviously must provoke in us some speculation about the role of the transitional object, the well-known "protective" animals, blankets, pillows, of human children, exemplified in the popular comic strip called "Peanuts." This features Linus, a little boy, dragging his blanket with him in every activity, mouthing it. One wonders whether children reared in less sophisticated cultures than ours do this also. Little Linus, presumed to be funny, is in effect an indictment of our child-rearing practices. For our children the wire-mother in the form of a bottle propper has practically become the rule. Through the centuries, we have progressively inhibited all body contact between child and mother, through clothing, through the crib, through the campaign against breast feeding. Our most recent achievement in the endeavor to deny any relation, physical or causal, between mother and child is to deposit newborns in hospital checkrooms, instead of keeping them next to

the mother's bed or, perish forbid, in mother's bed itself. This seems
to me a signal victory on the road to abolishing the link between sex
and survival, a major step toward Aldous Huxley's *Brave New
World*.

Harlow's findings prove experimentally what I have stressed for
a quarter of a century: the importance of breast feeding in establishing object relations does not lie in the fact that it assuages hunger
and thirst. That it stimulates the primal cavity, the oral region, is
also only part of its significance. As I see it, the major role of breast
feeding in the establishment of object relations lies in the fact that
it enforces the most consistent, the most multiform contact with the
mother's body. It takes all the perverse imagination of the human
animal to circumvent this necessity, as in the Balinese (Mead and
Macgregor, 1951) who nurse their babies holding them in a riding
position on their forearm; or in the case of the Albanians, who nurse
the baby tied to a cradleboard by bending over him and hanging
the nipple into his mouth (Danziger and Frankl, 1934). This is not to
say that the manifold stimuli provided by the breast-feeding situation
are experienced as isolated from one another. I consider the widely
different, but simultaneous sensory percepts during breast feeding
part of a total experience (Spitz, 1955a), from which single sectors
may or may not be segregated in the course of development.

Breast feeding thus re-establishes for a while the union with the
mother, which was lost through the precipitous process of birth, and
through the sudden cutting of the umbilical cord. It makes possible
the phylogenetically acquired slow and progressive achievement of
autonomy from the mother by imposing and facilitating massive
interchanges between the actions and sensations of the baby's body
and those of the mother's body.

I have pointed out earlier that at the adult level the picture
presented by Harlow's surrogate-raised monkeys is one of severe
disturbance, both in the social and in the sexual sector. Any attempt
to assess these disturbances in monkeys is strictly limited to the
observation of the animals' manifest behavior. That is a rather crude
indicator of deviations from the norm. The information afforded us
by this indicator therefore can only point up the more spectacular
disturbances. In man, verbal behavior and introspection provide us

with far more detailed, more numerous, and more sensitive instruments of investigation.

Moreover, we have nowhere as complete an inventory of the average behavioral development of the monkey baby as that available to us for the human infant. Furthermore, because of his lower evolutionary level, a number of highly complex, specifically human achievements are missing from the monkey's behavioral inventory. These particular achievements not only are of great diagnostic reliability, but represent also highly sensitive indicators of development and psychic process.

A human child who, e.g., in the second or third year of life has not yet acquired speech evokes our concern. He will be considered seriously disturbed if, in the absence of an organic defect, he does not acquire speech in the subsequent years. Thus the acquisition, the level, the proficiency, the form, and the content of the child's verbal communication are all obvious, exceedingly sensitive and informative indicators of the child's normal psychological development and of any deviation therefrom. Nothing comparable is available in the monkey.

Conversely, normal behavior patterns which the human child abandons at a certain developmental stage must remain part and parcel of the monkey's normal adult behavior. We would be gravely concerned if a human child continued his biting behavior, which is normal below the level of twelve months, into his fourth and fifth year. And we would be equally concerned if he were to continue at that age to revert consistently to locomotion on all fours. We would justifiably consider the survival of such archaic behavior an indicator (or a symptom) of serious underlying psychiatric disturbance—and it is irrelevant here to distinguish between its being endogenous or not. In the adult monkey, however, both behavior patterns belong in the animal's normal behavioral inventory.

Thus in evaluating the monkey's level of development, social and otherwise, we are limited to a few gross behavior patterns, manifest sexual behavior being among them.

The fact that sexual development is only a crude indicator does not detract, however, from its value for our orientation. In the human we usually can detect disturbances of object relations and of development long before sexual activity becomes disturbed. When it does become disturbed, it indicates spectacularly that other sectors are also damaged. In my own infant observations I have noted that deviant sexual patterns were highly correlated with severely disturbed or completely absent object relations.

Indeed, it is my contention that in the first eighteen months of life autoerotic activity (in the form of genital play or its absence) is a reliable indicator of the adequacy or inadequacy of object relations, just as age-adequate sexual activity (or its absence) would be in the adult.

Obviously, sexual activities will be different on these different levels. We do not yet possess sufficient objective data to be able to make systematic statements on the subject, *pace* Kinsey. However, in this behavioral sector of the personality we can discern something in the nature of the developmental lines of which Anna Freud speaks; we can trace a line of the unfolding genital behavior patterns. This line should not be confused with the successive stages of libido. The libidinal stages and the manner in which they are reached and mastered exert a decisive influence on the form which genital behavior takes at any given age. The following remarks, therefore, refer simply to the normally expectable genital behavior from birth to maturity.

INFANTILE GENITAL PLAY AND DEVELOPMENT

In a general way, one might say that some genital play should be expected in the infant by the end of the first year of life. In the toddler or the preschool child, a transition from genital play to masturbation is to be expected, the details of which have not yet been investigated either quantitatively or qualitatively.

I do not know enough about the latency child to pronounce myself on what to expect there; I believe that the forms and behavioral patterns of genital activities during this age period will vary considerably, for they are even more highly culturally determined than during the preceding stages. In puberty, masturbation should be considered a normal sexual activity, while in late adolescence the transition to intercourse will be considered as such .

Actually, as psychoanalysts, we have, I believe, become aware that a special pathology is present in those of our patients who assure us that they discovered masturbation only in their twenties. I have had occasion to study several cases of this kind; they were, on the whole, rather severely disturbed. As yet I am not prepared to say what particular form of pathology, or rather, what structure of the defenses, is responsible for this developmental retardation. I need hardly say that I am not speaking of those cases in which amnesia has obliterated the memory of masturbation.

I am aware that I will provoke many objections when I state that reasonably satisfactory object relations are among the conditions which make masturbation possible. It should be remembered that normal object relations do not *create* the drive. They channel it into its behavioral implementation, beginning with the means available on the own body and continuing on the "other's" body. Here again cultural influences play a major role in determining the measure in which the sexual drive is permitted satisfaction on the own body or on the "other's" body.

It should be added that when object relations do not channel the drive into its developmentally natural implementation, or when this implementation is inhibited, a variety of other solutions becomes necessary. The most elementary, the most undesirable solution is regression to archaic behavior patterns on the anal, oral, or even on the primary narcissistic level. We are all familiar with these regressions in neurotics, and particularly in psychotics, where in the more extreme cases infantile rocking and thumb sucking may be in evidence.

More desirable solutions compatible with genital play and subsequent masturbation are available. They may consist in the elaboration of specific defenses, such as reaction formation, sublimation, etc. In this process cultural forces become effective and significant.

It seems that so far there has been no systematic attempt to investigate the relationship between the age-adequate form of genital activity and the successive stages of development. It is true that this question has been approached by psychoanalysts at one time or another in a somewhat random fashion. Little has been published also about the influence of premature sexual gratification on the level of sublimation and of cultural achievement. Some of us do have the impression that in cultures which permit the unrestricted gratification of the sexual urge already in latency or prepuberty, the level of personality development is generally lowered and the activation of higher intellectual functions impaired.

This would not be surprising; I have always maintained, and Harlow appears to have demonstrated this, that the frustration of the drives is an indispensable prerequisite for developmental progress. By that I do not mean absolute frustration, but an optimal level of frustration, a middle road, as it were. "Optimal" applies to the age level at which frustration is imposed, to the duration of the frustration, and to the forms which it takes.

The problem of the frustration of the drive brings us back to the decisively important role of the sexual drive in the formation of social relations.

In Harlow's monkeys we have seen that the nature of object relations determines subsequent social relations. Normal mother-child relations will permit the monkey baby to develop normal relations with other monkeys of its kind—that means to acquire the capacity and the desire to deal with a whole spectrum of social relations with shifting and ever-changing roles. Being raised on a surrogate mother deprives the rhesus baby of those exchanges which make it possible to acquire this capacity. Being raised together with another monkey baby of equal age on a surrogate mother leads to mutual clinging of the two babies. An indissoluble closed system is formed which excludes all relations with others of one's kind.

Harlow's experiments show that a cloth-surrogate is not enough. If the rhesus baby is to achieve normal rhesus maturity, a living individual, a real rhesus mother, is needed. Her interaction with her baby opens the road to individuation, to social relations, and to sexual relations.

The findings made on monkeys are very similar to the findings made on infants totally deprived of object relations. Therefore we are justified in assuming that the presence or absence of age-adequate genital behavior patterns, and masturbation among these, are indicators of the nature of the object relations which preceded them. But their role is not limited to that of an indicator of what went before. Even more importantly, genital behavior and masturbation will influence the future personality. For their presence will interact with other developmental influences and have a significant role for the individual's relations to others.

Therefore, we have to investigate the possibility that in the human the defense mechanisms may undergo significant modifications when the sexual drive is not implemented in infancy, at the toddler age, or later.

Psychoanalytic theory rests on Freud's concepts of conflict and defense. The conflict arises between the demands of the instinctual drives and the obstacles to their gratification imposed by the environment in the form of external restrictions or internalized controls. The defenses are elaborated by the ego in the course of the process of domesticating the instinctual drives. In schematic terms: the domestication has to reconcile the demands of the drives with two factors, an outer one and an inner one. The outer one is reality, including environmental restrictions. The inner one is represented by the demands of the superego (that is, internalized reality). In both cases the outcome may be a compromise formation of one kind or another; in extreme cases, when there is no other way of simultaneously satisfying the drive, the environment, and the superego, the conflict may enforce the suppression of the demands of the drive.

Sublimation is a good example of compromise, hysterical anesthesia an example of suppression. Between the two, compromise and paralysis, there exists a whole gamut of solutions, the majority of them highly constructive. These solutions are attempts at adaptation and include the defense mechanisms of the ego.

Defense mechanisms are psychological devices for dealing with specific conflicts. They arise therefore in the wake of conflicts, and we may ask ourselves what will happen when one of the major reasons for conflict, namely, autoerotic behavior, is absent from the child's behavioral repertoire. What will happen if the main developmental line, which normally should proceed through the successive stages of libido development, is eliminated?

In our Western Protestant culture, this developmental line is the central axis of conflict and repression; it is the motor of the oedipus complex and of the formation of the superego. It is, I believe, worth while to speculate how different the structure of the system of defenses, of object relations, of oedipal development, and superego formation would be if sex activity in the toddler presented no educational problem because it was absent. Obviously this is a question which should be approached observationally, for instance, through the longitudinal study of orphanage-raised children. It should be checked whether such children achieve masturbation and when they achieve it, what its phenomenology is, its frequency, etc. At the present stage of our knowledge, we can offer only hunches in regard to the possible deviations to be expected when masturbation is absent or the tendencies to masturbate are missing in the toddler.

The "Good, Quiet Boy" Murderer

I wonder, for instance, about the overly docile, overobedient, the quiet, angelic, "no-trouble-ever" child. Even during the most turbulent years of latency and puberty, he never presents educational problems to parents or teachers, except for his distressingly inadequate learning performance. Could this be a concomitant of a history of absence of infantile sexuality? Everybody, the teachers, the school, the parents, the neighbors, consider such a child as particularly good, obedient, and problemless. He tries so hard in school, but does not seem to get anywhere. He does not have many friends either, and may be taken advantage of by the more domineering of his age mates, by those who relish an adoring, devoted slave. And then, one day, we read of the sudden, incomprehensible, murderous outbreak of an adolescent who had been this "good" boy.

In school he sat through classes meekly, friendless, without participating in group activities, unless so directed, and without appearing to absorb anything of the scholastic material. He was promoted, because he "tried so hard" (and because our school system considers it undemocratic that any child, however inadequate, should not be promoted like all the others). He ended up with a low I.Q., as a "dull normal," suitable for a trade or for menial occupation. Frequently he was rejected by the draft board.

It is quite probable that the I.Q. potential of such children is not as dim as routine testing results and school reports seem to indicate. But our ordinary educational methods are not equipped to deal with this kind of deficit, where deviation sets in too early to permit the school to reclaim such contactless children for society. Moreover, at the elementary school level, these children do not attract the attention of their educators. For they are colorless, inconspicuous, and do not even come into conflict with society, i.e., with their classmates. Conflicts arise from relatedness, not from lack of relation.

THE "GOOD LITTLE" PROSTITUTE

At first glance, it appears that the "good boy" murderer has no real counterpart in the female adolescent. I believe that he has, in the form of the "good little" prostitute, the classical female delinquent, who often tests as dull normal or below, and who is such a favorite heroine of our avant-garde, angry, Beatnik poets.

I have had the opportunity to study a large population of such female delinquents in the course of a five-year research in the nursery of a penal institution housing delinquent minors and their illegitimate infants. The former clergyman of this institution had reviewed the records of the 200 delinquent girls committed there in the course of a three-year period. He found that over 90 per cent of them came from broken homes. We may infer that the overwhelming majority of the delinquents housed in this institution had been deprived in one way or another of the opportunity to form normal object relations during infancy.

My own findings on these delinquent girls also support my proposition that normal object relations in infancy and childhood are of decisive significance for the development of the personality. By and large, these were harmless, not very bright girls, convicted under the Wayward Minors Act.

According to the proposition I voiced above, in their case, sexuality should have been conspicuous by its absence. Were these not individuals who had been deprived of object relations during infancy? Yet here we have girls who not only had achieved sexual activity, but whose downfall was caused by this very activity! The contradiction is only apparent. In Harlow's monkeys also it is females who ultimately are brought to sexual activity, even though, to quote him, "without enthusiasm or cooperation." One or two of them finally submitted relatively passively to active normal males.

It seems to me that in our delinquent subjects, the picture is that of the slightly stupid puberty girl, who does not know "what it's all about," but obediently does what she is told to do.

Any institution for delinquent girls houses a large number of such mentally and emotionally underprivileged; their absolute unselectivity and promiscuity in regard to their sexual partners are matters of common knowledge.[10]

ABSENCE OF INFANTILE GENITAL PLAY AND PERSONALITY FORMATION

Accordingly, I have postulated that a specific socially deviant behavior, in both boys and girls, is associated with early lack in object relations. This deviant behavior becomes conspicuous in a manner disturbing to the community only when the subject reaches puberty. At that age level an increased autonomy is expected from the individual; he is expected to give up his need for anaclitic support. At the same time, in exercising this autonomy, he is expected to show a modicum of conformity with social usage. In the case of the deviant boys, this leads to conflict with the need-gratifying objects; in the case of the girls, to an infringement of social mores through lack of object constancy and through the attempt to cling to ever new need-gratifying objects.

How are we to understand the psychic structure of such beings and the dynamics which lead to it? I have indicated earlier that with the absence of masturbatory practices a major source of conflict between parent and child has been removed. The sexual drive implements many of the child's activities, both manifestly sexual and nonmanifestly sexual, such as play, games with his age mates, etc. With the disappearance of sexual activity from manifest behavior, the child is not "bad" any more; not bad in "playing with himself," nor bad in playing with other children, for he does not even get that far. He does not form attachments or friendships. He may be a bit dull; but for the elementary rewards of food, warmth, closeness, he will do what the parents want him to do, and he will cling and be described

---

[10] I am not implying that every promiscuous girl, every prostitute, has subnormal mental equipment—even history would prove me wrong. But the personality of the intelligent prostitute, of the promiscuous intellectual, is a neurotic one, and has its origin in neurotic conflict. That is situated at a more advanced developmental level, at a later age, than that at which the "good little" prostitute was damaged. Neurotic conflict hardly arises in the absence of autoerotic activity. In this respect, the population of the penal nursery was moderately skewed, thus giving me the opportunity to observe a relatively large number of mentally somewhat underprivileged delinquents. Our laws and social institutions favor the commitment of the unintelligent. The intelligent prostitute will elude the police more easily; and it is not the bright girls, but the "dull normals" and the somewhat feeble-minded who get trapped by pregnancy.

as a "loving child." He is good in the sense of "Be good, sweet maid, and let who can be clever." But of such is not the Kingdom of Heaven.

When conflict is removed, so is frustration; with that, the incentive is absent for the adaptive development of the prismatic variety of sectors in the child's psychic apparatus. There are no problems to be solved, there are no obstacles to be overcome; there is just the road of least resistance, and the least resistance is to be a "good" child.

A major problem of these children is that the question of the defenses hardly arises. For the defenses are a powerful tool, perhaps the most powerful of all, in the instrumentarium of human adaptation, development, and progress. In these "good" children without sex activity, there is little to defend against, and at the oedipal stage no oedipus conflict is provoked.

For these "good" children the defense mechanism of choice is that of identification; it would probably be more correct to speak of introjective and projective mechanisms in the sense of "magic participation" as discussed by Edith Jacobson (1954). Her lucid analysis of the dynamics of becoming part of the omnipotent object covers many aspects of what I am describing. Perhaps Sperling's (1944) concept of "appersonation" should also be considered in this context.

Similarly, what the Kleinian School calls "projective identification"—the object exists simultaneously externally and internally (Klein, 1948) and the ego may become completely submerged at times—is also relevant to our topic. Here, however, Edith Jacobson clearly demonstrated that these Kleinian concepts refer only to prototypes which operate in earliest infancy. The mechanisms to be developed from them appear later; while processes analogous to the prototypes themselves can be observed only in psychotics and borderline patients. This is in good agreement with my own ideas. Though the later development of the subjects I have been discussing rarely falls into any of the conventional categories of psychosis, one surely would consider them borderline.

Of the other defenses, the mechanism of regression is obviously available from the beginning, as it is so close to the physiological prototype. How far introjection and projection operate, and whether repression is available, will have to form the subject of a special study.

It should be clearly understood that I am discussing only the extreme cases of mother deprivation in man, those which are comparable to Harlow's surrogate-raised monkeys. Bowlby (1960) recently alleged that such cases are no longer seen—an optimism which I cannot share. Man's inhumanity to man has not decreased that much. After all, the term which German ethologists are using for their "stimulus-deprived" animals is derived from human experience. They call them "Caspar Hauser animals"—a doubtful compliment to humanity.

Obviously the overwhelming majority of the cases which come to the psychiatrist's attention are less extreme. According to the amount of deprivation, its duration, and the age level at which the deprivation began, such cases present a wide spectrum of deficit ranging from the extremes of hospitalism to relatively inconspicuous defects.

I am, of course, not speaking of those cases in which the surround suppresses or restricts genital play and masturbatory activity. I am speaking of the *nonachievement* of genital play and masturbatory activity at the age-adequate level, as a consequence and an indicator of a significant deficit in mother-child relations. It is a symptom—and not the only one—of the deficit. The nonachievement of genital play and masturbatory activity is a developmental disturbance which damages, or does not permit, the emergence of one specific sector of the personality. This is a sector acquired through development (in the sense of Hartmann, Kris, and Loewenstein, 1946). The picture of this deficit has often been described quite unspecifically as developmental arrest; I am trying to be more specific. That is why I have at this point taken up the question of the defenses, which I consider as adaptive structures of the most far-reaching importance in the development of the ego.

From this point of view we have to ask ourselves what defensive mechanisms (beside the more primitive ones of regression, introjection, projection, repression, and denial) become available to the children who do not achieve manifest sexual behavior. This obviously depends on the severity of the case, and more precisely on the etiological factors already mentioned: on the degree and duration of the deprivation and on the age level at which it took place.

However, the degree of this impairment does not concern us here. Our problem is whether defense mechanisms will be produced in the absence of conflict. I believe that in these cases of impairment, defense mechanisms which ordinarily develop *after* the first year of life (reaction formation, isolation, undoing, even identification with the aggressor, etc.) will not be achieved.[11]

These are genuine ego defenses and contribute permanently to the structure of the ego and to personality formation. But the adaptive devices we can observe in these impaired children are not genuine, permanent ego defenses. They are impermanent identificatory

11 My distinction between primitive defenses and those developed later is based on a division of the concept of defenses into: (1) prototypes of defenses, (2) precursors of defenses, and (3) genuine defense mechanisms. (1) Prototypes of defenses I consider to be physiological behavior patterns and functions which serve, so to say, as models of later psychological processes. (2) Precursors of defenses are psychologically regulated behavior patterns. Unlike the prototypes, they involve psychological conflict either between the drives themselves or between the drives and reality. However, they do not yet involve structural conflict. (3) Defense mechanisms proper involve structural conflict. This structural conflict does not necessarily require the presence of a superego or even that of a forerunner of a superego. In its most archaic form the conflict may take place between ego and id.

In my opinion, defense mechanisms originate as adaptive devices. However, the adaptive function is not a useful criterion to distinguish defense mechanisms from their precursors or their prototypes. Both precursors and prototypes perform their adaptive function already in the first year of life, and often long before the psychological development of some of the true defenses.

I find unconscious processes the most useful criterion for establishing whether a given phenomenon involves defense mechanisms proper or only one of their forerunners. If what we observe is the outcome of an unconscious process; if it represents an attempt at psychological resolution of a psychological conflict, that is to say, of a conflict between the drives, or of a conflict between drive and reality (for instance, a conflict with the love object) and the outcome of this attempt is a device which from then on will serve as a model for dealing with comparable psychological conflicts—then we are dealing with a defense mechanism.

However, the various defense mechanisms do not develop at the same age level. When I speak of the primitive defenses, I am referring to those which in their whole structure are closer to prototypes and precursors than the later and more sophisticated defenses. From this point of view, regression unquestionably belongs among the primitive defenses, for not only is it present already in the first year of life, but it is also the most readily available device for dealing with archaic ego-id conflicts. Both incorporation and what I would call "ex-corporation" certainly are adaptive processes. But whether introjection is already operating at the early stages of ego development, toward the end of the first year of life is as difficult to decide as the question whether projection is in evidence at the same age level. But denial most probably is available at this early level; and it will be a question of personal opinion whether one wishes to posit the presence of repression at this early developmental level, or whether one should not rather situate it somewhere in the second year of life, as seems more probable.

maneuvers, pseudo defenses, transitory attempts at dealing with immediate situations. Accordingly, they are as easily abandoned as
acquired and do not exert a lasting influence on psychic structure
and character.

Therefore the problem I am discussing is the role of genital play
and masturbation in ego formation on the one hand; the arrest of
ego development, as manifested by a deficit in the implementation
of the sexual drive and in the formation of the defenses on the other.
One may well ask how the individual survives such deficits when
they become massive.

In the animal world, at the level of the primates, the individual
obviously will not survive, unless it be through fortuitous circumstances, such as being raised in a laboratory. In man, Western culture ensures such survival up to the point where the individual can
become self-supporting. In the extreme case, we have then the picture
of the individual to whom the autonomous functions of the ego
are available, but in whom some of the functions on the level of
secondary autonomy may be absent and in whom the higher, psychological functions involving control (defenses, oedipus complex, superego) are lacking.

In these individuals, ego identity may be achieved, but only to
a certain extent. It is questionable if identity of the self can be
reached—again, it should be remembered that this applies only to
extreme cases. In such cases, but also in many of the milder ones,
the boundaries of the personality remain fluid and shadowy. In my
opinion, the identity of the self is worked out through a delimitation
of the self from the nonself. That segregation is achieved through
cathectic displacements and investments within the systems of the
ego. The memory systems and the thought processes are particularly
important in this respect. The absence of firm boundaries between
self and nonself, between ego and id, and the inability to achieve
object constancy explain the compliance, the "goodness" of many
such individuals. Without having achieved a self, they, pliantly and
complyingly, become an extension, as it were, of the need gratifier.

But it should always be remembered that these individuals, who
become an extension of the need gratifier, do not have true object
relations with him. True object relations are the outcome of a pro-

longed developmental process. The vicissitudes of the drives, the stages of libido, the crucial points of development, such as the oedipus complex and its dissolution, latency and puberty—each of these contributes in its own way to the capacity to form object relations and to the durability of the relations thus formed.

The lack of sexual striving proper, the lack of masturbation, or the lack of fantasies connected with it, already preclude the oedipal conflict and modify the later vicissitudes of the drives. The clinging attitude of such children to the individuals of both sexes surrounding them should not be misinterpreted as object ties. It often becomes cloying, and it is precisely this cloying-clinging which precludes the oedipus relation. The need gratifier can be anyone—father, mother, aunt, uncle, brother, sister. The relation can shift from the one to the other; there is no competitor to take the object away, for our subjects have the capacity to become a part, an extension, of any individual toward whom drives or needs are directed, as long as the individual permits it.

Of course, it is rare to observe this picture fully. There are many variations and modifications; these result from the individual history of the child. The essence is that the sexual drive is either not implemented in terms of the genital organ, or, when it is, it is a secondary implementation in the nature of a drive discharge without concomitant psychological content, as would be infantile incontinence or a sneeze. Without such psychological content the oedipus situation does not arise.

In the absence of the oedipus complex, the formation of the superego cannot be expected. There are no imagos to be lost, and therefore none to be introjected. Indeed, the introjects are already there, primitive ones, and therefore not firmly anchored. They remain on the level of need fulfillment and are relinquished when they become frustrating. This explains the extraordinary ease with which such children accept new situations; it explains the shallowness of their attachment and, of course, the ineffectiveness of transference (Bender, in a discussion, remarked on what she calls the schizophrenic child's ready, anxietyless acceptance of a new environment). I have described one such individual in another context in "The Case of Felicia" (Spitz, 1955b). Evelyn, Felicia's mother, shifted without an instant's hesitation to that person who at the given moment offered her greater gratification.

That also explains the "good" little prostitute—without hesitation she shifts to the person who will offer her gratification, be that in the form of a drink, money, fondling, command, or a cup of coffee.

So much for the "good" little girl who becomes a "good" little prostitute. But what of the boy murderer? That does not seem a difficult question to answer. In most such cases, as reported in the papers, we find that a gratification, often trivial, had been denied. The boy was not permitted out of his room; he was denied the use of the car; he was scolded—time and again one is puzzled and bewildered by the incongruity between the frustration and the murderous response.

The answer, as I see it, is that the level of object constancy achieved by these individuals is and remains inadequate, and that their superego development is only rudimentary or nonexistent. The inadequacy of their object constancy becomes manifest in their readiness to change their ego ideal. Their rudimentary superego is a poor guide in making choices. As a result, they are unable to establish a hierarchy in their goals and to relate their actions to the decalogue of the surround.

The mode of their drive gratification fails to advance much beyond the level of the pleasure-unpleasure principle, and frustration tolerance remains low. When a prohibition is imposed, the resulting frustration is experienced as a total one. As soon as the need gratifier frustrates them, he loses his object attributes, such as they are. From a need-gratifying object he turns into a need-denying frustrator, an aggressor, and as such he becomes the victim of the delinquent boy's aggressive, destructive drive.

Conversely, in the girl, the moment the partner offers a gratification, he is accorded access to what he desires, though he does not become a true libidinal object on the genital level, but only a need-gratifying object. And the need he gratifies is not the sexual need, for the "good" little prostitute is frigid.

These considerations have carried us away from our original topic, the question of masturbation. If my speculations can be validated, some revision of our views on masturbation is in order. We will have to accept genital play in infancy as an indicator of satisfactory object relations. This implies also that masturbation during the preschool age, during latency and adolescence, is to be regarded as a necessary and logical developmental elaboration of this beginning. But, as we know from Freud (1905), the role and significance of infantile sexuality is vastly greater than that of being a mere indicator.

This becomes immediately clear when we remember that the child's urge to implement his sexual drive in the form of genital play provokes opposition from the surround and brings him into early conflict with socially accepted repression of sexuality. This opposition ranges from mild, loving "understanding" to harsh and sadistic measures (Spitz, 1952), with the avowed aim of eliminating the child's sexual activity. The child responds to this pressure with a variety of adaptive measures, ranging from superficial compliance to open rebellion, from latent pathology to severe personality disturbances. We are all familiar with the manifest behavioral changes so frequent at this age level. Occurring, as they do, in the period of anal stubbornness, they are bound to be fairly conspicuous; they may be, and they mostly are, manifested in sectors other than the overtly sexual one.

At the same developmental level, at the transition from the oral to the anal stage, a major dynamic shift takes place in the psychic economy. This is initiated by a maturational surge which increases powerfully the quantities of drive energy requiring discharge. The developmentally elaborated drive controls are still inadequate to cope with the increased drive pressure which arises from the newly invested anal zone and also from the harbingers of the incipient genital phase. The drive pressure is reinforced through the resistance offered by the environment's countermeasures to its manifestations.

One of the consequences of the conflict between drive pressure and environmental resistance is that it provokes a variety of fantasies, in which libidinal and anal-sadistic elements participate, the anal-sadistic ones predominating. The conflict between aggressive and libidinal fantasies provokes guilt feelings and concomitant anxiety. Attempts to deal with the latter lead to the elaboration of defense

mechanisms, such as identification with the aggressor, reaction formation, denial, etc. On the pathological side, these conflicts are liable
to lead to eating disturbances, infantile insomnia, and nightmares;
pavor nocturnus belongs among these disturbances: it is my opinion
that there are several developmental levels at which pavor nocturnus
is common. Of these the level of the second year of life appears to be
the earliest.

These stormy intrapsychic processes contribute importantly to
the shaping of the elements which enter into the still rudimentary
organization of the ego. They mark the transition from the achievement of secondary autonomy in the ego to the stage in which defense
mechanisms are elaborated; and through them, the character and
personality of the individual are determined. At this stage one can
observe identifications which represent the earliest outlines of the
ego ideal, and when probably even some dim rudiments of the
superego come into being. It is the stage at which the earliest archaic
images are conceived, the imagos destined to become the content of
the ego ideal on the one hand, and later to be introjected as the
formative elements of the superego.

These all too schematic comments on the vicissitudes provoked
in the psychic economy by the child's implementation of his sexual
drive indicate what a powerful force the child's early sexual activity
represents in the advancement of his development. This is a force
which transcends the individual's personal development, for it also
exerts an influence of the first magnitude on the individual's emerging social relations and on his adaptation to society.

Lest these comments be misinterpreted: I am not in any way
suggesting that masturbation should be encouraged. It must have
become clear that masturbation *as such* is not the prime force in
question. Far from it; I am stressing the role of masturbation in
eliciting the fantasies connected with it, the conflicts which it inevitably provokes, and the defense mechanisms which result from
these conflicts. I consider this process to be among the most potent
in making man into a social animal. With the help of the oedipal
conflict and its outcome, the superego, he is enabled to form social
relations and to integrate himself into the social order.

Looking back at my argument, I find that it has led me onto the
horns of a dilemna. On the one hand, I found that genital play in

infancy (or its absence) is an indicator of the nature of the child's object relations. Genital play will lead to infantile masturbation and to the fantasies connected with it. These fantasies contribute powerfully to the process of personality formation and to the elaboration of social relations. Both my own observations and animal experiments showed the undesirable consequences of the absence of sexual behavior in infancy and early childhood.

On the other hand, I am well aware that unrestricted permissiveness in regard to masturbation and sexual manifestations in childhood does not contribute to developmental progress. On the contrary, our psychoanalytic experience and knowledge indicates that it is the restriction of sexuality, and in particular of masturbation, which leads to such social and civilizatory human achievements as the superego.

Obviously, as always in evolution, a compromise must be found. From the viewpoint of our civilization, the consequences of masturbation without restriction are probably as undesirable as those of restriction without masturbation. Both lead to sterility, be it mental or reproductive.

We have no easy formula for the amount of frustration which should be applied in child rearing, beyond the basic principle *"est modus in rebus."*

Man is a unit born of compromise. But this unit cannot be divided from the larger totality, from society, from culture—which in their turn depend on man's individual development. In essence, man and his future, his survival as an individual, as well as mankind's survival as society and civilization are as dependent on the child's relation to his mother as they are dependent on the way in which the individual deals with his drives. Ultimately, mankind and its works depend on how man deals with his offspring, with his children.

Paraphrasing the words of the poet: Man, "a stranger and afraid in a world he never made," can survive and achieve his destiny only if he is led by the hand into society by the twin gods of Eros and Aggression.

BIBLIOGRAPHY

Benjamin, J. D. (1961), The Innate and the Experiential in Child Development. In: *Lectures on Experimental Psychiatry*, ed. H. W. Brosin. Pittsburgh: Pittsburgh University Press.

Bowlby, J. (1958), The Nature of the Child's Tie to His Mother. *Int. J. Psa.*, XXXIX.

—— (1960), Grief and Mourning in Infancy and Early Childhood. *This Annual*, XV.

Danziger, L. & Frankl, L. (1934), Zum Problem der Funktionsreifung. *Z. Kinderforsch.*, XLIII.

Diskussion der Wiener psychoanalytischen Vereinigung (1912), *Die Onanie*. Wiesbaden: Bergmann.

Ford, C. S. & Beach, F. A. (1951), *Patterns of Sexual Behavior*. New York: Harper.

Freud, S. (1905), Three Essays on the Theory of Sexuality. *Standard Edition*, VII. London: Hogarth Press, 1953.

Harlow, H. F. (1958), The Nature of Love. *Amer. Psychol.*, XIII.

—— (1959), Love in Infant Monkeys. *Sci. Amer.*, CC.

—— (1960a), Primary Affectional Patterns in Primates. *Amer. J. Orthopsychiat.*, XXX.

—— (1960b), Affectional Behavior in the Infant Monkey. In: *Central Nervous System and Behavior*. [Transactions at the Third Conference]. New York: Josiah Macy Jr., Foundation.

—— (1960c), Development of the Second and Third Affectional Systems in Macaque Monkeys. Manuscript.

—— (1960d), The Maternal and Infantile Affectional Patterns. Manuscript.

—— (1960e), Nature and Development of the Affectional Systems. Manuscript.

—— (1962), The Heterosexual Affectional System in Monkeys. *Amer. Psychol.*, XVII.

—— & Zimmerman, R. (1959), Affectional Responses in the Infant Monkey. *Science*, CXXX.

Hartmann, H., Kris, E., & Loewenstein, R. M. (1946), Comments on the Formation of Psychic Structure. *This Annual*, II.

Hermann, I. (1936), Sich-Anklammern—Auf-Suche-Gehen. *Int. Z. Psa.*, XXII.

Jacobson, E. (1954), The Self and the Object World. *This Annual*, IX.

Klein, M. (1948), *Contributions to Psychoanalysis, 1921-1945*. London: Hogarth Press.

Lampl-de Groot, J. (1950), On Masturbation and Its Influence on General Development. *This Annual*, V.

Mahler, M. S. (1952), On Child Psychosis and Schizophrenia. *This Annual*, VII.

Mead, G. H. (1934), *Mind, Self, and Society from the Standpoint of a Social Behaviorist*. Chicago: University of Chicago Press.

Mead, M. & Macgregor, F. (1951), *Growth and Culture: A Photographic Study of Balinese Childhood*. New York: Putnam.

Simmel, E. (1948), Alcoholism and Addiction. *Psa. Quart.*, XVII.

Sperling, O. (1944), On Appersonation. *Int. J. Psa.*, XXV.

Spitz, R. A. (1945), Hospitalism: An Inquiry into the Genesis of Psychiatric Conditions in Early Childhood. *This Annual*, I.

—— (1946), Hospitalism: A Follow-up Report. *This Annual*, II.

—— (1952), Authority and Masturbation: Some Remarks on a Bibliographical Investigation. *Psa. Quart.*, XXI.

—— (1955a), The Primal Cavity: A Contribution to the Genesis of Perception and Its Role for Psychoanalytic Theory. *This Annual*, X.

—— (1955b), Childhood Development Phenomena: 1. The Influence of the Mother-Child Relationship and Its Disturbances. 2. The Case of Felicia. In: *Mental Health and Infant Development*, ed. K. Soddy. New York: Basic Books, 1956.

—— (1956), Countertransference: Comments on Its Varying Role in the Analytic Situation. *J. Amer. Psa. Assn.*, IV.

—— & Wolf, K. M. (1949), Autoerotism: Some Empirical Findings and Hypotheses on Three of Its Manifestations in the First Year of Life. *This Annual*, III/IV.

Winnicott, D. W. (1953), Transitional Objects and Transitional Phenomena. *Int. J. Psa.*, XXXIV.

Yerkes, R. M. (1943), *Chimpanzees*. New Haven: Yale University Press.

—— & Eider, J. H. (1936), The Sexual and Reproductive Cycle of Chimpanzees. *Proceedings of the National Academy of Science*. Washington.

CLINICAL CONTRIBUTIONS

PATTERNS OF AGGRESSION IN
SCHOOL PHOBIA

JOHN C. COOLIDGE, M.D., ELLEN TESSMAN, PH.D.
SAMUEL WALDFOGEL, PH.D., MARY LOU WILLER, M.S.W.

(Boston)

The central importance of the mother-child relationship in the genesis of school phobia was first noted by Johnson, et al. (1941) in their pioneering study of this syndrome. These writers clearly recognized that the fear of school was a manifestation of the child's anxiety at separating from the mother stemming from a long-standing hostile dependent relationship.

Subsequently, a number of clinical investigations have analyzed the nature of this relationship in greater detail. Eisenberg (1958) in an illuminating paper on the direct interaction between mother and child described the behavioral cues by which they communicated anxiety to one another under the threat of separation, and elucidated the transactions that serve to reinforce the neurotic pattern. Waldfogel, Coolidge, and Hahn (1957) dealt with the influence of parental behavior on the child's ego development and the relationship of this to symptom formation. Estes, Haylett, and Johnson (1956) underscored the fact that the child's neurosis never exists in isolation but is "always intimately associated with a complementary neurosis in the mother." They further suggested that since the fear of school is really a fear of separation, shared by both mother and child, it might better be labeled "separation anxiety." Their position was that this term had the twofold advantage of more adequately reflecting the underlying dynamics and of including those cases where the child

From the Judge Baker Guidance Center, Boston, Mass.

This work has been conducted with the partial support of the United States Public Health Service. During the initial period of the study (1953-1955) support was received through Mental Health Grant MH661, and subsequently through Mental Health Grant M826.

somehow manages to attend school, but experiences acute anxiety in other situations involving separation. Although we agree that there is a genuine merit in this suggested revision in nomenclature, we have continued to employ the more familiar term because of its widespread acceptance.

Although these papers have added considerably to our understanding of the dynamics of the hostile-dependent relationship that was first adumbrated by Johnson and her collaborators (1941), it seems to us that there are still significant gaps in the total picture. It is certainly clear, for example, that the mother's guilt about her own hostile impulses underlies a similar concern in the child and is the source of his prodigious anxiety. At the same time the processes by which the guilt around hostility is transmitted from mother to child seem not to have been as clearly formulated. Since all observers agree on the fundamental importance of these unresolved feelings in the genesis of school phobia, it seemed worth while to re-examine in detail the origins and development of the hostile impulses in the parents and children, the vicissitudes of these impulses and fantasies, and the consequent disturbance in their control and expression.

The ideas developed in this paper originate from our observations of more than fifty children with school phobia studied at the Judge Baker Guidance Center over a six-year period. Although this report will focus on the importance of hostility as a genetic agent in the formation of the symptom, we do not wish to imply that it is the sole agent or outweighs in importance the erotic components. The two, of course, are interrelated. The seductiveness which is so patently present in such a large proportion of these families will not be discussed in this paper.

There is abundant evidence that the mother's hostility toward her child is derived from her unresolved dependency upon her own mother. Yet we regard as too simple the formulation (Johnson, et al., 1941) that her rage at her child's demands stems fundamentally from the fact that she resents giving emotionally when she feels that she has not received enough herself. To begin with, it should be recognized that these mothers, in spite of unresolved ties to their mothers, often have many strengths and during their adult years may have experienced periods of great satisfaction. Many held jobs after completing school and looked back upon this period as a time in which they were self-sufficient and free of old family ties. It was during this period of relative freedom that many of these women married, and some of them continued to work after their marriage until forced to stop by the birth of their children. However, on closer scrutiny, and often from the parents' own spontaneous accounts and self-observations, one quickly senses undercurrents of insecurity and patterns of dependent relationships which were subtly or overtly transferred from one key person to another. These included their superiors at work and often their husbands. As long as this dependency balance was maintained (although often not consciously recognized) the mother felt fulfilled and functioned well, but if this external support was withdrawn or denied, the sense of satisfaction was easily threatened and dormant feelings of deprivation and resentment were quickly aroused.

Although these reactions are of an oral nature, the mothers themselves would not be classified as oral characters. The undertones of orality are nevertheless strongly evident in the mother's child-rearing practices, and are manifestly present in her ideals of what a perfect mother should be.

In order to clarify more clearly the disturbance which takes place early in the relationship between mother and child, it would be well to review briefly the psychoanalytic theory of the transition from the stage of primary identification and magical thinking to the beginning of object relatedness and reality testing. This has been succinctly described by Winnicott in his paper, "Transitional Objects and Transitional Phenomena" (1953):

> The mother, at the beginning, by almost 100 per cent adaptation affords the infant the opportunity for the *illusion* that her breast [herself] is part of the infant. It is, as it were, under magical control. . . . Omnipotence is nearly a fact of experience . . . the breast is created by the infant over and over again out of the infant's . . . need. . . . The mother places the actual breast just there where the infant is ready to create, and at the right moment [pp. 94-95].

Gradually, as the infant matures and according to his ability to deal with increasing increments of frustration, his mother's active adaptation to his immediate needs becomes less and less. She actually disillusions the child in the sense of not conforming by the reality of her behavior to the child's illusion of creating just this behavior. The frustration caused by the discrepancy between the child's illusion and the mother's manifest behavior is a powerful force for the beginning development of reality testing. The infant deals with the failure of his mother (and his own omnipotence) by employment of autoerotic satisfactions, remembering, reliving, fantasying, dreaming, and the integration of past, present, and future.

> *If all goes well* the infant can actually come to gain from the experience of frustration, since incomplete adaptation to need makes objects real, that is to say hated as well as loved [Winnicott, 1953, p. 94].

The fostering of the initial illusion of the infant requires an easy unresented and pleasurable devotion to the infant. It appears that some of the mothers in our group were able to do just this and report that the earlier phases of the child's life went smoothly and serenely. With other mothers in the group, anxiety and ambivalence stifled the maternal spontaneity and in its place there was a conscious, labored attempt at "perfect" mothering. The frequent history of early infant irritability, sleep and feeding disturbances bore witness to the imperfect dovetailing of the child's needs and maternal adaptation.

For this latter group the subsequent renunciation of infantile privileges which had never been freely gratified augmented the difficulties and seemed to increase the already-present tension and guilt in the mother.

In the former group matters begin to go awry only when the step-by-step withdrawal of the early infantile privileges is realistically called for. It is then that the mothers' anxiety arises and that they feel increasing conflict. To these mothers, the disillusionment of the child's omnipotence is not recognized as dissolution of an already outmoded infantile process of relating, but is perceived unconsciously as leading to the destruction of the child. As a consequence the maternal active adaptation to the child's needs continues for years to a degree well over and above the demands of reality. It is not that the baby is not weaned and toilet trained at the usual times, but that the mother's demeanor toward the child is to pave his way, remove obstacles for him, and generally to attempt to detoxify the noxious agents, as she sees them, in the real world around the child. She thus fosters herself as an obligatory and essential partner for the gratification of his needs and for the protection against internal as well as external stresses.

The origins of the mother's difficulties, as mentioned earlier, stem from her own oral difficulties. Confused and conflicted by her own needs the mother cannot see the ordinary needs of her baby in proper proportion. The infant's normal wish for relief of tension and for his needs to be met is equated with yearnings of extraordinary insatiability. Therefore, the mother fears that she will be unable to supply what is in fact an ordinary amount of nurturance and care. We repeatedly find indications of two haunting interrelated fears: one is the fear of the bottomless demandingness of the child; the other is the fear that the mother in some incomprehensible way cannot provide enough for the child. For example, one mother reported the acute anxiety she had felt that her child was not getting enough milk during breast feeding, which led her to give it up in favor of the bottle after a few weeks despite the child's satisfactory gain in weight and reassurances by her pediatrician. In another instance, a mother reported a repetitive dream that had occurred during her pregnancy, of her baby crying to be fed and of her own powerlessness to help it. This same mother also revealed how she was haunted by guilt at having missed a single feeding for her child while she was busy with his sick brother. This incident was magnified out of all proportion to its actual significance, and she attributed most of her child's subsequent difficulties for the next twelve years to this one experience of privation.

Such exaggerated interpretations of the infant's needs are an expression of the reawakening of the mother's own infantile feelings of unfulfillment. Although aroused, the yearnings still tend to remain unconscious and are projected onto the baby, who is then seen as the devouring part of herself. The mother now perceives the child's anger toward her to be as dangerous as she had originally felt her anger toward her own mother had been, and conversely as her mother's anger had been toward her. This simultaneous double identification is a phenomenon which Benedek (1959) has lucidly described in her paper on the earliest relationships between mother and child:

Just as the positive balance of transactional processes leads to confidence in the child and to self-confidence in the mother, so we can recognize the effects of the negative balance of the transactional processes in the mother and in the child. The frustrated infant frustrates his mother; by this he induces a regression in the mother which intensifies the aggressive components of her receptive needs. . . . The regression stirs up in the mother preverbal memories of the oral-dependent phase of her own development. If the recathexis of the infantile relationship with her own mother activates in the mother confidence and hope, she will overcome the actual disappointment and frustration, secure in her wish to love the child and to take care of him as she herself was loved and cared for. But if the crying fits of the infant or signs of his feebleness stir up not only justified concern, but beyond this, anxieties which originate in the mother's oral-dependent conflicts, the psychodynamics of the mother's response "can best be formulated by stating that both levels of her identification, that with her mother and with her child, turn negative. This means in terms of herself that she becomes the 'bad, frustrating mother' of her child, as well as the 'bad, frustrating infant' of her mother again. In terms of the infant it means that the 'bad, frustrating infant' becomes the irreconcilable 'hated self'; and at the same time her infant now becomes, as her mother once was, the needed and feared object. Just as she could regain emotional equilibrium as a child by satiation through her mother, her emotional balance can now be re-established only by 'reconciliation' through the thriving of her child. As a child, when the mother was the *receiving part* of the symbiotic unit, her frustration led to the incorporation of the ambivalent core in her personality organization, and now when she is *the active, giving part of the symbiosis,* her infant's frustration mobilizes the 'ambivalent core' of her personality (Benedek, 1956, pp. 405-406)" [1959, pp. 396-397].

From this nucleus of oral ambivalence arises the mother's distortions of the child's wishes. Even the frustration of minor wishes is perceived as tantamount to sadistic deprivation and becomes the emotional equivalent of withholding the breast from a hungry infant. The infant's angry cry falling on the mother's ears is heard, not as a protest, but as an accusation and even an indictment. In order to protect herself from the devastating onslaught of guilt, the mother, through overcompensatory care, attempts to deny the existence of her own hostility and simultaneously to eliminate all expression of the child's anger. Her conscious goal is to keep the child's frustration and tension at a minimum and to protect him from fear, pain, and suffering. Implicit in her efforts is the underlying fear that anger is a nihilistic force which will destroy the love object or drive it away. She cannot conceive of love and anger as coexisting, and there is no assurance that tender feelings that are put aside will inevitably come to the fore again once irritation subsides. As a consequence neither the mothers nor the children have the opportunity to experience the quantitative expression of anger in doses appropriate to reality events in daily life, and thereby learn that the fantasied dangers do not follow. Anger, when expressed, usually erupts inappropriately, and is accompanied by guilt, discomfort, and the anxious expectations outlined above.

Because of their limited tolerance for any manifestation of hostility it is hardly surprising to find that the mothers encounter a good deal of trouble in discipline and control. When a parent acts firmly with a child, he demonstrates that he is stronger than the child and thereby can influence the child's behavior against his will. However, with these mothers firm limit setting with the necessary "bending of the will" is construed as a cruel frustration of the child's wishes and is regarded as damaging to the child. The child's inevitable angry reaction to parental discipline is likewise perceived way out of proportion. Both the firmness (wrongly meaning "hurting") and the child's hostile response (which to the mother means, "I'm not a good mother because my child hates me") must be avoided.

Because the role of disciplinarian is so repugnant to her, the mother finds it almost impossible to act in a properly authoritative manner. When the child does not yield to her requests the mother tries vainly to "reason" with him and implores him to behave. The mother is trying to convey that she is really not angry with the child, but he, sensing the hostility beneath her professed "nonviolence," continues to thwart her. In her helplessness she has no recourse except either to back down or to explode in anger. If her fury does finally break out, it leaves her exposed to her guilt which she is apt to handle by compensatory undoing. This serves to confuse the child even further and adds to his own burden of guilt at being so wicked when mother is patiently trying to do all she can for him. By unloading some of her guilt onto the child the mother succeeds not only in relieving her own burden but also is able indirectly to find an outlet for some of her resentment toward him. The difficulty in control is compounded when both parents attempt to act in a concerted fashion. Each mistakenly sees the attempt of the other to control the child as a sadistic act, and the mother, identifying with the child as a victim, rushes to his "rescue." This behavior effectively negates the attempted limit setting of the other parent and further confuses the child.

This interplay may persist for a matter of years before the actual symptoms in the child break out. It is a period of precarious compensation in the mother-child relationship. During this period both mother and child receive sufficient gratification to prevent the outbreak of the dormant oral frustration with all its aggressive implications. As mentioned above, the child feels the tenseness and precariousness of the situation, however, and closer scrutiny quickly reveals that he has always been unduly concerned about separation, has need for more than the usual amount of reassurance in new situations, and has often felt uneasy about going to school.

The final rupture of the equilibrium, leading to the outbreak of the acute phobia, is usually precipitated by two psychologically important events occurring simultaneously, one for the parent and one for the child. For the child, this may involve a new step in separation from the mother, such as entering school or the birth of a sibling, or it may consist of some traumatic life experience such as an illness or a death in the family. For the mother, the stress may result from a crisis in her relations with her own mother or with her husband, leaving her feeling abandoned and helpless. The coincidence of these experiences reinforces them and arouses regressive wishes for protective closeness in both mother and child. However, because of the ambivalence around dependency, these wishes trigger off strong aggressive feelings. The anger, which is equally unacceptable, is not consciously experienced but is transformed into anxiety and concern about loss and abandonment. As anxiety in the relationship mounts, the child finds it more and more difficult to separate from the mother. The mother, who shares his concerns, is not only unable to help him but unconsciously supports and fosters the manifest regression in the child. By taking the active position as the "protector" of the helpless one, she is able to some degree to ward off her own re-aroused oral-sadistic impulses and prevent a more total regression in herself.

This interplay is demonstrated by Patricia and her mother, Mrs. O. Patricia, a large girl of twelve, developed a fulminating school phobia the day after her twelfth birthday, which occurred several months after her menstruation had begun. Her birthday party unexpectedly developed a strong sexual tinge when an aggressive girl friend took over and set the stage for kissing games. Patricia's reputation for giving fast parties spread in the community in a matter of hours. The following day Patricia became panic-stricken and from that day on could not return to school.

It soon became apparent in treatment that Patricia's mother was deeply involved in Patricia's difficulties. Mrs. O.'s reaction toward Patricia's school difficulties was intensely ambivalent. She condemned her ruthlessly for not attempting to go to school, yet would instantly rise to her protection against the supposed aggression of others, for instance, shielding Patricia from her father's anger by not informing him that Patricia had missed a tutoring session. She grudgingly gave in to Patricia's demands upon her for closeness, yet resented Patricia's hovering around her like a puppy dog. She was furious when Patricia wheedled a pair of skates from her father that she herself had negativistically refused to buy, saying, "Why should I buy her skates so she can have a good time when she just hangs around me and won't go to school." In the next breath, she described with real feeling the sympathy she felt for Patricia in her loneliness, and how sad Patricia's suffering made her feel. It elicited a sense of closeness and a wish to protect her. Mrs. O. was very envious of Patricia's fondness for her father and their mutual pleasure. This became readily apparent in her interview when she complained that father should recognize her own needs and want to give more freely to her. In the same vein she was furious that her older sisters did not give her support. She refused to make even realistic requests of them and kept repeating, "They ought to know and want to give. Am I asking too much? Tell me." She little realized how actively she promoted Patricia's regression, who at this time was physically leaning against her during mealtime and was hoarding Cokes, milk, and other food in her room.

The function of mother's preoccupation with the regression of

her daughter as a defense against a similar regression in herself
became patently clear in the second year of treatment, after Patricia
had returned to school and in general was functioning better. It was
only at this time that the mother's true panic came to light and she
could reveal how terrified she was of menopausal symptoms which
had started several years before. Gradually, she expressed fears of
losing her husband's love, and finally spoke of her fear of impending
insanity. Interwoven with these concerns was massive anxiety about
her own mother's deteriorating condition. This was so threatening
to her that she was forced to deny the obvious recurrence of a cancer
which had been operated upon several years before. Anger at her
cold and aloof mother had always been checked or displaced onto
other targets. With the threatened loss, the anger became uncontrollable and she burst out in rages at her husband, children, and
older sisters.

Only in retrospect did it become clear just how disturbed the
mother herself had been at the time of the eruption of her daughter's
manifest symptom. Mrs. O. never could adequately grasp the connection between her resentment of Patricia's demandingness of her
for time, attention, and even her body, and her own ungratified
wishes for just these things from her own ungiving and now dying
mother.

Turning to the general effects upon the child, we find that the
mother's methods of dealing with her own aggression, notably her
confusion about omnipotence, and the consequent patterns which
she established with her child, influence the child's ego development
and determine the mechanisms he uses in dealing with his own
aggressive impulses. The central disturbance in the ego development
of the child lies in the area of magical thinking and in the carry-over
of an exaggerated sense of infantile omnipotence. As described
earlier, the orderly progression toward reality testing in the area of
his relationships to his parents is not encouraged by the mother but
is actually hindered. There follows, then, a tenacious conviction of
"owning" the mother, and the child acts as if her *raison d'être* is
solely to take care of him. He continues to see himself as powerful
and as important to his mother as she, in fact, fears him to be. He
expects her to carry out his wishes and be at his side whenever he

needs her. When frustrations arise or when the child is faced with the need to share the mother he reacts with intense rage toward her, feeling that she has willfully failed to maintain her end of their neurotic bargain.

Concurrent with the continued illusion of omnipotence—and really the natural consequence of this illusion—is his equal conviction of helplessness when faced with the prospect of dealing with internal or external stresses without his mother. This too is reinforced from without and within. By her own concern for the child's welfare the mother fosters in him a sense of helplessness in mastering new situations independently and forces him to rely on her for continued help in areas which he is actually mature enough to handle independently.

When thwarted from external help and called upon to act assertively the child feels helpless not only on the basis of inexperience, but also in the face of the anger which is immediately generated and which itself is magically feared as having destructive and annihilatory power. The magic then functions as a double-edge sword. Fearing he cannot cope with the anger, he resolves the crisis usually by regressive maneuvers and increasing the demands for assistance from his mother. In effect, he re-establishes the illusion of omnipotence, and thereby obliterates the source of the frustration.

The resultant generalized vulnerability of the ego shows itself whenever the child is faced with the need to act independently. It is no wonder, then, that the child perpetuates the special importance of the mother, and clinically we see frequent expressions of the underlying fantasy that without her he will perish. Although these feelings are greatly intensified with the outbreak of the symptom and with the rapid regression which ensues, even at other times in the child's life the exaggerated importance of the mother is also present.

We have not yet made a systematic review of our cases to study the presence or absence of transitional-object phenomena in the children's past history, but we believe such a review would throw light on the general problem of development of separateness from the mother and help to measure the degree of dissolution of omnipotence. Two examples reveal the tentativeness of attempts to separate from their mothers. One child carried a big floppy-eared dog to school and demanded its constant presence beside her at her desk. The teacher correctly sensed intense emotional need for this object and the necessity of its presence and put up with the inconvenience and annoyance rather than demand its exclusion which would have led to a stormy scene and the risk of the child's withdrawal from school.

In contrast to this child who used a transitional object to an intense degree for protection is an adult who as a child used the thought and image of her mother in a transitional-objectlike way. She vividly recalled her panic in early school years and her fear of being away from home. When frightened in the classroom she consciously and deliberately imagined the presence of her mother at the side of the classroom, and then, believing her to be really there but just out of sight, felt safe. To her it was both real and pretend. As an adult when upset she still occasionally found herself saying out loud, "Poor baby," in the same tone her mother had used when she had been a small child. These unplanned-for utterances were most confusing to her rational self.

The central concern in the child is the fear of abandonment by the parents. The child fears that some danger from the outside world will befall the parents, particularly the mother, and that thus abandoned, he will either die of lack of care or because of lack of protection be a victim of violence from the outside world. This underlying fear is considerably intensified at the outbreak of the symptom, bringing with it an increase in the dammed-up aggressive fantasies which stem from murderous wishes toward the parents. These are experienced as too dangerous, and the child defends himself by regressing to increased dependence on the mother while displacing the anger associated with his hostile wishes to the outside world, notably the school.

It is abundantly apparent why the child has considerable difficulty in expressing overt anger, particularly toward the mother. The characteristic mode of expressing his hostility toward her is to control her. Because of the child's acute sensitivity to frustration, even the slightest deprivation by the mother is perceived as evidence that she does not love him. This stirs up the child's fear of abandonment, and he then tries to control the mother through clinging, teasing, bossing, and temper tantrums, to get her to give in to his wishes and thereby avoid the fantasied consequences. Simultaneously he is really discharging copious amounts of hostility toward mother for not freely giving in to his every whim and for not freely gratifying all his dependency needs. At the outbreak of the symptom the child reacts to every threat of separation with vigorous conscious and unconscious impulses to control the parents to prevent separation from them. The child may or may not be aware of feeling anger toward the parents at such a time, but he is unaware of the hostility of his controlling actions.

As has been indicated above, the mother tends to further the child's dependence on her. She may also readily bolster his displacement and projection of hostile wishes onto the school because of her own anxieties about school. For example, one mother who had recently lost her own mother described her daughter's school as being like a "dark, dank basement" and felt as if she were "leading a lamb to slaughter" when taking her to school. Or the mother may support the displacement by augmenting the child's distortion about his teacher or school by verbally agreeing with him or even acting out against the school. One mother sat in the back of the class "editing" the teacher's remarks and after class accused the teacher of making sixteen hostile statements to the class. Needless to say, this made the teacher exceedingly anxious and had the desired effect of arousing her anger. The mother quickly convinced herself that her child was, in fact, in a hostile milieu.

The difficulty of renunciation and intolerance toward sharing are manifestly present in the relationship to siblings. Just as the parents themselves tend to displace their own hostility and unconsciously encourage the child to displace hostility toward the school, so is there much encouragement of the child's displacement of aggression toward the parents onto their siblings. This happens particularly when it serves to discourage oedipal rivalry. Linda, a twelve-year-old girl, stated repeatedly that she got into fights with her younger sister when she "feels mad at mother, because I know I can win with Judy, but I can never win with my mother." Linda's mother showed a similar pattern of displacing her own anger from maternal grandmother toward her sisters. It is quite striking that for the group as a whole a marked contrast exists in the manifest expression of aggression toward siblings on the one hand and parents on the other.

Although friction, fights, and other elements of open competition may be expressed toward siblings, such actions bring little or no relief of tension and actually arouse much guilt. There is outright fear of parents' disapproval for even having such feelings. Since much of the hostility expressed toward the siblings is really intended for the parents, the guilt associated with the hostile outbursts is great. The child's feelings of guilt are further enhanced by the parents' inability to tolerate overt expression of aggression or feelings of jealousy in their children, even while unconsciously encouraging them.

Much has been said about the frailty of ego functioning in the area of aggression, the lingering of omnipotence, and the proclivity for rapid regression in the identification between parent and child to an oral level, and about the primitive aspects of oral-destructive fantasies that this implies. We wish to indicate, however, that in many of the younger children, this is a neurotic process involving only one part of the ego, and only one segment of the relationship with the parents. There are also many conflict-free areas and strong assets. The parents, by and large, feel positively toward their children and have given them many strengths. In the younger age range, the majority of the children show evidence of this in their colorful personalities, their capacity for rich fantasy life, their reasonably good peer relationships, and their ability to learn well in school.

In other children, including a few of the younger and a larger proportion of the older (Coolidge, et al., 1960) the lines of demarcation between neurotic and conflict-free areas are not so clearly drawn. A more diffuse anxiety is present and to a lesser or greater degree other psychic functions and activities may become invaded by the neurotic process, influencing such areas as learning and peer relatedness. In the severely disturbed younger children the conflicts are held in check by great ego restriction with impoverishment of fantasy life and inhibition of activity with a consequent severe limiting of rewarding outlets. Some of the adolescents who are severely limited in their outlets remain virtual prisoners at home and indulge in a fantasy life paralleling the actual lives of peers in the outside world and talk about their aims with a pseudological conviction. Regardless of the degree of spread of the neurotic process and the variety of defenses called forth, the underlying dynamics with regard to aggression seem fairly constant from case to case.

BIBLIOGRAPHY

Benedek, T. (1956), Toward the Biology of the Depressive Constellation. *J. Amer. Psa. Assn.*, IV.
—— (1959), Parenthood As a Development Phase: A Contribution to the Libido Theory. *J. Amer. Psa. Assn.*, VII.
Coolidge, J. C., Willer, M. L., Tessman, E., & Waldfogel, S. (1960), School Phobia in Adolescence: A Manifestation of Severe Character Disturbance. *Amer. J. Orthopsychiat.*, XXX.
Eisenberg, L. (1958), School Phobia: A Study of the Communication of Anxiety. *Amer. J. Psychiat.*, CXIV.
Estes, H. R., Haylett, C. H., & Johnson, E. M. (1956), Separation Anxiety. *Amer. J. Psychother.*, X.
Johnson, A. M., Falstein, E. I., Szurek, S. A., & Svendsen, M. (1941), School Phobia. *Amer. J. Orthopsychiat.*, XI.
Waldfogel, S., Coolidge, J. C., & Hahn, P. B. (1957), The Development, Meaning and Management of School Phobia. *Amer. J. Orthopsychiat.*, XXVII.
Winnicott, D. W. (1953), Transitional Objects and Transitional Phenomena. *Int. J. Psa.*, XXXIV.

VISUAL HALLUCINOSES IN YOUNG CHILDREN

AARON H. ESMAN, M.D. (New York)

The proximity of young children to the primary process, the fluidity of their defensive organization and of their capacity for reality testing, the ease with which they regress, and the theoretical importance of introjective and projective mechanisms involving the visual sphere in their ego development would lead one to expect that visual hallucinatory phenomena would be a frequent occurrence. In fact, however, the literature contains few references to visual hallucinoses in young children, and hallucinations are described as more or less incidental phenomena in personality disturbances.

Within a period of seven months five cases of acute visual hallucinosis were admitted to the Nursery Unit of the Children's Psychiatric Service of Bellevue Hospital Center.[1] These children ranged in age from two and a half to six and three quarter years; four were boys, one was a girl; four were Negro, one white. In no case were toxic or metabolic factors demonstrable as pathogenic agents (Toolan, 1962).

1. Alice, a six-year-old Negro girl, was admitted to Bellevue Hospital in December, because she had suddenly developed hallucinations of a rat biting her. She was diffusely anxious, crying out, and frightened. After her admission she continued to hallucinate; in addition, she described introjected[2] rats in her abdomen which, she said, were biting her from the inside.

The home situation was disorganized; Alice's mother was a patient in a tuberculosis sanitarium, and her maternal aunt had just

---

[1] I am indebted for the clinical material cited herein to the staff of The Children's Service, Bellevue Hospital Psychiatric Division, and particularly to Dr. Peter Ferber.
[2] See Furer et al. (1957).

returned from one. The family was dominated by the maternal grandmother, a matriarchal, authoritarian figure. There was a swarm of children in the home, all out-of-wedlock progeny of Alice's mother and aunt, all being cared for by the grandmother.

In the hospital, Alice's hallucinosis subsided only gradually over a two- to three-week period, despite medication with chlorpromazine, and it tended to recur under stress. She was initially clinging and dependent, but as the hallucinosis cleared she appeared withdrawn and silent; this was followed by a phase of aggressiveness. Verbal communication was negligible throughout, though there was no speech disorder per se. She often walked down the hall holding her dress out before her in what seemed to be an imitation of a pregnant woman. Psychological test data indicated severe disturbances in reality testing and body image.

2. Later in December, Tommy, aged two and a half, was admitted on an emergency basis because of an acute hallucination that a dog was biting him. He had awakened with this complaint at 4 A.M., after a day marked by some sluggishness and a demand for the bottle at bedtime. He was brought immediately to the hospital, and sent home with chlorpromazine medication. The hallucinosis did not clear, however, and he was admitted later that day. He appeared to be a chubby, well-developed child, who related well. He responded readily to approach from interviewers, but would suddenly grasp his foot and scream, "Dog, dog," flinging himself into adult arms in terror.

He had a mild upper respiratory infection, with temperature never going above 100.4. There was no evidence of any toxic factor, and extensive search of the home showed no significant toxins. The symptoms cleared gradually over a ten-day period. Tommy was the fourth of five siblings. His history was unremarkable, except for a game with his father involving mutual dog fantasies, in which each would in turn "be" a dog and pretend to bite the other. The parents appeared to be rather rigid disciplinarians. Attempts at follow-up after discharge were unsuccessful.

3. Jimmy, a Negro boy aged four years and three quarters, was admitted in April, with a history of sudden nocturnal onset of hallucinations of roaches and snakes in his bed, on the floor, and in his ears. Initially, there was intense anxiety, which subsided the next

day despite persistence of the hallucinations. Jimmy was the second of two siblings; at the time of admission his mother was near term with a third pregnancy. The parents had been separated for two years, but his father, a former drug addict, returned to the home occasionally to fight with his wife, have intercourse with her, and attempt to exterminate the many roaches in the apartment by spraying them with an aerosol bomb. Jimmy had seen this activity many times, and probably the others as well. The day before admission a nine-year-old playmate of Jimmy's had thrown a pail of sand at him, saying it was snakes. Jimmy had believed it for a while and been quite frightened. His development was remarkable for a slight delay in onset of speech (two and a half to three years) and for the mother's frequent use of rigid discipline with strapping and abrupt deprivations "because you have to teach them." She described Jimmy as a very serious, quiet child.

In the hospital he appeared to be a charming, friendly, responsive child, who spoke well and related easily, though somewhat immaturely. He expressed the fantasy that he had a baby in his tummy. The hallucinosis cleared after six days, and three days later he denied having any pregnancy fantasy, saying that he knew only ladies could have babies. His mother delivered shortly thereafter; and when Jimmy was informed of it, he was able to express his ambivalent feelings about it. He was discharged to his family with referral to a child guidance clinic, which reported several months later that he appeared quite well and showed no evidence of disturbance.

4. David, a white boy aged four and three quarter years, was admitted in May, as an emergency after he woke screaming at 3 A.M. that roaches and snakes were crawling all over him. For two months previously he had been waking every night but without overt anxiety. There had been some occasions when he had said, in his sleep, "Take them off"; his mother attributed this to the effects of a recent tonsillectomy and adenoidectomy, and assumed he had been talking about the ether cone. David's previous history was marked particularly by maturational disturbances, especially in the area of speech. He did not speak until age three, and at the time of admission his speech was still immature. It appeared, however, that he suffered from a moderately severe hearing loss, and he was at that time being evaluated for a hearing aid.

The family background showed disturbances. David's father had deserted the family when David was eighteen months old; and the paternal grandfather who had supported them likewise deserted about nine months prior to David's admission. His mother was a rigid, depressive, masochistic woman, who severely inhibited aggressive behavior in both David and his nine-year-old brother. She was clearly hostile to males and intolerant of any masculine activities on the part of her children.

In the hospital, David was at first passive and withdrawn. His hallucinosis cleared quickly, but occasionally recurred briefly. After a few days he blossomed into an outgoing, friendly, sometimes aggressive child, who showed only speech immaturity as a behavioral manifestation of pathology. His play was preoccupied with fantasies of being eaten, destroyed, and flushed down the toilet. He was observed for a year after discharge, and hallucinations did not recur.

5. Daniel, a Negro boy, was six and three quarter years when he was admitted to the Children's Service in June, following the onset of an acute hallucinatory episode involving the perception of a shadow, further defined as a butterfly. This was reported to be the second hallucinatory episode in this child's life; the first had occurred one and a half years earlier, shortly after the birth of his youngest brother. At that time he awoke from a nightmare about a rocket to see the rocket flying around his room, through his axilla and cut his back. It appears to have occurred during a clouded state of consciousness, and may well have been part of a pavor nocturnus. The present episode occurred after his mother had slapped him in the face with a wet washcloth following his persistent failure to tie his shoes. He promptly saw a shadow, which became an orange and black butterfly which flew at him and, he feared, was about to take his "pa—clothes off" (as he told it on admission). He was extremely anxious and unable to sleep. His hallucinations persisted during his first day at the hospital, but then cleared and did not return. He appeared anxious and impulsive at first, but soon quieted, related well, spoke freely and easily, played well and with sustained attention, and revealed a rich fantasy life largely preoccupied with mutilation and veiled sexuality.

About the hallucinations, he reiterated that he feared the butterfly would pull his clothes off. The middle part of the butterfly looked like a snake, and this was the part that would do it, though he did not know how. When asked with what it would do it, he said, "With nothing."[3] In his play, he constantly removed parts from toys and dolls, showing considerable anxiety at the possibility that they could not be restored. He did not like the woman doll because "she's ugly and has long hair." His three wishes were for a gun, a cap pistol, and a popgun. He once picked up a Negro doll baby and said, "He's all covered with kaky. He's crying. Somebody hit him. His mother hit him. This is me."

Daniel's mother, a thirty-three-year-old Negro woman, was described as compulsive, narcissistic, and alternately seductive and punitive toward Daniel. She habitually went about the home nude before the children. Daniel was conceived out of wedlock with a mulatto father. Mrs. J. was disappointed that he was dark like her rather than light like his father. The relationship to Daniel's father terminated before Daniel's birth, but two years later she met Mr. J., a white man, by whom she shortly became pregnant, again out of wedlock. However, Mr. J. offered to marry her, and she reluctantly accepted. Eight years her junior, he was described as passive, dependent, and chronically depressed.

Daniel was born prematurely by Caesarian section. After his period of incubation his mother was warned about the possibility of retrolental fibroplasia, and though he never showed any evidence of visual difficulty, Mrs. J. was quite preoccupied about this and frequently took him for eye examinations. Mrs. J.'s initial reaction to him was quite negative. He was hyperactive from early infancy. She went to work when he was seven months old, and he was cared for by an aunt who began toilet training at nine months. When he was twelve months old Mrs. J. was hospitalized for removal of a fibroid tumor, and Daniel was boarded out until sixteen months of age. On his return he was nervous and began having nightmares, which continued to the time of admission, increasing in frequency at age four following the birth of a younger brother. Shortly after the birth of his second brother, when Daniel was five years old, the first quasi-hallucinatory episode occurred; at that time he also developed fears of bugs, the dark, and separation from mother. Mrs. J. said she had

_____
[3] As pointed out by Lewin (1948), this strongly suggests the hallucinated image of the female genital.

never seen him masturbate and was sure he did not because "he knows I wouldn't let him get away with it." Daniel was very frightened of school. Toward his siblings he was overprotective, to the extent of happily beating up younger children who picked on them. At the same time, he preferred to be with younger children because, his mother said, "He's so mild and sensitive that he's pushed around by kids his own age."

Daniel was discharged in his mother's custody, and was referred to the outpatient department for psychotherapy. Mrs. J. did not, however, follow up this referral.

DISCUSSION

As indicated earlier, the psychiatric literature on visual hallucinoses in childhood is scant.

Weiner (1961), after remarking that "visual and tactile hallucinatory states . . . are quite uncommon in the absence of delirium associated with intoxication or infection," offers a brief description of just such a case, which resembles those cited here in many respects. He explains such phenomena as "attempts to deal with internal emotional stimuli by translating them into concrete perceptual material that will allow the child to utilize his previously learned stimulus-response patterns"—i.e., as regressive phenomena in response to traumatic conflict.

Several authors, among them Despert (1948), Bender and Lipkowitz (1940), Toolan (1962), have discussed hallucinations in children, but the bulk of their material deals with auditory hallucinations, which are indeed far more common. The paper by Bender and Lipkowitz is of particular interest, however, because it considers the clinical phenomenon seen in our group, namely, the greater incidence of hallucinations in Negro than in white children. Though conceding that the studied population (similar in composition to this one) is skewed in the direction of economically and culturally deprived Negro children, they nonetheless state that "the fantasy life of the Negro child appears to be richer" and that "the Negro child is constitutionally endowed with a more facile fantasy life." The available evidence does not sustain these suggestions. What appears to be more probable is that many Negro children, due to

well-defined sociocultural influences, suffer from significant deviations in ego development, particularly in the area of reality testing
and impulse control, so that the pathways to direct discharge and
loss of differentiation are more open to them. There is nothing to
suggest constitutional racial differences in "fantasy life," but much
to suggest cultural differences in the mode of its expression.

Brenner (1951) offers a fascinating account and interpretation
of a case descriptively similar to some of those reported here. He
finds, as in our cases, that concerns about pregnancy and wishes to
have a baby were crucial predisposing fantasies, and that his subject's hallucinated bugs represented the little girl's conception of the
"male seed." According to Brenner, it was the knowledge of the facts
of penile penetration that precipitated the child's hallucinosis. Nothing is said of possible visual exposure to primal-scene experiences,
but the cultural background of the family makes this less likely than
in our cases.

Modell (1958) has recently reviewed the psychoanalytic contributions to the theory of hallucinations, beginning with Freud's earliest
references to the subject in his letters to Fliess (Freud, 1887-1902).
Of particular interest here are Freud's observations in "A Metapsychological Supplement to the Theory of Dreams" (1917); he said
that the voices of the schizophrenic reflect a hypercathexis of the
verbal representation of objects. As Freud points out elsewhere
(1900), such excitation leads to overpowering of the censorship;
"the unconscious excitations overwhelm the Pcs., . . . [and] forcibly
bring about hallucinatory regression. . . ." These conceptualizations,
though primarily related to auditory phenomena, can, as will be seen
later, readily be applied to the visual hallucinations under consideration here.

Bychowski (1956) sees the hallucinated voice as the projection
of a previously introjected object. In his view, the patient's basic
problem is the reconciliation of the wish to cling to the object
and the concomitant wish to destroy it. The problem is solved by
a split in the ego and a projection of the ambivalently cathected
introject. Modell, too, regards the hallucinated voice as a projection
of the internalized parental object. He emphasizes particularly the
importance of the primal-scene experiences in the genesis of the ego
disturbance, with the hallucination representing an attempt at mas-

tery by re-creating perceptually the primal scene in relation to internalized objects.

Isakower (1939) describes the role of the auditory sphere in the development of the superego, which, following Freud, he suggests, is projected and raised to hallucinatory intensity in auditory hallucinations. It appears that in our cases it was not the auditorily determined superego introjects, but visually determined ego introjects that were so treated. This is consistent with the observations of Modell (1958), who found it difficult to differentiate ego and superego processes in the hallucinations of his patients.

Of the five cases described in this report, only one seemed to be a clinically psychotic child (Toolan, 1962). In the other four instances, the hallucinosis appeared to be a manifestation of an acute anxiety state. In two instances, it was manifestly associated with pregnancy fantasies; one of these children had been almost continually exposed to pregnancies in her aunt and mother, while the mother of the other child was pregnant at the time of the child's acute illness. In these instances, there were anxiety-laden, ambivalent identifications with the pregnant mother and projected hostile fantasies toward her and the anticipated younger sibling who was seen as dangerous and menacing the child's status in the family.

Daniel, our best-studied case, exemplifies many of the common features of the group. There was a history of repeated early visual exposure to sexual scenes and adult genital organs, with, I suggest, a consequent conflict-laden hypercathexis of the visual sphere of perception. The menacing object was in many ways suggestively symbolic of the female genital. Quite prominent in the patient's history were symptomatic or behavioral reactions to the birth of several younger siblings. The acute onset of his symptoms represented an acute ego repression clearly related to an onslaught of anxiety-laden rage directed at the mother. This was defensively projected in the form of a visually perceived symbolic representation of the previously introjected aggressive, castrating mother. (In the case of Tommy, the introject appeared to be that of the father.)

Though adequate historical information regarding the role of the visual sphere in the development of these children was not obtainable, in at least three cases there were indications of maturational irregularities involving certain essential ego functions, which suggest at least the possibility of an imbalance in the range of perceptual modalities in favor of the visual. This was enhanced in the case of Daniel by the mother's preoccupation with his eyes, plus the above-mentioned experientially determined hypercathexis common to the group. David, on the other hand, with his auditory deficiency, may have used visual modalities in a compensatory fashion.

In any event, it is likely that both constitutional and experiential determinants of development of the normally autonomous function of visual perception play a role in the predisposition of these children to experience their reprojected destructive introjects in the visual sphere. This is parallel with Freud's previously cited formulation regarding auditory hallucinosis; *in these children, however, precipitated by overwhelming excitation into acute ego regression, it was the visual, rather than the verbal representation of objects that was hypercathected to hallucinatory intensity.*

Though it is not the purpose of this paper to deal with the management of hallucinatory states in children, one observation on this subject is necessary. In several of our cases, attempts had been made by misguided emergency-room personnel to "dispel" or "drive away" the hallucinated animals. Intended to reassure the child, such a procedure serves only further to impair his reality testing and to confirm his fears. When a supposedly authoritative adult appears to share his perceptual experience, the anxious child has little alternative to accepting its reality. The adult should rather firmly but comfortingly assure the child that nothing is there, that his experience is the product of anxiety, and that it will pass. Though it may not serve fully to reassure the child, such a stand will at least help to reinforce reality testing rather than to undermine it.

Summary

Five cases of acute visual hallucinosis in young children have been observed within a relatively short time. The hallucinoses appeared to represent acute regressive reactions in response to overwhelming anxiety. Restitutive efforts involved the projection of a destructive parental introject, which was then perceived visually. Background factors for the choice of visual perception of the projected object are discussed.

BIBLIOGRAPHY

Bender, L., & Lipkowitz, H. (1940), Hallucinations in Children. *Amer. J. Orthopsychiat.*, X.

Brenner, C. (1951), A Case of Childhood Hallucinosis. *This Annual*, VI.

Bychowski, G. (1956), The Ego and the Introjects. *Psa. Quart.*, XXV.

Despert, J. L. (1948), Delusional and Hallucinatory Experiences in Children. *Amer. J. Psychiat.*, CIV.

Freud, S. (1887-1902), *The Origins of Psychoanalysis.* New York: Basic Books, 1954.

—— (1900), The Interpretation of Dreams. *Standard Edition*, V. London: Hogarth Press, 1953.

—— (1917), A Metapsychological Supplement to the Theory of Dreams. *Standard Edition*, XIV. London: Hogarth Press, 1955.

Furer, M., Horowitz, M., Tec, L., & Toolan, J. (1957), Internalized Objects in Children. *Amer. J. Orthopsychiat.*, XXVII.

Isakower, O. (1939), The Exceptional Position of the Auditory Sphere. *Int. J. Psa.*, XX.

Lewin, B. D. (1948), The Nature of Reality; the Meaning of Nothing; with an Addendum on Concentration. *Psa. Quart.*, XVII.

Modell, A. (1958), Theoretical Implications of Hallucinatory Experiences in Schizophrenia. *J. Amer. Psa. Assn.*, VI.

Toolan, J. (1962), Hallucinations in Children and Adolescents. Unpublished manuscript.

Weiner, M. F. (1961), Hallucinations in Children. *Arch. Gen. Psychiat.*, V.

EGO SYNTHESIS OF A LIFE-THREATENING ILLNESS IN CHILDHOOD

JEROME KAVKA, M.D. (Chicago)

Despite numerous studies in which psychoanalytic insights have been brought to bear upon the relation between illness and character development, students of child psychopathology, including Anna Freud, have alluded to the absence of exact observations on the psychological effects of illness. In a recent panel on the psychological consequences of physical illness in childhood, Edith Buxbaum offered a partial explanation: people, in general, do not like handicapped children or adults. This attitude is based on a deep-seated horror of and resentment against illness, feelings which are also expressed by parents toward the sick child. In support of this she noted how often curative measures take a restrictive form. Similar attitudes, she suggested, may account for the reluctance of psychoanalysts to observe the effects of bodily illness (see Calef, 1959).

The following report is based on the supposition that by a detailed study of the evolution of the transference neurosis, the analyst can secure reliable information regarding the integration and synthesis of physical events in the life of the child as reflected in the ego's adaptation to these events. Re-enactments and reconstructions of extreme traumas, such as serious physical illness, may provide instructive examples not only of ego synthesis but of the related interpersonal transactions, and thus help to affirm or modify current theories of character development and neurosis.

The psychoanalytic treatment of an adolescent boy revealed the mechanisms used by his ego to integrate a life-threatening illness, which began at the height of the oedipal period of development. The combined traumatic assault of the illness, the required medical treatments, and the alarm reactions of his parents were superimposed

Presented before the Chicago Council of Child Psychiatry, October 11, 1961.

on an unconscious castration threat. The obvious danger to his life was in the center of the parents' conscious interest. This emphasis as well as their consequent attitudes and behavior were later used by the patient as the main, though preconscious, focus in the evolution of the transference neurosis. In other words, there was a constant concern about physical health and disease and preoccupations with disaster and death. The data of the treatment ultimately tended to confirm the classical theory that castration anxiety underlies the fear of death.

SUMMARY OF DEVELOPMENTAL HISTORY

A highly intelligent nineteen-year-old university student was referred to me because of decreased interest and poor performance in academic work which seriously threatened his career. According to his parents, he was chronically irritable and doubted his career choice; but their main concern was that he engaged in daring physical activities, such as extremely long walks in bad weather, lifting heavy weights, etc., which could result in the flare-up of a chronic disease. The parents as well as the referring analyst informed me that a diagnosis of reticulum cell sarcoma (Hodgkin's disease) had been made following the biopsy of an enlarged lymph node when the patient was five years old. He had received intensive X-ray radiation and nitrogen-mustard treatments at the time and again at the age of eleven years. At the time of referral, there had been no recurrence for a period of eight years. The patient had never been told the truth about his illness. When one of his vertebrae was involved during puberty, he was told he had osteomyelitis, which euphemism he would use to refer to the events of his illness. Presumably, he was not conscious of the gravity of his past illness.

After an evaluation I agreed to accept the patient for psychotherapy, eventually perhaps for psychoanalysis, under one condition: since I had been informed of the diagnosis, I would be ruled by honesty and discretion in my conduct with him; while I would make no effort to reveal unsolicited information to him, should he directly ask me what I knew, I would feel obliged to tell him what I had been told. The possible consequences of panic, depression, and rage to the parents were discussed with them. They agreed to the condition and the therapy proceeded.

The dormant physical illness with its implications of fatality presented, along with the compact made with the parents, possible countertransference difficulties. For the most part, however, I felt comfortable in my dealings with the patient. While sensitive and empathic at more intense periods, I did not become helplessly involved with sympathy and identifications in matters pertaining to the illness. There were no direct manifestations of the disease process during the four and a half years of the treatment.

I shall summarize the patient's developmental history as it unfolded in the treatment and shall focus mainly on the important memories and the fantasies associated with them.

The patient had distinctive physical features: he was thin, pale, and had a slight hunch in the upper back due to the spinal involvement. He was gawky in his movements, and, in general, gave the impression of an unsturdy physique. Not until later in the treatment did the bespectacled scholar substitute gazing at girls on his way to the office for reading the books constantly in his hand.

Frightened at first, he assumed a cautious, if respectful attitude. He resented his parents for having suggested psychiatric treatment and viewed his referral as another step in his mother's campaign to restrain his independence. Nevertheless, he soon avowed his dissatisfaction with himself, and expressed a desire to become comfortably independent of his parents, to do well in school, establish a career, and to have more satisfying relations with his peers. As he talked, his confidence in me increased to the point where he was soon able to confess perverse fantasies and fetishistic preoccupations, which he preferred to communicate in a written note:

> When I was a rather small boy, certainly before I was ten years old, I became obsessed with the horror of suffocation in general and hanging in particular. It was really a pseudo-erotic stimulation, and has persisted until the present with, I think, less poignancy. As a matter of fact, this realization was the original reason why I came to despise capital punishment. This is my own declaration to myself that my mind can discipline its own impulses.
>
> My strongest memory, which may have something to do with this, is of the time that my mother took to telling me "go hang yourself" when I irritated her. She says this was when I was eleven. I thought it was sooner. She still thinks she was righteous.

Like the other, this preoccupation has not affected my interest in women. However, I have only dreamed of girls twice or so in my life, and neither of these dreams was a true "erotic" dream since they provoked no discharge. My true erotic dreams have all been concerned with this perversion. However, even in dreams, the sadism has been muted. Sometimes it is masochistically expressed.

My other claim on hell is, since childhood, in various forms, depending on age, a fascination with handkerchiefs, especially neckerchiefs, which brings this into some sort of relation to the above. As a boy, I used to watch Westerns. At that time, the neckerchief was a symbol of masculinity. Since puberty, the significance has reversed and preserved itself, depending on the circumstances. When I was in kindergarten or first grade, I refused to carry a handkerchief, to my mother's chagrin which is always ready at hand. One day, when she and my sister escorted me to school, I was forced to carry a woman's handkerchief, which mortified me. That is all I can recall relating to this.

It seemed to me that this form of communication, with its exhibitionistic display of language and forced intellectual style, represented during this early phase of treatment a carry-over from the academic sphere and implicated the treatment in a student-teacher relationship with overtones of supplication for acceptance. The content, nevertheless, revealed his intelligence, his attempt to establish psychological connections, and some capacity for insight. One may note the masculine-feminine struggle and the anticipatory association between male pride, castration anxiety, and, as he called it, mortification. The tone of the communication, while tinged with masochistic self-pity, was assertive and individualistic and contained unveiled antagonism to his mother.

He cooperated during the exploratory phase and revealed that he had been somewhat prepared for help from outside the family, having for years turned to a physician friend of his parents for guidance and inspiration, which he felt he had now outgrown. As he looked back on it, he now regarded this guidance as overmoralistic, pushy, and too reminiscent of his parents' excessive stimulation. This evaluation seemed to express a certain wariness concerning the possible influence of his parents on me; it also reflected some degree of conscience anxiety which was apt to be mobilized in the permissive environment of the office.

He freely criticized his parents, especially his mother, who, he said, "babied" him. In this he was not incorrect, although in his rationalizations he obviously overlooked both his own provocativeness and his submissiveness. During later, critical phases of the treatment, the mother, a compulsive character with hysterical qualities and a whining voice, often sought help from me, especially when the patient was "acting up" with her. Separation from him increased her fears for his health. Yet she was able to leave on her occasional vacations with the feeling that he was in safe hands.

The father was a highly successful professional man of compulsive character make-up, a sensible and kindly person, if formal and stiff. Two recurrent notions were often associated with the father: as a youngster the patient was discouraged from entering his father's study and this had disappointed him; he could not imagine his father "unbending enough" to enjoy sex.

The only sibling, an older sister, left for an out-of-town college when the patient was eight or nine and returned when he was thirteen. She left home permanently shortly thereafter to marry and raise a family. She was remembered mainly as being seductive inasmuch as she and mother often walked about the house half-dressed and without regard for the excitement which this caused in him.

In reviewing the history as it emerged, piecemeal, throughout the analysis, traumatic incidents and screen memories of traumas dominated the dated remembrances. The few preoedipal memories consisted essentially of some excitement around a miscarriage of the mother when he was between one and three years of age. Details remained obscure, but fears and anxiety related to blood were relived and recalled. Reconstructions and some memories revealed an ambivalent attachment to a "nanny" who cared for him between the ages of one and six years and who was responsible for his toilet training. Considerable urinary and anal aggression was expressed, reconstructed, and re-enacted in the course of the analysis. His expletives were urinary or anal (pissed off, shit) until later in the analysis when they assumed a more phallic, aggressive character.

Beginning with age four years, fears of expanding objects such as balloons and umbrellas screened anxiety over erections. There was a recollection of tumescence at age five when he had masturbated in his mother's presence; she had voiced various warnings to stop and told him to "go hang himself." On one occasion she struck him for masturbating, and he was filled with murderous rage. Fears of a magician and his kerchiefs necessitated his fleeing home from school at the onset of latency. Also, an invitation to a father-and-son dinner aroused fears in him that he and his father would be hung when they got there.

A number of memories dating from the ages of five to six years appeared to be screens for the biopsy of a lymph node which had resulted in the diagnosis of his physical illness and fearsome radiation therapy. He recalled his parents' fears for his life when he had what he referred to as "measles" characterized by "lumps." Measles was obviously a euphemism for the enlarged nodes, just as osteomyelitis later became the euphemism for the spinal involvement. His fright of the radiation machines was expressed in oral-cannibalistic anxieties as he recalled being taken to a hospital where he seemed to have seen "a big cruel turtle eating a dead bird." Exposed to separation and danger in the hospital, the idealized mother came to his aid in a fantasy; "I am a goldfish in a bowl of cold water. A beautiful girl comes to the edge of the water and talks to me and I talk back."

Between the ages of six and nine years, and following his hospitalization, loving memories of both parents emerged, including nostalgic reminiscences of summer vacations and the warmth of sleeping beside his mother. These pleasant memories concealed some anxiety since he sought his mother's side because of nightmares. Also, he recalled embarrassment over her return of his affection. The latency memories revealed a fascination with a hanging in a Western movie he attended with his mother at age seven. The theme of a Western-style hanging later became the framework of pubertal and adolescent masturbation fantasies. The fetishistic and obsessional preoccupation with kerchiefs, necks, and hanging was embellished and varied in many ways, but most importantly by the eventual addition of his fantasied rape of the bereaved wife during or after the hanging of her husband. This fantasy thus disclosed the oedipal theme barely disguised.

On the whole, and as would be expected, the latency period was relatively quiescent by comparison with the periods immediately preceding and following it. However, a dramatic and violent end to the latency period was ushered in by a sudden hospitalization at age nine years when the patient developed pneumothorax requiring a two- to three-month stay at a hospital for treatment and observation. At that time, he consciously feared for his life and regressed to urinary incontinence. The seductiveness of the hospital experience was exemplified by a later urinary retention when he was embarrassed over mother pouring water on his genitals to stimulate urination.

At the age of eleven years, the patient developed a more intense fascination with neckerchiefs which to him symbolized masculinity. Further hospital treatment at the age of twelve years, when his ego was stronger, was no longer fraught with terror. At the age of fourteen years, while ambulating with crutches, he developed a direct interest in real women. His later adolescent memories, from ages fifteen and seventeen years, included his grandmother's death of apoplexy and mother's hysterectomy.

The Course of the Analysis

The first seven months of treatment were preparation for analysis. The therapeutic approach was cautious because he had not come of his own accord and resented his parents' suggestion of psychiatric treatment. Furthermore, he was initially somewhat cynical; his "what can this do for me" attitude reflected rebellion against authority and a continuation of a self-destructive pattern evident in his academic work, in his personal relations, and in his attitude toward his body. In his somewhat being "eased" into analysis, he resembled the frequently reluctant adolescent who will characteristically attempt to deny defects, deformity, and mutilation of body or character by evasion, displacement, projection, or other defensive devices. However, with sufficient distress, good intelligence, and increasing trust in me, regular analysis was instituted. He came four times weekly, used the couch and free association, and abided cooperatively with the external rules of analysis to the end.

The diagnosis at the beginning was that of a character disorder with immaturity, emotional inhibitions, and neurotic manifestations, but with the evolution of the analysis an obsessional neurosis became more evident; there was the history of preoedipal precocity and regression to pregenitality when at the height of the oedipal period he was faced with extreme danger to his life—a trauma which was repeated at the prepubertal and pubertal periods.

Soon after treatment was initiated he began to masturbate compulsively and defiantly continued as he moved from autoerotism to object relatedness. Sadistic phallic fantasies with the penis as a hurting organ emerged, and he challenged me to stop his masturbation as his mother had done with her threats. On the other hand, he feared attack by me and implored me not to punish him as his mother had done. Confronted by my noninterference, he made spontaneous efforts to be a "good boy" by controlling masturbation. As a substitute, however, he shed his shoes, wrist watch, and keys, and picked at his clothing while on the couch. His desire to be close to me alternated with withdrawal as he felt he was getting too excited by sadistic and masochistic fantasies. In a fairly rapid regression from the phallic position, his actual shedding of clothes and his attempts to use free association recalled early toilet-training experience. Getting things "off his chest" was similar to going to the toilet, while revealing his thoughts and feelings was a form of nakedness and recalled diapers and dirtiness. Elements of phallic anxiety were mixed with anal anxieties as he recalled his fears of the magician and his disappearing act—now it's here and now it isn't. He attempted to provoke arguments with me, while in reality the number and intensity of his arguments with his mother diminished considerably in the first year.

With the approaching first long vacation from analysis, he feared losing control of his emerging phallic sadistic impulses in the absence of the analyst as controller. I was seen as the abandoning mother whom he wanted to shoot. The second line of diversion was an attempt to convince me not to go away since vacations were "whoring, bad, dirty." As his efforts to change my plans failed, he regressed to the arch weapon—illness; he developed a cold and "needed" a doctor to remain with him.

When the analysis was resumed three weeks later, he reported that during the vacation he had had back pain which recalled the hospitalization during puberty—the whole experience now summarized as punishment, mutilation, and castration. Oedipal fantasies now were associated with masturbation. Murderous, choking impulses toward the father were rationalized as due to the father's sadism; father, being a biologist, tore wings off insects. Though the patient began to assert himself with a girl, his fantasies while "necking" were of an incestuous nature. These fantasies were rationalized as "not too bad" since his mother was able to arouse every kind of excitement in him in the past except desire for sexual intercourse. Under the increasing tension of urinary and phallic impulses with simultaneous remembrances of feelings toward his parents, he made an important anticipatory remark at this point in the analysis: "A wonderful thing has happened to me since I came here. Remembering makes my life seem whole again."

Following a series of alternating pleasurable regressive fantasies—head on mother's lap, nursing, looking up into her face—and frightening suffocation fantasies, he reached a high point of emotional tension after one year of treatment. After masturbating with fantasies of women's scarves, intense castration anxiety was ushered in with the dream of a tornado. Sex was connected with death and hanging with deprivation—loss of love. While there was no evidence of guilt feelings, there was a fear of reactivating the old "infection." I understood this to refer to the reactivation of the infantile neurosis. Strong attraction to older women and a dream about an older woman aroused intense fears for his penis and recalled radiation therapy, which he equated with punishment for his phallic impulses. As he unfavorably compared his penis to that of older men, he concluded that radiation, used as punishment, made him impotent. During fantasies of hanging, choking, and dying, he recalled the anesthesia experience too as punishment for phallic impulses. From the analytic material it appeared that his illness had occurred before the period of phallic primacy and while urination had represented the only permissible cathexis of the penis. Phallic impulses had just been emerging and genital primacy had not yet been inaugurated.

In the transference situation, he recalled his mother's love for him when he was six or seven years old. He had experienced this as exceptional permissiveness and now expressed it with simultaneous disparagement of me. Strong sadistic feelings erupted under great pressure of incestuous fantasies. At this time a dream representing an attempt to deflect sexual feelings away from the incestuous object initiated an effort to find a girl in real life. He began to "neck" more aggressively with girls. At the same time, the father reported by telephone that the patient was recklessly exposing himself to cold weather; this behavior represented a counterphobic denial of his vulnerability displaced onto the weather. As he enjoyed necking, his fears of being punished increased in intensity. The oedipal conflict became obvious as he expressed satisfaction over the death of a gorilla in the local zoo and simultaneously experienced "puzzling" hostility toward me. Castration anxiety was most intense when he introduced the gorilla's death; he commented that he was now learning things about himself he should have known long ago, by which he referred to the reactivation of death wishes toward his father now displaced onto the analyst. Following another entreaty for me to interdict his masculine endeavors, a dream revealed that he had conceived of the X-ray therapy as a castration threat and punishment for his sadistic impulses. Until that time he had occasionally used regressive homosexual defenses to ward off intense castration anxiety, but now a sexual interest in my wife ushered in a more consistent use of passive, submissive devices. He regularly began going to toilets in the building, hoping to meet me there sometimes. He then switched to violent attacks on his mother and began to see me as his mother who refused to accept his love in the place of the father's love. In a continuous homosexual flight from castration anxiety, the father now was all good and the mother all bad. He envied people's closeness to each other, yet feared being crushed in sadistically conceived primal scenes. Thus, at the end of the second year of treatment, he was switching back and forth between heterosexual impulses directed to girls reminding him of his mother and homosexual impulses induced by regressions. With each increase in masculine assertiveness outside the office, he showed a corresponding increase in apparent maturity in the office. He now felt more adult, and for the first time was able to place his coat in the closet instead of throwing it down casually. However, assuming a more adult role again increased his castration fears and revived fantasies about radiation and how it may have affected his potency. He began to wonder about his sperm, which he studied under a microscope. He visited his physician for information, but was quite hesitant and vague in seeking it. It was apparent that he was not yet ready to accept the truth of his past experience. The desire to know something from adults continued, but in the disguised form of seeking advice on the choice of a career. Increased interest in his career and improved studies also represented identification and rivalry with adults—he too could have what adults have.

Upon reaching twenty-one years of age, he made heroic attempts to be a man. He changed his style of clothing to a more mature one and proudly announced that he had registered to vote. At the same time, he realized that his notion of being adult implied cruelty and destructiveness to women as he indulged in sadistic fantasies toward women in the waiting room. His aggressiveness had mobilized hostility instead of affection.

The first murmurings about leaving occurred in the third year of analysis. Independence meant relief from incestuous fantasies which were diminished only after a great struggle and augured another round of oedipal fantasies. Now I was identified with his father; this became clear in a dream. After a brief vacation in which he feared for my safety, he had open fantasies about caring for his mother after his father died. When his father undertook a plane trip, he feared for the father's safety and called his mother ugly in an attempt to deny his attraction to her. This attempt was unsuccessful, because he could not get his mother off his mind while he masturbated compulsively day and night. Again the retaliative fears appeared, this time in the form of fearing a recurrence of the "bone thing"; so he had himself X-rayed.

After a longer vacation, regressive homosexual devices again came to the fore. He wanted to be accepted as a girl. Many pre-genital anxieties appeared—rape, murder, and choking fantasies; fetishistic preoccupation with scarves, polymorphous-perverse mani-festations—in an attempt to avoid increasing attractions to women in the waiting room. He struggled intensely to give up masturbation. While reviewing pubertal anxieties over his illness, suicidal impulses were overcome by a strong life-preservative tendency. He referred to "a little nodule of feeling coming out" which showed how difficult it was for feelings to emerge, and also that he associated the illness and castration. It was becoming clear that he had experienced the removal of the nodule as a punishment for phallic impulses. He also recalled castration fears in the form of dissolution feelings with the nitrogen-mustard injections.

As the phallic impulses toward women and the phallic rivalry with me in the transference increased, the intensity of castration anxiety also increased and manifested itself in a remarkably strong fear of renewed medical treatments. He feared lung collapse and radiation; he developed spots before his eyes and anticipated the return of all his previous illnesses. In an effort to divert the image of his mother and sister in his masturbation fantasies, he turned to women in the office and the analyst's wife, and even to his father's former secretary. With each diversion, the anxiety mounted and he again anticipated the end of analysis. One year before termination, he developed an attachment to a physically handicapped woman. Overt sexual exploration of the female body gradually replaced the frightening incestuously toned masturbation. His intellect was freed and his course work improved as he looked forward to ten years of productive work.

After several months of regressive shifts related to sadistically conceived primal scenes, he began to make realistic statements: "Life is not going to be a bed of roses. I want to be a man, but I fear getting sick." Following a triumphant dream, "I made it—a great accomplishment," there was intense excitement involving love for the mother and hatred for the father with a subsequent fear of dissolution in orgasm. His parents' solemnity during his first illness was related to his feelings toward his parents at that time. Acting outside the analysis, he began to manipulate the girl's genitals with fantasies that both parents would die. Soon phallic preoccupations assumed a more genital character.

The oedipal neurosis reached a full climax in the fourth year of analysis as he began to have erections on the couch and strongly controlled his impulses to masturbate in the office. In a dream he asked a girl "where to put the fluid." A great deal of hostility was displaced from the genitally refusing mother onto me. He viewed me as refusing his penis and therefore his masculinity. This he associated to his mother treating him as a weakling and as if he were going to die. Dying was related to castration in a dream of his teeth falling out.

After failing to fulfill his oedipal attraction to mother in the transference, the other aspect of the family romance was relived in his affects and re-enacted. He became strongly competitive in and outside the analysis and was very eager to have heterosexual relations. Simultaneously, he pursued his studies diligently and secured an advanced degree. With his academic triumph, he planned slowly to abandon the analysis, insisting upon reducing his hours and arranging a termination date, which was agreed upon.

Several weeks later, he had intercourse for the first time in his life. He was relieved not only because his penis remained intact, but also because he was able to give a woman pleasure in this way. He now felt he could make plans for leaving home, his euphemism for abandoning infantile claims, and he even began seriously to consider marriage. These plans to marry resulted in apprehensions regarding his health. He felt his parents had misinformed him about the dangers of sexual intercourse, and he had now disproven these apprehensions. This led to associations to other forms of misinformation and he spontaneously connected his fears for his life with fears of castration. "I used to believe doctors were taking retribution and now I realize they saved my life." The link between his illness and castration was still preconscious. As he planned marriage more seriously, he told his girl friend of his "osteomyelitis" and arranged a visit to his physician to obtain an opinion concerning his physical status. It dawned on him that I was a doctor and in the course of asking my opinion, he casually asked whether I knew anything about his state of health. In an ensuing discussion, I told him what I had been told: that he had been treated for Hodgkin's disease as a child. The name was unfamiliar to him, and he remained calm as the general nature of the illness was discussed briefly and discreetly. I suggested that he could now talk more freely with his medical consultant. His reaction after this hour was considerable relief, even mild euphoria. "I feel very good, like after I passed my exams. Before, I felt things were done without any reason. Now, I don't have to feel bitter. While I am tempted to use this information as a club, I feel more responsible and less like a child. I feel very grateful to you, but I want to see Dr. X as soon as possible." This exchange took place one month before the previously established date of termination of the analysis and was most likely influenced by the pressure of the anticipated separation from me.

Although he seized upon the diagnosis in an obsessional way, that is, he now had a magical word to grapple with, he was, in a long discussion with his physician, finally able to come to terms with the facts of his life. He was told by his physician that in view of the quiescent course of his illness in recent years, the original diagnosis remained in doubt, although at the time it was made there was no doubt. The patient, in the face of increasing frankness, changed remarkably. He felt more secure and made the poignant remark, "Every day I live is an act of defiance of my folks. I wanted the privilege of worrying about my own life."

Until then independence had meant the death of his parents. Now he wanted to be recognized as a man and not be prevented from leaving the analysis. After some vacillations and renewed fears that a node in his neck similar to that which had precipitated his illness at age five might reappear, he fearfully anticipated leaving the analysis but remained undaunted in his desire to separate. A number of rebirth fantasies emerged toward the end. In his last hour, he expressed phallic defiance: "My penis is better than yours."

The patient still had to accomplish a number of tasks: to be more independent from his parents, to establish and maintain an adequate heterosexual adjustment, to work effectively over a sustained period, and to have meaningful interpersonal relations. At the conclusion of the analysis, signs of movement in these directions were clearly evident. He had by this time become a serious student, secured an advanced degree, and progressed toward a definite career, the latter interestingly in a field involving the study of basic life processes.

While I would have preferred a more extensive period of working through, particularly of the preoedipal aspects of his neurosis, the patient was not tolerant of the need to continue at the time. On the other hand, the analysis had achieved definite structural changes in his personality. He had made his first satisfactory heterosexual adjustment, which ultimately led to marriage, though the fact that he chose a girl with a physical handicap suggests that compromises were being made. He cared for his health in a more realistic fashion, no longer feeling compelled to indulge in extensive counterphobic maneuvers. Also, he improved in his family relations to the point of more realistic, if not more pleasant, adaptations. He developed capacities for insight of which he had previously been afraid or unaware. There was a marked softening of a severely critical superego. He was able to tolerate separations with little or no anxiety, although this was now tempered by the new, marital attachment. He found more direct means of satisfying his instinctual impulses, which were no longer expressed in symptoms or masturbation, and he increased his capacity to sublimate. Finally, his ability to test reality was shown in his ability to deal with the facts of his past illness without the extensive use of denial.

The analysis of his oedipal neurosis as well as of his equation of fears of dying with castration fear enabled the patient to accept his current reality and the unique meaningfulness of his own personal life history. As a consequence of his unresolved obsessional neurosis with traumatic features, he had been afraid to live. In this, he had been encouraged by the well-intentioned protectiveness of his parents. He had complied with his parents, and implicitly with me, not to know the facts of his life.

DISCUSSION

In studying the after effects of childhood operations, Anna Freud (1952) found that in a male child it was not the castration fear but the feminine castration wish which was most frequently responsible for serious postoperative breakdowns or permanent character changes. In these instances, she suggested, the surgical attacks on the body act like a seduction to passivity, to which the child either submits with disastrous results for his masculinity or against which he has to build up permanent pathologically strong defenses. In my patient, struggles against passive submission were strikingly evident in the amplitudes of his swings from submission to assertion, the latter often of a counterphobic nature. Anna Freud was so impressed by the importance of the submission factor that she felt the reactions of boys in the oedipal stage to bodily pain could provide a useful key to the differential diagnosis between genuine phallic masculinity and misleading manifestations of reactive, overstressed phallic behavior designed to ward off the passive feminine castration idea. The masculine boy, she stated, is contemptuous of bodily pain, which means little to him. The boy who has to defend himself against passive leanings cannot tolerate even slight amounts of pain without major distress.

Emmy Sylvester indicated that early insults cripple the development of the ego, while traumas which occur after consolidation of the ego and of object relations affect ego functioning (see Calef, 1959). I would say that in my patient, his physical illness influenced the manner of ego functioning rather than crippled his ego development.

The emphasis on phallic imagery in this patient's associations was determined by the time of onset of his illness, the phallic-pregenital period. At that time the phallus was already cathected, and the anxiety concerning his body was therefore phallic anxiety. The clinical evidence suggests that dissolution anxiety was related to somatic experiences, particularly those caused by radiation. He also reacted to panic states in the parents, the manipulations and restrictions necessitated by the gravity of the illness. Various aspects characteristic of the illness such as nodal enlargement were symbolically incorporated into the infantile anxieties and later emerged in the course of the transference. Something could be said about the relevance of pregnancy fantasies in relation to having a node removed in a passively disposed boy. Considerable preoccupation with a miscarriage of the mother when he was one to three years of age was not elaborated in this account, but fantasies were worked over a number of times in regard to this supposed event.

Unresolved pregenital conflicts strengthened the fixation points to which he regressed in life and in the transference situation. There were many manifestations of polymorphous-perverse sexuality, fetishism, and accented urinary and anal sexuality. The frequent shifts of pregenital cathexes gave evidence of an unstable refuge in pregenitality into which he had been pushed by his mother's overstimulations. Upon entering the phallic and oedipal periods, he was "dropped" by his mother inasmuch as she did not accept his more mature sexuality. This attitude of his mother's as well as his incapability of achieving adequate discharge left him in an unresolved oedipal neurosis. This neurosis was further fixated by his illness which by overwhelming the ego prevented further mastery and which led to increased infantilization by the parents.

Among his regressive manifestations, one is struck most by the intensity and chronicity of his fetishistic fantasies and behavior both in his life and in the treatment. All his fetishistic preoccupations could be traced back to the period following the onset of his illness. The earliest ones, dealing with mother's underpants, women's kerchiefs, and magicians' scarves, reflect anxiety over erections, the anatomic differences between the sexes, and separation from the mother. His latency and pubertal preoccupations disclose conflicts over masculinity and the unsuccessful integration of libidinal and aggressive drives. These resulted in the delayed appearance of orgasm and the related fears of dissolution. The patient recalled infantile masturbation which he resumed during the treatment in late adolescence, but he did not recall pubertal masturbation. The analysis of his fetishistic fantasies accompanying masturbation revealed a high degree of overdetermination, some degree of accidental association, and some degree of anxiety-influenced misperceptions. Two examples will illustrate the latter. "As a child, I thought HAND-KERCHIEF was HANG-KERCHIEF." This misperception, he felt, was influenced by his mother's curse, "go hang yourself." He also confused the words "scarves" and "scars," an obvious reference to surgery. Again, balloons were part of the anesthesia experience as was the feeling of choking.

Greenacre (1953, 1955) and Socarides (1960) in their studies of fetishism suggest that the fetishist has a body-image disorder. According to Greenacre, internal traumas, rage, spasms, fevers, and anesthesia create severe disturbances of the bodily sense of self, with feelings of immanent dissolution. In her cases she also found disturbances in the phallic phase which led to an exaggeration of the oedipus complex. The clinical material reported here seems to be an apt illustration of these conclusions. The traumatic assault of surgical experience, radiation, and chemical suffusion, as well as the fact that these events took place in a climate of understandably frightened parents lent reality emphasis to the unconscious fears of retaliation for unconscious impulses. Synthesis of an adequate body image in this patient was made particularly difficult by two factors: reality events lent support to his worst unconscious expectations, and he reached the phallic and oedipal phases without having consolidated his pregenital development.

While more genuine masculinity provides protection from the insult of pain and illness, immaturity, whether chronologic, fixated, or regressed, results in a state of helplessness which precludes effective mastery of reality or even of unconscious fantasy. Anita I. Bell stated that mastery requires a fusion or neutralization of aggressive and libidinal instinctual energy—processes which free the ego for reality testing and object relations. Excessive defused aggressive energy is used masochistically or sadistically (see Calef, 1959). According to Lucie Jessner, the crucial issue in illness is the struggle to maintain the bond to the loved person: "The effect of illness is that libidinal investment of objects suffers a narcissistic regression altering body and self-images. The image of the parents changes. The parents' helplessness, anxiety, and incapacity to protect the child become painfully clear. The powerful protector turns into an archaic devouring monster in retaliation for the child's impulses. Identification with the parents becomes disturbed" (see Calef, 1959, p. 158).

After the establishment of genital primacy death fears represent castration to the ego and in such a predisposed individual may reflect castration anxiety. Threats to the organism before the establishment of genitality are threats to the whole body as well as to the developing ego which is still relatively helpless. This patient experienced considerable conscious relief after he learned the facts of his medical history. Perhaps because he had not known them, he appeared to be less concerned with the actual threat to his life except in so far as he equated it with castration. Eissler (1955) indicates that the fear of castration is so great, presumably after genital cathexis, that the destruction of one's self appears preferable. "Man's reaction seems to be, with surprising frequency: rather dead than castrated." He implies that man cannot tolerate life without the prospect of pleasure.

This patient's discovery of his illness, in addition to the resolution of his infantile neurosis, constituted a mastery by the ego which could now facilitate a psychological freedom where he had not even that before. His ego's need to maintain an unbroken representation of the future (Eissler, 1955) probably led to his marriage.

BIBLIOGRAPHY

Calef, V. (1959), Report on Panel: Psychological Consequences of Physical Illness in Childhood. *J. Amer. Psa. Assn.*, VII.
Eissler, K. R. (1955), *The Psychiatrist and the Dying Patient.* New York: International Universities Press.

Freud, A. (1952), The Role of Bodily Illness in the Mental Life of Children. *This Annual*, VII.

Greenacre, P. (1953), Certain Relationships Between Fetishism and Faulty Development of the Body Image. *This Annual*, VIII.

—— (1955), Further Considerations Regarding Fetishism. *This Annual*, X.

Socarides, C. (1960), The Development of a Fetishistic Perversion: The Contribution of Preoedipal Phase Conflict. *J. Amer. Psa. Assn.*, VIII.

ON THE PSYCHOLOGY OF CHILDHOOD TONSILLECTOMY

SAMUEL D. LIPTON, M.D. (Chicago)

The purpose of this essay is the study of tonsillectomy from two separate standpoints. The first is the standpoint of clinical psychoanalysis. A review of relevant literature is cited to demonstrate that the operation can have important psychological repercussions, and then clinical material is cited to confirm and expand this fact. The second standpoint is that of applied psychoanalysis. In that approach the long history and present status of the operation is reviewed, and on the basis of extensive documentation the argument is advanced that this operation is scientifically invalid. Finally, a unitary hypothesis based on psychoanalytic principles is advanced to account for the persistence of the operation.

The demonstration of the scientific invalidity necessitates a protracted excursion into the pertinent medical literature. While the detailed documentation of this evidence is important to the thesis, it may not be of interest to each reader. For that reason it is relegated to an appendix so that it can be studied by those who wish to evaluate it critically and will not burden those readers who wish to devote their attention to the main psychological thesis.

While tonsillectomy is done in adults, the usual practice is to perform the operation in childhood, and the important psychological repercussions occur when it is done at this time. For this reason the psychological study is confined to tonsillectomy performed in childhood.

I

In the literature there are many valuable contributions to both surgery in general and tonsillectomy in particular in children. Anna

---

Presented in shortened form to the Chicago Psychoanalytic Society on March 28, 1961.

Freud's observations (1952) are cited first because of their broad applicability. She writes that the evaluation of this problem is hampered by the division of the material between various fields such as pediatrics, child analysis, nursing, and teaching, so that there is little or no opportunity for the trained worker in one field to function even as an observer in the others. The psychologically oriented do not see the child ill; the organicists do not see him well; and the mother is personally involved and therefore hardly an objective observer. This is clearly true, and I would add only that there is a factor in addition to opportunity. Custom dictates deference to the specially trained physician so that, opportunity and experience notwithstanding, independent judgments outside one's specialized field may evoke an unenthusiastic reception.

She points out that hospitalization involves an anxious separation which inevitably obscures the effect of the illness. The child cannot distinguish suffering originating in the body from that imposed from without. I would add that tonsillectomy is done when the child is feeling well, a factor which adds to its psychological repercussions since no immediate bodily suffering explains the various procedures. It is my opinion that this particular circumstance is of great importance in encouraging the development of a fantasied cause for the procedure and increases its psychological impact on the child.

The change in the emotional climate is most important, Anna Freud continues. The mother may be more concerned or more permissive than usual. The nursing care, bodily exposure, helplessness, new attention to excretion and similar factors may be experienced as a loss of mastery and ego control. Restriction of movement has most significant repercussions.

Concerning operations she writes: "By now it is common knowledge among analysts that any surgical intervention with the child's body may serve as a focal point for the activation, reactivation, grouping, and rationalization of ideas of being attacked, overwhelmed and (or) castrated." The importance of the operative experience depends on "the type and depth of the fantasies aroused by it," not on the seriousness of the operation itself. Among such fantasies are retaliatory attack by the mother, a sadistic conception of the primal scene, or mutilation for exhibitionism or masturbation. "In the phallic phase, . . . whatever part of the body is operated on will take over by displacement the role of an injured genital part. The actual experience of the operation lends a feeling of reality to the repressed fantasies, thereby multiplying the anxiety connected with them."

In considering how to lessen the traumatic effect of the three main factors in surgery—hospitalization, anesthesia, and operation—she notes that preparation should be long enough for the ego but not too long for the id; that is to say, mastery should be fostered without fostering fantasy formation. In the literature there are many more sanguine comments about the value of preparation. My own experience has left me convinced that preparation is of value in aiding mastery of the immediate anxiety, but I am skeptical about its long-range effect.

In his essay Menninger (1934) writes, "Certainly there is nothing in the practice of medicine so barbarous and so fraught with psychological danger as the prevalent custom of taking a child into a strange white room, surrounding him with white-garbed strangers, exhibiting queer paraphernalia and glittering knives, and at the height of his consternation pressing an ether cone over his face and telling him to breathe deeply. The anxiety stimulated by such horrors is probably never surpassed in the child's subsequent life." Menninger comments on the wish for surgery in adults, suggesting several mechanisms such as a masochistic wish toward the surgeon or a focal self-destructive offering. To his account one can add that such wishes can be displaced onto the child and that parents may seek operations on their children for their own neurotic reasons.

Helene Deutsch (1942) points out that reconstructions in analysis of the psychic reactions to operations are particularly reliable because the analysis itself is conceived of as an operation and attitudes toward it are vividly mobilized. She finds that the surgically removed organ can become a disguised persecutor in the external world. She writes, "I have noted that operations performed in childhood leave indelible traces on the psychic life of the individual." Deutsch cites a number of fantasies evoked by operative procedures and their later repercussions, which are by no means regularly remediable.

Miller (1951) describes two cases in which childhood operations had repercussions on later ego functioning. In his first case the operation was a tonsillectomy; the second patient had an operation for a dislocated hip at age two and a tonsillectomy at age eight. Miller attributes greater importance to the former, but his clinical material suggests the possibility that the second was quite important.

Beata Rank (see Jessner and Kaplan, 1949) states that in her practice she has seen cases in which tonsillectomy was the precipitating cause of a severe disturbance. In another discussion (Jackson, 1942), she states that following a tonsillectomy without preparation, a three-year-old girl refused to speak to anyone except her parents for five years.

Pearson (1941) cites a number of unfavorable reactions to surgery and notes that tonsillectomy is used as a treatment for neurotic symptoms. He too speaks of these procedures leaving a permanent mark. In diametrical contradiction to those who claim that the tonsils are responsible for nightmares, Pearson finds that tonsillectomy can be responsible for nightmares—and he is not alone in finding this.

A large number of papers describe the anxiety the child suffers in connection with hospitalization and after and offer suggestions for the preparation of the child. Beverly (1936) cites examples of the facetious, chilling callousness of the staff which unfortunately occurs in hospitals: an interne casually stating in front of the child, "Give me the scissors and I'll cut them out"; a nurse telling a crying child after tonsillectomy that she would be taken back to the operating room and have her throat tied up. He cites the case of a well-prepared seven-year-old girl, having had the procedure fully explained, escorted to the operating room by her father and left there comfortable, then a few minutes later screaming in terror and "requiring" forcible restraint to be anesthetized. Postoperatively she was irritable and had nightmares. Ultimately the explanation for this changed behavior was disclosed. At the very last moment the surgeon had decided to take another, final look at the child's throat; had approached her and put a tongue blade in her mouth. The child was terrified because, as it later became known, she thought he was about to remove her tonsils without anesthesia. Beverly writes that the surgeon could not explain his action. I would add that Beverly does not comment on why the father, having gone as far as he did, had to leave the operating room, and I wonder if his leaving at that late point contributed to the child's anxiety.

Coleman (1949, 1950) is an unusual otolaryngologist who has

interested himself in the psychological problems of tonsillectomy. He pleads for considerate treatment of the child and notes the bad effects which can follow the operation. He specifically mentions a lifelong fear and distrust of doctors, hospitals, anesthesia, and surgery as well as acute reactions including nightmares. He notes that the child behaves better if kept isolated from the parent, but in contrast to all experienced psychiatric evaluations, he overemphasizes the value of this coerced compliance. Similarly he advises only one or two days' notice of the operation, in contrast to experienced child analysts, Fries (1946), for example, who found one or two months necessary.

Jackson (1942) cites severe psychological reactions in carefully studied cases. Levy's paper (1945), which is often quoted, is based on a large experience and documents anxiety, phobias, behavior problems, and unfavorable personality changes following the operation. He found "manifest" sequelae in 25 of 124 cases. Such unfavorable results are often ignored or passed over in the literature of the proponents who indeed may recommend the operation for these difficulties. Other papers (Huschka and Ogden, 1938; Langford, 1948; Pillsbury, 1951; Proctor, 1960) discuss aspects of psychological disturbance and its prevention. One gains the impression that the obviousness and simplicity of many remedial measures are an unfortunate index of the unfavorable conditions that sometimes prevail.

Jessner and her collaborators (1952, 1949; Kaplan, 1952) studied the reactions of 143 children to tonsillectomy by means of interviews with the child and mother preoperatively and postoperatively for as long as four years in some cases. However, the method is one of direct study, and the authors state that the long-range effect of the experience could not be determined. One is reminded when confronted with these limitations of the relevance of Deutsch's opinion, cited above, and Kris's similar statement (1951) that the reconstructive method remains the best to establish the etiologic importance of experience.

Possibly another limitation in this study was the fact that the realistic validity of the operation was taken for granted. This leads the authors to interpret certain responses of the child as more influenced by fantasy than might actually have been the case if they could have determined the extent to which the child was simply repeating the statements of adults. For example, when William, aged four years two months, is anxious to see if after operation he can eat a whole meal and swallow better, the authors comment that he expects a change that would make him capable of unlimited intake. The significance of this conclusion, however, may be linked with the fact that just such indications and expectations can be found in the medical literature, and the child might learn it directly. Similarly, the expectations of some mothers that tonsillectomy would help a schizoid condition, alleviate feeble-mindedness, cure enuresis and asthma are not to be described merely as fantasies or credulous expectations because they are culturally sanctioned, scientifically documented results to be expected.

Regardless of the limitations of their study, Jessner and her collaborators make a contribution of great value. They are able to present evidence which confirms the conclusions of analytic reconstructions—that the operation is regularly an event of great psychological significance. This holds true whether the result is construed to be constructive or not. In this regard the authors view as constructive the identification which an eight-year-old girl formed with a nurse; one might demur since more data about the ultimate advantages of this identification are necessary to evaluate it. From the same broad standpoint they consider it to be constructive that the operation allowed the acting out of hatred by a mother with a subsequent amelioration of the unfavorable relationship with the child.

Their observations showed that the children experienced separation anxiety, loneliness, and disturbances of identity; that they conceived of the tonsils as enemies and demons to be exorcised and that they unconsciously equated them with other organs such as the testes, eyes, and teeth; that anesthesia threatened death, punishment, and loss of control; that the removal of the tonsils was conceived of as castration, mutilation, change of sex, and giving birth; that the operation was viewed as an initiation rite. These observations are in accord with the data of individual analysis and are, at least in my view, largely correct descriptively, but they may not be accurate economically. In analysis one gains a more convincing insight into the irretrievable impact of the organization of such fantasies around the vivid experience of an operation. Consequently one must view with an element of caution these authors' conclusion that the emotional consequences are not serious in most children. It is likely that the authors mean that the consequences in terms of persisting, troublesome symptoms in the child are not regular and that the late ego modifications may not be prominent.

A discussant, Work, states that tonsillectomy is the cultural cure for everything and wonders how many children improved or how many mothers felt better because the operation was done. A pediatrician, Butler, notes that in at least half of the cases seen in his clinic for clearance for tonsillectomy recommended by the otolaryngologist, no indication for the operation could be found (see Jessner and Kaplan, 1949).

The problem of parental hostility and the advantages or even necessity of a ritualistic, culturally sanctioned release alluded to in the discussions above is directly discussed by Fries (1946) and Mead (1959). Fries makes the important point that our society has built a system of defenses that attempts to deny the existence of parental hostility. In this connection it is interesting that parental pressure is now cited by pediatricians as one of the "indications" for tonsillectomy. Furman (1959) published a valuable essay precisely on this issue in an effort to aid pediatricians who are confronted by this problem. It seems to me that irrational idealization of the child and corollary insistence on ideal adaptation are among the important areas of culturally sanctioned hostility.

Analytic experience has convinced me of the correctness of these psychological data. Repeatedly psychoanalytic evidence has shown that a childhood tonsillectomy had profound, lifelong, and sometimes irreversible repercussions. The type of effect I have in mind is far too pervasive, too much imbricated with ego development, to be categorized in any simple manner or to be classified as "good" or "bad." I do not mean the anxiety which so commonly may follow the operation and which may be soon mastered. A minor example of the type of effect I refer to is the particular avocation chosen by a girl. She became interested in ballet dancing, acquired a degree of skill that permitted her to give a number of performances in public, and found this most gratifying. She keenly enjoyed her cognizance that she was illuminated by bright lights and was the object of continuous attentive watching by a group of people whom she could scarcely see and only indistinctly hear. She felt confident that she could keep their attention and evoke their response, a burst of applause, at a time that was precisely geared to the conclusion of her performance. Late in her analysis she was able vividly to recall one episode from her tonsillectomy in her fifth year. She was lying on a table under bright lights. She heard the dim mumble of voices around her and occasionally glimpsed an unfamiliar form. She felt intensely that she was being watched. In a sense she knew that she was about to have a tonsillectomy, but there had been many puzzling events and she was afraid of some unknown danger. She hoped to ward off this danger by lying *perfectly still*, only pleading with her eyes, hoping that her perfect behavior would result in evoking *no* response from the shadowy, threatening figures around her.

What I am attempting to show is that the pervasive, subtle effect of the trauma had a long-range organizing effect on the ego and extended broadly into areas of adaptation remote from the original trauma.

I shall present further evidence from her analysis on the effect of the tonsillectomy, but first a few general statements are necessary. The analysis lasted four years, and the fact of the tonsillectomy did not come up until three years had elapsed. During the first period as the transference neurosis developed and became clear and as many of the facets of inferiority feelings, penis envy, and its displacements and other defenses became conscious, the historical determinants lacked the precision that was added only later. It follows that during this time the patient was more convinced that she was correct in her current evaluation of reality and less able to recognize the transference distortions. In retrospect I can say that she had a stable ego, and the analytic contract was a secure one. During the analysis I was not always that certain. I consider the sequence of the development of this material of the utmost importance. It turned out that attitudes toward the parents and siblings were revealed first, while the more intensely affect-laden experience of the tonsillectomy was concealed. In discussions the point was suggested that the tonsillectomy itself was a screen experience, but I do not think that was the case. I have the impression that the screen concept can be misused and applied to *any* experience until some arbitrarily determined chronologically early experience is finally postulated as not being a screen.

Having heard of the ballet-dancing-operation link, one probably will not be surprised to learn that during the first part of her analysis she lay immobile on the couch, spoke in rather measured tones, and expressed no feelings other than occasionally anger. She intensely hoped that I would make no spontaneous comments but would after careful deliberation make an "interpretation" which would serve to conceal my feelings. She would then think of the content as a disguise and evaluate my underlying response by various clues. Indeed, for some time she was convinced that I actually spoke in this deliberate and hypocritical way, using as evidence my usual silent expectancy at the outset of the hour.

On the other hand when it seemed to her that she could predict and control the timing of my response and keep its content within the rigidly prescribed bounds that she had established, she would insist on a reply. One method was to ask me a practical question, one to which her right to a reply was quite reasonable or even indisputable, for example, "When are you taking your vacation?" However, as ingenious and rational as her questions were, she could rarely hit on one that would not keep either until the end of the session or for a few days. In other words, she might require a response but not at the moment she asked. The cogent point that we were able to confirm was this. When she did get the response that she presumably was so intent on after some period of delay but well within the requirements of reality, she no longer had any interest in it at all! This was further confirmed when after she was told and realized herself that my silence indeed indicated that I would not answer promptly, she would still insist that I state that fact. Relevantly in her sexual life, it was essential to her that she and not the man initiate the relationship; the timing had to be in her control. She learned to be clever about this and to leave her partner with the impression that he had started it; at least so she thought.

Her concept of my thinking as an analyst allowed her to form the conviction that I had a secret sadistic purpose which I could keep masked if not provoked. The secret purpose could be represented by my wish to catch her off guard and make a sudden penetrating comment which would elicit an uncontrollable response much to my enjoyment. Or it might be a sudden reaction of disgust to an unpleasant idea she had exposed, which would lead me to indicate my conviction that such an idea was harmful and had to be eradicated.

These equivalents of the fantasied piercing and biting phallus were represented in her thinking.

This area of the patient's thinking can be viewed as a symptom complex within the transference neurosis. Gratification and defense were combined in the symptom with sexual conflicts displaced onto thinking. In this conception my thoughts were regressively perceived as concretized, as erections which could penetrate or bite, or be timed entirely to her own use, or harmlessly ejaculate having missed her entirely. Put to an unfair disadvantage by the obligation to associate she could even the score by provoking a reaction from me which I could not avoid. The reaction itself equated orgasm and incontinence and was the object of amusement and derision. The roots of these conflicts lay in the broad area of the castration complex and penis envy. The instinctual sources are well known, and there were also a number of environmental reinforcements. Parents and siblings had important parts in her history. Nevertheless I think the tonsillectomy had an important consolidating and organizing part. For example, I suspect that it had its place in accentuating the upward displacement of sexual wishes and that the unconscious fantasy of the mind as a phallus with speech as its ejaculation might well have been encouraged by this procedure.

Turning to further consideration of the tonsillectomy, there are two general points that are true for this patient and others as well. First, the time chosen for the operation is when the child is healthy, and the causal link becomes tenuous. It is difficult for the child to conceive of an operation for illnesses past and possibly almost forgotten or for future ones it may never have. Consequently the assumption of a cause in fantasy such as punishment for masturbatory wishes is reinforced. I have not found this factor given attention in the literature, but I suspect that procedures carried out on the subjectively healthy child tend to be more serious psychologically than those which are directly related to a current, subjectively verifiable illness or injury.

Second, the exact timing of the operation is usually based on the requirements of adults. Hospital routine tends to take on a machine-like inexorability, and the child may well realize or indeed discover that his attempt to gain a delay of even a few minutes will be frowned on or forcibly overcome. In reading about the distress of those who dislike forcibly overcoming a child's resistance, I did not find anyone who stated that he delayed or deferred the operation for that reason. I was reminded of my own experience in treating acute injuries and the observation, confirmed I suppose by many others, that the child confronted with a frightening surgical procedure will often put even a short delay to good use.

However, as I said, these factors may well have had their part in this patient, but they were not unique. It turned out that a most important trauma did not take place at the time of the operation at all but had its basis in her conclusions about the preliminary examination. It was then that a strange doctor had stuck something in her throat, and she immediately and responsively gagged! Here was the answer! She *subsequently* concluded that the reason for the tonsillectomy was gagging. Here lay the proof that there was indeed something wrong with her throat. Obviously she should have been able to accommodate the doctor's long instrument without such an unpleasant reaction. Now the doctor was led to do something again, and do it without meeting her response. Here a response directly related to a stimulus led to catastrophic results. The timing of the response had been entirely out of her control; subsequently defenses against such responses became internalized.

The sexual nature of the doctor's maneuver as the child considered it in fantasy has already been alluded to. A part of the hospital procedure tended to reinforce this idea, namely, that her clothes were taken away, a puzzling measure for a throat operation. A particularly ominous sign of the severity of the contemplated procedure was the fact that she was being turned over to a stranger. If indeed something had to be done to her, it seemed more natural to the child that her parents should do it themselves. In the transference she was convinced that I had a secret purpose and concealed my enjoyment of carrying out this procedure; in further corroboration of the two ideas mentioned, she believed that I wanted and indeed might actually interest myself in all areas of medical care. She would complain that her physician was not understanding, hurried, or taciturn, and would expect me to fill in the gap.

This concern with response and timing was prominent both at the beginning and end of the analysis. Immediately after we agreed to begin she demanded that I write a letter to certain military functionaries to explain that her husband's presence in Chicago was necessary because in order to be analyzed she must lead a normal life. I was surprised, hesitant, and explained that I did not think I understood the basis for her request and would do nothing promptly. This response was adequate for her unconscious purpose, and the demand for the husband's presence was soon dropped. At the conclusion, the day before we had agreed to stop which was a Friday, there was an outburst of recriminations. She felt bad, she was not through, I was hurrying her out, I was foolish to think that her analysis had done anything at all, she needed more time. Again surprised and puzzled I asked what she was thinking, how much more time she needed. She replied she needed—one more hour! She wanted to alter the time from Friday to Monday. It turned out that there were a number of reasons that underlay her request, among them a special therapeutic "victory" which she had planned hopefully for the week end, but also included was the matter of her unilateral domination of timing.

In this material I have attempted to show how elements of the tonsillectomy experience had become integrated into the adaptation to reality and were used as an externally validated framework for the organization of sexual fantasies from different levels of development. The particular facets of the immensely complex experience which were selected for emphasis were those which dovetailed with fantasies; they could not have been predicted and developed unexpectedly in the analysis. I think this is an important point in several ways. In analysis itself it follows that one's predictive capacity is sharply limited. It also means that the preparation of the child for the operation cannot be entirely effective, and it means that the direct observation of the child later cannot reveal the future vicissitudes of the organization of the trauma.

There were other areas of confirmation and elaboration of this theme in the analytic material. Dreams of attack, exposure, desertion, and death were again and again associatively linked with the operation. Unexpected details came up repeatedly in such associations. The first phobic symptoms were found to go further and further back until she recalled her terror after the operation that burglars would enter the house while she slept. The unconscious equation of the self-tonsil-phallus-feces-baby idea gained particular vividness during pregnancy when she felt that I had a peculiar fascination with the fetus, that I wanted it removed (delivered), that it was dead, and that it would be taken from her prematurely by an overeager doctor, that it would be deformed because of her masturbation. During her pregnancy there was no interference with the analytic work. I suspect that when there is an interference during pregnancy the analyst should be alert for a countertransference intrusion based on the idealization of the pregnant woman. In my experience, the pregnant woman is no more engrossed in the fetus than the mother is with her children, and she uses this concern for similar unconscious purposes.

Another source of confirmation was daydreams and some acting out. She had the capacity to fascinate a man, evoke his intense interest, and suddenly cut him down to size. In fantasy she would slash a man with a razor so deftly that he would not realize what had happened until he noticed he was bleeding. The anesthesia proved to be one of the important determinants.

Various memories were confirmatory. For example, a year or so after the operation at a movie she was grief-stricken and in tears over the death in a conflagration of a minor character, a "little, unimportant, old man whom no one cared about." She agreed with me that this was the personified tonsil, and other material at the time fitted this idea. I might conclude this résumé by reminding the reader that all this material is distilled. It was developed against the healthy resistance of this intelligent and skeptical patient and involved a step-by-step process starting from, "I had a tonsillectomy just like any other child. It was a sort of custom, and I thought nothing of it."

I shall very briefly cite two other patients; this does not exhaust my material but will suffice.

In the analysis of a second patient, the fact that she was sent to the hospital for her tonsillectomy (again disclosed late in analysis) along with her much younger brother proved to be a key point of validation and organization of her fantasy. Already the father's favorite because she was the first and only girl in the sibling group, she had the fantasy that this last belated child stemmed from her father's growing love for her, that he had compromised for reasons of propriety which had forced him to settle for his second choice, her dull and prosaic mother. She felt her main role was to comfort the younger child and that for this reason they had both been sent to the hospital at the same time. For his benefit she was impelled to be casual, conceal her fear, and take it all as a matter of course.

One of her important characteristics was that she was a desperate good sport. She felt bound not to complain despite such provocation as illness, injury, and significant personal distress. When she was seriously injured she shrugged it off and started to walk away; not long after she had to have surgical treatment. In the analysis she indicated that she felt I might have to be cautious with my other patients but need not be troubled about her, that if I wanted to cancel a session, change it, delay it, or talk on the phone, I should be assured that it was all right.

A third young woman, more seriously disturbed, spent nine years in analytic therapy with me. For the first few years she was unable to speak spontaneously and could respond only to my speaking; later she could express herself better. She made some significant gains, but her relationship with me became irretrievably fixed on the basis of a fearful idealization. She had had two tonsillectomies, one at the age of two which she barely recalled and one two years later which was a terrifying experience. She unconsciously equated analysis with tonsillectomy in many ways. However, I wish to cite only one confirmatory point. Years have passed since the conclusion of this analysis. She writes to me now and then, appreciates my responses to her letters, and wants to be sure of my continued interest. Yet she cannot bring herself to visit me! That would be the *second time*, and the thought terrifies her. She wants me to be assured that once was enough.

I shall not give further examples. I should state that I have analyzed patients who had had tonsillectomies and in whom I did *not* find pervasive results, although I do not think they would necessarily come into focus in every analysis. My clinical data are confined to women with just one exception, but I cannot draw any conclusion from this.

The organizing effect I stress can occur only in the child old enough to have an internally organized fantasy system which can impel the perceptive apparatus to seize on elements of external reality for validation. In the very young child the effect of the trauma is more likely to be disorganizing. My third patient who was the youngest at the time of her operation had suffered the most. Her defenses were the most pervasive and crippling. Her inability to speak spontaneously reminds one of the child described by Rank (in her discussion of a paper by Jackson, 1942).

In conclusion, the data of psychoanalysis supported by data based on other methods of psychological study demonstrate that tonsillectomy in childhood can have extensive psychological repercussions. These repercussions may be in the form of the rapid accession of anxiety with or without the mobilization of defenses depending in large part on the age of the child; or there may be delayed results hinging on the organization and validation of fantasies and modifications of the ego. It is important to emphasize that the results can be conceptualized in some instances as good if one resorts to a behavioral frame of reference. This view is often propounded in the medical literature, in which various authors cite as an advantage some amelioration of troublesome behavior; in fact, some go so far as to consider the tonsils the *cause* of bad behavior. Delayed repercussions may of course have a superficial appearance of good or bad adaptation. The patient cited who had become a "good sport" at first thought of this characteristic as favorable and in fact had often been praised on that basis.

The data also demonstrate that the long-term results are unpredictable and that the value of preparing the child is limited by the fact that it is almost or entirely impossible to predict what elements of the immensely complex experience will be seized on by the child's observational capacity which is influenced by the force of fantasies.

Here, then, is a procedure of great psychological importance which therefore is of interest to the psychoanalyst. Yet traditionally the procedure itself lies in the field of organic medicine. It is the purpose of the next section of this essay to demonstrate that the traditional basis is ill-founded.

II

I shall now critically evaluate the medical literature on tonsillectomy, utilizing both medical and specifically psychoanalytic information and judgment, or, putting it differently, applying psychoanalytic knowledge to the critical evaluation of relevant medical data.

However, before proceeding to the issue it is necessary to acknowledge certain serious difficulties inherent in this task and also
objections and criticism that accrue to it. First, is this topic a proper
one for the author, a psychoanalyst, to discuss? Is he not obliged to
confine his discussion to the sphere of psychology? Should the issues
arising from the operation itself not be left to the more proper
authorities, the otolaryngologists who are experts at carrying out the
operation and the pediatricians and internists who are experts at
evaluating its presumed indications?

These questions merit careful consideration. It is indeed exceptional for the specialist to cross the barriers of custom and presume
to formulate an opinion contrary to many specialists in another field.
Ironically the only common exception is psychoanalysis itself which
is considered by some neurologists, neurosurgeons, internists, and
organically minded psychiatrists to be fair game for the most intense
if uninformed criticism. For the psychoanalyst to intrude on a
medical specialty seems strange.

In considering these objections it is important to recognize that
some have broad applicability but can be inaccurate in specific situations. For example, it is assumed that scientific medicine is constantly
advancing and that the specialist tends to lose contact with other
fields. I have been criticized on that basis for a presumed lack of
familiarity with modern management in this area of medicine. In
reply I would say that while many areas of medicine are advancing,
some do not, and in regard to tonsillectomy there has been no basic
advance. My acquaintance with the current literature shows, as will
be demonstrated in detail, that there has been no shift in the major
issues. In a similar vein, another objection can be answered. There
are no questions here that are beyond the comprehension of the
physician; no questions that require specialized knowledge to form
an opinion. On the contrary, the central issues can be readily identified and judged by anyone with a medical background, and similarly
the reader of the medical literature can easily identify the boundaries
of his independent evaluation and the point at which he defers to
superior judgment or knowledge. In any event, deference to authority is of little enough use in the tonsillectomy controversy since
diametrically opposed opinions can easily be uncovered.

Yet these objections, lack of specialized or modern knowledge, are rather formal and open to rebuttal. More serious is the true extent of the problem itself. Actually only one part of it is reflected in the immense bibliography on the subject. According to one estimate (quoted by King and Story, 1959), there were 100 papers a year published from 1942-46, a period when all publication was curtailed because of the war. This is only the number of direct references; innumerable others have relevance. Since an exhaustive review was out of the question, I have attempted for this essay to assemble a representative sampling of the literature. This is not too difficult a task because much of the literature is repetitious. This bibliography has the merit of being broader in scope than any found in the literature because it covers areas that tend to remain separate. On the whole, pediatricians refer to other pediatricians, otolaryngologists to other otolaryngologists, while psychological matters are given scant attention by either.

I would emphasize that the limitation that is thus forced on one studying this problem—the fact that it is practically impossible to read every paper on tonsillectomy and literally impossible to read all the potentially relevant literature—does not *in itself* mean that one can reach no conclusion. The literature is extremely repetitious, and the selection I cite provides, in my opinion, an accurate basis for a conclusive evaluation. After all, this operation is carried out hundreds of times every day, and its proponents are not keeping their justification a secret. No one can take the position that he is immune to error, but one can sometimes avoid the error of equivocating when one's conclusion is clear. The documentation of the data allows the reader to make his own evaluation.

However, the huge potential bibliography does not accurately delineate the scope of the problem. A crucial difficulty lies in the fact that many fields of medicine impinge on it. Not only pediatrics, internal medicine, and otolaryngology, but anatomy, histology, embryology, pathology, bacteriology, immunology, epidemiology, and psychiatry all have areas of importance in this problem. This complexity stems in part from the fact that at one time or another the operation has been recommended for a tremendous range of illnesses of all types. Such claims have rested on the single type of *post hoc ergo propter hoc* observation on which indeed the operation is based; that is to say, the observation reported is that subsequent to a tonsillectomy the patient improved. At times such claims seem tenuous indeed. After the operation, some illness—acute or chronic, serious or minor—improved. The difficulty then arises that the disproof is far more laborious and far less dramatic. For example, balanced against the reiterated, dogmatic statements that list nephritis as one of the indications for tonsillectomy there is the report of a methodical study of 300 cases over an eleven-year period, a report which indicated that the effect of the operation was, if anything, harmful (Illingworth, 1939).

This sort of data will be more extensively documented later. Here I am trying only to illustrate the nature of the particular difficulty that arises when one attempts to evaluate the results of a procedure which has become institutionalized and entrenched. A disproportionate amount of effort must go into the more rigorously scientific disproof than went into the initial conclusion. Indeed it would be a most naïve observer who could fail to note that the scientific quality of the work which has led to opposition to the operation tends to be superior to that of its proponents. To cite one example of the latter, in a report of 1,136 cases of enlarged tonsils and adenoids, Rolleston (1939) baldly states, "Enlarged tonsils and adenoids are the cause of considerable retardation in education," and, "There is no more debilitating disease than acute tonsillitis. . . ." The upshot is that while the operation is performed quite readily, the disproof of its validity is extremely arduous.

To summarize the reply to certain objections to undertaking this study, I would contend that the problem is a comprehensible one to the physician; that it does not require specialized knowledge in many of its ramifications; that it extends beyond specialty barriers; and that there is extensive disagreement among those who claim specialized knowledge in any case.

The position of the psychoanalyst merits particular consideration. Among psychoanalysts themselves there is some disagreement concerning the definition and scope of psychoanalysis. In its early development psychoanalysis was considered a psychology of the unconscious with its data deriving from the psychoanalytic situation (Waelder, 1960). Other aspects of psychology were acknowledged but not considered the special province of psychoanalysis. However, in addition, psychoanalysts interested themselves in the far broader area to which the findings of psychoanalysis had some relevance and the field of applied psychoanalysis has thus been extremely broad. As Mead (1959) puts it, "Freud took the world as his province."

In more recent years there has been a systematic effort to expand psychoanalysis to a comprehensive psychology. To some extent this effort tends to incorporate the former field of applied analysis into the area of analysis proper. This may be having the repercussion of narrowing the sphere of the analyst's interest to those matters which are already classified as psychological. It is expected that the analyst's interest in psychology is unitary and that he has mastered a single field. In the broader concept of applied psychoanalysis it is necessary that the analyst have a dual viewpoint, that he acquaint himself with a different field and bring psychoanalytic principles to bear on it. In such a position he has both more leeway for investigation and a greater possibility of error since he is not necessarily fully expert in the ancillary area.

Possibly this sort of conceptual shift accounts for the fact that Mead (1959) criticizes the apparent narrowing of the analyst's interest, as does Wheelis (1958) who maintains that psychoanalysis may be entering a "stage of scholasticism, becoming increasingly preoccupied with the abstruse, the minute, and the unverifiable." Be that as it may, the attempt is made in this essay to study an area of what is usually claimed to be organic medicine and bring to bear on it certain hypotheses from psychoanalysis. My position is more favorable than that of those who would reverse this process, because I have no objections at all to organic medicine while the organicists are often opposed to psychoanalysis on principle. To put it diagrammatically, I maintain I can comprehend organic disease and neurosis, while the organicists often cannot comprehend the psychoanalytic theory of neurosis.

It is clear that the old dichotomy between psychic and somatic or organic and functional is followed here. A detailed defense of this position would become discursive and tangential. Suffice it to say that I think this distinction is methodologically sound regardless of the unity of the person, that it is a method commonly used in the practice of medicine and that its implications are clear. In an ultimate sense the mind-body unity is evident, but methodologically at any given time the physician addresses himself to one aspect or the other.

For the convenience of the reader the documentation of the review of the medical literature is relegated to an appendix. There follows here a résumé in necessarily categorical form of the salient features uncovered.

From the medical literature there emerge two crucial conclusions regarding the rationale of this operation. First, psychological factors are almost universally ignored or misunderstood. Second, far from being an accepted procedure, the operation has been highly controversial for a full century. A mass of critical scientific work has been done which again and again has impeached the validity of the procedure and its results. One need go no further than selected papers in this literature to conclude that the procedure is *largely* or *frequently* unscientific.

While the first point becomes obvious to any psychoanalytically oriented reader, the second of course requires a critical selection of the articles in the literature. In carrying out such a selection, it is clear that opposition to the operation cannot itself be used as a criterion of a rational outlook or sound scientific judgment. Obviously irrational motives can be used to justify opposition to the operation just as readily as they can be to advocate it.

Actually the evidence against the operation is clear and adequately documented. While this is quite remarkable, the really astounding fact is that it has had so little effect. It is astonishing to learn of the number of meticulously disproved indications for the operation that have remained in effect. I shall offer an explanation of this enigma, but first I wish to summarize the data of the medical literature.

Broadly, there are two crucial clues in the history of the operation and a series of current criticisms. First, the operation is some 2,500 years old. More precisely, tonsillotomy is that old, while its current follower, tonsillectomy, was initiated only in the twentieth century when anesthesia and improved technique permitted control of hemorrhage. However, in principle the operations are the same. During this period which so long antedates scientific medicine as we know it, the indications for the operation appear now to be obviously irrational, yet good results were claimed just as they are now. Indeed, some of the symptoms used as indications in the distant past linger unchanged in the medical literature of today.

Second, the introduction of adenoidectomy in 1868 and its subsequent ill-founded coupling with tonsillectomy compromised a rational evaluation of the results of either operation. In addition, the entrenchment and cultural sanction of tonsillectomy has hampered research immeasurably.

From the standpoint of its current status, one can say:

1. The medical research on tonsillectomy is inadequate on several bases:
   a. Direct scientific observation is poor. The most glaring example is the myth that the tonsils obstruct respiration or deglutition.
   b. Control studies are inadequate. For example, the idea that the tonsils are responsible for either local or general infection is disproved by control studies as is the moribund focus of infection theory.
   c. The significance of maturation is not adequately recognized. Changes in the child occurring at the time of the second dentition are erroneously attributed to the operation.
   d. Complex epidemiologic factors are ignored in evaluating the incidence of infections.
   e. The obscurity and complexity of upper respiratory illnesses are not appreciated, and the tendency to designate a heterogeneous group of such disorders as tonsillitis if the tonsils are present and inflamed gives the diagnosis a spurious certainty.
   f. The natural status of the tonsils in both appearance and function is inadequately appreciated.
2. There is an almost complete failure to comprehend basic psychological principles:
   a. Psychogenic symptoms are not recognized, and the childhood neurosis seems almost unknown. When recognized, such symptoms are often attributed to organic causes, such as toxins from the tonsils.
   b. Correspondingly, the psychological effects of the operation are unrecognized. Many of the so-called good results are clearly the behavioral repercussions of the anxiety and defenses

against it aroused by the operation. A dramatic historical example of this obliviousness is the fact that Meyer, the originator of adenoidectomy, attributed his superlative results to the removal of the adenoids, not recognizing the impact of the fact that he used no anesthetic!

c. A further corollary is a naïve acceptance of the complaints and evaluations of parents and a startlingly uniform failure to communicate with the child.

3. The multiplicity of indications has led consistently to the apparently judicious exclusion of many by the individual physician. In fact, no indication withstands scientific scrutiny.

The upshot is that tonsillectomy as a method of organic therapy is not supported by scientific evidence. As stated, the concept that the operation is irrational is nothing new and has long been amply documented. The real enigma is the perpetuation of the operation in the face of its scientifically conclusive disproof. The reason, I believe, is that there is a fatal flaw in the whole impressive mass of scientific criticism. The flaw is this: while author after author has been able to conclude that the operation is *largely* or *frequently* unscientific or irrational, none has been able to conclude that it is *entirely* irrational. Each critic of the operation is therefore forced to leave a logical loophole in his argument; each assumes there *must* be *some* scientific rationale. The trouble is that not one of them indicates an adequate knowledge of the basic principles of psychoanalysis; none recognize the power of the unconscious or the extent of irrationality. Conversely, no psychoanalyst has studied the problem and attempted to bring psychoanalytic knowledge to bear on it.

The crux of my argument and the essence of the contribution I am attempting are exactly the addition of this final step. I believe that tonsillectomy is a psychological matter entirely and that the whole tangled web of indications and results of the operation can be readily explained on that basis. I believe it is clear that the operation is rooted not in science but in tradition; that the presence of the tonsils is probably beneficial and at worst harmless; that their removal is at best useless and at worst harmful; and the results are all explainable without resorting to postulating some malign attributes of the tonsils themselves.

III

Once the organic basis of the operation is proved invalid, it is clear that what remains is an elaborate, institutionalized, cryptic ritual. The only basis for its perpetuation must be intense and persistent psychological needs. It is this conclusion that I consider the central contribution of this essay. It is a conclusion reached by studying medical data with both medical and psychoanalytic viewpoints or by applying psychoanalytic scrutiny to an ostensibly medical area, and I submit that my conclusion can be confirmed, or at least evaluated, by any analyst on the basis of the documented data.

The remaining question is the positive explanation for the perpetuation of the operation, but the answer certainly must lie in the domain of psychology. What I now add are hypotheses which I suggest may answer this question.

In the first place it seems clear that the claim of good results on which the continuation of the operation rests is a rationalization. The so-called good results are explained either by inaccurate, too brief, or uncontrolled observation, or are unrecognized psychological repercussions. For example, better behavior and increased alertness obviously do not derive from the elimination of tonsillar tissue. Equally clear are the effects of the shift in the libidinal economy of the family. The psychological factors have been discussed fully, and it remains only to state explicitly that they account for so-called good results as well as unrecognized bad ones.

In so far as the culturally sanctioned, ritually bound discharge of hostility to the child can redound to its benefit, the psychological element is re-emphasized. However, it should be noted that the operation is not avowedly a ritual but rather is ostensibly a rational and scientific procedure. Whatever may be the advantages of a ritual, it would appear that they are jeopardized by the fact that exactly the ritualistic aspect is denied. The recognition of a ritual allows for the suspension of critical judgment, while its denial enforces the acceptance of falsifications of reality and compromises intellectual functioning.

If one grants that the results are used as a rationalization, then I suggest there are three factors of general importance which underlie the implementation of more specific fantasies.

First, there is the dread of passivity. This fear is generally recognized and requires little discussion. The need to take action may reach great intensity in the parents when the child's vulnerability to illness threatens their narcissism or when the child's maladaptation jeopardizes their own defenses. The alternative to the active step that tonsillectomy offers against a host of ills is inactivity and the tolerance of suffering. The alternative to doing something is generally the uninviting prospect of doing nothing or undertaking the far less dramatic and more arduous task of viewing the problems psychologically. It may be added here that the child is sometimes only the incidental object of the action, while the main issue is a disguised transference-countertransference relation between the parent and the physician. Prototypic is the parent who unquestioningly follows the physician's orders with slavish devotion.

A second factor is the culturally reinforced, irrational idealization of the child which is accompanied by a complementary denigration of disavowed undesirable attributes. The result is the mobilization of aggression against the child as he exists in the effort to convert him into the projected ideal.

It seems that some aspects of the child's ego development have entered the public domain to even a less extent than childhood sexuality. The child's capacity for hatred of both himself and others seems hardly known, and the result is that many adults continue to believe that on the whole *children are happy*. This is a really remarkable illusion since it can be dispelled by simple observation. For example, almost any child who dares give an honest answer will indicate that he is waiting for better days when he grows up. Objectively the environmental intrusions in our culture on the lives of children are impressive, ranging as they do from contemplated or actual indiscriminate slaughter to lesser evils. However, even in a favorable environment there is a constant maturational struggle which precludes happiness as the term is usually construed. The illusion seems to rest on the defenses of the parents and their own narcissistic idealization of childhood.

The illusion of the happy healthy child interferes with the recognition of the child as he is, often unhappy and unhealthy, and progressing from one difficult maturational phase to the next. The inevitable childhood neurosis and the inescapable childhood illnesses which are so often concurrent or possibly related are thus more likely to be construed as severe and abnormal conditions requiring drastic action and can more readily become projected representations of repressed impulses in the parents.

The third common factor underlying the specific fantasies which determine the perpetuation of the operation is the unique nature of the tonsils themselves. They impinge on an important orifice and are easily visible, readily accessible, dubious-appearing, questionably useful organs which can be extirpated with apparent impunity. They can therefore serve with singular efficacy as the regressively concretized representations of the undesirable impulses or attributes so commonly projected onto the child.

It seems to me that on these three bases are constructed the specific sexual and aggressive fantasies that are individually determined. This specific material is beyond the scope of this essay.

In conclusion I append a statement about the operation as a practical matter, mainly because this issue has come up in discussions. To me the issue seems academic since I have neither authority nor responsibility in carrying out the operation, and advancing my opinion is the logical limit of my contribution. Beyond this it seems clear that one cannot anticipate that anyone can accept the idea that tonsillectomy is irrational unless he accepts the view that relevant psychoanalytic principles are rational. Therefore, granting that the thesis is correct, one can expect only the slow results that may accrue to the dissemination of the underlying psychological principles.

While my position is that the operation is irrational, I do not automatically equate irrational with bad. For example, pediatricians now cite parental pressure as an indication for tonsillectomy. I do not consider this a rational, scientific indication. Rather it is akin to the convictions of certain cultists who oppose some medical measure such as blood transfusion. However, I would not conclude that doing the operation for this indication is necessarily bad, and I have cited results which can be considered good. Of course these results are not explained, in my opinion, by the removal per se of the tonsils. My view is comparable to that which might hold with any irrationality, that sometimes the wisest course is to join the game.

Appendix

It is one of the curious and intriguing facts of the history of medicine that the surgical excision, in part or totally, of one particular organ, the faucial tonsil, has retained its status as a valid medical maneuver from the Hippocratic period, 2,500 years ago, up to and including the present time. This single procedure has thus survived the entire development of medicine from its origins to its present stage of scientific development. This historical fact considered alone would lead one to assume that correspondingly there has always been some clear and obvious indication which accounts for the continued use of this procedure. However, a study of the history of medicine shows surprisingly that quite the reverse is the case. It is the operation itself which has survived rather than the indications. It would appear that some unrecognized necessity has dictated that the operation must be done, and indications seem to have been found and adapted to this need. Actually over the span of centuries the accumulated indications have been truly protean encompassing at one time or another a huge segment of all known illnesses. Furthermore, the indications have been unstable, constantly being disproved, and repeatedly shifting to new or rediscovered bases. Not only has the operation persisted in this remarkable manner, but in addition it has successfully weathered the criticism of a small minority of physicians who for over a century have been presenting evidence published in the medical literature that raises the most serious question as to its scientific validity. It is surprising to find how little this mass of evidence is given credence or even acknowledged in the pertinent literature. It is no wonder that H. Bakwin, a pediatrician, who has written an extensive review of the subject (1958) terms the prevalence of the operation an enigma.

This enigma is by no means an academic issue; on the contrary, it is a matter of great practical importance from many standpoints. It has been estimated that the operation comprises one third of all the surgery done in the United States (Lederer, 1952). It is stated that the operation comprises one half of the surgical procedures done on hospitalized patients under twenty years of age and two thirds of those done on children under ten (Anonymous, 1957). Some two million tonsillectomies are performed annually in the United States at a cost of one hundred fifty million dollars (Bakwin, 1958). While there is great variation depending on such factors as social and economic status, it is not unusual to find in surveys of children that half or more have had tonsillectomies.

The procedure is by no means innocuous. There is a small mortality rate, particularly unfortunate because quite customarily the patient is in good health at the time of the operation. Precise statistics are hard to come by and must be construed cautiously because there is variability in the conditions of the operation and the skill and experience of the surgeon. Not all operations are done in hospitals, and the otolaryngologists do only some fifteen per cent of the total number. Furthermore, there is a lack of uniformity in reporting the cause of death. All in all, it would seem that Bakwin's (1958) estimate of some two to three hundred deaths annually is conservative being in fact a lower ratio (1:10,000) than estimates which are commonly cited for anesthesia alone.

Not catastrophic but much more frequent are the complications and repercussions of the surgery. Of these probably hemorrhage either immediate or delayed is the most common. Systemic infections, exacerbations of various illnesses, pulmonary infections, and otitis media are reported. Ironically the last is often cited as an indication for the operation. All the complications have been extensively and meticulously studied and are continuously being reviewed; there are a great many reports on this subject in the literature (Abrahamson, 1931; Anonymous, 1955; Bakwin, 1958; Beverly, 1936; Beecher and Todd, 1954; Keen, 1932; King and Story, 1959; McKenzie, 1953; McLemore, 1959; Pembleton, Walker, and Gill, 1959; Rhoads, Sibley, and Billings, 1955).

For all these reasons alone the operation merits the careful judgment of the physician. Yet there is still another area of great importance though almost unrecognized, the psychological repercussions discussed in Section I. While immediate anxiety is recognized, the sphere of ego modifications and characterological deformations remains outside the boundaries of traditional medicine and is not even conceptualized, let alone recognized, by most physicians.

A most valuable historical source has been Jonathan Wright's *The Nose and Throat in Medical History* (1898), and extensive use is made of it here. Among the interesting facets of Wright's work is his recognition of the great psychological importance of the nose and throat. His observations are in full accord with modern clinical practice and the host of neurotic manifestations that involve breathing, swallowing and regurgitation, and speaking. The symbolic importance of this area and its functions is recognizable in ancient literature.

In the Hippocratic period the brain itself was conceived of as a respiratory organ, inspiring air through the nose and discharging it through the skull sutures. It was thought also that the brain discharged secretions into the nose through the cribriform plate of the ethmoid which acted as a strainer. It was supposed that mental processes were sluggish in those whom faulty secretion led to a clogging of the brain with mucus. The Greek word, *coryza*, meant both a cold in the head and a fool or driveler. (Incidentally Hippocrates' remedy for habitual catarrh was coitus which would supposedly effect a cure in three days.) In this period a clean nose connoted mental acuity, an obstructed nose, dullness. It is most interesting to compare these ideas with the observations of Meyer that his adenoid cases had an expression of stupidity and with the later reiterations of the notion that there is in fact mental defect resulting from hypertrophied adenoid tissue.

It is possible that operations on the tonsils were done by the ancient Hindus. They did do uvulotomy and may also have done tonsillotomy but possibly only the incision of peritonsillar abscess. Hippocrates recommended avulsion of the tonsils if they were enlarged. Asclepiades, circa 200 B.C., scarified the tonsils and fauces. Celsus avulsed large tonsils with his fingers or a hook. Aetius warned against hemorrhage from tonsillotomy. In these ancient accounts the symptomatology is not clear.

Paulus Aeginata, writing in the early part of the seventh century, A.D., left a compendium of medicine as it was then known. His books, translated by Francis Adams, in 1844, are an important source. He writes that inflammation of the tonsils causes difficulty in deglutition and breathing. He advises that operation be undertaken only after the inflammation has subsided and warns of the danger of hemorrhage from red, spongy tonsils. He recommends piercing the tonsil with a hook, pulling it outward as far as possible, and cutting it out by the root with a curved scalpel. Paulus also recommended uvulotomy and stated that an elongated uvula could cause cough, sleeplessness, and suffocation.

Evidently Paulus was searching for a precise local cause of the difficulties he described. Perhaps his observation of difficulty in deglutition and breathing was limited to acute inflammations but possibly he meant it more broadly. In any case, such interferences are still to this day attributed to the tonsils even without acute inflammation as if in the intervening centuries no broader view of these problems had emerged. What Paulus blames on the uvula is shifted to the tonsils, which centuries later are blamed for nightmares and fear of suffocating.

Greek medicine reached the Arabs, and tonsillotomy is described in some detail by Albucasis. Then with the advent of the Dark Ages scientific attempts in medicine became unknown. The knowledge of the Arabians became one of the sources of scientific recovery in the Renaissance.

Berenger del Carpi, who taught at Bologna from 1502 to 1527, denied that the cribriform plate of the ethmoid was pervious to cerebral fluid. Later Vesalius supported this view, but he still thought that brain secretions percolated through the base of the skull. However, it was not until the seventeenth century, long after the work of Massa in the sixteenth century, Varolus in 1572, and Spigelius in 1627 had finally led to the recognition and identification of the olfactory nerves as we now know them, that Conrad Schneider disproved the cerebral origin of catarrh. However, as will be seen, some of the current views on the tonsils and adenoids suggest that such a connection retains its appeal.

J. T. King (1956) records an interesting episode, a report of Wiseman, surgeon to King Charles II, in 1686. It is perhaps the first record that reveals the psychological response of a child to tonsillotomy. Wiseman describes his patient as a Person of Honor, aged ten years, having for some years been diseased with preternatural swellings on her tonsils. At one point in the procedure the child choked, apparently having aspirated a piece of tonsil. Wiseman coolly extracted it, and the choking was immediately relieved. The child, recovering, cried, "Shall I live?" Centuries later methodical research indicated that the question of this forthright little girl, who retained her self-possession under the impact of a tonsillotomy without anesthesia at least to the extent of making a direct and relevant inquiry, was indeed a central question in the minds of the untold numbers of children who had undergone the modern version of this procedure.

At about this time, there was already a physician objecting to the operation. Dionis, circa 1700, considered the operation cruel and the results uncertain. Long anticipating an argument to be advanced with much more evidence, he claimed that tonsils had an important function which should not be sacrificed. In his view, this function was "to separate and filtrate serosities which moisten the tongue, larynx, and esophagus," and to aid in "tempering the air in the lungs and sliding the nourishment into the stomach." Behind what we would now think of as a naïve and archaic concept of function is a broad point of view which can be recognized through the whole area of the tonsillectomy controversy. On the one side are a group of physicians like Dionis who seem to be fundamentally committed to the concept of the functional value of the intact human organism, who exercise their ingenuity in the direction of discovering and validating unknown or unrecognized functions, and who often are opposed to excisions and amputations. On the other side are those who seem to be committed to the fundamental concept that illness is wrong or bad, that the body contains disease potential, and that their task is to identify the malign areas and extirpate them. It seems likely that in so far as such deep-seated attitudes exist, they stem from unconscious complexes and exert great influence on theoretical viewpoints.

Apparently the first precisely accurate anatomical description of the tonsils was Kölliker's in 1852. He considered them ductless glands. Waldeyer's description of the ring of lympoid tissue which surrounds the entrance to the respiratory and alimentary passages was published in 1884. In 1857 and 1858 Türck and Czermak popularized the laryngeal mirror. However, Wilhelm Meyer's discovery of the "adenoid vegetations," though published in 1868, was not due to his use of the mirror. Meyer depended on digital examination.

A brief reference to some of the major landmarks in the history of medicine is useful here (Sigerist, 1933). It should be kept in mind that tonsillotomy was popular all through the nineteenth century and that good results were claimed, while the era of scientific medicine as we now know it did not begin until the latter part of the nineteenth century. The work of Semmelweis on the infectious nature of puerperal fever we now recognize as valid, but in 1847 when he published it it was violently repudiated. Pasteur's definitive disproof of the theory of spontaneous generation was in 1860. Koch's work on the anthrax bacillus was published in 1876 and his other important work later. Joseph Lister became professor of surgery at Glasgow in 1861, and it was in the subsequent years that he applied Pasteur's work and introduced the era of antiseptic surgery which was followed fairly soon by aseptic technique. Thus the development of the germ theory did not reach its climax until the last decade of the nineteenth century. Parenthetically, although general anesthesia was discovered before 1850 by Morton, Long, and Wells, it did not come into general use until several decades later. Local anesthesia was first described in 1884 by Koller.

With this background in mind, it is most interesting to note the report of an enthusiastic advocate of tonsillotomy, James Yearsley of London, writing in 1868. Basing himself on experience with several thousand cases over a period of twenty-five years, he reports his results in a monograph which has an admirably descriptive title and subtitle. He calls it: *Throat Ailments, More Especially the Enlarged Tonsil and Elongated Uvula in Connection with Defects of Voice,*

Speech, Hearing, Deglutition, Respiration, Cough, Nasal Obstruction, and the Imperfect Development of Health, Strength, and Growth in Young Persons. The most interesting and significant point of Yearsley's monograph is that so much of it could be fitted without important modification into the current textbooks of otolaryngology. It is therefore worth while to record some of his specific views so that they may be compared with later references.

Yearsley calls tonsillotomy the most uniformly successful operation in surgery. This conclusion is an extremely valuable one, based as it is on long and extensive experience with the use of the operation in a heterogeneous group of disorders. His results are as good for tonsillotomy as any claimed much later for tonsillectomy and therefore cast grave doubt on the later assumption of the importance of the total extirpation and the presumed danger of tonsillar remnants. Furthermore, his claim of favorable repercussions on general health are much the same as the later claims that rest on modern theories of infection; and he reports good results in disorders which much later were attributed to the adenoids and not the tonsils at all. It is evident that Yearsley made the same basic error that was made by every subsequent advocate of the operation, that is, to predicate a causal relation between certain events subsequent to operation and the removal of the tonsils. This *post hoc ergo propter hoc* basis and no other remains the central justification for tonsillectomy. Yearsley thought that the function of the tonsil was to secrete mucus and that enough remained after tonsillotomy to fulfill this function.

He describes three effects of enlarged tonsils. Again his concepts, though apparently archaic, resemble ideas advanced currently. (1) Pressure on the carotid decreases the flow of blood to the brain, thus diminishing nervous energy and retarding corporal development. (2) Food is imbued with foul secretions, the food does not reach the stomach in a pure state, the viscus becomes disordered, and general health suffers. (3) Air is tainted on its passage to the lungs so the patient is living essentially in an unwholesome atmosphere. Almost a century later one finds that similar sweeping connections between the tonsils and health were made, connections which are now authenticated on different bases.

In addition to these general effects, Yearsley believed there were specific repercussions of enlarged tonsils. Various forms of dysphonia ranging from severe hoarseness to minimal voice fatigue, poor enunciation, and slurred speech were not only attributed to the tonsil but interestingly cured by the operation. (Cf. Bunker [1934] on the psychological importance of the voice.) Of particular interest is Yearsley's concept of laryngospasm. He writes that children get violent spasmodic attacks of closure of the glottis at night. They have severe dyspnea and are afraid of suffocating. These children are afraid to sleep alone, and often the parents have to sit with them. This is then an early description of the tonsillar origin of night terrors.

Yearsley writes that deglutition is interfered with, that the child may have a tendency to return his food from the fauces to the mouth to remasticate it, and that this disorder should be suspected if children spend too much time at their¯ meals. Chronic nausea and vomiting, otorrhea, tinnitus, and decreased acuity of hearing are also attributed to the tonsils. Subsequently, some of the difficulties in speech, respiration, and hearing which were then presumed to be caused by enlarged tonsils and relieved by tonsillotomy were relegated to the adenoids and treated by adenoidectomy.

One of Yearsley's cases is a useful illustration. The patient was a fourteen-year-old girl with "a variety of painful and distressing symptoms such as confirmed tonsillary disease can alone produce." Thick snuffling speech; defective hearing; respiration much affected especially at night when she would awake with a loud scream from the impending danger of suffocation; chest pains, headaches, dimness of sight, and other evidence of disordered circulation of the brain; great susceptibility to colds and sore throats; difficulty in swallowing; retardation of growth—all this of ten years' duration and all completely cured with tonsillotomy and some associated medical treatment.

In other cases cited, snoring was stopped, stammering was relieved, and a constant dread of suffocation was cured. Finally, prominent authorities of the time are cited who concur in the views of the author.

It is most interesting to find that a century ago such difficulties as snoring somehow stirred the physician to drastic action. Throughout the literature on tonsillectomy one finds snoring and mouth-breathing referred to repeatedly, always as a self-evident reason for the operation. Just why these habits are deemed sufficiently malign to merit such drastic intervention is never explained; nor can one find any plausible explanation of how the tonsils can be the cause. The obstruction myth looms large in both the old and recent history of tonsillectomy. It is unsupported by proof and is even cautiously questioned. Denzer and Felshin (1943) cite Brennemann's statement questioning whether the tonsils ever obstruct air or food.

One finds in the current literature reiterated and emphatic references to the supposed obstruction caused by the tonsils, but diligent search has failed to unearth the *mechanism* by which such an obstruction is supposed to be possible. Since the faucial tonsil abuts medially on the pharyngeal cavity itself, it can expand in that direction without meeting any resistance. It is inconceivable that thus without leverage it could impinge on the circulation of the well-protected carotid an inch away. Similarly it seems mechanically impossible for the tonsil to impinge on the relatively remote auditory canal. Direct obstruction to either deglutition or respiration is not validated by objective evaluation. Instances in which the tonsils almost meet in the midline are cited in patients without complaints. It is most remarkable that conceivable objective examinations and comparisons are not mentioned. All these presumptions of obstruction are repeated to some extent in the current literature, yet one searches in vain for roentgenologic evidence which might be obtained with fluoroscopic observation of swallowing an opaque meal. One reads of the tonsil obstructing the airway when the child lies supine without any accompanying observation of the child lying supine in fact. It is startling to find that in paper after paper in which obstruction to swallowing or respiration is postulated one cannot find a reference to the child's subjective description of these presumed difficulties. In fact, the

absence of communication with the children themselves is one of the most
remarkable and surprising facets of the whole tonsillectomy problem. A personal
experience lent a particularly precise validation to this point. In a discussion
with an otolaryngologist I inquired of what proof he knew that the tonsils ever
obstructed anything. He replied that it appeared obvious when a mother
reported that her child ate too little, the child was in fact undernourished, and
the tonsils were large. As far as one can determine, the whole obstruction
concept is a deduction based entirely on the relief of certain symptoms subsequent to operation. Barring acute inflammation and the complicating presence
of dysphagia the objective evidence which would demonstrate the existence of
obstruction is lacking, and the facts of anatomy speak eloquently against this
possibility.

Returning to further historical considerations, it is of interest to compare
Yearsley's views with those of William Harvey, published in 1850. Harvey states
that his purpose is to show that tonsillectomy does not relieve deafness and that
misery often results from the operation. However, his conclusions go further
than this. His data are a collection of 116 cases, either his own or those of friends
on whose judgment he could rely.

Harvey is convinced that tonsillar enlargement is a local sign of a morbid
condition of the entire pharyngeal mucous membrane. He therefore believes that
general medical measures, among them cod-liver oil, are preferred therapy. He
does not consider chronically enlarged tonsils a cause of symptoms either in
speaking, swallowing or hearing. His book contains a drawing of a pair of
greatly enlarged tonsils, meeting in the midline, taken from a patient who had no
symptoms of any kind. While Harvey thinks their function is secretory, he believes
they may have other important functions not yet understood, comparing them
to the thyroid, spleen, and suprarenals. In his opinion, the removal of the tonsils
may unfavorably affect speech, hearing, and nutrition. His own historical research goes back another century to the work of French surgeons, which is an
interesting index of the prevalence of the operation before the germ theory. He
cites a number of bad results which he observed. He concludes, referring to
the prevalence of tonsillectomy, "Such errors are so commonly and heedlessly
committed that they may be considered to have become contagious; there are
those persons who are urged almost instinctively to follow the beaten track. . . ."
Some of the cases he cites demonstrate an unfavorable course after tonsillotomy.
However, Harvey's own conclusions also veer far into a post hoc propter hoc
reasoning, now in a negative sense, in that he attributes many difficulties to the
presumed loss of tonsillar function. When Harvey's and Yearsley's reports are
compared they form a potent argument against this deductive fallacy.

With the dissemination of bacteriological knowledge and with the development of the focus of infection theory, tonsillectomy gained a most important
rationale, even though it was already soundly based on empirical results. In a
series of lectures published in 1916, Frank Billings, one of the foremost proponents of this theory, presents the history and rationale of this idea. Many of
these ideas still prevail and can be found in current textbooks.

He defines a focus of infection as a circumscribed area of tissues infected with pathogenic microorganisms. Since many microorganisms are found in the mouth and upper air passages, he considers their presence as indicative of infection in a pathogenic sense. "The presence of these infectious microorganisms in the mouth and upper respiratory tract indicates unhealthful surroundings and individual uncleanliness." This statement remains an operational theoretical landmark in current medicine. The concept that microorganisms are bad is a conviction of many physicians, and the concept of a normal bacterial flora is not regularly accepted. Although his thesis concerns infection, he also adds that hypertrophy of the tonsils and adenoids interferes with respiration and causes deformity of the chest and thorax. The statement is unsubstantiated.

Concerning the relative rarity of systemic infection in comparison with the frequency of foci, Billings writes that the explanation is natural and acquired immunity. Rheumatic fever and endocarditis "are undoubtedly due to focal infection of the mouth and throat." He adds, paradoxically, that the presence of foci can probably excite additional defenses and prevent the evolution of systemic disease.

Rosenow's work on the isolation of pathogenic bacteria from various exudates or excretions or foci and the production of lesions in animals is cited in some detail. It was considered of great importance at the time. With this as a basis and results as support, a tremendous group of illnesses were brought into supposed connection with focus of infection. It is most interesting that the results of the removal of foci were buttressed with what Billings referred to as building up the natural defenses of the body. This included mental and physical rest, nourishing food, cheerful environment, good air and sunshine, exercise, and calisthenics; all in all a regime that would hardly be demanded if the removal of the focus were of such conclusive value.

In line with this theory, Judson Daland, professor of medicine at the University of Pennsylvania, was invited to present a paper on focal infection at a symposium of a joint meeting of otolaryngological societies at Montreal in 1926. Citing twenty-five years of experience, he listed the following diseases as due to chronic infection of the tonsils or sinuses. More precisely, so-called "infected tonsils" were found in the listed illnesses, and an etiologic relationship was assumed: (1) Nervous System: meningitis, encephalitis, bulbar palsy, chorea, neurasthenia, psychoses, diseases of the spinal cord, cranial and peripheral nerves; (2) Bones, Joints, and Muscles: arthritis, osteitis, periositis, synovitis, tendovaginitis, myositis; (3) Alimentary System: gastric, duodenal and intestinal ulcer, gastritis, enteritis, cholecystitis, gallstones, cholangitis, hepatitis, pancreatitis, and appendicitis; (4) Circulatory System: pericarditis, myocarditis, endocarditis, aortitis, thrombosis, embolism, anemia, and pernicious anemia; (5) Genitourinary System: nephritis, pyelonephritis, calculus, prostatitis, seminal vesiculitis, endocervicitis, and sterility; (6) Respiratory System: bronchitis, bronchiectasis, pneumonia, bronchopneumonia, lung abscess, pleuritis, and asthma; (7) Skin: acne, furunculosis, alopecia, herpes, herpes zoster, urticaria, pruritus, dermatitis, and ichthyosis; (8) in addition, conjunctivitis, keratitis, corneal ulcer, iritis, optic neuritis, uveal tract disease, impaired hearing or deafness, tinnitus, vertigo, and Ménière's disease; also, focal infection complicates tuberculosis, syphilis, influenza, and diabetes.

All these diseases require the surgical eradication of the focus in the tonsils or sinuses. Daland states that the tonsils once infected are a menace and should be removed. He tells the ear, nose, and throat specialists that their specialty's importance has doubled with the recognition of the principles of focal infection and warns them against the preventable tragedies of conservative management. A typically tragic history, according to Daland, is one of childhood tonsillitis, diphtheria, or scarlet fever and apparent recovery; occasional bouts of tonsillitis; then at age fifty—systemic disease! A pea-size mass, he writes, can cause fatal illness.

In current standard textbooks of otolaryngology, Ballengers' 1947 edition and Lederer's 1952 edition, one finds Daland's list still cited. Nor does Daland's list form a complete record of the diseases for which this procedure has been attempted. From Moore's modern monograph (1928) and its exhaustive review of the literature can be added toxic goiter, diabetes, lichen planus, and epilepsy. All have been "benefited" by tonsillectomy.

In this monograph Moore lists nineteen symptoms of "enlarged or diseased" tonsils. Note that it is the tonsils, not the adenoids, Moore refers to, although it is true he later attributes some of the same symptoms to the adenoids: (1) Vacant expression; (2) Mental impairment, shown by contracted and narrow nose, swollen lips, the lower one frequently everted; (3) Mouth breathing; (4) Nocturnal mouth breathing and resulting dyspepsia; (5) Thick, muffled voice; (6) Snoring; (7) Nightmares, night terrors, and screaming. This is due to interference with respiration and resulting disturbed cerebral oxygenation; (8) Colds, frequent and prolonged; (9) Hacking cough; (10) Interference with deglutition and vomiting; (11) Chest deformities, pigeon breast, etc.; (12) Impairment of digestion and nutrition. Retarded growth. This is due to want of oxygen and swallowing decomposed secretions from the crypts; (13) Foul breath, from decomposed secretions in the crypts; (14) Anemia—"one of the direct results of enlarged tonsils"; (15) Impairment of hearing—the Eustachian tube is obstructed by pressure on the posterior pillars of the fauces; (16) Impairment of sense of smell and taste; (17) Reflex phenomena—pains in the ear, cough, vomiting and epigastric pain; (18) Fever of uncertain origin; (19) Enlargement of the cervical glands.

The reader should keep in mind that Moore's monograph was published in 1928. It might therefore be of interest to record his summary of the "symptoms and results of neglected adenoids": defective growth and backwardness, aprosexia (the inability to fix attention!), nasal obstruction with the adenoid facies— open mouth, "stupid" expression, thick lower lip, high arched palate, crowded teeth, and collapsed alae nasi. To this he adds rickets, chorea, nocturnal enuresis, stammering and stuttering.

A note on the result of surgical treatment is appended and is most informative. One might suppose that all the breathing difficulties supposedly due to obstruction by the adenoids would be relieved by their removal. However, on the contrary, it then becomes advisable to "encourage" nose breathing with a chin strap, and a whole series of breathing "exercises" are advantageously added.

Additional concepts in Moore's thesis are of interest because they are commonly cited. Regarding the function of the tonsils, he cites some of the work done in the last century supporting the quite generally accepted idea that they are a protection against infection. From this work he, like many others, states that healthy tonsils should not be removed but adds that healthy tonsils are exceptional after the first or second year of life.

An earlier monograph on the tonsils, written by Barnes (1915), is more soundly based scientifically and offers some similar and some contrasting ideas. Barnes takes up embryology, histology, physiology, and pathology. It is interesting that the tonsillar fossa originated from the second branchial pouch. The Ballengers (1947) expand this point, stating that this is similar to the development of the thymus from the third, thyroid from the fourth, and parathyroid from third and fourth branchial pouches. This origin distinguishes the tonsil from other lymphatic glands and suggests it may be distinguished functionally from otherwise comparable tissue. This point is an intriguing one. In repeated discussions about the possible danger of destroying some defensive function with the removal of the tonsils, authorities regularly cite the fact that they form only one element in Waldeyer's ring of lymphatic tissue. Yet this is apparently not precisely true from the standpoint of this unique ontogeny, and in so far as it is true the special localized surgical extirpation would not be easy to defend. The assumption has to be added that the tonsils have a special predilection or susceptibility to infection. Yet one wonders if the deciding issue is not the more practical matter of accessibility. At any rate, no other lymphoid tissue in the body is thus assumed to "lose" its defensive function.

Barnes presents the crucial argument regarding the infection thesis. He states that various microorganisms can be cultured from the tonsils regularly, the basic "infection" datum, but that there is no cultural, morphological, or pathogenic distinction between organisms recovered from the crypts of the tonsils of healthy controls and those from patients suffering from some illness. Nevertheless Barnes writes, "it is almost universally admitted" that the tonsils are a portal of entry for systemic infections. He lists as examples of such systemic infections arthritis, endocarditis, pericarditis, acute and chronic nephritis, neuritis, osteomyelitis, appendicitis, peritonitis, and infectious jaundice. Again returning to the basis of scientific skepticism he writes that neither the clinical, pathological, nor bacteriological evidence is entirely conclusive; moreover, the most convincing evidence that the tonsils are primary foci comes from postoperative results. In the individual case the clinician can seldom "say with certainty" that the tonsils are at fault. Finally he cites the dramatic improvement in that form of chronic toxemia or septicemia evidenced by "general malaise, anemia, loss of weight, etc., but without distinctly localized lesions."

The vacillation between scientific data and the weight of dogma seems quite clear in this passage. Worth noting is the fact that although Barnes wrote in

1915, the tell-tale intrusion of such dogmatic statements as the presumed "universal admission" runs through the literature to the present. Here in the passage cited one can discern the facts which Barnes recorded with scientific precision and the assumptions based on the interpretation of results. The elusive "toxemia" or "septicemia" without lesions is the familiar catch-all term still in use in place of an illness that cannot be precisely diagnosed. One is reminded of the "subclinical" entities, the diseases just beneath the threshold of recognition, indeed of the perennial hapless sophomore who states he "almost palpated" the liver, when confronted with these indeterminate entities.

In regard to function, Barnes states that probably the best evidence of their importance is that their greatest cellular activity is during the most active period of growth; he assumes that their function is the same as lymphoid tissue in general. However, this is a difficult and controversial question. A great deal of experimental work (cf. V. J. Schwartz in discussion of Dean, 1959; Editorial, 1943; Griffith, 1937) suggests a specific *local* defensive function. This is supported by the evidence on poliomyelitis which will be cited in greater detail.

The first suggestion of a link between tonsillectomy and poliomyelitis was probably P. A. E. Sheppard's comment in 1910. In his report of a study of an epidemic he states he saw "one or two" cases in which paralysis seemed to have been precipitated by tonsillectomy. He briefly mentions the two cases, a five-year-old boy who developed paralysis a day after tonsillectomy and a six-year-old boy who developed it twelve days postoperatively. He suggests that it might be injudicious to remove inflamed tonsils during an epidemic. However, he does not stress the point, nor does he mention it in his conclusion. In later publications (1913, 1916) he makes no reference to this (see also Brues and Sheppard, 1912). Consequently it is quite understandable that his observation remained sterile. Thirty years passed and much further work was done before this observation was rediscovered and validated, and the increased vulnerability to poliomyelitis after tonsillectomy was established (Aycock and Luther, 1929; Faber, 1949; Francis et al., 1942; Lucchesi and LaBoccetta, 1944; Sabin, 1938; Siegel et al., 1951; Top and Vaughn, 1941).

The whole problem illustrates both an area of the evidence which indicates that the tonsils have a specific local defensive function and the tenacious convictions concerning the value of the operation. I am not competent to form an opinion about the specific defensive function of the tonsils. The above evidence and some to be presented does seem to indicate that it is distinctly possible that they have such a function.

Some additional comments on the pharyngeal tonsil may be of interest since the removal of the tonsils and adenoids is so commonly done at one operation.

Prior to 1868 there was almost no attention paid to the pharyngeal tonsil or adenoids, as it came to be known. At that time Wilhelm Meyer published his results; two years later they were published in English. Meyer's description of the results of what he called adenoid vegetations has become a classic and the principle of treatment that he suggested has remained the same. It is unusual in medical history that one paper should have had such a result and it merits careful scrutiny. Meyer reported that he found a speech defect and hearing defect commonly associated. The particular speech defect is an inability to pronounce the nasal m and n. The patients would say "cobbod" instead of "common," "sogg" instead of "song," etc. They could not breathe through the nose and kept the mouth open. The voice lacked resonance and sounded dead. These patients would twist and pout their lips in a way which added to the stupidity of their countenance. The nose is thin, flattened from side to side, and the nostrils are collapsed. Other symptoms include a foreign-body sensation in the posterior nares. There is often a pharyngeal secretion of thick green or gray mucus. There is a transitory or permanent decrease in auditory acuity and often otitis media.

Meyer found in such cases that a digital examination of the nasopharyngeal cavity revealed a soft mass which felt like earthworms and which almost filled the cavity. The examination would cause bleeding. He treated this condition by crushing or scraping off these tumors as close to the base as possible. There was free bleeding but apparently no serious hemorrhages. His results were remarkable in that all of his first 102 cases seemed to be successful. The good results appeared quite quickly. The voice becomes sonorous, the pronunciation clearer, respiration is through normal channels, and the facial expression changes "in a surprising manner." He states that "aftertreatment" was nevertheless continued, though why he thought it necessary was not clear. The majority of his patients were between five and fifteen years of age; only three were under five and only nineteen over twenty.

There is a most noteworthy accompaniment of Meyer's procedure which might be connected with his amazingly good results—an accompaniment on which he understandably did not comment: he used no anesthetic! I have seen no mention of this in the literature, and yet if one conceptualizes the traumatic effect of an adenoidectomy without anesthesia, one can envision quite extensive symptomatic repercussions on a psychological basis alone.

Subsequently the diagnosis has become less certain, the treatment open to criticism, and the results questioned. In one instance that attracted my attention, the case was cited of the son of a surgeon who had six adenoidectomies (symposium, 1950). Otolaryngologists in that symposium (see also Proctor, 1960) state that the operation is often badly done. It is very difficult to remove lymphoid tissue which is close to the orifice of the Eustachian tube, and injuries have resulted. For this reason irradiation was used, but malignancy is feared. Careful studies of auditory acuity in children have cast serious doubt on the pathogenic significance of adenoid tissue (Bordley, 1950; Bordley and Hardy, 1955). (For further critical evaluations, see Birdsall, 1939; F. H. McGovern, 1950; Crowe and Burnam, 1941; Tumarkin, 1937.) The opinion has been advanced (M. Yearsley, 1939) that the so-called adenoid facies is due primarily to a particular cranial formation; if there is any association, it is that a high palate causes adenoids. However, the central issue became one of confusion. The two operations, tonsillectomy and adenoidectomy, became paired and their individual evaluation confounded. Occasional efforts at doing adenoidectomy alone (see

McLemore, 1959) have been disappointing but have not led to a systematic re-evaluation. The dogmatic tenacity that adheres to tonsillectomy seems to be shared in regard to its companion procedure.

From this historical survey it seems clear that surgical attacks on the tonsils have been validated for centuries for a variety of shifting reasons and in the face of serious criticism. The next step is the evaluation of current practice. For this purpose a critical examination of modern textbooks and a representative sampling of current literature follows.

A detailed account from one textbook (Lederer, 1952) is useful as a proto-type. The author states that chronic tonsillitis is the most common of all throat diseases. He considers hypertrophy, hyperplasia, and cryptic retention as patho-logical changes. He begins his account of the symptomatology by stating that *at times there are no symptoms.* Thus by inference the diagnosis is made by examination of the tonsils. He continues that large tonsils cause a sense of full-ness or local irritation in the throat and difficulty in swallowing and breathing. (One wonders how consistently those complaints are psychogenic.) He adds that bad breath is due to retention in the crypts.

Following this, Daland's list, taken from the 1926 paper cited earlier, is quoted verbatim with the explanation that these diseases are caused by "absorp-tion into the general circulation." The author makes the surprising claim that "Tonsillectomy has met with unequivocal world-wide acceptance." (In fact, there have been consistent criticisms for a century, but they have not come to the attention of the author; though in this respect his position is not remarkable.) Acknowledging that the tonsils have a function, he states that the real problem in medicine is the baneful effect of diseased tonsils in undermining health. He adds that a relationship to endocarditis, nephritis, and arthritis is generally accepted, although in fact such a relationship is controversial at best.

Ten indications for tonsillectomy are listed. The list is partly repetitious but is cited because it adds certain conditions and is quite representative (My com-ments are added in brackets).

1. Frequent attacks of acute tonsillitis.
2. Recurrent peritonsillar abscess. [Very rare in children according to Bak-win (1958).]
3. Systematic or focal infection [A huge area!]
4. Chronic otorrhea or repeated otitis media [often cited as due to ade-noids].
5. Recurrent or persistent cervical adenopathy.
6. Failure of children to gain weight.
7. Diphtheria carriers.
8. Mechanical obstruction giving rise to alterations in speech and difficulty in breathing and swallowing. [This typical citation seems to rest entirely on the propensity to attribute these symptoms to presumed obstruction. One searches in vain for any objective evidence that indicates that the tonsils are in fact an obstruction.]

9. Frequent colds. Mucopurulent rhinitis.
10. Pathologic tonsils. [This terse indication evidently refers to examination and the evaluation of the size of the tonsils or the presence of caseous material in the crypts. It is apparently considered an indication for tonsillectomy even in the absence of any symptomatic criteria.]

The indications for adenoidectomy are: (1) mouth breathing, day or night; (2) chronic mucopurulent rhinitis; (3) frequent head colds; (4) spasmodic cough; (5) cervical lymphadenopathy; (6) frequent earaches or aural discharge. Interference with hearing is mentioned elsewhere. No explanation is given of the overlapping of the indications.

Finally, when the author comes to prognosis after tonsillectomy, he seems to base himself more directly on his experience and adds some most significant comments. He states that the real value of the operation cannot be determined in the first two years inasmuch as the apparent benefits are not so pronounced except over a longer period. It is clearly most difficult for the unbiased observer to accept the idea that such a protracted period, especially in the development of a child, should have any favorable developments explained by the operation. Such a protracted period is suspect. Other authors cite immediate, dramatic results which are equally suspect since one must then consider the effect of the psychological trauma.

The author also adds, again evidently from experience, that endocarditis is not aided, that polyarthritis may be initiated, that myocardial infection may spread, that kidney disturbances may be aggravated, and that remaining lympoid tissues can be a focus of infection. The last point is apparently intended to explain the presence of infection allegedly due to foci when the tonsils are absent.

Three other textbooks (Ballenger and Ballenger, 1947; Litchfield and Dembo, 1947; Watkyn, 1953) present lists of indications and comparable unsubstantiated statements. "Headache," "cough," and "neurasthenia" are among the ailments attributed to absorbed toxins from diseased tonsils. In these texts one can learn of no scientifically founded rationale. The claims made are clearly traditional, based entirely on assumptions regarding results, and without convincing evidence of relevant pathological mechanisms. A survey of the current literature might be expected to add more light, but an examination proves to be disappointing. In view of the customary coupling of the tonsils and adenoids, citations are given from opinions about both.

Alexander (1956) writes that "a marked anemia develops from diseased adenoids." He states that the consequences of diseased adenoids include snuffling, nasal obstruction, nasal catarrh, sinusitis, cervical adenitis, gastrointestinal disturbances, defective growth, aprosexia (an esoteric term used mainly by otolaryngologists to designate an inability to fix attention—another surprising intrusion into psychological matters), neuroses, systemic infections, middle-ear disease, and auditory impairment. He writes that few surgical procedures produce such good results, but in describing them he refers to a personality change rather than the cure of all the indicated illnesses: the dull, listless, and even stupid-looking child becomes bright, active, and healthy-appearing with a new enjoyment of life. The most obvious supposition would be that such a sharp personality change is the result of increased anxiety and the attempt to master it. One wonders how such a conclusion as Alexander's can be reached without any subjective confirmation by the child.

Barnes (1915) considers the high palatal arch a *cause* rather than an *effect* of adenoids, an opinion shared by others, but he also believes that enlarged adenoids result in deficient aeration of the blood and consequently in mental backwardness from cerebral anoxia. He states, "The mental sluggishness of many chronic mouth breathers disappears in a remarkable manner after the removal of an obstructive adenoid. . . . The general health and vigor of the child usually changes wonderfully for the better, the amount of improvement depending of course on the extent to which the mouth breathing was responsible. . . ." And yet he adds that mouth breathing, having become a habit, may persist. Thus by circular reasoning the operation is defended against failure.

Baron (1956) asserts that speech defects are associated with hypertrophy of the tonsils and adenoids. The mechanism of such a defect is explained no more than it was a century before.

Bass (1934) cites his personal opinion that tonsillectomy helped 88 per cent of 150 children whom he carefully selected.

Crookes (1957) sent a questionnaire to fifty physicians on whose children he had done tonsillectomies. He found that forty of them were satisfied with the results of the operation. One may conclude that physicians respond as most parents would.

Dean (1959) considers the tonsils a focus of infection, but adds that tonsillectomy does not prevent rheumatic fever. This statement is important coming as it does from a proponent of the focus of infection theory. Again and again one finds specific experience opposed to the theory, while the theory as a whole is not impeached. In "toxic malnutrition" secondary to infection of lymphoid masses he finds the return to normal almost miraculous. Simple hypertrophy may necessitate removal to restore normal breathing. Dean writes that he never saw a permanent deleterious result of tonsillectomy. One may construe this as the sincere opinion of a physician who is oblivious of the realm of psychology. Yet, in the discussion of his paper, F. R. Spencer states that the tonsils may be ductless glands because some children of four or five change after the operation as if they were suffering from hypothyroidism. This observation merits attention in contrast to the more common reports of increased alertness. E. C. Mitchell offers the opinion that recurrent tonsillitis tends to decrease in severity spontaneously. He questions one of the most consistent indications. Referring to enuresis as a kidney disease, he does not find the results consistent.

An Editorial (1947) in the *Journal of the American Medical Association* cautions against leaving a focus of infection in a tonsil stump.

Ersner and Lerners (1956), otolaryngologists, state that ". . . toxemia may prevail without giving rise to clinical manifestations." This type of toxemia is linked to the tonsils. They maintain that reflex symptoms of diseased tonsils are nightmares, night sweats, cough, and occasionally enuresis. Often overlooked, in their opinion, is retarded mental development due to anoxemia. They state that the psychic trauma of the operation is greatly exaggerated.

Farrow (1956) writes that in children who habitually sleep on their backs, the relaxation of the throat muscles during sleep may allow the tonsils to fall backward and downward and cause the child to awake with a sudden sense of suffocation. This is not an uncommon cause of night terrors in children, and involuntary bed wetting may occur at the same time. This statement warrants comparison with Burton's observation reported by Jones (1931): those who are witch-ridden, if they lie on their backs, suppose an old woman sits hard on them so they are almost stifled.

Fowler (1934) states that 95 of 100 children lost their heart murmurs after tonsillectomy.

Kaiser (1952) includes as indications for tonsillectomy interference with breathing, swallowing difficulties, colds, and also unexplained malnutrition, unplained anorexia, cyclic vomiting, and retarded mental development. In other studies (1931, 1940) Kaiser presents statistics that cast some doubt on the efficacy of the operation though his own conclusions do not so state. While Kaiser's study was based on 4,400 children, his conclusions are based on very small samplings. For example, he writes that nephritis occurred only one third as often in children who had tonsillectomies. Yet this is based on a total of thirty-four cases of nephritis. In this group only nine had tonsillectomies.

Hall (1937), in his textbook, states that marked weight gain often follows tonsillectomy, from which he concludes that malnutrition is a sequel of infected tonsils. He considers difficulty in swallowing, choking, "fits," and mouth breathing as due to mechanical obstruction.

In a study of charts, LeRiche and Stiver (1957) found that physicians' calls for acute upper respiratory infections decreased after tonsillectomy. One can hardly draw any conclusion other than the bald fact that once a tonsillectomy has been done, the parents are less likely to call a physician.

Francis McGovern (1959) adds a highly controversial point in recommending the operation for sinusitis. Others disagree. He cites Dean, though in the reference given Dean does not recommend the operation for that purpose, claiming only that he often found sinusitis at the time of the operation. McGovern makes the interesting observation that the average emotionally balanced child looks upon the operation as an exciting new adventure, thus by inference establishing this response as a criterion of normality and by the same token authenticating the "normality" of the operation.

McLemore (1959) cites one of the usual groups of indications, among them rheumatic fever. He has tried adenoidectomy alone but was embarrassed to find the child returning with "absolute" indications for tonsillectomy. He states frankly that he tells parents that when there have been repeated attacks of tonsillitis the tonsils have lost their protective function but that he himself has no way of deciding when this has occurred.

Incidental to another study (Nesbitt, 1934) is the observation that snoring was cured in all but 58 of 798 operations. The author does not comment on the need to cure snoring.

A questionnaire survey of 3,400 pediatricians elicited twelve indications (Wolman, 1956). These were (1) recurrent or chronic otitis media; (2) prominent mouth breathing or snoring from hypertrophy; (3) recurrent or chronic tonsillitis; (4) early hearing impairment; (5) recurrent or chronic cervical abscess; (6) previous peritonsillar abscess; (7) recurrent or chronic asthma from respiratory infection; (8) "tendency" to rheumatic fever; (9) recurrent or chronic sinusitis; (10) recurrent or chronic lung infection; (11) scarred or cryptic tonsils; (12) large size alone.

In regard to results, 64 per cent of the physicians find emotional changes lasting more than two weeks either absent or rare, but 0.4 per cent find them as a rule. They report certain nonspecific benefits: weight gain (83%), increased appetite (82%), improved growth (52%), improved social attitudes (32%), better school grades (30%). In concluding, Wolman states that almost all the evidence in favor of tonsillectomy is *post hoc ergo propter hoc* in essence.

A pediatrician, McLendon, states, "It is frequently the case that one finds misbehavior situations in children as the result of diseased tonsils. There is no doubt that this behavior is frequently associated with the toxemia and the accompanying malnutrition. Such behavior expressed in maladjustment and anxiety frequently improves with the nutritional state postoperatively. I found that one should be careful not to overemphasize the psychological disturbance of these children during this period of lowered physical status" (see Jessner and Kaplan, 1949).

With this the survey of the representative current literature which supports the operation is concluded. The reader cannot escape serious questions about the quality of this work; moreover, as will be seen, it compares unfavorably with that of opponents. Repeatedly one finds such cases as this paradigm (Rock, 1944): a patient with septicemia was vigorously treated with chemotherapy. Organisms found in the blood were cultured from the tonsils. Certainly this might have been expected. A tonsillectomy was done during the acute illness. The patient recovered. From this evidence it is suggested that the tonsils were the source of the septicemia.

It requires specific emphasis that the issue raised here is exclusively one of scientific validity and has no connection whatsoever with integrity. This point must be explicit because occasionally even in the literature and not uncommonly informally one hears that the operation is done to make money. There is no scientific evidence to support such a conclusion, and such an abuse would be entirely an ethical problem having no connection with this essay. Indeed it is true that the incidence of tonsillectomy tends to increase in proportion to income (Mertz, 1954), but this is apparently a matter of the accessibility of medical care. Among those in the upper-income group with the higher proportion of tonsillectomies are the children of physicians themselves, a fact that demonstrates that the indications for the operation are a matter of sincere conviction.

The practicing physician will also recognize that the literature does not do justice to the acumen of the clinician. To begin with, physicians are not often gifted writers and find it difficult to describe the nuances of clinical judgment that may enter into a decision to operate. No textbook is an accurate guide to practice; in fact, textbooks tend to be indicative more of recent history than current practice. Probably not a single clinician would concur in all the indications cited or even in the majority of them. It seems most plausible that the clinician is aiming at satisfactory results and utilizes all his capacities to predict good ones and avoid the bad. It requires emphasis that the thesis advanced here is that the operation is based empirically, as Wolman (1956) states, on results and on what are considered good results. However, I contend (1) that what are commonly construed as good results are open to careful scrutiny, (2) that bad results are not adequately conceptualized, and (3) that the results altogether are not due mainly to the extirpation of the faucial tonsil itself as a somatic entity but are in fact explained by the nature and circumstances of operative intervention in a nonspecific sense and the symbolic rather than somatic significance of the surgical attack on this particular organ.

A representative survey of the literature which casts doubt on or opposes tonsillectomy is now cited. The bases of such skepticism are diverse. One method of investigation is the comparison of large groups of individuals who have had tonsillectomies with those who have not. Four such studies (Forsythe, 1928; Gafafer, 1932; Mertz, 1954; Smiley, 1924) showed minor differences, but such as they were favored those who had retained their tonsils. The evidence on poliomyelitis tends to support this point. The examination of a large group of children, 4,000, of whom only 2 per cent had had tonsillectomies, showed that they were in good health and quite free of the presumed ill effects of the presence of tonsils (Ellis and Russell, 1937). These children were Basques and had not had access to the most modern medical care. The examiners were clearly most favorably impressed with the courageous behavior of the children under catastrophic conditions but this bias need not have influenced their opinions of the children's physical status.

Two points regarding these and other statistical studies merit attention. On the whole, they seem to show minor differences which are rather unconvincing because of the great margin of error inherent in the evaluation of any single patient. Subjective evaluation of health is most important, and the evaluation of the health of children by parents is notoriously inaccurate. The clinician is not really surprised to listen to a parent's history of a delicate, frail child, and then be confronted with a young colt bursting with vitality. In the face of these and comparable uncertainties, nuances in statistics are unimpressive. Furthermore, since tonsillectomy is traditionally a promoter of health, subsequent illnesses are likely to be minimized. Finally, there is a glaring gap in research. The possibilities of more extensive, more careful, and more conclusive control studies are immense. No comparisons of autopsy statistics were found; nor are there studies of large fixed populations—state hospitals, prisons, military forces —comparable to the studies on tobacco in relation to cancer. Control studies on psychological repercussions are lacking, although here again data could be easily available. In summary, I could not find a broad statistical study which demonstrated that a clear advantage adhered to tonsillectomy.

The protean indications for the operation dictate almost necessarily that its incidence will be capricious. Many studies prove this and show the degree of individual dogmatism that enters into the decision to operate. One of the best known of these studies is one in which nineteen physicians gave their opinion of the need for tonsillectomy in a large group of school children (American Child Health Association, 1934). Each child was examined by three physicians independently. Then the results were arranged statistically so that the examinations appeared to be sequential rather than concurrent. By this means it was found that a given physician would tend to decide that very roughly 45 per cent of a group of children required tonsillectomy. If the remaining 55 per cent were examined, the decision was still that 45 per cent needed the operation; and the examination of the remainder, now with the tonsillectomy candidates twice weeded out, indicated that still 45 per cent needed the operation. This study also showed that about one half of the children with severe untreated dental and visual defects had already had tonsillectomies. Another study (Dey, 1952) demonstrated that on re-examination, after tonsillectomy had been postponed for a long time because of a polio epidemic, one third of the children were no longer thought to require it.

Since benefits have been claimed for tonsillectomy in so many diseases, it has been necessary for the specialists in those particular areas to make specific investigations. These results are most important from several standpoints. First, as documentation will show, confirmation of the benefit is lacking. This is by no means an unweighted difference of opinion, but is as a rule the considered and careful opinion of the investigator in a particular field as opposed to the traditional and unsupported claim of the tonsillectomy proponent. Perhaps the weakest point in the argument of the otolaryngologists who are fully convinced of the operation's value is that they are thereby so consistently forced to expand their opinion into fields in which they are not expert. The otolaryngologist is indeed in a tenuous position when he insists that tonsillectomy produces beneficial personality changes or when he insists on this operation as the rational treatment of choice in neuroses. One notes that there is some development in the direction of considering the otolaryngologist's contribution to this problem mainly that of special technical skill in the operation itself.

Not only in psychiatry but in many other areas we find specialists disputing claims of benefit. Ironically while the pressure of such evidence may gradually force the abandonment of the operation for a particular condition, the accumulation of this evidence never seems completely to impinge on the rationale of the operation. Thus any physician would today discard much of Daland's list (1926) cited above; yet the method of deriving such a list is unitary and if some elements are demonstrably false, then logically the whole list is useless since there is no method of distinguishing one component from another.

Still another facet of this issue is the tendency of the proponents to make broad claims which overlook careful research and meticulous classifications. How can one evaluate the claim of benefit in "nephritis" in the face of painstaking and ingenious research on the complexities of the nephritides? How can one compare a recommendation about frequent "colds" with the mass of epidemiologic, nosologic, and etiologic research into these illnesses?

The following papers are representative examples of the type of work discussed. Further examples are given in more detailed reviews. In a study of 403 children who had tonsillectomies and a control group it was concluded that tonsillectomy offers no protection against rheumatic fever and may render the child more vulnerable (Wallace and Smith, 1936). A careful study of 300 cases of nephritis in childhood over an eleven-year period led Illingworth (1939) to conclude that the operation might increase the risk of nephritis, might be fatal if done during the illness, and was of no benefit. Studies of sinusitis lead to the conclusion that tonsillectomy has no beneficial effect (Birdsall, 1939; Crooks, (1938). Another author (Tumarkin, 1937) concludes that it is a useless procedure in ear and sinus disease. Careful studies with controls have indicated it is not of value in allergies, particularly asthma (Glaser, 1956; J. P. McGovern, 1959).

Griffith (1937) reports that the operation is not helpful in middle-ear disease, that sinusitis becomes more common, and cites other poor results. M. Yearsley (1939) offers various skeptical considerations but concludes that both obstruction and sepsis are indications. He mentions his own long-maintained view that the so-called adenoid facies is a peculiarity of cranial development and is not due to nasal stenosis.

A Symposium (1940) of the Royal Society of Medicine included diametrical differences of opinion. On the one hand the focus of infection theory and obstruction were advanced so that the operation was advised for poor nutrition, poor stamina, poor body tone, enuresis, rheumatism, and nephritis. Others stated that the operation was useless or harmful in rheumatism, pulmonary disease, and sinus disease; that spontaneous resolutions of cervical adenitis and sore throats were the rule; that deferment and re-examination often indicated the operation was no longer necessary; and, finally, that many children seem to breathe through their mouths, although there is no respiratory obstruction. This last comment is unusual. I have not been able to fathom the mouth-breathing, snoring mystery. Why either of these "symptoms" becomes the cause for such concern and drastic action is nowhere spelled out. Only rarely does one encounter a comment like the one above which raises the question of why one must take these matters as a sort of medical emergency.

Turning now to more detailed consideration of specific contributions, the first to be reviewed is that of Sanford Blum, a pediatrician, published in 1915. He had become skeptical of the results. In 100 unselected cases in his practice he found that he had recommended the operation twice and had one good and one bad result. The remaining 98 children had recovered from their various illnesses and were doing well. In his observation of a group of 100 clinic patients with more frequent tonsillectomies he noted that in three instances asthma began after the operation and three other children developed mastoiditis later. He found that when the operation had been done because of enlarged cervical glands, they remained enlarged anyway. He judged that the children with tonsillectomies suffered more frequent upper respiratory infections.

Blum noted that the multiplicity and heterogeneity of indications for tonsillectomy ranging from mouth breathing and colds, to the size and appearance of the tonsils and the material in the crypts, to obscure stomach trouble, would suffice to recommend removal of all tonsils. He stated that tonsillectomy had become a menace. He cited studies which indicate that hypertrophy is not a problem and that other indications are dubious. He remarks that the throat specialist is not best able to judge results, and he considers some of the favorable developments subsequent to tonsillectomy to be due actually to maturational events connected with the second dentition, broadening of the jaw and larger respiratory passages. He felt that the tonsils had a function in combating infection and was one of the contributors of experimental data in support of this thesis. He mentions as indications for the operation malignancy, possibly recurrent peritonsillar abscess or evidence of serious local or systemic injury. Logically his position on the last point is open to question from his own argument. Many of Blum's data and arguments seem valid to me, and it is noteworthy that in the intervening half century they have gained so few adherents.

Bradley in 1930 reported on a careful study of 289 boys in an English school. He presents arguments which are of crucial importance in connection with one of the indications for tonsillectomy which is currently in vogue, sore throats. In the first place, the frequency of sore throats or upper respiratory infections in general cannot be reasonably evaluated on the basis of the individual child. *alone.* In part this is an epidemiologic problem and is linked with the density and virulence of the particular microorganisms to which the child is exposed. In addition, general hygienic factors have a place in such an evaluation. Second and most important, he points out that the precise diagnosis of the myriad group of acute respiratory infections in children is both extremely difficult and impractical. With inflammation of the upper respiratory passages and a systemic reaction accompanied by fever and perhaps headache and vomiting, a whole group of diagnoses, flu, pharyngitis, bronchial catarrh, gastroenteritis (and currently virus infection) as well as tonsillitis, are conceivable. They have a practical descriptive value but cannot be exact etiologically.

This argument is most important because recurrent attacks of acute tonsillitis is one of the indications currently in use for tonsillectomy. Since the designation of such a diagnosis cannot be precise but depends in part on the weight the physician gives to tonsillar inflammation in the presence of evidence of more diffuse illness, this indication itself is subject to great uncertainty. Even granting a prominent tonsillar inflammation, it is by no means evident that the tonsillar reaction is provocative rather than defensive. On the contrary, Bradley states that with the tonsils present, there are somewhat more frequent localized sore throats, but with their removal there is an increased incidence of non-descript febrile reactions which are far more difficult to classify. I have not found this point acknowledged in the usual literature, even if only in an attempt to refute it, yet it is of obvious importance since the one difficulty that tonsillectomy indubitably prevents is tonsillitis. This seems to be a distorting factor in statistics since any less well-recognized illnesses are more likely to be overlooked.

In Bradley's opinion, the appearance of the tonsils in the entity called acute follicular tonsillitis is explained by the particular architecture of certain tonsils and is not otherwise a clinical entity. The debris in the crypts is no more important than wax in an ear or smegma behind a prepuce, and the appearance of beads of puslike debris in the crypts during a sore throat does not indicate a more serious illness.

Bradley found the appearance of the tonsils different in different seasons, often large in winter and small in summer. He considers operation for hypertrophy useless and adds that compensatory hypertrophy of other lymphoid tissue in the neck suggests there is an optimal amount necessary for protection. He states that tonsillectomy offers no protection against otitis media or upper respiratory infections and leaves the patient more vulnerable to serious infection. He deems it a most elementary form of symptomatic treatment which obscures research. Nevertheless he finds it necessary to recommend it in most exceptional instances, about one per cent of the children he saw, in which he felt that auto-infection from a chronic focus produced recurrent inflammation. Like Blum's, his thesis is weakened by the inadequate delineation of this exception.

Epstein (1937), reporting on 540 tonsillectomies and adenoidectomies, correlated various factors. Of 1,200 cases, this number had remained under observation for two years. He found 92 per cent free of cervical adenitis, 79 per cent cured of mouth breathing, 73 per cent free of cough, and 36 of 40 free of otitis media; 60 per cent had complete relief of complaints. The best results were in the six-to-ten age group, next in the ten-to-thirteen, and worst under six. He found that 66 children developed new complaints, 40 persisting during the period of observation. He could find no relation between the results and the size of the tonsils, whether deeply embedded or not. The pathologic changes were correlated neither with complaints nor with results. Some evidence of pathological changes that could be classified as destructive was quite regular. (I have not expanded this study into the area of histology and can only note the apparently consistent observation that the tonsils as they exist in fact do not seem to fulfill the requirements of the pathologist to be designated as a normal organ.) Epstein could not find any correlation with the appearance of the tonsils and concluded that the "infected tonsil" so-called cannot be identified.

He palpated the adenoid while the child was under anesthesia in a number of cases. Seventy-nine children with obstructed pharyngeal spaces complained of mouth breathing. (Presumably the parent complained.) However, this complaint was also present in 20 of 37 children who had no obstruction; and of this group of 20 whose mouth breathing was *not* explained by pharyngeal obstruction, 6 were nevertheless cured by the operation.

The protracted observation leaves in doubt the relationship between the favorable changes and the tonsillectomy; moreover, the mechanism of change is not evident. The puzzling relation of cough to tonsil, for example, is not explained. The lack of correlation with objective findings is most interesting.

Glover (1938, 1948) documents the extensive eccentricities in the incidence of the operation. There was a great rise after the First World War, a reduction after a series of critical papers in the early 30s, and then a rise. In the discussion of this paper (1938) Layton states he has seen children living in unfavorable, overcrowded conditions go downhill and die after tonsillectomy.

Glover shows that in immediately contiguous and similar geographical areas there was a fivefold variation in incidence of tonsillectomy depending on the opinion of the physician. While in certain cases the operation seemed to have brilliant results, but he concludes that (1) incidence is excessive. (2) The age incidence suggests that the operation is done because of physiological, immunologically useful enlargements. (3) Clinical examination cannot demonstrate disease or infection [a most important viewpoint which asserts that the *appearance* of the tonsils is of no importance]. (4) The operation has its own morbidity and mortality. (5) Frequently repeated attacks of acute tonsillitis are the most useful indication. (6) It is useless in colds, chronic nasal catarrh, and otitis media, and harmful in bronchitis, asthma, and nephritis. (7) It is of no value as a prophylaxis against common infectious diseases. (8) It is never urgent. A six-month observation period is indicated. (9) More control studies are necessary. (10) Finally, Goodhart already said in 1885 that it is comparatively seldom that an operation is necessary. [Children outgrow the "symptoms." By fourteen or fifteen chronic enlargement ceases to be of importance (Goodhart, 1885).]

A study by a British group (Medical Research Council, 1938) could find very little value in the operation. A group of 364 boys who had had tonsillectomies seemed to be sick less often than expected. However, their figures leave the reader somewhat skeptical. In regard to specific illnesses, there was no favorable influence on scarlet fever, rheumatism, or otitis media. The authors thought the operation might be detrimental: "One cannot avoid the conclusion that there is a tendency for the operation to be performed as a routine prophylactic ritual for no particular reason, and with no particular result."

Paton (1943) studied the medical records of 909 school girls, 57 per cent of whom had had tonsillectomies. Those who had had tonsillectomies were more likely to have otorrhea and enlarged cervical glands, and lost slightly more time because of illness. In general, he could not detect beneficial results of the operation.

Denzer and Felshin (1943) report that the mere establishment of a preoperative clinic for tonsillectomy to make adequate differential diagnosis and collect adequate records led to a lowering of the incidence of the operation by 50 per cent in a year. Results were difficult to evaluate. Tonsillitis was eliminated, but other infectious illnesses were not known and the falling curve of illness after the seventh year was a factor. These authors eliminated allergy; mouth breathing from malocclusion (they alone cite *that* cause); bad oral hygiene; mental disorders; malnutrition, underweight, and anorexia, taking into account poverty, ignorance, and bad eating habits. They eliminated a large group who came only because a teacher, mother, or friend thought it should be done. They ended up deciding that 17 per cent of those referred required tonsillectomy.

As indications they selected chronic otitis or defective hearing; apparent interference with respiration from size; frequent infection with large tonsils; and rheumatic disease, only for the lack of anything better to do. However, in connection with their own criteria, they report that they saw tremendous tonsils with no mouth breathing. Thus they are among those who confirm Harvey's 1850 report.

They cite the capricious incidence previously mentioned, particularly referring to the reduction in operations from 2,316 in 1930 to 164 in 1937 in a single locale by Ash. They cite Brennemann who stated, "I am not sure that large tonsils ever cause a deleterious obstruction to either air or food, and who can tell when a given tonsil has grown large from true hypertrophy in the rendering of yeoman service or is harboring organisms that menace the host?"

Fry (1957) considers the operation valuable in selected cases but leaves few enough indications. One is intransigent parental pressure. This curious, but understandable reason is often cited. Fry includes among the indications recurrent otitis media and tonsillitis, but in regard to the former he states that patients who did not have the operation got along well and that recurrent tonsillitis declines naturally after age nine.

Fry has never been convinced of obstruction, nor of the focal infection theory, nor of the importance of cervical glands. He observes that certain children have repeated colds, coughs, earache, transient deafness, and some debility, and that all these difficulties tend to decline after the age of seven or eight.

He considers the fact that certain conditions become irritating, trying, and demoralizing for the child, family, school, and doctor, and lead to the need for operation. Yet he asks if the operation is a fashionable and misguided procedure carried out in a desperate attempt to treat a normal phase of child development, a phase which will subside in two to three years. Fry's statement most closely approximates my thesis, since it is compatible with the factor unknown to the organicists—the ubiquitous childhood neurosis.

Bakwin's careful study (1958) assembles the mass of evidence that leads him to characterize the continuing frequency of the operation as an enigma. Much of the evidence he cites has already been referred to, but a brief recapitulation will be given. He discusses the extremely variable frequency of the operation and its direct relation to economic opportunity. He points out that at present the most common reasons for the operation are parental pressure, the large size of the tonsils or adenoids, and frequent upper respiratory infections. In regard to the latter he writes that all the available evidence indicates that the operation is at best useless. He cites the dangers and complications. Here, he states, is a "disease" with no mortality and a therapy with a potential danger which is proved in relation to bulbar poliomyelitis and may exist for other neurotropic viruses.

However, having disposed of the arguments in favor of the operation, Bakwin finds it necessary to qualify his conclusion in a way which undermines his own thesis. He states, "The careful studies in the literature, although showing beyond doubt that by and large tonsillectomy and adenoidectomy has no favorable influence on the health of children, cannot be interpreted as proving that the operation does not help in certain isolated cases." This statement is something of an enigma within an enigma, since one cannot escape the hypothesis that Bakwin has demonstrated precisely that the benefits that are thought to occur in certain cases cannot be explained on any organic basis. His own position answers at least in part the subsequent question as to why the practice is continued indiscriminately as he puts it. The answer is that no individual physician avowedly removes tonsils indiscriminately, each uses judgment and selection, and quite commonly the individual physician takes pride in the judicious exclusion of unsuitable cases. The issue seems to lie in the limitation of the span of individual experience rather than in indiscriminate operation.

This latter factor has been most forcibly impressed on me in the course of discussions with a number of physicians during the past year while I have been preparing this essay. Repeatedly I have been told of a single case, sometimes a son or daughter, in which it was presumed that the results of tonsillectomy were favorable. Apparently the factor cited by several authors (Blum, 1915; Denzer and Felshin, 1943; Fry, 1957), that children become particularly susceptible to infections during the period roughly from the fifth to the ninth year, possibly connected with exposure in school, possibly connected with the childhood neurosis, is either not known or not accepted. This period of vulnerability tends to come to a sharp conclusion before puberty, and infections decrease in frequency and become more adult in character. The concept of the child outgrowing his vulnerability to illness is in the public domain. Yet ironically the proponents of tonsillectomy have "discovered," and the point is made repeatedly, that the best "results" are obtained if the operation is not done early and tend to avoid the operation before the child is six. If the operation is done at that point and the two years which Lederer (1952) recommends be allowed to pass before the results are evaluated, then a normal maturational process has been submerged and its results attributed to an irrelevant operation.

With the scope of divergent opinion documented above, it is rather surprising how often one finds that the operation is not even recognized as a controversial one. Such recognition might stimulate further research which is so deficient.

With this I bring to a conclusion the data which I have assembled to document the hypothesis that tonsillectomy as a method of organic therapy is not supported by scientific evidence. The mechanisms by which the presence of the tonsil is presumed to be detrimental are not adequately explained but rest on deductions derived from the results of their removal. Neither remote infection, local infection, nor obstruction prove to be well-founded concepts. The so-called results of the operation prove to be deceptive. In the first place, despite the fact of the antiquity of the operation, the results are still inadequately documented; the traditional sanction that the operation enjoys has impeded accurate and imaginative research. Secondly, in so far as the documented results can be evaluated, leaving aside the identified complications and considering what are construed as favorable results, they seem to be explained by two quite separate factors. First, significant maturational changes regularly take place rather rapidly after the usual time of the operation, and no long-range development can be attributed to it without control study. Control studies do not tend to confirm this causal connection. The second factor explaining the results is the unrecognized psychological repercussions. In neither case need one assume that it is the removal of the tonsils *themselves* which explains the results.

BIBLIOGRAPHY

Abrahamson, L. (1931), Subacute Bacterial Endocarditis Following the Removal of Septic Foci. *Brit. Med. J.*, II:8-9.

Alexander, L. W. (1956), The Adenoid and Its Relation to the Ear. *Trans. Amer. Laryngo., Rhino., & Otol. Soc.*, LX:431-444.

American Child Health Association (1934), *Physical Defects—The Pathway to Correction.* New York, pp. 80-96.

Anonymous (1955), Committee on Deaths Associated with Anesthesia in Tonsil-Adenoidectomy. *Anesthesia*, X:218-220.

—— (1957), Statistical Bulletin, Metropolitan Life Insurance Co. (April).

Aycock, W. L. & Luther, E. H. (1929), The Occurrence of Poliomyelitis Following Tonsillectomy. *New Eng. J. Med.*, CC:164-167.

Bakwin, H. (1945), Pseudodoxia Pediatrica. *New Eng. J. Med.*, CCXXXII:691-697.

—— (1958), The Tonsil-Adenoidectomy Enigma. *J. Pediat.*, LII:339-361.

Bakwin, R. M. & Bakwin, H. (1942), *Psychologic Care During Infancy and Childhood.* New York: D. Appleton-Century.

Ballenger, W. L. & Ballenger, H. C. (1947), *Diseases of the Nose, Throat and Ear.* Philadelphia: Lea & Febiger, pp. 228-237, 272-273, 291-309.

Barnes, H. A. (1915), *The Tonsils.* St. Louis: C. V. Mosby.

Baron, S. H. (1956), Indications for Adenoid and Tonsil Removal in Children. *Rocky Mountain Med. J.*, LIII:999-1003.

Bass, M. H. (1934), Results of Tonsillectomy in Private Practice. *Laryngoscope*, XLIV:780-783.

Beecher, H. K. & Todd, D. P. (1954), A Study of the Deaths Associated with Anesthesia and Surgery. *Ann. Surg.*, CXL:2-33.

Beverly, B. I. (1936), Effect of Illness on Emotional Development. *J. Pediat.*, VIII:533-543.

Billings, F. (1916), *Focal Infection.* New York: D. Appleton.

Birdsall, S. E. (1939), The Symptoms, Signs and Treatment of Nasal Sinusitis in Childhood. *J. Laryngol. & Otol.*, LIV:549-564.

Blum, S. (1915), The Proper Position of Tonsillectomy in Pediatrics. *Arch. Pediat.*, XXXII:817-836.

Bordley, J. E. (1950), Indications for and Results of Irradiation in the Naso-pharynx. *Trans. Amer. Acad. Ophth.*, LIV:492.

—— & Hardy, W. G. (1955), The Efficacy of Nasopharyngeal Irradiation for the Prevention of Deafness in Children. *Acta Oto-Laryngologica*, Suppl., CXX.

Bradley, W. H. (1930), The Tonsils and Nasopharyngeal Epidemics. *Arch. Dis. Child.*, V:335-360.

Brues, C. T. & Sheppard, P. A. E. (1912), The Possible Etiological Relation of Certain Biting Insects to the Spread of Infantile Paralysis. *J. Econ. Entomology*, V:305-324.

Bunker, H. A. (1934), The Voice As (Female) Phallus. *Psa. Quart.*, III:391-429.

Coleman, L. L. (1949), Psychosomatic Aspects of Diseases of the Ear, Nose and Throat. *Laryngoscope*, LIX:709-720.

—— (1950), The Psychologic Implications of Tonsillectomy. *N.Y. State J. Med.*, L:1225-1228.

Crookes, J. (1957), Tonsils and Adenoids: Evaluation of Removal in 50 Doctors' Children. *Practitioner*, CLXXVIII:215-222.

Crooks, J. (1938), Nasal Sinusitis in Childhood. *Brit. Med. J.*, II:935-938.

Crowe, S. J. & Burnam, C. F. (1941), Recognition, Treatment and Prevention of Hearing Impairment in Children. *Ann. Otol., Rhin. & Laryngol.*, L:15-31.

Daland, J. (1926), Chronic Focal Infection of Tonsils and Accessory Sinuses in Adults. *Ann. Otol., Rhinol. & Laryngol.*, XXXV:1064-1072. Read by invitation as part of a Symposium on Focal Infection at a joint meeting of the Amer. Laryng., Rhinol. and Otol. Society, the Amer. Otol. Society, the Amer. Laryngol. Assoc., and the Amer. Bronchoscopic Society, Montreal, May 31-June 2, 1926.

Dean, L. W. (1959), The Tonsils, Their Function and Indications for Their Removal. *J. Amer. Med. Assn.*, CIII:1044-1049.

Denzer, B. S. & Felshin, G. (1943), The Pretonsillectomy Clinic. *J. Pediat.*, XXII:239-249.

Deutsch, H. (1942), Some Psychoanalytic Observations in Surgery. *Psychosom. Med.*, IV:105-115.

Dey, D. (1952), Quoted by L. Dods: Some Aspects of Australian Pediatrics. *Pediatrics*, X:364.

Editorial (1943), The Tonsils and Antibodies. *Lancet*, CCXLV:575 (November 6).

—— (1947), Tonsil Stumps. *J. Amer. Med. Assn.*, CXXXIV:698.

Ellis, R. W. B. & Russell, A. E. (1937), 4,000 Basque Children. *Lancet*, CCXXXII:1303-1304 (May 29).

Epstein, I. M. (1937), Factors Influencing the Results of Tonsillectomy and Adenoidectomy, *Amer. J. Dis. Child.*, LIII:1503-1520.

Ersner, M. S. & Lerners, S. S. (1956), The Unsolved Problem of the Tonsils and Adenoids. *Med. Clin. N. Amer.*, XL:1749-1760.

Faber, H. K. (1949), Adenotonsillectomy and Poliomyelitis (Editorial). *Pediatrics*, III:255-257.

Farrow, R. (1956), *The Surgery of Childhood for Nurses*. Edinburgh & London: E. and S. Livingstone, p. 89.

Forsythe, W. E. (1928), The Health Record of University Students As Related to Tonsillectomy. *Public Health Reports*, XLIII:560-562 (March 9).

Fowler, R. H. (1934), Progress in Tonsil Surgery. *Laryngoscope*, XLIV:769-779.

Francis, T., Jr., Krill, C. E., Toomey, J. A., & Mack, W. N. (1942), Poliomyelitis Following Tonsillectomy in Five Members of a Family. An Epidemiologic Study. *J. Amer. Med. Assn.*, CXIX:1392-1396.

Freud, A. (1952), The Role of Bodily Illness in the Mental Life of Children. *This Annual*, VII:69-82.

Fries, M. (1946), The Child's Ego Development and the Training of Adults in His Environment. *This Annual*, II:85-119.

Fry, J. (1957), Are All T's and A's Really Necessary? *Brit. Med. J.*, I:124-128.

Furman, R. (1959), Handling Parental Pressure for the T. and A. *J. Pediat.*, LIV:195-199.

Gafafer, W. M. (1932), Adenotonsillectomy and Diseases of Upper Respiratory Tract in Adults. *J. Infect. Dis.*, LI:489-492.

Glaser, J. (1956), *Allergy in Childhood*. Springfield: Thomas, pp. 228-232.

Glover, J. A. (1938), The Incidence of Tonsillectomy in School Children. *Proc. Royal Soc. Med.*, XXXI:1219-1236.
—— (1948), The Pediatric Approach to Tonsillectomy. *Arch. Dis. Child.*, XXIII:1-6.
Goodhart, J. F. (1885), *A Guide to the Diseases of Children.* Philadelphia: P. Blakiston, Son & Co., p. 109.
Griffith, I. (1937), The Function of the Tonsils and Their Relation to the Etiology and Treatment of Nasal Catarrh. *Lancet*, CCXXXIII:723-729 (September 25).
Grulee, C. G. & Eley, R. C. (1952), *The Child in Health and Disease*, 2nd ed. Baltimore: Williams & Wilkins, pp. 640-649.
Hall, I. Sampson (1937), *Diseases of the Nose, Throat and Ear.* Baltimore: William Wood, pp. 132-156.
Harvey, W. (1850), *On Excision of the Enlarged Tonsil and Its Consequences* [etc.]. London: Henry Renshaw, 356, Strand, Hunton, York.
Huschka, M. & Ogden, D. (1938), The Conduct of a Pediatric Prophylaxis Clinic. *J. Pediatrics*, XII:794-800.
Illingworth, R. S. (1939), Tonsillectomy and Nephritis of Childhood. *Lancet*, II:1013-1016.
Jackson, E. (1942), Treatment of the Young Child in the Hospital. *Amer. J. Orthopsychiat.*, XII:56-67.
Jessner, L., Blom, G. E., & Waldfogel, S. (1952), Emotional Implications of Tonsillectomy and Adenoidectomy on Children. *This Annual*, VII:126-170.
—— & Kaplan, S. (1949), Observations on the Emotional Reactions of Children to Tonsillectomy and Adenoidectomy. A Preliminary Report. In: *Problems of Infancy and Childhood* [Transactions of the Third Conference], ed. M. J. E. Senn. New York: Josiah Macy, Jr. Foundation, pp. 97-156; Discussion, pp. 118-156.
Jones, E. (1931), *On the Nightmare.* New York: Grove Press, 1959, p. 50.
Kaiser, A. D. (1931), The Relation of the Tonsils and Adenoids to Infections in Children. *Amer. J. Dis. Child.*, XLI:568-581.
—— (1940), Significance of the Tonsils in the Development of the Child. *J. Amer. Med. Assn.*, CXV:1151-1156.
—— (1952), Tonsils and Adenoids. In: Grulee & Eley (1952), pp. 640-649.
Kaplan, S. (1952), A Child's Reaction to Adenoidectomy. In: *Case Histories in Psychosomatic Medicine*, ed. H. W. Miles, S. Cobb, & H. C. Shands. New York: Norton, pp. 178-188.
Keen, J. A. (1932), Medical and Surgical Complications of Tonsillectomy in Childhood. *J. Laryng. & Otol.*, XLVII:1-34.
King, H. C. & Story, S. R. (1959), Blood Loss During Tonsillectomy. *Arch. Otolaryngol.*, LXX:153-157.
King, J. T. (1956), Tonsillectomy: Two Millenia of Hemorrhage and Controversy. In: *Trans. of 60th Meeting of Amer. Laryng., Rhinol., & Otol. Soc.*, pp. 569-575.
Kris, E. (1951), Opening Remarks on Psychoanalytic Child Psychology. *This Annual*, VI:9-17.
Langford, W. S. (1948), Physical Illness and Convalescence: Their Meaning to the Child. *J. Pediat.*, XXXIII:242-250.
Lederer, F. L. (1952), *Diseases of the Ear, Nose and Throat.* Philadelphia: F. A. Davis.
LeRiche, H. & Stiver, W. B. (1957), 1000 Cases of Tonsillectomy in a Prepayment Plan: Pre-operative and Post-operative History. *Canad. Med. Assn. J.*, LXXVII:109-115.
Levy, D. M. (1945), Psychic Trauma of Operations in Children. *Amer. J. Dis. Child.*, LXIX:7-25.
Litchfield, H. R. & Dembo, L. H., eds. (1947), *Therapeutics of Infancy and Childhood*, 3rd ed. Philadelphia: F. A. Davis, II:1112-1114.
Lucchesi, P. F. & LaBoccetta, A. C. (1944), Relationship of the Tonsils and Adenoids to the Type of Poliomyelitis: An Analysis of 432 Cases. *Amer. J. Dis. Child.*, LXVIII:1-4.

McGovern, F. H. (1959), Advances in Adenotonsillectomy [Condensed from] *J. Int. Coll. Surg.*, XXXII:668-672.

McGovern, J. P. (1959), Management of Asthma in Infants and Children. *Chicago Med. Soc. Bull.*, LXII:165-170 (September 5).

McKenzie, W. (1953), The Risks of Tonsillectomy. *Lancet*, II:958-960.

McLemore, C. S. (1959), A Review of 1,150 Consecutive Tonsillectomies and Adenoidectomies with a Glance at the Literature. *J. Florida Med. Assn.*, LXIV:427-433.

Mead, M. (1959), Cultural Contexts of Puberty and Adolescence. *Bull. Phila. Assn. Psa.*, IX:57-79.

Medical Research Council (1938), *Epidemics in Schools.* London: His Majesty's Stationery Office.

Menninger, K. A. (1934), Polysurgery and Polysurgical Addiction. *Psa. Quart.*, III:173-199.

Mertz, J. C. (1954), Tonsillectomy and Respiratory Illness in the Populations of Two Communities in New York State. *Milbank Memorial Fund Quart.*, XXXII:5-18.

Meyer, W. (1868), On Adenoid Vegetations in the Naso-pharyngeal Cavity; Their Pathology, Diagnosis and Treatment (communicated by John Marshall). *Medico-Chirurgical Trans.*, LIII:191-217, 1870.

Miller, M. L. (1951), The Traumatic Effect of Surgical Operations in Childhood on the Integrative Functions of the Ego. *Psa. Quart.*, XX:77-93.

Moore, I. (1928), *The Tonsils and Adenoids and Their Diseases.* St. Louis: Mosby.

Nesbitt, B. E. (1934), The Post-operative Complications and Results of Tonsil and Adenoid Operations in Children. *Brit. Med. J.*, II:508-513.

Paton, J. H. P. (1943), The Tonsil-Adenoid Problem in Relation to the Health of a Group of School Girls. *Quart. J. Med.*, XII:119-128.

Paulus Aeginata, *The Seven Books of Paulus Aeginata*, tr. F. Adams. Printed for the Sydenham Society, 1844.

Pearson, G. H. J. (1941), Effect of Operative Procedures on the Emotional Life of the Child. *Amer. J. Dis. Child.*, LXII:716-729.

Pembleton, W. E., Walker, T., & Gill, J. A. (1959), Anesthesia for Tonsillectomy and Adenoidectomy. *Arch. Otolaryngol.*, LXX:48-52.

Pillsbury, R. M. (1951), Children Can Be Helped to Face Surgery. *Child*, XVI:122-125.

Proctor, B. (1960), Indications for Surgery in Middle Ear Deafness. *Ill. Med. J.*, CXVII:72-74.

Prugh, D. G., et al. (1953), A Study of the Emotional Reactions of Children and Families to Hospitalization and Illness. *Amer. J. Orthopsychiat.*, XXIII:70-106.

Rhoads, P. S., Sibley, J. R., & Billings, C. E. (1955), Bacteremia Following Tonsillectomy *J. Amer. Med. Assn.*, CLVII:877-881.

Rock, J. E. (1944), Staphylococcic Septicemia, Tonsillar in Origin. *J. Iowa Med. Soc.*, XXXIV:10-13.

Rolleston, C. (1939), Observations on 1,136 Cases of Enlarged Tonsils and Adenoids. *Brit. J. Child. Dis.*, XXXVI:253-260.

Sabin, A. B. (1938), Experimental Poliomyelitis by the Tonsillo-Pharyngeal Route, with Special Reference to the Influence of Tonsillectomy on the Development of Bulbar Poliomyelitis. *J. Amer. Med. Assn.*, CXI:605-610.

Shapiro, A. K. (1959), The Placebo Effect in the History of Medical Treatment (Implications for Psychiatry). *Amer. J. Psychiat.*, CXVI:298-305.

Sheppard, Philip A. E. (1910), A Study of an Epidemic of Infantile Paralysis (Acute Epidemic Poliomyelitis) in Springfield, Mass. in 1910. On pages 95-140 of a pamphlet entitled *Infantile Paralysis in Massachusetts during 1910, together with Reports of Special Investigations Made in 1911 Bearing upon the Etiology of the Disease and the Method of Transmission.* Boston: Wright and Potter Printing

Co., State Printers, 18 Post Office Square, 1912. (On the pamphlet itself the statement is made, "Reprinted from Monthly Bulletins of the Mass. State Board of Health for 1911." This statement is an error which has been perpetuated in subsequent references. In fact Sheppard's paper was not printed in the Monthly Bulletin.)

—— (1913), The Distribution of Stomoxys Calcitrans. A Note on Its Possible Etiologic Relationship to Acute Poliomyelitis. *Amer. J. Clin. Med.*, XX:228-230.

—— (1916), Acute Epidemic Poliomyelitis. A Contact Infection. *N.Y. State J. Med.*, XVI:442-446.

Siegel, M., Greenberg, M., & Magee, M. C. (1951), Tonsillectomy and Poliomyelitis. I. Studies on Incidence in 1949. II. Frequency of Bulbar Paralysis, 1944-1949. *J. Pediat.*, XXXVIII:537-557.

Sigerist, H. E. (1933), *The Great Doctors*. New York: Norton.

Smiley, D. F. (1924), A Study of the Acute Infections of the Throat and Respiratory System. *J. Amer. Med. Assn.*, LXXXII:540-541.

Symposium (1940), Discussion on the Indications for Removal of Tonsils and Adenoids in Children. *Proc. Royal Soc. Med.*, XXXIII:347-356.

—— (1950), Irradiation of Lymphoid Tissue in the Nasopharynx. *Trans. Amer. Acad. Ophth. & Otolaryngol.*, LIV:479-530.

Top, F. H. & Vaughn, H. F. (1941), Epidemiology of Poliomyelitis in Detroit in 1939. *Amer. J. Pub. Health*, XXXI:777-790.

Tumarkin, A. (1937), Deafness: Prevention vs. Palliation. *Lancet*, CCXXXIII:782-784.

Waelder, R. (1960), *Basic Theory of Psychoanalysis*. New York: International Universities Press.

Wallace, H. L. & Smith, A. B. (1936), The Effect of Early Tonsillectomy on the Incidence of Acute Rheumatism. *Edinburgh Med. J.*, XLIII:452-457.

Watkyn, F. W. (1953), *Diseases of the Throat, Nose and Ear*. Springfield: Thomas.

Weiss, H. (1934), Relation of Portal of Entry to Subacute Bacterial Endocarditis. *Arch. Int. Med.*, LIV:710-719.

Wheelis, A. (1958), *The Quest for Identity*. New York: Norton, pp. 152-153.

Wolman, I. J. (1956), Tonsillectomy and Adenoidectomy. *Quart. Rev. Pediat.*, XI:109-132.

Wright, J. (1898), The Nose and Throat in Medical History. St. Louis: L. S. Mathews.

Yearsley, J. (1868), *Throat Ailments, More Especially the E..larged Tonsil* [etc.]. London: John Churchill and Sons, New Burlington Street.

Yearsley, M. (1939), The Present Position of Tonsil Operations. *Brit. J. Child. Dis.*, XXXVI:1-15.

THE DEVELOPMENT OF A PREOEDIPAL PARTNERSHIP BETWEEN AN ADOLESCENT GIRL AND HER MOTHER

MARJORIE P. SPRINCE (London)

Anna Freud has described the value of simultaneous analysis of mother and child, both from the point of view of therapy and for research purposes.[1] As a therapeutic tool it has become the method of choice for those carefully selected cases of children whose forward moves on the developmental scale have been held back because of unconscious interplay between themselves and one of their parents. In the cases reported so far, the parent concerned has been the mother, although in many cases and certainly in the case reported here, there is evidence of more than a compliant attitude on the part of the father.

Debby was twelve and a half years of age when she started her analysis. During the first two years of treatment her extreme tendency to regress because of the intensity of her preoedipal fixations was noted. It seemed likely that there was a connection between this fact and the partnership which appeared to exist between mother and child and from which neither could extricate herself. Therapeutic insight in the child alone could not, it seemed, counteract the pull exerted by this partnership.

When Debby was just under fifteen years of age the mother accepted treatment for herself. It was hoped that simultaneous analysis would not only offer us insight into the nature of the

This paper forms part of two research projects entitled "Simultaneous Analysis of Mother and Child" and "Enquiry into the Analysis of Adolescents" respectively. The analysis of Debby and her mother, and the coordinating work attached to it, have been financed by the Ford Foundation, New York, by a grant to the Hampstead Child-Therapy Clinic.

[1] See Introduction to "Simultaneous Analysis of a Mother and Her Adolescent Daughter" by Kata Levy (*This Annual*, XV, 1960).

mother's unconscious influence on the child's pathology, but also enable the former to abandon fixed positions in relation to her daughter which would facilitate forward moves.

In 1960 Kata Levy reported on the simultaneous analysis of Debby and her mother from the point of view of a mother who consciously wished to loosen the ties by which she and her adolescent daughter were attached to each other but who had been unable to do so. The paper described Debby as an adolescent who had been through all the upheavals characteristic of her age and yet at the time of the report had shown no urge or ability to sever the attachment from her original objects.

The mother's analysis was continued until Debby was seventeen and a half years old—Debby's own daily treatment terminated six months later. While simultaneous analysis enabled my patient to lose many of her presenting symptoms and finally to achieve at least a partial removal from her preoedipal objects, the outstanding feature has been an inability to use much of the insight gained or adequately to sustain forward moves which would enable her entirely to relinquish preoedipal fixations. This has been so in spite of a conscious wish for independence, a cooperative attitude in treatment, and a capacity for examining unconscious motives in herself.

I would suggest the following explanation for the fact that it has been unusually difficult for my patient to sever her ties from the original object or to lose completely those symptoms which were based upon preoedipal conflicts. It is likely that she may be one of the cases described by Greenacre (1952, 1960) in which an early and prolonged infantile trauma, such as is associated with long, drawn-out body stimulation, results in a permanent and possibly irreversible tendency to tension in addition to a persistent preoedipal fixation. Furthermore, one can argue that such a traumatic infantile experience might have irremediable repercussions on ego formation because it results in a lack of resistivity to sexuality and aggression.

This paper sets out to study, from the point of view of the child's analysis and in the light of the mother's analytic material, the basis for these assumptions. It also sets out to show that in cases where very early ego disturbance may have led to permanent ego damage, the decision for simultaneous analysis of mother and child may have to be undertaken with a limited aim. Such ego damage may be expected, among other things, to interfere with a totally successful severing of the object tie at adolescence.

DEBBY

Symptoms

Debby, an only child, was referred to the Clinic at the age of twelve and a half years because of a school phobia which had been incipient since her nursery-school days and had become full-blown a year after starting grammar school to which she had gained a free place. A year previously she had developed a fear of sickness which had resulted in night panics and an inability to go out without her parents. She had also developed a number of knocking rituals.

During treatment it became evident that this child was crippled by many symptoms which included acute separation anxiety, and obsessional symptoms and rituals demanding her mother's constant participation. She had to be washed, bathed, and dressed, and her bowel movement supervised. Food fads and fear of sickness necessitated special meals at special times. She could not eat with the family and often had to eat in bed. Magical actions and formulas had to be repeated to ward off sickness and other hazards. She would spend hours at night making noises in the lavatory and when panic threatened, her father had to leave his bed so that Debby could sleep close to her mother. Temper outbursts coupled with extreme demandingness made family life intolerable and social life impossible. When frustrated in her demands, Debby blamed her parents for upsetting her and causing her illness. Thus she entirely dominated and controlled her parents' existence. At a Clinic conference the intolerable existence these symptoms created for Debby's family was discussed. So controlling and demanding was she, in fact, that we questioned how any parents could bear to be enslaved in this way. We asked ourselves what pathology one would expect to find in parents who were willing and able to submit to such demands.

In spite of an I.Q. of 156 on the Stanford Revision of the Binet, Debby's headmistress considered her dull and was not anxious to have her back at school. When treatment started, her school life had come to a standstill. She had one friend who was tiring of her because she would never go out; her activities and interests were limited to week-end riding, to which her father took her by car and with which she was compulsively preoccupied.

Background Information

Knowledge about this family has been obtained from three sources: my interviews with both parents, Debby's analytic material, and the mother's personal analysis. During the first two years of Debby's analysis, I saw her mother at frequent intervals. When the mother herself started treatment there was a regular interchange of information between Mrs. Levy and myself. Thus any conclusions I have reached about this mother's role in the partnership are based upon my own observations, the communications made by Debby in the course of her analysis, and the findings which Mrs. Levy published (1960). I am, moreover, indebted to Mrs. Levy for some of the additional information which is relevant to this study.

The parents.—Both parents come from middle-class Jewish English backgrounds in which family ties were extremely strong and religious observances important. They were married during the war and were together for the early part of it, after which the father was called to the forces and the mother returned to her own parents. The mother's personality, her strong competitive relationship with her second youngest sister, Pen, with whom she identified Debby, and the difficulties she experienced in finally leaving her own family have been described in detail by her analyst.[2]

Mrs. G. was an attractive, well-dressed woman with a slim figure. Her physical form would not justify the preoccupation with slimming and the careful consideration she has always given to regulating intake and preventing obesity. Her interest in clothing and her concern about foundation garments, which she has shared with Debby since I knew her, seems to have been something of a family characteristic. Apart from clothes and social activities, Mrs. G. appeared to have few interests. Neither she nor her husband have ever played with their daughter or introduced intellectual pursuits which would have encouraged sublimations.

---

[2] Mrs. Levy describes how the sister Pen achieved just such a privileged position in the family by bad behavior as Debby did. Mrs. G. had displaced her oedipal rivalry onto this sister, knowing that while her mother preferred Pen, her father preferred her. In identifying Debby with Pen, her own unsolved oedipal conflict became entangled with that of Debby's.

Mrs. G. spent much of her childhood nursing a sick mother and sister. She herself was an anxious mother who has always fussed over the slightest body complaint in herself or others. Until the time of her analysis she suffered from migraine and indigestion which compelled her to retire to a darkened room. Illness in this family justified very special consideration—thus Mrs. G.'s migraines entitled her to the prerogatives of the sick, special food, medicines, and her husband's sympathy and attention.

Mrs. G.'s father was an orthodox Jew who strictly followed the Jewish dietary laws. He had a predilection for Andrew's Liver Salts—a remedy passed on by Mrs. G. to my patient, whose use of it was such that it could be compared to an addiction. In addition, the old man had magical beliefs such as the power of the "evil eye" the effects of which only a rabbi could counteract.

Mr. G. was not analyzed and initially treated his daughter's analysis with a mixture of jocularity and suspicion—he had been in the R.A.F. and used the term "Trick cyclist" for psychiatry. His dry, humorous manner covered considerable anxiety. He had badly bitten nails. He was the youngest of four brothers, all of whom were extremely attached to their family and have done well in their professions. Mr. G. prided himself on being a respectful good son to his orthodox parents. He was a journalist but now has business interests which provide greater security. One brother, who is referred to later, had always been considered selfish and emotionally disturbed, and Mr. G. feared that this might explain his daughter's abnormality.

Mr. G. always stressed his all-male background to explain the fact that he was totally unable to visualize his daughter's interests or feelings or to understand why she could not share such sports as rugger with him.

The possibility that the father might have hoped for a son would be supported by his marked feelings of failure at not having attended a university and his conscious wish that his daughter should achieve what he missed. It seemed that once it became clear to him that Debby was not destined for academic success, he lost interest in her entirely and this made him feel very guilty. He compensated for this by an overindulgent attitude and an inability to refuse her demands. The father attributed his academic failure to the fact that his education had been interrupted at the age of twelve, when he had been kept in bed for a year with what he thought had been anemia. This break in his education at the age when Debby's school phobia became acute is interesting, and in view of the vagueness of his illness one wonders whether this too could have been a school phobia.

During the latter part of Debby's treatment the father told me that he suffered from a feeding disturbance necessitating the avoidance of all food which ever contained bones. In addition, a bowel prolapse at about four years of age which involved treatment with enemas and purgatives left him with the conviction that regular bowel movement was imperative to health. He described how failure to pass a daily motion left him stricken with anxiety until purgatives had restored the routine. The father considered himself a coward troubled by premonitions and superstitions.

Personal Development.—Two years before Debby was born her mother gave birth to twin daughters who died two days later. Since Mrs. G. was said to belong to the Rhesus Negative blood group, her pregnancy with Debby was an anxious one. In addition, she vomited throughout and had to spend quite some time in bed.

Debby was born during her mother's evacuation, while her father was working and living in London. When she was three months old mother and daughter rejoined the father, but distress about Debby's feeding and digestive problems caused Mrs. G. to return to her mother for advice and protection, where she stayed until Debby was three. Mr. G. was called to the forces when Debby was fifteen months, but he could spend most week ends with his wife and daughter, finally settling in the country with them. It is likely therefore that he participated quite considerably in early feeding and habit training.

Breast feeding continued until the eighth month, but Debby was always difficult about food, and weaning was prolonged because she refused solids. At two years of age she was said to have suffered from an intestinal illness making her allergic to milk and fat; after eating either she was said to have vomited. This illness was never investigated or treated medically. But a special nonmilk diet was initiated and continued throughout latency.

Habit training was equally problematic—the mother believed a daily bowel movement was essential and training was started immediately after birth. Since Debby was breast-fed, bowel movements were relatively infrequent; the mother therefore administered daily oral purgatives until at three months the family doctor intervened. Examinations of bowel products, however, continued until treatment commenced, and Debby was still given frequent suppositories. At about six years of age, after a bout of constipation, Debby was taken to a hospital for unmarried mothers of which an aunt happened to be matron and was given an enema by a strange nurse in the absence of her mother. She remembered this incident and the fact that she had messed and lost control over her bowels with anger and horror.

At about two years of age, possibly earlier, Debby was given an injection against whooping cough. The needle broke off in her arm. Wartime conditions resulted in abortive attempts to remove it with and without anesthetic until operative measures in the hospital became necessary. Debby is said to have developed a fear of men from that time.

Two months after the father's discharge from the army, when Debby was three, mother again became pregnant but miscarried shortly thereafter. She was taken to the hospital suddenly and Debby was sent away to relatives where she was extremely homesick and where she stayed for two weeks instead of the three days she had been promised. Shortly after her return and because of her mother's weakened condition, she was sent to nursery school. There she cried bitterly when left, and ran away in an attempt to find her way home alone.

Debby's school life had never been happy. She had difficulties in work and was unpopular with teachers. She had few friends. This was to some extent counteracted by her large family of girl and boy cousins with whom she was often together and by whom she felt more easily accepted.

THE PARTNERSHIP BETWEEN MOTHER AND DAUGHTER
AS SEEN IN TREATMENT

Debby was a good-looking, dark-haired girl, with a pleasant face which could look sullen and petulant. Her nails were badly bitten and she played with her hair continually, winding it round her fingers. Her speech was quick and compulsive, often inaudible, and she brought a profusion of material, one thought interrupting another. Intellectual arguments, rationalizations, and aggressive attacks were all used in support of her main defense mechanism—denial.

For the sake of clarity and continuity, the order and manner in which the material was brought has had to be sacrificed. The profusion of material and the disorder in which it emerged, reflected the extent of inner confusion and anxiety.

Oral and Anal Development

A reconstruction of Debby's developmental history based upon her analytic material indicated that the partnership between mother and daughter was founded upon a mutual interest surrounding digestive processes and body care. Orality and anality overlap in the reconstruction, and one is reminded that bowel management was a concern of the mother from birth and that purgatives were administered orally from that time on. Feeding difficulties appear to have started equally early. The intestinal illness at two years of age, whether real or imaginary, provided Debby with body care which may be said to have established a permanent pattern. Intake of food soon became a process which endowed her with considerable power, for it could result in vomiting and an immediate state of concern on the part of her parents. Thus body attention and her parents' exaggerated concern came to represent evidence of love.

The connection between intake and expulsion was emphasized by scenes re-enacted and recollected during treatment. Debby described how she sat on a pot for hours at a time waiting for purgatives or suppositories to work—a biscuit or sweet ready as a reward, while mother, in the neighboring kitchen, awaited a knock on the wall to summon her to examine the product. Mother's concern could be characterized by Debby's description at thirteen years of age: "When I'm ill mother is wonderful, she will sit up all night and wipe my bottom for me."

Vomiting was anticipated as the result of a single day without passing a movement. Debby at fifteen still remained convinced that whatever was taken in by mouth must be expelled at one end or the other the selfsame day.

In treatment Debby would use threats of vomiting to ward off unwelcome interpretations, just as at home any frustration had to be avoided in case it made her sick. Anal battles were re-enacted in every sphere of Debby's life: time arrangements were never suitable and never kept; punctuality or regularity meant "giving in" and "if I'm good you'll want more and more of me."

There were fantasies of "oneness"—e.g., that the therapist and Debby were menstruating at the same time—and these found their counterpart in mother's frequent remarks to her analyst that she and Debby had parallel experiences: "I was settled and Debby was settled"; "I was constipated and Debby was constipated."

Mrs. G.'s attitude to illness in her daughter can be better understood in the light of her unresolved childhood conflicts. Mrs. Levy has described how this mother's love for her only child, rooted as it was in an unconscious conflict over death wishes and defenses against them, had to take the form of overprotectiveness. That this overprotectiveness should be expressed in anxiety about health is not surprising when we recollect that Mrs. G. spent much of her childhood nursing a sick mother and sister against whom she harbored unconscious death wishes. In her own childhood, hostility was associated with the need to make sacrifices for the ill person who was invested with special importance by virtue of her guilt in relation to them. In her married life the role of the ill person was clearly defined; thus Debby told me, "In our family the sick person is the important person." Debby's worst outbursts occurred at times of illness in the family, until finally intense anger and jealousy caused her to become more ill than the sick person from whom she invariably managed to wrest all attention. Even Debby's migraines could be more severe than mother's.

The analytic facts about Mrs. G.'s relationship to her father help us further to understand her unconscious difficulties in handling her daughter's oral and anal development. We know that her oedipal conflict with her orthodox Jewish father remained unresolved. We also know that this father, with his magic beliefs, had influenced his daughter to anticipate punishment for disobeying the dietary laws. One might suspect that in passing on to Debby her father's favorite "Andrew's" the mother was also demonstrating the persistence of her father's attitudes in herself. Mrs. G. told me of an unreasonable anticipation that God would punish her if she ate non-Kosher food.

Her own analysis enabled her to tolerate Debby's emancipation and to allow Debby to eat freely, but it did not enable Mrs. G. to do so herself.

Indicative as these hints are, they are not enough to explain the intensity of the body-bound partnership between Debby and her mother.

The Father's Role in the Partnership

While Debby's material points continually to parental preoccupation with digestive and bowel activities and leads one to anticipate oral and anal fixation in the mother, there is no evidence of such fixation in the mother's analytic material. On the other hand, it is a fact that Debby's communications indicate that it was by no means only mother who was interested in her early feeding and habit training; father was concerned as well. This is confirmed by many memories, including one in which mother inserted a suppository while father held her down. In all these memories, however, Debby blamed mother for involving father in such activities.

It will be remembered that this father suffered from a severe feeding disturbance as well as compulsive and obsessional attitudes toward bowel functioning. It is, I would think, of considerable significance that Mrs. G. has been able to accept her husband's feeding and bowel attitudes so completely that no mention was ever made of them in her own analysis. This, I suggest, would imply that they did not appear unusual or disturbing to her.

Debby's father was an orthodox Jew whose food phobia went hand in hand with food rituals similar to those followed by Mrs. G.'s father. We know from Mrs. G.'s analysis that she identified her husband with her father. Debby's material about her father and grandfather also pointed to this and suggested that the identification could in part be on the basis of the father's feeding and bowel disturbance. It would fit in with Mrs. Levy's findings that this mother's oedipal fantasy of Debby as her own father's child made it necessary for her to take over unquestioningly her husband's feeding and bowel attitudes as if they were her father's. If this is so, we would be justified in relating the intense libidinization of Debby's digestive tract to the effect upon Debby of the unconscious interplay between father and mother's respective pathological needs.

Thus it can be argued that father's disturbance was in some way responsible for setting the partnership between Debby and her mother in motion, or at least for facilitating it. It is possible that father's guilt about his ambivalence toward Debby compelled him to make reparations by demonstrating his love in the only way he knew—by renewed concern for her bodily functions. It certainly led him to bouts of overindulgence and explains an inability to set limits.

However it came about, from the point of view of Debby's material it may be said that concern for digestive and bodily processes appears to have been unconsciously exploited by both parents as the one way in which they could *share* in the upbringing of their only child. From the point of view of pathology, the prolonged and massive stimulation was perpetuated and continued into latency and must be considered to constitute a severe trauma. It would further explain Debby's reluctance to move forward to levels at which this joint expression of love would be denied her.

Phallic Development—Penis Envy

During the latter half of her first three years, Debby was brought up together with a boy cousin, Steven, of her own age. In her analysis her overwhelming penis envy and her swing between masculine and feminine identifications appeared less related to this early experience than to a deep conviction, which showed itself in the transference, that mother would have preferred a boy child, but could not have one because she was a sickly woman. Mrs. G. made no secret of her difficult confinements and of the death of twin girls two days after their birth. It was only in the very last weeks of her own analysis that Mrs. G. admitted that she would have preferred a son. Debby in her analysis once told the story of a widowed mother who, disappointed at the birth of a malformed daughter with two amputated fingers, imagined killing the child and making it appear accidental. This story is revealing not only in this context but also as an indication of how Debby projected her aggression onto her mother.

Debby's insatiable demand for a penis found its way into all her activities and relationships; there was a constant need to have whatever her friends had, even before they had it themselves. She was convinced that her mother's interest in her feces indicated a wish to find and take from her an anal penis. Her "sublimations" appeared to depend almost entirely upon activities giving opportunity for exhibitionism and the acquiring of equipment which she equated with the possession of a penis. Her hopes that she might magically achieve one was well demonstrated by one of her obsessional rituals in which she had to masturbate with one hand, while stroking every new possession with the other. Many of her food fads could be traced to rivalry and identification with her father whose special diets she envied. In this family where illness was so highly valued, symptoms and indeed her very illness itself compensated for the penis she lacked.

Debby's exhibitionism was acted out in the transference. At times she arrived dressed in borrowed boy's clothes and in trousers; at other times, wearing six underslips at once, she would try to persuade me to look at her knickers, feel her waist, or examine her brassiere. Her attempts to re-establish in the transference a body-bound relationship was equalled by her determination that I should discover in her qualities which were as good or better than any boy's. That Mrs. G. herself experienced a considerable problem over penis envy has been pointed out by her analyst. Her own tendency toward exhibitionism could be seen in her need to share the toilet with Debby, and in her inability to lock toilet doors. It would explain why she could not impose such limits on Debby who feared being overheard urinating but also used the toilet with the door open.

Debby at the age of thirteen so feared the onset of menstruation that she would not go to the cinema in case it caught her unawares. She kept a small bag prepared for the eventuality much as a pregnant mother prepares for entering the hospital. During her analysis Mrs. G. revealed that at her wedding dinner she had unexpectedly started to menstruate and had soiled her wedding dress. Debby knew of this experience. One wonders whether she understood what it had meant to her mother in the way the mother revealed it in a dream to her analyst. The dream was about a poor girl who like her mother was unlucky enough to start her period on her wedding day, thereby discovering that however much she wanted to become a boy, she could never escape the fate of having been born female.

It seems that the combination of penis envy together with guilt and disappointment over having created a girl child contributed to this mother's difficulties in handling phallic development and explains something of her need to share and participate in Debby's attempts to solve her problem of penis envy. Thus a typical joint situation occurred shortly after the commencement of Debby's analysis. The family had gone to the Midlands to celebrate a cousin's Barmitzvah. Debby, unable to tolerate the boy's importance, sought attention and limelight for herself by vomiting throughout the celebration supper. She forced both parents to sit up with her all night, so that on the day of the ceremony the mother was exhausted and developed migraine. They both retired to bed and were thus protected from witnessing the boy's triumph.

Debby's feelings of inadequacy were so gross that she could only compensate by the use of reversal and withdrawal into fantasy. Thus she would imagine herself of the blood royal and walk through the streets nodding regally to passers-by. Since she could not risk normal competition, she developed a method of becoming famous for bad characteristics, insisting that "it is better to be top of the bottom than never to be top at all." She had fantasies of being discovered as an infant prodigy.

The fact that so many of Debby's narcissistic fantasies threatened to become permanent must be pointed out here. There was a marked "as if" quality about her—an impulse to translate fantasies into reality and an inability to distinguish between these fantasies and practical possibilities and achievements. Touching upon this was the shallowness of her object relations. Her temporary but enthusiastic friendships were invariably based upon the wish to emulate often imaginary characteristics.

Phallic Development—Masturbation and Castration Anxiety

The partnership between Debby and her mother which has been traced through one area of phallic development can be followed throughout the phallic level. The need to share her mother's bed and later her bedroom, with which both parents complied, had many ramifications. It must be considered not only as a source of additional stimulation but also as an indication of the mother's part in the union. Debby's masturbation fantasies indicate that mutual masturbation was the outcome of the close and satisfactory body-bound relationship between mother and child which Debby repeatedly sought to re-establish both in fantasy and in fact. Her guilt about her masturbatory fantasies may have reinforced the need to share the guilty activity with another person.

A very early relationship to a maid seems to have been her first experience, and subsequently all her girl cousins and friends became partners in this activity which was both anal and genital in character and in which each partner took the active and passive role in turns. Pencils and similar objects were used for penetration. There was also evidence of developing perversions. Debby described how she used the dog's penis to masturbate with and to replace her own missing organ.

At school her relationship with her teachers was tinged with a strong sexual coloring associated with guilt about masturbation (for which she was openly chided) and connected with her secret homosexual fantasies. One such fantasy was of a woman teacher locking her into a cupboard and torturing her by sticking witches' thistles up her vagina.

With the cessation of mutual masturbation in the second year of treatment, Debby was enabled to discuss her fear of masturbation as such—a fear which continued into adolescence and which determined some of her sleeping difficulties. These included a dread of ghosts, and the need to have the door open, the light on, and the wireless playing so that it could be heard until she fell asleep and when she awoke.

In the fourth year of treatment she brought memories of a repeated childhood hallucination. A number of times she awoke to find "broken bits of worms" on her bed and her panic was such that no one could calm her. Even when describing the experience in her analysis she remained convinced that the worms had been a reality. In fact, they had their origin in the picture of Little Bo Peep and its border of broken tails which hung over her bed and which she observed while touching her genitals. Her mother had frequently chided her for masturbating while sharing a bed with her.

Even in the early part of treatment the connection between food intake and mastery over sexual excitement was evident. When frightened in her sessions Debby would eat chocolate; her disturbed nights were calmed with "Andrew's" and chocolate biscuits which she longed for continuously but felt she ought not to eat because they made her fat. As her treatment proceeded and many of the obsessional rituals disappeared, the conflict was almost entirely expressed in a symptom which had many other meanings as well—that of a compulsive preoccupation with controlling food intake by dieting, of which I shall speak more fully later.

Oedipus Complex—Seduction

It is often difficult to distinguish between preoedipal and oedipal material. Most of Debby's symptoms served the purpose of separating her parents and ensuring that neither think of the other but only of her. The oedipal conflict seems to have been so intense and disturbing to her that it had to be defended by regression to preoedipal satisfactions. Thus the material could be seen as a constant swing between the two levels, each regression cementing more firmly the homosexual attachment to the mother. One of the aspects of her school phobia was the fear that if she could do without mother, mother would learn to do without her—if necessary, by taking a substitute.

This regression became understandable when in the first year of treatment, Debby confessed to a seduction by her paternal uncle at about five years of age. While otherwise feeling compelled to tell her mother everything, this had been kept a secret from both parents and remained so until she was eighteen. The seduction took place in a double bed in her grandmother's house when the unmarried uncle invited the child to suck his penis as if it were chocolate and to manipulate it, imagining it to be bandaged. The incident was interrupted by the grandmother's voice and Debby promised the uncle not to tell. This happening throws light on the compulsive longing for chocolate biscuits and their significance as a means of reliving and controlling the traumatic experience. The story has never varied in her reports, although at times Debby has wondered whether fellatio actually took place or whether the whole thing could have been fantasy. She feared discovery at the time, yet felt pride at "having a man like mother had." She believed she bragged of her experience to friends and longed to do so to her parents; she had fantasies of publicly blaming her uncle for her illness and thus drawing her father's attention to her attractive qualities. The parents' description of the uncle's oddness, his very late marriage, and his later behavior to Debby would confirm the reliability of her memory. Moreover, when at eighteen Debby did tell her mother of the happening, the mother seemed quite unsurprised.

The fact that Debby did not tell her parents until she was eighteen stemmed from the unconscious conviction that she was responsible for seducing the uncle just as she had wished to seduce her father. In daily life and in the transference, temper outbursts could frequently be traced back to the dread of being left alone with father and finding him like uncle, unable to resist her seductive behavior. Fantasies of being raped, impregnated, and left alone with her widowed father accompanied exhibitionistic behavior and aimed at demonstrating that she was as much of a woman as her mother.

Understanding of these fantasies through the transference cleared up a number of phobias concerned with going out or being left alone.

The oedipal situation followed her into her school life. Friendships were invariably triangular and the dread of being left out caused her finally to withdraw entirely. Her inability to compete at work stemmed from the same conflict. Debby could not attempt to do anything which had already been done better by someone else, for it reminded her that mother had married father before she had had the chance—success was therefore out of reach. On the other hand, the dangers of her love for father made it quite impossible for her to acknowledge her interest in him for any length of time. Any glimmer of awareness of her feelings for him pushed Debby back into homosexual preoccupations, and this too entered into her school life and made working with women teachers impossible. When her school phobia made home teaching advisable, Debby was overtly seductive with the women tutors and then became terrified of their maternal responses. She had fantasies of phallic and attacking women, and her symptoms of sickness and anxiety increased so that lessons had to cease. At the age of thirteen her feelings for a young lame girl, five years older than herself, with whom she imagined sharing a horse, or whom she imagined saving from an accident, became so strong that she commented, "My trouble is that I love girls, not boys."

Mrs. G. seems to have been aware of her daughter's homosexual problems. She reported to me (before beginning her own analysis) that she had noticed something suspicious about Debby's games with other girls, but that she had avoided too close an inquiry and had not discussed it with her husband lest he think his daughter mad. Before Mrs. G. commenced her own analysis, I discussed with her the question of stimulation in connection with sharing a bed with Debby and the joint use of the toilet. There was an odd lack of affect and concern about the whole matter. The quality of Debby's transference, which clearly pointed to the mother's seductive behavior to her daughter, together with Mrs. G.'s need to deny the problem to the extent of ignoring it, led me to suspect unsolved homosexual conflicts in the mother; however, these were not confirmed by the mother's analytic material.

It should be noted here that Debby appears to have experienced no solution of the oedipal conflict and that her attempts to solve it continued without cessation through what should have been a latency period until puberty set in.

Aggression—Death Wishes—The Battle for Control

The fear that neither parent could help Debby to control her fury and destructive outbursts enhanced her feelings of omnipotence and could be observed at each stage of development. From the oral point of view, it is possible that early feeding difficulties and her mother's anxieties over them did, in fact, cause her bodily discomfort, some real hunger, and helpless sensations of rage. Certainly Mrs. G.'s fear that her baby would starve covered her own unconscious hostility toward her child and introduced a battle over feeding and expulsion that set the character of their sadomasochistic relationship. Food and anxiety over feeding were, for Debby, concrete evidence of love, of which she could never be sure of obtaining an adequate supply unless she drew attention to her needs. Her greed and aggressive, demanding behavior expressed some of her sense of deprivation and were repeatedly worked through in the transference.

Anal attacks in the form of enemas, suppositories, and purgatives were experienced by Debby not only as acts of intimacy but as controlling and proprietary behavior expressing mother's belief that Debby's performances were mother's successes: "When I've had a movement she says, 'good girl,' as if it were her limelight, not mine." This concept of being an extension of mother played its part in

Debby's determination not to succeed if success at any level brought credit to her mother. The two aspects of the anal situation, submission and rebellion, pin-point the ambivalence so characteristic of Debby. They equally indicate the qualities she both feared and longed for in her mother—the loving attentive mother who reacts to libidinal domination by increased intimacy and "oneness," and the mother who offers signs of real authority and strength. Often Debby's outbursts developed into panic-stricken pleas for control, which were no less sincere for the fact that the very plea contained an attack against mother's weakness. In her analysis Debby described her obsessional habits as "the sort of barbed wire with which a mother should surround her child to protect her against herself." Thus she had to do for herself what she felt her mother failed to do.

Debby was greatly relieved when her mother's analysis enabled the latter to be firm and authoritative and to detach herself from involvement in her daughter's rituals. She dreaded a return to the old weakness, commenting that there must be a point where mothers were firm, and even suspecting herself of always trying to find that point. With mother's new-found firmness, Debby was able to express her aggression more openly in words and to experience it in the transference. This culminated in her verbalizing the fear that she might discover the most terrible thing about herself—the fact that she really wanted to kill her mother.

Killing is a word that both mother and daughter used easily to express their aggressive drives. They both shared fantasies of strangling or being strangled. Debby's fantasies of mother's aggression toward her repeatedly appeared in the transference and may be understood in terms of projection of her own aggressive feelings and actions and the anticipated retaliation. At times it seemed that they were also an expression of Debby's awareness of mother's underlying hostility displaced as we know from her sister to her child. Both aspects were expressed in a story Debby told of a mother who tried to strangle her daughter. She commented that it must be terrible not to be able to trust your own mother. Implicit in this was her admission that her mother could not be expected to trust her.

Mrs. G.'s tendency to separate her husband from his daughter was experienced by Debby as an attempt to show her that father belonged to mother, not to Debby. In a story in which she reversed roles, Debby likened herself to a mad mother who exploited her madness to dominate her children, thereby preventing them from marrying or having a life of their own. Thus Debby indicated that her "mad behavior" was a weapon with which she could dominate and separate her parents.

The Effect of the Partnership upon Adolescence

The adolescent process itself is a driving force toward change and maturation, a process which in spite of its characteristic upheavals constitutes a step toward healthy development.

As we have seen throughout Debby's analytic material, forward moves toward health, resulting from increased insight, invariably came into conflict with the regressive pull toward infantile gratifications. At a developmental stage characterized by the resurgence of pregenital drives and newly acquired genital ones, it was not unexpected to find an intensification of the central conflict.

From the age of thirteen and a half years a gradual disappearance of many of the most disturbing rituals and obsessional symptoms could be observed, and this was accompanied by indications of progression toward age-adequate aims and attitudes. In treatment Debby made greater efforts, at home she became more independent. She began to make friends, went out alone, and was no longer troubled by separation anxiety. She could be left when her parents went on holiday. Her interest in her appearance, clothes, and boys appeared characteristic for her age. At the same time, however, new symptoms appeared which, although slightly less crippling and disturbing socially, could be seen to reflect the old partnership with her mother in new but related forms.

The continued pull toward preoedipal gratifications revealed itself in the way in which Debby utilized her age-adequate interests in the service of her regressive urges. Thus her interest in boys and clothes was used almost entirely to achieve new forms of intimacy and excitement with mother. Intimate "cosy talks" about these matters now replaced the former compulsive discussions about sickness. Debby's demands for new clothes were insatiable. She gazed at herself continuously in the glass, calling her mother for consultation as she changed her clothes five or six times before leaving for school.

Analytic treatment aimed at maintaining a constant watch on these new or changed symptoms to recognize and make conscious their repetitive character and their role in impeding development. At the same time treatment worked toward supporting healthy forward moves so that adolescence could proceed as smoothly and fully as possible.

If we examine Debby's analytic material from the point of view of this conflict between the progressive and regressive forces, it enables us, I believe, to evaluate not only her adolescent development but also the extent to which analysis exerted a counterinfluence upon the effects of the partnership.

Dieting As an Overdetermined Symptom

It was through her overwhelming preoccupation with her figure and the need to reduce and become skinny and flat that Debby came nearest to re-establishing the infantile position in which her digestive processes again became her mother's main concern. Her method was ostentatiously to refuse food or demand diets until she became so hungry that she could speak of little else. In her imagination the dieting led to illness and would result in the longed-for concern on my and her family's part. Finally she would succumb to an orgy of eating, particularly chocolate biscuits, following which she would have to stay away from school, ballet, and even treatment, until a dose of "Andrew's" had emptied her out and made her thin again.

This rhythm of abstinence and orgy followed by guilt reflected, in addition, the infantile affects surrounding her need to control masturbation and the orgastic experience. It also represented a compulsive repetition of the seduction, and the conflicts surrounding the invitation to fellatio. Pregnancy fantasies were also evident.

It can be seen that although the dieting had as its main function the purpose of drawing everyone, and especially her mother, into her narcissistic fantasies, it was overdetermined and had acquired even further implications. It had the purpose of mastering adolescent body changes and sensations which were felt to be overwhelming. At times it was also experienced as a means of controlling masculinity and femininity. Moreover, it served a function similar to the "barbed-wire habits" by providing an external control which the internalized mother, like the real mother, failed to supply.

Finally, the dieting served an aggressive function toward her mother, and it is significant that twice when angry with her mother, Debby took an overdose of aspirin "to make her take notice." The turning of aggression against the self is characteristic of such extreme dieting.

Seductive and Exhibitionistic Behavior—The Fight Against Homosexuality

The pull toward a normal social life and the wish to enter a group outside the family became stronger as analytic work enabled Debby to understand her motives behind the school phobia. Even then, attempts to return to school (a new coeducational one) were finally successful only when the mother's own analysis enabled the latter to support and encourage Debby's still uncertain drive toward emancipation.

Once at school, however, the pull toward infantile forms of gratification presented a constant threat to the maintenance of this forward step. In her treatment she revealed how precarious her daily school attendance was and how it depended upon exhibitionistic strivings for limelight associated with her ballet class. This exhibitionism had its roots in a fantasy of her mother looking with admiration at Debby's athletic body, much as if it represented the admired penis. In this fantasy Debby identified both with her father and with the boy she imagined mother wished her to be.

The battle between the healthy move away from her mother and the primitive need to hold on to her could now be followed a step further. Debby attempted to ward off her mother by transferring her feelings for her onto other mother figures. This mechanism of displacement is not unusual in mother-daughter relationships of this type and might be considered a positive step toward severing the infantile tie. Thus Debby's exhibitionism in ballet was partly motivated by her interest in her ballet teacher, which in turn was based upon the close bond between the teacher and the teacher's mother, who was the class pianist. Similarly, a dancing friendship with a girl of her own age was determined by interest in her friend's mother, who, separated from her husband, showed an enviable interest in her daughter's dancing and slimming. Debby displaced onto this mother all the affect belonging to her own, responding to criticism or rejection with disproportionate pleasure or distress. Debby's first holiday away from her parents was with this lady and her family.

It was as a result of these strong emotional experiences, accompanied by similar transference manifestations, that Debby became more aware of her homosexual feelings and how greatly they distressed her and interfered with normal friendships and activities. Her fear that she might have inherited homosexual leanings was colored by her impression that her mother was now frightened of her own feelings toward Debby and therefore treated as repulsive signs of affection which in the past she had invited. It was not surprising that an attempt to move from her coeducational school to a girls' college ended in failure. Debby could not achieve this advance since she could not deal with her relationship to the teachers and girls, and there were no men in the environment to whom she could take flight.

Debby's reversion to preoedipal and negative oedipal positions was, as we know, an attempt to resolve her oedipal conflict. As analysis proceeded, oedipal behavior became increasingly evident. Her seductive and exhibitionistic manner to teachers and boys bore the imprint of her seduction experience at the oedipal level. Success as much as frustration at this level could be seen to push her back to earlier modes of satisfaction. She would stay away from school with an imaginary illness and retire to bed. One could thus observe the ease with which she still swung from one level to the other.

This was well illustrated when a susceptible male teacher responded to an offer of a bite of Debby's apple. She could not understand why she became so anxious until she recognized her "Evelike qualities" and likened the teacher to the uncle who had seduced her. She longed to expose his unteacherlike behavior to the headmaster, whose rocklike strength against her seductiveness made her feel safe. As with the uncle and for the same reason, she did not report the teacher concerned. Her fear was that the headmaster would recognize her motives—the attempt to point out to him that she was desirable to another man and had played a part in seducing him.

Debby's seductive behavior with boys and her overwhelming preoccupation with falling in love and having sexual intercourse fall into place in relation to her oedipal conflict, her homosexual fears, and her excessive penis envy. It was, I believe, the careful analysis of all these factors which made it possible for her to arrive at any lasting heterosexuality. Without analysis it is doubtful whether she would have done so.

The process of reaching heterosexuality was characterized by the flight from homosexuality and her tie to her mother and a compulsive denial of her own femininity. Debby had to chase boys to prove that she was not homosexual and because possession of a boy meant possession of a penis. Conquest was followed by lovemaking which terrified her and was complicated by the intrusion of a fellatio fantasy related to the seduction. At seventeen and a half the fear that she might really be homosexual led to a single unsatisfactory sexual act with a delinquent boy she hardly knew. It was a repetition of the original seduction as well as a counterphobic act in which she controlled the terrifying situation. This time she brought the experience to her mother's notice by leaving her diary about and used the occasion for a dramatic confession of the original incident. In this way she utilized heterosexual development for preoedipal gratifications. It is interesting that in spite of the mother's emotional response to Debby's confession, the mother decided to conceal both incidents from Debby's father.

A Career—Difficulties in Sublimation

The continued regressive pull and its ramifications were of course reflected in Debby's approach to sublimations. As might be expected, her conscious wish to pursue the academic career justified by her high intelligence was impeded by her need for exhibitionism and her inability to tolerate failure or frustration or to work toward long-term aims. She had no hobbies.

One interest, that of a stage career, continued to attract her, but for a long time guilt about its basis in her exhibitionism hindered all practical efforts in this direction. A positive forward move was noticeable when increasing insight into the nature of her exhibitionism enabled her to reduce the sexual aspect of the gratification to manageable proportions. The activity became more sublimated and less guilt laden, so that through her own efforts she was able to gain admission to a reputable stage school where she enjoyed the work, made friends, and was well thought of.

TERMINATION OF ANALYSIS

Debby's break with analysis was not the result of a planned decision, but the outcome of the intolerable pull between her forward moves toward severing her object tie and the primitive need to hold on to her mother. It reflected the struggle in the transference between adolescent maturational strivings, and attitudes determined by her unresolved oedipus complex and the resultant homosexual urges.

While the transference had been surprisingly free of the characteristic adolescent rebellion, at home Debby had provoked her parents beyond endurance with bohemian behavior and extreme temper outbursts. But although she had gone through all the motions, there had in fact been no indication of any true "removal" (Katan, 1937; Anna Freud, 1958).

Two factors now influenced the nature of the transference. On the one hand, Debby's extreme acting out at home was scrutinized and discussed in terms of the conflict over severing the tie with her mother. It became clear that the opposing pulls were dealt with by a splitting process which enabled her to displace her infantile wishes onto me while keeping the formidable demonstration for home where implementation would not be encouraged. These interpretations enabled Debby to bring her need to free herself into the transference. These discussions coincided with the termination of the mother's analysis, an event which enhanced Debby's fantasies of homosexual danger. There were hints that she both hoped and feared that her mother would look to the old intimacy with her to replace the lost relationship with her analyst. In addition, Debby feared that without her analyst's support, her mother would be unable to maintain her detached role.

Three months after the mother's analysis had come to an end the whole conflict was brought fully into the transference and a marked ambivalence became apparent. Infantile demanding and seductive attitudes could be seen side by side with attempts to establish distance. Debby became secretive and rebellious. She criticized and mistrusted analysis and resented being influenced by it. While declaring that treatment was her lifeline and pleading for it to continue, she missed sessions for weeks on end without canceling, and asked for appointments which she did not keep. It became clear that treatment would have to cease, and contact was kept by weekly inter-views. Debby was just eighteen and a half years.

When weekly treatment commenced, Debby's relationship with her parents had greatly improved—at least from the point of view of her behavior. Outbursts of temper had largely disappeared as had the compulsive dieting. Some degree of obsessional behavior remained, and Debby still kept a measure of control over her parents by sleeping with the door open and under stress demanding to be comforted at night.

The First Extrafamilial Heterosexual Object

The positive implications of a serious heterosexual relationship for Debby are obvious and may be evaluated as an analytic achievement. Its interest for us is that it reflects the shift away from the infantile tie while at the same time illustrating how the remnants of her central conflict caused her to establish a new partnership based on many of the old features.

Debby met Joe two years ago when she was eighteen and he was twenty-eight. Through him she was able to satisfy some of her intense oedipal rivalry with her mother, thereby decreasing her guilt in relation to the latter and improving their relationship. Apart from his age, Joe was considered to have many qualities in common with her father, particularly his desirability to other women, his attachment to his own parents, his defensive and cynical attitude to psychiatry and emotional disturbance, and his possessive, somewhat condescending attitude to Debby. He was highly acceptable to the family and embraced as a member of it.

From the outset the quality that most attracted Debby to him was his demand for a docile and dependent partner, for it satisfied the two aspects of her anal character, the need to submit and rebel. Together with the oral features, the alliance soon took on a familiar form, that of a relationship based upon constant verbal rows and reconciliations. Debby bitterly resented Joe's demand that she prove her love, dependence, and readiness for marriage by abandoning her professional training in favor of a job. Soon the sadomasochistic relationship with the mother was repeated in the endless battles for power between Debby and Joe. This was further complicated by Debby's unconscious determination to endow Joe with the authority and firmness she had failed to find in her mother, and her genuine enjoyment of her training and a wish to succeed in it.

The conflict over the drama school revived many aspects of the school phobia, for, as in the past, Debby believed that interest and pleasure in anything but the object of her love would result in loss of the object. She feared Joe would find someone else, just as she had imagined her mother would do in the past, and would then discover that he could manage without Debby and thereby remove himself from her control.

Debby's ultimate decision to prove her love for Joe by giving up acting was overdetermined and illustrated the strength of the backward pull exerted by the infantile tie. It coincided with her decision to terminate treatment entirely; this decision to give up acting stemmed in part from her aggression toward Joe, now turned against herself. It could be traced to her need to assuage her guilt for successfully competing with him, for he had been her coach in amateur theatricals and had played the lead while she had had minor parts. Her continued problem of inadequacy was further reflected in the fact that having a man to whom she was engaged provided her with a sense of possession and importance which she herself equated with the longed-for penis. It compensated for past failures and ensured against future ones. Finally, it could be ascribed to her familiar calculations, based upon oedipal strivings, that a rival might steal her limelight. Marriage would enable her to withdraw from a competitive situation without losing face.

Joe's attitude toward sexual matters made him additionally attractive to Debby, for his behavior seemed to play into her counterphobic defenses and enable her to feel in control of him. This need to control her partner stemmed from her continued seduction fantasy in which she gained possession of the seducer's penis. Joe appeared to make few sexual demands beyond petting, while Debby twice initiated sexual intercourse. She emphasized that in bed with him she felt that it was she who was in power. At the same time the prospect of marriage increased her night terrors which were all associated with fantasies of sexual violence. On three occasions at the age of nineteen, these night terrors drove Debby back to her mother's bed from which her father was then excluded. On one occasion she slept with her mother for a week. Thus the swing between heterosexuality and homosexuality could clearly be seen.

Although both in the transference and with her mother, the complications of her relationship with Joe were used initially to justify "cosy discussions" based on the old intimacy, this has more recently been balanced by more positive indications. Not the least important aspect of the tie to Joe has been an increasing conscious reassurance about her heterosexuality. At the time of writing Debby reports that her night fears have disappeared, that she has held a job in advertising for five months (work that is related to both father's and Joe's profession), and that she hopes to marry in less than a year.

To sum up, we see that while removal from the original object has taken place and heterosexuality has been achieved, it appears to be labile and to break down under stress. Not only does the relationship with the new object repeat many features of the infantile partnership, but the displacement appears to depend upon the new object being brought into the family orbit. It can be argued that what we are observing is the process of severing the object tie in development. This, I think, is true, but Debby, unlike other adolescents, appears to remain suspended in this stage of development, still unable to make the final forward move.

DISCUSSION

In her paper on "Pregenital Patterning," Phyllis Greenacre (1952) elaborates on the effects of an early and prolonged trauma which may produce so massive a stimulation as to suffuse the whole organism. In a later paper (1960) she adds that such unfavorable conditions, if long sustained, may establish a permanent tendency to tension which cannot be relieved by analysis, although the patient may learn to deal with its secondary effects. These observations seem to apply to Debby.

It is possible, in Debby's case, that excessive oral and anal stimulation, beginning almost at birth, resulted in a state of primitive erotization and genital stimulation which required all channels available for discharge and even those channels not yet fully developed. This excessive body care in infancy was, we know, followed by exaggerated dietary and bowel concern until well after the oedipal phase. The stimulation owed its strength and persistence to the interplay between mother and father's unconscious needs and the fact that body-bound attention of an oral and anal quality was the only way in which these parents could *share* in the upbringing of their only child. The mother's analysis has established that her unresolved oedipal conflict caused her to identify her husband with her father. Thus the need to comply with her husband's food fads and bowel attitudes, as she complied, and still does, with her father's food rituals, may have contributed to the nature of the identification and its effect upon her child.

It is further suggested that body-bound interests of this character form the essential bond between mother, father, and daughter, and that therefore the pull toward continuing this state of affairs even into adolescence was very great.

We can assume that the mounting tension on the oral and anal level, for which at the time she had no adequate discharge capacities, caused Debby to battle with early and excessive masturbation problems; and it is likely that this factor influenced not only the nature of her later genitality but also increased her castration and penis-envy problems. This was emphasized by the mother's wish for a boy child, and Debby's envy of her boy cousin, whose genitals, according to the mother, she openly coveted. It may have been further accentuated by the injection-needle incident.

Whether healthy growth processes would have enabled Debby, in spite of her bad beginnings, to resolve her oedipal conflict, we shall never know. We can ask ourselves whether the seduction at the height of the oedipal phase would have taken place at all had her previous experiences not led to excessive tension, precocious erotization, a strong oral fixation, and extreme exhibitionism. That it did take place was the turning point in her development, and it ensured a regression from that point on the libidinal ladder to a level toward which a strong pull already operated. It added to her symptomatology the compulsive need to act out ritualistically the actuality of the trauma and her responsibility for it.

Both in her infantile relations to her mother and in the seduction incident, Debby experienced not only the reality of her seductive powers but the confusing fact that in some cases her frightening fantasies of omnipotence were borne out by reality.

Debby's perversion can be traced to her preoedipal development and the intensity of sexual confusion that followed the early stimulation and the seduction. Apart from mutual masturbation and the use of the dog's penis as if it were her own, there were examples of the confusion of sexual identity and impaired reality sense reflected in her other compulsions, such as the need to use all new possessions as if they were a penis. Thus one could observe the development of what could have become fetishism.

Greenacre points out that these traumatized children become more than ordinarily prone to strong bisexual identifications and that this influences the resolution of the oedipus conflict. Indeed, she suggests that in the case of girls who have undergone severe traumatization, there is no solution at all and the whole question is deferred until puberty when the castration problem arises with extreme intensity.

These findings are confirmed in Debby's case. It has been pointed out that this is a child who experienced no cessation in her sexual and aggressive conflicts between the oedipal phase and the onset of puberty; indeed, the oedipal battle continued unabated, and it might be said that there was no latency period at all.

As predicted in Greenacre's paper (1952), adolescence brought with it a heightened castration problem, which influenced her sexuality and could be seen in her wish to possess a man so as to possess his penis. In Debby's case, penis envy had oral coloring—of significance too in connection with her feeding and dieting symptoms.

Debby abandoned the perversions during treatment, but at no time during adolescence could she entirely resolve her oedipal difficulties. She swung continuously between the homosexual wish to re-experience the intimacies with mother while at the same time seeking to separate the latter from father and have both for herself. Not only had she to live out these conflicts in every sphere of life, but equally all men had to be tested again and again to see whether they, like her uncle, would submit to her overtures.

Anna Freud's paper on "Adolescence" (1958) is responsible for my attempt to trace Debby's oedipal and preoedipal fantasy life through what should have been the latency period into adolescence, in the hope of demonstrating how these fantasies have been colored and lent frightening reality by the reawakened pregenital urges and the newly acquired genital ones. In her paper, Anna Freud emphasizes that to the adolescent, the danger is located not only in the id impulses and fantasies but in the very existence of the love objects of the oedipal and preoedipal past, and that the anxieties which arise center around breaking the tie with them.

We have followed Debby's struggle in that direction—a struggle made more difficult by her parents' own pathology—and have seen how problems concerned with severing the tie were finally instrumental in bringing about the termination of her analysis. This termination may be viewed both as an expression of a homosexual conflict too dangerous to face and as a healthy sign of an attempt to loosen the infantile object tie.

I have further tried to illustrate how Debby found herself suspended in a process of severing an infantile tie which she could not finally break. I have attempted to show how labile any new relationship was, how for its continued existence, it depended upon being brought into the family orbit, and how many of its features are characteristic of the preoedipal and oedipal object relationship.

It seems reasonable to conclude that the long drawn-out infantile stimulation followed by the subsequent trauma described in this paper may be held responsible for ego deviations causing such far-reaching disturbances. But ego deviations are not necessarily irrevocable. Why then has it not been possible sufficiently to strengthen this patient's ego to enable it to play a greater part in resisting infantile sexuality and aggression?

Freud wrote in "Analysis Terminable and Interminable" (1937) that every normal person is only approximately normal; that his ego "resembles that of the psychotic in one point or another to a greater or lesser degree and its distance from one end of the scale, and proximity to the other, may provisionally serve as a measure of what we have indefinitively spoken of as 'modification of the ego'."

It appears that the amount of help that we can expect from the ego in assisting recovery or defending against regression is related to its ultimate position on that scale. It would be equally true to say that the degree of ego modification we can hope to achieve, and which will ultimately be decisive in the battle against infantile sexuality and aggression, depends upon the extent, depth, and quality of ego damage, or distortion, and how soon after the trauma treatment is undertaken.

Phyllis Greenacre (1960) refers to work in recent years, examining conditions under which ego formation is weakened and distorted at its inception. She speaks of how "special exigencies of the young ego may influence the selection and nature of later defence mechanisms." She points out that a repeated high pitch of fear and anxiety at a time when the defenses are less well developed must interfere with those ego functions which are *in statu ascendi*.

We know that the earliest fantasies of merging with the mother by means of oral incorporation is the foundation upon which all future types of identifications are built. It follows that true and lasting ego identifications presuppose a gradual transition from oral fantasies of fusion with the mother, to the establishment of ego boundaries and the awareness of self as a separate entity. It is recognized that internalization of the parental images, leading to ego-ideal and superego formation, is essential for the building up of a well-integrated personality.

We may ask ourselves whether Debby's earliest oral and anal experiences, arousing states of rage, acute anxiety, and probably erotization of anxiety, may have been responsible for a disturbance in identifications. In connection with a defect in internalization one must consider the symptoms concerned with intake and expulsion which persisted into adolescence. Her shallow object relations with their "as if" quality are also relevant here.

It is certain that the inconsistent and indulgent mothering she received deprived her of the support and security necessary for the growth of control and the canalization of sexual and aggressive drives in the service of the ego. This support, dependent upon secure love, oedipal frustration, consistent parental demands, etc., facilitates solid identifications and the establishment of aim-inhibited personal and social relations. It is a process essential for the formation of a healthy superego and a functioning and self-reliant ego, and the support was lacking in Debby's environment. It would not surprise us if these deprivations alone had resulted in an ego unable to deal with drive and thus environmental demands.

To all this we must add the effects of the seduction and the continued parental pathology which caused a continuous regressive pull to operate right into adolescence, so that internal tension was repeatedly met with external stimulation. Thus an already fragile ego found itself further weakened by the need to use every defense that it could muster in the battle against instinctual urges.

Accurate methods of measuring ego strength and weakness have not yet been devised, and it is likely that assessment becomes progressively more difficult the nearer on either side to the center of the scale the ego is. We may asume that lack of resistivity of ego functions against regression constitutes a true ego defect in itself. Hartmann (1955) points out that an ego swamped by insufficiently neutralized instinctual energy may result in pathological development and an interference with the capacity to sublimate. The question of interference in sublimations is also associated with disturbed identifications. Debby's very limited capacity for sublimation is significant from the point of view of the ego's capacity to neutralize instinctual energy, since it seems likely that this too may be an indication of ego strength or weakness.

Glover (1931) emphasized that ego strength or weakness is exclusively due to the extent to which other systems (such as id or superego) encroach upon the ego. In Debby's case, one must consider not only the strength of drives, toleration of frustration, anxiety, and guilt, but also the fact that she uses almost every known defense mechanism to battle against her instinctual urges. While defenses may demonstrate relative ego strength vis-à-vis drives, Freud (1937) himself emphasized that these very defenses might cause exhaustion of ego strength.

How does the assumption of irreversible ego damage influence our attitude to treatment? From the point of view of the mother the aim of simultaneous analysis remains the same—that of reducing the involvement in the child's pathology to the extent of minimizing the pull toward infantile gratifications. From the point of view of the child, our aims may have to be modified. We may be satisfied if we can strengthen the damaged ego to the limits of its capacity, bringing it further along the scale and thereby reducing the danger of psychotic illness. If the need for infantile gratification is substantially reduced and replaced by new and more stable object relations, the capacity for heterosexuality, and the achievement of some sublimations, we hope that our patient may function with greater safety, even if a final severing of the infantile object tie seems improbable.

BIBLIOGRAPHY

Beres, D. (1956), Ego Deviations and the Concept of Schizophrenia. *This Annual,* XI.

Freud, A. (1958), Adolescence. *This Annual,* XIII.

Freud, S. (1937), Analysis Terminable and Interminable. *Collected Papers,* V. London: Hogarth Press, 1950.

Glover, E. (1931), Sublimation, Substitution and Social Anxiety. *Int. J. Psa.,* XII.

Greenacre, P. (1952), Pregenital Patterning. *Int. J. Psa.,* XXXIII.

—— (1960), Regression and Fixation. *J. Amer. Psa. Assn.,* VIII.

Hartmann, H. (1955), Notes on the Theory of Sublimation. *This Annual,* X.

Hellman, I. (1960), Simultaneous Analysis of Mother and Child. *This Annual,* XV.

Jacobson, E. (1954a), The Self and the Object World. *This Annual,* IX.

—— (1954b), Contributions to the Metapsychology of Psychotic Identifications. *J. Amer. Psa. Assn.,* II.

Katan, A. (1937), The Role of 'Displacement' in Agoraphobia. *Int. J. Psa.,* XXXII, 1951.

Kris, E. (1955), Neutralization and Sublimation. Observations on Young Children. *This Annual,* X.

Levy, K. (1960), Simultaneous Analysis of a Mother and Her Adolescent Daughter. *This Annual,* XV.

Reich, A. (1954), Early Identifications As Archaic Elements in the Superego. *J. Amer. Psa. Assn.,* II.

THE "EVOCATION OF A PROXY"

A Psychological Maneuver, Its Use As a Defense, Its Purposes and Genesis

MARTIN WANGH, M.D. (New York)

In recent years psychoanalytic theorists have shifted their interest from primary narcissism to the primal mother-child unit. Freud (1921) said that the embryo *in utero* lived in a state of "absolutely self-sufficient narcissism" ending at the moment of birth. Present-day views partially prefer to assume a continuance of a symbiotic mother-child relationship for a period after birth. It is characterized by interfunctioning of mutual needs and a fusion of body images (A. Freud and Burlingham, 1944; Greenacre, 1941, 1960; Mahler, 1952; Mahler and Gosliner, 1956; Winnicott, 1960; *inter alios*). My introduction to this paper reconsiders the Freudian statement and stresses in particular the significant kinetic qualities of the prevailing assumptions.

We all share the opinion that the process of individuation, ideally culminating in an independent self, capable of sharing life in tolerant interchange with other like selves, proceeds gradually and with many chances for relapse as the infant emerges from the mother-child mesh. The processes and functions that contribute to the final establishment of such a self are multiple. Their occurrence is so nearly simultaneous and their mutual reinforcement so immediate that, with our present means of observation, no true sequence can be constructed. For instance, the building up of object representations is contemporaneous with the evolution of self-representations, and this whole process of image formation is as much causative of, as caused by, the separating out of the infant from the mother-child unit.

The intermingling ebb and flow of self- and object-discernment in these initial phases of individuation has been the subject of several contributions by Edith Jacobson (1954a, 1954b). She accepts Melanie Klein's conceptualizations of "good" and "bad" self- and object images, and also her view that both introjective and projective mechanisms participate in the constitution of object representations. However, Jacobson stresses that with the growth of ego independence, identifications arise. These are processes to be distinguished from representation formation.

Introjection and projection prevail when reality testing is still weak; then ego boundaries shift easily and self- and object images merge, as well as split facilely. ". . . for some years the child feels himself to be only an extension of the mother and participates in her imagined omnipotence or, the reverse, regards the mother as part of his omnipotent self. . . . Evidently, such experiences of merging with the love object are always connected with a temporary weakening of the function of perception, i.e., of the awakening of the sense of reality," writes Jacobson (1954b, pp. 241, 242).

In elastic progression the sense of reality and the sense of identity develop as manifestations of the pressures of maturing. These delineate the young individual out of the mother-child unit. As is the case with all other psychological processes, these two ego functions are not neatly distinguishable from each other; they overlap—a fact that facilitates their mutual sustentation. Reality answers the question, "What operates, where, and how?" and identity, that of "Who?" However, it is as necessary for the definition of the sense of identity to establish the locus, inside or outside, the "where" of a stimulus source as it is for the sense of reality that a "who," a "self," be discerned from its environment.

The maturational propulsion to cleave self from nonself is opposed not only by fluctuating returns to fusion but is also moderated by more stable compromise formations. The invariably paired "omnipotent self-extensions" and "submersions of the self in the omnipotent maternal image" are of this order. They are transitory psychological structures in normal growth, but as pathologically persistent features they pervert the process of individuation out of symbiosis into one of parasitism. The object exists then exclusively for the subject's use. But only when a self already exists, if solely as a core with unsteady delimitation, can we speak of a truly narcissistic state, where regard for the object does not play any role.[1]

The relationship of the infant and of the young child to the "transitional object" (Winnicott, 1953) seems to be a good example of what I have in mind here. Its character as a self-extension is confirmed by these facts: (1) that very often the transitional object must be suffused with the child's own body odors; (2) that no adaptations to it are necessary; and (3) that it is used and abused at will. Winnicott (1954) also calls it "the first possession . . . created by the infant" and found "in the environment for the infant's use." "And sometimes," Winnicott (1953, p. 91) says, "there is no transitional object except the mother herself." The imaginary companion of later childhood may be a second edition of the early "transitional object." In any case, we are dealing here with a thing, a person, or an image, created and invoked to play a role in the service of the self without any regard for the object involved.[2]

Residues of transitional object relationships persist normally throughout life. Pathological manifestations of them will be illuminated in the main body of my paper through clinical examples. In particular, I shall endeavor to show how another person may be used by the ego for defensive purposes. I shall describe the structural and economic aspects of such a defensive maneuver, and I shall suggest that its genetics proceed from a persistence of narcissistic object relationships. This complex unconscious defense will be called "Evocation of a Proxy." Essentially it represents an enlargement of Anna Freud's (1936) concept of "altruistic surrender." I shall make clear later on why I speak of "evocation." A "proxy" shall be

[1] The concept of symbiosis emphasizes interadaptation and interfunctioning within the mother-child unit, though an embryonal, and infantile biological, narcissistic core must be presumed to exist at the same time. Ever-present automatic processes regulate the adaptation of the baby's narcissistic needs to that of the mother's and vice versa. For instance, during harmonious nursing the production of milk may depend on the quality of the baby's sucking, just as the quality of the baby's sucking may depend on the milk production. In a psychological sense, the term narcissism might more logically be reserved for a time when a self has emerged which is strong enough, if only for a brief period, to function on its own and which is capable of demanding subservience to its wishes without adaptation to the needs of the object.

[2] See Annie Reich's (1953, p. 22) summary of Freud's view on narcissism: "Objects, at that level, are 'selfishly' used for one's own gratification; their interests cannot yet be considered."

defined as a person other than oneself who is used to experience feelings, exercise functions, and execute actions in one's own stead.

Altruism and the Evocation of a Proxy

Anna Freud (1936) has pointed to the defense by proxy in the chapter entitled "A Form of Altruism" in *The Ego and the Mechanisms of Defense*. She discusses how natural it is for the ego of little children to use the mechanism of projection when punishment is feared or guilt is to be experienced. Another child, or person, or an animal, or even an inanimate object is equally useful for this purpose. Our own jealousy and aggressive acts can by means of this mechanism be attributed to other people. Presumably fear of loss of love, of castration, or of the superego promotes this defense. Anna Freud also states that a normal and less conspicuous form of projection might be described as "altruistic surrender" of our instinctual impulses in favor of other people. In this instance, a person evades the pressures of his superego by participating through unconscious identification in the instinctual gratifications of another person. Anna Freud's patient "found some proxy in the outside world to serve as a repository [for her forbidden, unconscious impulses]. . . . The surrender of her instinctual impulses in favour of other people had thus an egoistic significance, but in her efforts to gratify the impulses of others her behaviour could only be called altruistic." To protect the proxy's participation even otherwise forbidden aggression may be mobilized. "In most cases the substitute has once been the object of envy. . . . This surrender of instinctual wishes to an object better qualified to fulfill them often determines the relation of a girl to some man whom she chooses to represent her—to the detriment of any true object relation." In such cases egoism and altruism may be blended in varying proportion. The same phenomenon is so clearly observed in the attitude of parents toward their children.[3]

Otto Sperling (1944) uses Bleuler's term "appersonation" to stress the extension of ego feeling beyond the actual self. What Anna Freud calls "proxy" he labels "appersonand." He is mindful of the distri-

---

[3] See Flügel (1921, p. 168) for normal aspects of this: ". . . the parent identifies himself with the child, as it were incorporates the child into his larger self and is thus able to take pleasure in the increasing powers of the child as if they were his own."

bution of narcissistic libido involved and states that appersonations may "appear as a resistance" and "as a mechanism of defense against, or for the satisfaction of the most varied instinctual impulses." His discussion of the difference between appersonation and identification is particularly concise.

Many other authors have emphasized one or another aspect of what Anna Freud has described in the chapter quoted. Therese Benedek (1937) illustrates how a patient may try to use the analyst as his superego, and Annie Reich (1953), elaborating Freud's theories on the narcissistic object relations, reviews the subject in terms of a pathology of the ego ideal. Martin Stein (1956) examines such phenomena in the marriage bond, and Marcel Heiman (1956) in the bond between a man and his dog.

Ruth Eissler (1949) has pointed out that society may use some of its members as executors of its own forbidden impulses—"the scapegoats of society"—while Johnson and Szurek (1952) describe how the parent may be vicariously gratified by the (mis-) behavior of the child. The relationship that develops then has "the twofold purpose of allowing vicarious gratification of forbidden impulses as well as expression of hostile, destructive impulses toward the child."[4] Though these authors do not explicitly state it, their case material often implies active, though unconscious, incitement of the child's actions by the parent.

In an individual setting, I shall seek to demonstrate that for purposes of unconscious defense, in addition to the arousal of id impulses, both ego experiences and ego functions can be mobilized in others. Specifically, affects such as anxiety or jealousy, functions of impulse control and of reality evaluation, instinctual discharges of both a libidinous and an aggressive nature can all be evoked in an alter ego. This may occur (1) in response to anxiety aroused by the threatened loss of a narcissistically cathected object,[5] (2) by the threat

---

[4] Warren Brodey (1959) has similar processes in mind. He calls "externalization" a mechanism of defense defined as projection plus the selective use of reality for verification of the projection; and "narcissistic object relationship" is, to him, a relationship with a projected part of the self, as mirrored in the behavior of another.

[5] William A. Greene (1958, 1959) discusses such "proxy mechanisms" in the context of vicarious object functioning. He describes the need for the existence of the vicariously functioning object and states: "When the proxy mechanisms are no longer feasible . . . these patients become somatically sick."

of unmanageable regression in reality testing,[6] or (3) by the threat of loss of control over impulses. I postulate that, in the cases to be cited, there occurred defective dissolution of the early symbiotic tie to the mother, and with it a lagging development of the sense of identity. Additionally, later childhood experiences of a seductive character interfered with the proper development of the enumerated ego functions, offering a further push toward the patient's use of the defense by "evocation of a proxy." In brief, I shall try to investigate the structural and economic aspects of this defense, its resistance effects in analysis, and its genetic background.

Case Illustrations

My first example stems from direct child observation. A six-year-old frightens her younger sister by telling her scary tales. She does this when their parents are out for the evening. When the younger one becomes upset, the older one assumes the role of the protector; she pets and reassures the little sister.

These bare facts easily invite the interpretation that the older sister herself had been anxious, that she had gotten rid of her anxiety by arousing this emotion in her younger sister. By assuming a parental and consoling role, via unconscious identification with the little sister, she was able to deny her own fears about being abandoned. In this circuitous way she assuaged the instinctual tensions which would presumably have led to the increasing development of anxiety within herself. It should be especially noted here that we are dealing not with a simple *projection of fear upon an apt object* but with an act aimed at the *creation* of a proxy who then, *in reality*, carries the projection affixed to it.

Two other examples come from the analytic treatment of two adult female patients. Mrs. L. is a fifty-year-old woman, married for over twenty years to an artistic, relatively impotent, passive and narcissistic man. Throughout the years of marriage she had succeeded in keeping her husband from any affectionate relationship with their daughter, by now eighteen years old. A few years ago the patient had sought analysis in the fearful anticipation that the pubescent girl would soon be grown up and leave the household.

[6] In contrast to temporary artistic regression which is manageable.

Now the long-feared separation had occurred. However, as one might expect under these circumstances, the news from college was not good. The girl was failing scholastically and my patient learned that she was quite promiscuous. At this point Mrs. L. involved her usually excluded husband. She incited his rage against the girl. But while he railed over the phone at his wayward daughter, the mother, on the extension line, assumed a reassuring role. Afterward she berated him for having been such a bad, critical, and absent father.

The actions of a second patient, Mrs. T., were not much different. She had come for analysis because of a severe agoraphobia. Her past history included one period of depression and two episodes of mania, for which she had been hospitalized. When her sixteen-year-old son began to stay out late at night, she would wait up for him for a while. Then she would wake her husband, a severe hypochondriac, from his barbiturate-induced slumber. She easily aroused his anxiety to the point that he would storm out of the house, pace up and down the sidewalk for hours, engulfed alternately by waves of rage and anxiety, until the boy came home. In the meantime, Mrs. T. herself retired to sound sleep, from which she was awakened only when her snarling husband and truculent son staggered into the bedroom. Then she would get up and chat with the boy about his evening's adventures over a late night snack.

Essentially, then, what happens is that anxiety is induced—or evoked—by one member of a couple in the other, and we learn from our analytic examples that the husbands consequently become not only agitated but also angry against a third person, their progeny. In contrast to the partner's agitation and rage, the older sister and the wives remain calm and assume a benevolent and protective attitude. In this way, the two mothers seemingly maintained a "good" relationship with their children.

We have already heard how Mrs. L. had dreaded the coming separation from her daughter, and when Mrs. T.'s son went off to college she would not admit any feelings about his absence. Both women had the inclination to react with icy withdrawal from the absent object, but both were filled with destructive fantasies against it, especially when jealousy was awakened. Mrs. L. fantasied thrusting her arms into her daughter's vagina and ripping out her uterus, while Mrs. T. saw her son drowned many times over when he pre-

ferred a fishing trip with some classmates to a visit home. The increment of libidinous charge is self-evident in Mrs. L.'s fantasy of
raping her daughter, and when the analysis succeeded in piercing
Mrs. T.'s denial of feelings, we glimpsed that any awareness of feeling of longing brought in its wake a rush of incestuous fantasies in
this sexually frustrated woman. I could thus observe that separation
and separation anxiety stimulated aggressive as well as libidinous,
genital impulses, which in turn heightened the level of anxiety.
Projections occurred, straining the ability for reality testing in both
these patients. Mrs. L., particularly during the first year of her
analysis, on the subway ride from home to the analyst, constantly
felt that people went out of their way to bump into her, and the
major content of Mrs. T.'s agoraphobia revealed itself as a fear of
encountering on the street men of whom she might think that they
were her dead father. Separation thus represented the traumatic
situation for these patients. It readily evoked their anxiety, to which
they responded with regression of ego functions, particularly involving the sense of reality. This reaction, however, resulted only in
further increase of anxiety. At times these women developed fears
of a paranoid character. These fears in turn promoted aggressive
impulses which threatened the ego's control over the latter. I could
observe that by means of the defensive maneuvers of proxy creation,
these patients not only rid themselves of any consciousness of their
own impulses by arousing them in someone else, but also freed themselves in moments of crisis from anxiety by evoking it in another
person.

In what follows I shall give further information to illustrate that
these patients' impulse control and ability to test reality were extremely tenuous. I shall also show that their childhood experiences
interfered with a proper development of their individuation, and
that excessive libidinous and aggressive stimulation impaired impulse control, sense of reality, and sense of identity.

After periodic previous disappearances, Mrs. L.'s father ab-
sconded forever when she was eight years old. Her memories of her
father were all filled with sadistic content. He would force the patient and her sisters to play gin rummy with him for endless hours
and when they misbehaved he would have them undress completely,
and he would beat them with a strap. Her mother was a spiritualist

who used the little girl as her medium at occultist sessions. It became quite clear in the course of the analysis that she in turn tried to use her daughter as an extension of herself as she had been used by her own mother. The girl was to fulfill Mrs. L.'s own exhibitionistic aspirations by becoming an actress and Mrs. L.'s cultural aspirations through brilliant scholastic performance. Mrs. L. led her daughter into libidinously charged situations and wanted to hear all about the subsequent experiences. When the girl rebelled the patient would usually withdraw icily, but it was a shattering experience to the mother when this defense failed and, in response to some minor provocation, she lost control one day and slapped her adult daughter with all her might. A strong paranoid trend was recognizable in Mrs. L.'s complaint that people in the subway were always bumping into her, or that her husband was steadily elbowing her in his sleep.

The other patient, Mrs. T., had an equally ominous background. Her father was a severe compulsive neurotic, limited by many rituals. Moreover, he preferred the company of his adolescent daughter to that of his wife. Thus he took his daughter with him to the theater and for a prolonged business trip out West. He was involved in shady business affairs, and at one time there was good reason to fear that the young daughter might be kidnaped by a rival group. Until the age of fourteen, she never left the house without being accompanied by an adult. Mrs. T.'s mother was an infantile person, utterly dependent on her own overwhelmingly controlling mother. My patient was told early in her life by the family physician that she was to be her mother's "window to the world." One night, when returning from an outing with a disapproved suitor, the patient, then eighteen years old, was mercilessly thrashed by her mother. After enduring this without any attempt at self-defense she sank into a severe depression. Recovering after about two months, she fled into marriage. Her husband turned out to be a man whose religious strictness incarcerated her even more. The two manic attacks during her marriage were, in part, the regressive expression of dammed-up rage and of the renewed wish to run away, a wish blocked by an utter inability to dare to do so.

Mrs. T.'s tendency to "loss of impulse control" and impairment of reality testing is illustrated further by a later episode. It occurred some time after her analysis had been interrupted because her hus-

band "refused to spend any more money on her"—a truth of highly
equivocal character in a proxy-creating patient like Mrs. T. She came
to consult me again when she was troubled about their son. He was
in his last year of college, and his initially good work had deteriorated
to such a point that the school authorities had been alarmed and
had recommended psychotherapy. Moreover, he had become involved with a girl, not of his faith, whom he was all set to marry—
to the utter consternation of his religious father. My patient claimed
that *she* did not feel upset like her husband; to the contrary, she had
invited the girl to the house, had been a friendly hostess, while her
husband had been extremely rude to the guest and had had violent
scenes with their son. So it went on for several weeks (I saw her
weekly, or twice a month, at the time), and the date of the wedding
was approaching. The patient's husband, though very saddened, had
become more and more resigned to the inevitable. Once, some time
before, in his frenzied search for a way out, he had thrown out the
idea to her that one might offer the son's psychotherapist a bribe to
dissuade the boy from entertaining the misalliance. The patient
discussed this as a harebrained scheme with me at the time. She was
all on the side of reasonableness; being so well acquainted with
matters of the mind and of psychotherapy, she saw clearly how
absurd the proposal was and how damaging to the boy's therapy and
health such interference would be. Yet now, when her husband
calmed down, she herself did what was so utterly out of touch with
reality. She called the doctor, made the offer, was duly rebuffed, and
the son was informed. This action probably contributed to the
eventual breakup of her son's engagement, but it also broke up the
therapy. The son barely graduated, and shortly thereafter became
overtly psychotic.

My patients obviously felt compelled to use their children in
order to repeat actively the traumatic experiences with their own
parents. By identification with their children, however, this break-
through of instinctual impulses caused them anxiety—the more so
since, due to their insufficient individuation, detachment from the
vicarious object was felt as a severe narcissistic injury. When the
regressive defenses mobilized by the anxiety lead to the danger of
loss of control over impulses and to a disturbance in the reality
orientation, the projection of the anxiety as well as that of the im-

pulses which caused it becomes economical. Under such circumstances, anxiety and aggression were usefully assigned to another person whose ego, though weak and easily aroused to anxiety, was *in toto* more resistant to the regression of its functions.

DYNAMICS

At this point I shall attempt a further, detailed dissection of the qualities, causes, and effects of the composite defense—evocation of a proxy. I think that in order to get past the formidable resistance which this defense offers in analysis, it will be useful to have knowledge of these elements. In the main, I shall deal with three phenomena: (1) a defusion of aggressive and libidinous strivings takes place by means of projection and evocation of the former in someone else and by retention in the self of the latter; (2) the *actuality* of seeing anxiety and rage in the partner serves to bolster the sense of reality endangered by regression; and (3) the involvement of the marital partner offsets to some extent the threatened loss of one extension object by replacing it with another.

From our material first emerges the idea that the evocation of a proxy has the purpose of preserving a good relationship with a narcissistically cathected object, the daughter or the son respectively in the case of the two women patients, and, by inference, the parents in the case of the little girl. This relationship seems to be endangered by the aggression mobilized against that object when the latter seeks to free itself from its tight bond to the subject. This sudden increment of aggression against the object produces anxiety which augments the chronically persistent, potential separation anxiety in the persons under discussion.

Projection of this aggression seems to offer a way out. However, the question arises, why does the patient not stop at simply projecting his impulses and feelings; why must a proxy be produced that portrays all the features of anxiety and breathes the fumes of aggression? The function of reality testing is certainly involved here. My patients again and again countered any attempt to bypass their defense with the emphatic argument, "But my husband *is* that anxious and he *does* get so furious."

From the sampling presented, we saw what happens when the

proxy fails to function—the ability of these vulnerable egos to test reality and to control their drives breaks down. Therefore, the so oft-repeated assertion, "but he *is* so," seems to reflect the need of these patients to assure themselves that *their sense of reality* is unimpaired—it implies an unconscious alert to danger. By arousing the omitted emotion in the partner, by inducing the repressed aggression in the proxy, the patient concomitantly relies on an auxiliary ego for control, and yet also affirms to himself his own sense of reality. The perception in the other of these emotional and instinctual manifestations then serves for denial, too; as, in similar manner, the witness's credence does in pseudologia fantastica (Fenichel, 1939). With the ridding of aggressive pressures against the love object, the patients' own actions are expressive of libidinous strivings only, which they demonstrate, albeit by an overbalance of seductive behavior. What we witness is a splitting off of libidinous and aggressive strivings by a process in which the latter are aroused in another person, who thus appears to be a "branch" of the self. One may add, somewhat parenthetically, that the phenomenon ordinarily seen in connection with such splitting—namely, the division into loved and hated object—is present in the circumstances described, too; the vicious incitement of anxiety and rage in the partner is certainly a discharge of aggression against him, displaced from the object toward which it was originally directed.

During a discussion on twins,[7] Anna Freud recently made a statement that fits here as well: "Through the emotional surrender, object relationship is increased. Such persons fuse with the object. This is not an ego operation, but an id process." One may put it in our present context in these words: Through the creation of a proxy, vacillating object cathexes are stabilized.

In summing up this section I offer the following formulation: "Altruistic surrender" to—or mobilization of—a proxy serves to reinforce ego control, to maintain reality testing, to ward off the loss of an important external object relationship, and to retain a measure of internal object constancy by temporarily finding a new fusion object.

Finally, a few remarks on terminology are in place here. Anna

[7] Discussion on Twins, Affiliated Staff, New York Psychoanalytic Institute, September 18, 1960.

Freud, in using the term "altruistic surrender," underscores the passive renunciatory nature of the process involved. My emphasis is on an *active* quality, equally unconscious. That is why I say "evocation" rather than "surrender."

If one is once alerted to the observation of the creation of proxy relationships many instances spring to mind. In a paper which I wrote on the play *Othello* (1950), I made the point that Iago needs to rid himself of an intolerable jealousy and succeeds in doing so by arousing the selfsame affect in Othello. All of us who have analyzed homosexuals know that it is a kind of game among them to stimulate the jealousy of the constant or temporary partner. On close examination, we find how much they suffer from jealousy, that, in fact, the need to avoid this emotion has driven them to abandon the prime object, the mother. Anna Freud emphasizes how much the mechanism of altruistic surrender is used by passive homosexuals, just as it is normally present in any husband-wife relationship. Remarkable, too, is how specific the actions of the proxy have to be in order to preserve the equilibrium of the subject. One of my homosexual patients became greatly perturbed when his partner temporarily began to work in an art form different from the one through which, had he dared, the patient would have expressed himself.

TRANSFERENCE MANIFESTATIONS

It now is necessary to ask ourselves how this defense becomes manifest in the analytic situation and where, in the transference, the analyst is placed in the process of proxy evocation. In doing so, I keep clearly in mind that this is, of course, only one aspect of the wishes involved in the transference situation.

There are at least two possibilities: the therapist may represent the original self-extension object which is to be preserved, or he may stand for the proxy interposed in the previously illuminated way. Dramatization of events and of associative sequence may be used to achieve these ends. Every analyst has heard from his patients how badly the patient's wife or his friend talked of the analyst, or of analysis, and how the patient came to the analyst's defense. This approximates the situations of Mrs. L. and Mrs. T. in their manipulation of their husbands in regard to the daughter or son, respectively. It is the analyst who is thus placed in the latter category. He is the precious object with whom a relationship has to be preserved; he stands for the child to be protected. Upon careful listening it may, however, become evident that the reported conversation, stimulating the spouse's or friend's antagonism against psychoanalysis, had been directed by the patient. Often one hears oneself fearfully misquoted, so that the desired cooperation of the proxy may be aroused. Children may be particularly inclined to this mode of defense. To work it through may remove one of the causes of interference with the analysis by the child's parent or the adult's marital partner.

There is also the other variant, wherein the patient aims to arouse the anxiety or anger or passion of the analyst in connection with some third person whom he seeks to persuade his analyst to see in consultation. This may be an attempt to draw the analyst into a relationship in which the patient himself fears to engage. The patient wants the analyst to experience in his stead the anxiety or the feeling of guilt linked to this attachment. This behavior can of course also be observed in the patient's regular life pattern. In both heterosexual and homosexual couples one partner at times leads the other into a relationship to a third person, often directly representing the primal love object.[8]

Occasionally one may be able to demonstrate to a patient how the sequential organization of his associations reveals his unconscious intentions regarding the analyst. Mrs. L. was among those patients who may tell, in the first part of the session, of some financial or family crisis that has occurred since the last analytic hour. Only later on in the session would she let me know that the problem had come well under control in the course of the previous day.

If the only purpose of this sequence were to arouse anxiety in the analyst, we might call this a defense by reversal—turning the passive position into an active one—or a defense by identification with an aggressor. But if the aim is to mobilize the analyst's concern for the patient and the wish to entice the analyst to intervene against the threatening object in the patient's stead, then we are dealing with a maneuver of proxy evocation. In the end, such is the tech-

[8] Dr. Rudolph M. Loewenstein called my attention to the operation of these factors in the dynamics of complicity.

nique which every successful storyteller employs. The ability to involve an audience in such a fashion is the mark of the dramatist.

GENESIS

The maneuver of evocation of a proxy is no doubt a universal one; everyone at one time or another resorts to it. Society abuses some of its members by this method, and, in the intercourse of nations, it has long played a role. There are, however, individuals who are particularly inclined to incite others to function as their proxies. I believe that some characteristic genetic events can be recognized in these persons. I have talked before of their highly narcissistic object relation, of their failure in establishing an independent identity, and have made reference to similar fusion phenomena in twins (Anna Freud). Jacob A. Arlow (1960), examining the mythology of twins, writes, "[they] work as a unit and by the complementary relationship of their attributes lend strength, wisdom, and alertness to each other, especially at critical moments when they either protect, save or augment the forces of the other." In other sections of this paper he demonstrates through clinical material these interchanges of id, ego, and superego functions between twins. Joseph and Tabor (1961) postulate a "twinning reaction," which consists of interidentification and mutual fusion of self and object representations. The authors believe that this reaction can be found not only in twins but also among siblings and couples who have been married for a considerable time. The two children cited in the present paper as well as the couples, L. and T., could be considered such pairs. Analytic data from *both* partners are unfortunately not available to confirm with definiteness the mutuality. When I go into the history of my patients I can see that they have persistently needed a fusion relationship with a partner. At the hub of that need seems to stand an insufficient individuation experience which should have occurred at the point when the symbiotic mother-child relationship is normally dissolved. In the case of the six-year-old girl, a series of traumatic events at birth and in the first year of life had retarded the timetable of this maturational process, and then the birth of the sibling intervened before individuation had been sufficiently accomplished. In the case of Mrs. L., we have learned how much her mother considered her a part of herself and used her as a medium; and in the case of Mrs. T., I could still observe her mother's clinging to her as "her window to the world."[9] From several patients I learned to appreciate that this initial disturbance in the maturational time-table of the mother-child relationship may develop into a strong coupling with an available sibling.

The sisters of two of my patients were only two years older, but they had early in life functioned as replacements of their mothers for many of the anaclitic needs of their younger siblings.

Another patient dreamed of a fish with two heads. It led him to speak of himself and his sibling as Siamese twins, a conception that reflected the easy shift of undesirable affects, actions, and opinions onto the sibling, and later, through further displacement, onto the marital partner. Greenacre (1960, p. 583) also believes "that pro-longed and unrelieved contact of an infant . . . with another indi-vidual, usually another child, leaves a permanent effect of diminished differentiation of the self from the other, and consequently weakens and confuses the sense of identity, producing an effect somewhat simulating twinning."

It is my hypothesis that the defensive maneuver of inciting others to function as proxies has its ultimate genesis in an insufficiency of the mother-child relationship in the symbiotic phase. If this maneu-ver is prominently used, some pathology of either mother or child, or both, at that period is indicated. Concomitantly, fixation to such a developmental disturbance facilitates regression of the ego func-tions of identity, reality testing, and impulse control. Yet, the defense by "evocation of a proxy" is too complex a formation to be ascribed *in toto* to this period. Ego maturation must have proceeded from this point forward to a considerable degree. However, subsequent in-fluences, among them primarily the use by the mother of the child for fulfillment of her own needs, left a particularly strong noxious imprint upon identity development; other traumatic experiences of a grossly aggressive and libidinous nature added to the impairment of the functions of ego control, sense of reality and of identity. Considering these elements, it is not astonishing to find that the anxiety potential of these patients is higher, that they suffer markedly

[9] Compare also Annie Reich's cases (1953, p. 33).

from separation anxiety, and that they are prone to travel phobias and agoraphobias. Of course, from a genetic point of view one can also say: children who were treated as narcissistic objects will in turn treat others in the same way.

I am fully aware that in the foregoing I have given almost no room to castration fear and feelings of guilt as factors which might cause the initiation of the defense "evocation by proxy." These factors did indeed, as they do in any analysis, play an immense role in the analyses of the cases cited. The need of sharing fear and guilt with others is a general phenomenon; any group formation must serve such purposes. Castration anxiety and guilt are the starting point for defensive and regressive moves. In my description of this defense, however, I have focused on its elements and economics and on the fundamental fixations involved.

CONCLUSION

In this paper I have elaborated on the defense which Anna Freud called "a form of altruism," by stressing the active quality of this defensive maneuver. I have given reasons why I prefer to name it "evocation of a proxy." I have hypothesized that in the cases cited, the inclination to resort to it is genetically tied to a persistence of symbiotic needs and to the failure in the proper development of a sense of identity.

I have postulated that the insufficient dissolution of the early symbiotic tie to the mother produces weak spots in the development of the sense of identity, of the sense of reality, and of the ability to control impulses by offering fixation points in a period when such reliance upon another individual for the exercise of these functions is quite the normal order. In patients such as those discussed here, regression of these functions may therefore occur under stress. This is particularly apt to happen when later traumatic libidinous and aggressive experiences and continuous identity-confusing influences weaken these ego functions even more.

Separation from any object that has prevalently served as a narcissistic extension of the self, that has functioned more like a transitional object and less like a true object, becomes, under these circumstances, a particularly grave threat to the integrity of the self.

The "evocation of a proxy" utilizes such symbiotic and transitional foundations for defensive purposes. Another person is mobilized to function as an "alter ego." Selected superego qualities, ego functions, and id manifestations are evoked in and assigned to a partner. The anxiety aroused in the proxy stirs him—instead of oneself—to actions, emotions, judgments, and controls. A splitting off of aggressive from libidinous strivings occurs intrapsychically, a process which has various consequences. The value of actually evoking these emotions and actions in another person lies, among other factors, in a reinforcement of the subject's sense of reality which was endangered by regression. This can be noted particularly in the great stress these patients lay on the assertion that the proxy actually shows the behavior and emotions in question. Furthermore, teleologically, it appears that in these persons with weak egos, the whole sequence from anxiety to aggression and its control is, in moments of crisis, indeed more safely left in the hands of an alter ego, which is *in toto* less liable to regression of its functions.

I have tried to show that these patients, throughout their lives, have had the tendency to use others, often siblings, as their proxies, and I have tried to demonstrate at least two ways in which these patients unconsciously attempt to involve the analyst in the transference in the proxy-creating process. The wish may be to make him represent the precious narcissistic extension object which needs to be protected against the attack of an incited outsider, or the wish may be that the analyst himself become the attacking or seducing proxy. In order to dissolve and work through this defense of proxy creation, the splitting of instinctual drives, the need for bolstering the sense of reality, and the need for a fusion object have to be considered.

SUMMARY

The "evocation of a proxy" is a defense which is, as other defenses, promoted by anxiety. In the face of regression, it serves to reinforce ego control, to maintain reality testing, to ward off the threatened loss of an essential narcissistically cathected, external object relationship, and to retain a measure of internal object constancy by temporarily resorting to partial fusion with a new object.

BIBLIOGRAPHY

Arlow, J. A. (1960), Fantasy Systems in Twins. *Psa. Quart.*, XXIX.

Benedek, T. (1937), Defense Mechanisms and Structure of the Total Personality. *Psa. Quart.*, VI.

Brodey, W. (1959), Some Family Operations and Schizophrenia. *Ā.M.A. Arch. Gen. Psychiat.*, I.

Eissler, R. S. (1949), Scapegoats of Society. In: *Searchlights on Delinquency*, ed. K. R. Eissler. New York: International Universities Press.

Fenichel, O. (1939), The Economics of Pseudologia Fantastica. *The Collected Papers of Otto Fenichel*, II. New York: Norton, 1954, p. 129.

Flügel, J. C. (1921), *The Psycho-Analytic Study of the Family*. London: Hogarth Press, p. 168.

Freud, A. (1936), *The Ego and the Mechanisms of Defense*. New York: International Universities Press, 1946, pp. 132-146.

—— & Burlingham, D. (1944), *Infants Without Families*. New York: International Universities Press, p. 7.

Freud, S. (1921), *Group Psychology and the Analysis of the Ego*. London: Hogarth Press, 1948, p. 104.

Greenacre, P. (1941), The Predisposition to Anxiety. *Psa. Quart.*, X.

—— 1960, Considerations Regarding the Parent-Infant Relationship. *Int. J. Psa.*, XLI.

Greene, W. A. (1958), Role of Vicarious Object in the Adaptation to Object Loss. I. Use of a Vicarious Object as a Means of Adjustment to Separation from a Significant Person. *Psychosom. Med.*, XX.

—— (1959), Role of Vicarious Object in the Adaptation to Object Loss. II. Vicissitudes in the Role of the Vicarious Object. *Psychosom. Med.*, XXI.

Heiman, M. (1956), The Relationship Between Man and Dog. *Psa. Quart.*, XXV.

Jacobson, E. (1954a), The Self and the Object World. *This Annual*, IX.

—— (1954b), Psychotic Identifications. *J. Amer. Psa. Assn.*, II.

Johnson, A. M. & Szurek, S. A. (1952). The Genesis of Antisocial Acting Out in Children and Adults. *Psa. Quart.*, XXI.

Joseph, E. D. & Tabor, J. H. (1961), The Simultaneous Analysis of a Pair of Identical Twins and the Twinning Reaction. *This Annual*, XVI.

Mahler, M. S. (1952), On Child Psychosis and Schizophrenia. *This Annual*, VII.

—— & Gosliner, B. (1956), On Symbiotic Child Psychosis. *This Annual*, X.

Reich, A. (1953), Narcissistic Object Choice in Women. *J. Amer. Psa. Assn.*, I.

Sperling, O. (1944), On Appersonation. *Int. J. Psa.*, XXV.

Stein, M. H. (1956), The Marriage Bond. *Psa. Quart.*, XXV.

Wangh, M. (1950), Othello: The Tragedy of Iago. *Psa. Quart.*, XIX.

Winnicott, D. W. (1953), Transitional Objects and Transitional Phenomena. *Int. J. Psa.*, XXXIV.

—— (1954), Introduction to Olive Stevenson: The First Possession. *This Annual*, IX.

—— (1960), The Theory of the Parent-Infant Relationship. *Int. J. Psa.*, XLI.

APPLIED PSYCHOANALYSIS

A CAUSERIE ON HENRY JAMES'S "THE TURN OF THE SCREW"

M. KATAN, M.D. (Cleveland)

I was asked by the editors to add a short preface to my "Causerie." To attempt to give a summary of James's story will neither do homage to the little masterpiece nor be of assistance to those readers who are not acquainted with it. This preface, of course, does not do away with the advice to read the story for oneself.

On Christmas Eve in an old house, a strange tale is told of an apparition "of a dreadful kind, to a little boy sleeping in the room with his mother and waking her up in the terror of it; waking her not to dissipate his dread and soothe him to sleep again, but to encounter also, herself, before she had succeeded in doing so, the same sight that had shaken him."

This "strange tale" causes Douglas, one of the people present, to promise an even more gruesome story, in which two children are involved. Douglas had acquired the written account of this story from the woman to whom it happened.

This woman, the daughter of a vicar in the province, as a girl of twenty, had been newly employed by a bachelor to bring up two orphans, his nephew and his niece, for whom he was the guardian. He had stipulated that she should never in any way bother him with problems arising from this task. The children lived at his country place, Bly, where the governess found a staff of servants under the direction of a motherly woman, Mrs. Grose. The little girl, Flora, aged eight, immediately captivated the governess with her lovely appearance. The boy, Miles, was still away at school. Already on the second day the difficulties of the governess began when she

---

At the request of Dr. William Wallace, head of Pediatrics at University Hospitals of Cleveland, I discussed with him, several other doctors, and a group of students this short story of Henry James's. It was selected for discussion by Dr. Ralph Wedgwood. The story had previously been unknown to me.

received from the bachelor a letter written to him by the headmaster of Miles's school. This letter, which the guardian had refused to open, contained the message that the boy had been expelled from school.

Next, the ghost of a man appears twice, and the governess learns, through the discussion of this strange event with Mrs. Grose, that this man, Peter Quint, was a former valet who had died. The story gains in momentum when the governess discovers that the children have an intimate relationship not only with the ghost of Peter Quint but also with the ghost of Miss Jessel, the previous governess, who apparently had committed suicide. The story hints that these two, when alive, had had a sexual relationship. James masterfully leaves it undecided whether the ghosts appear to the children, too, or whether the governess merely imagines that the ghosts appear to them. The governess directs all her efforts toward freeing the children from the demoniacal power under which they seem to live. The result is terrifying: the little girl turns against the governess, and the boy dies.

Before embarking upon what is still for me a foreign adventure in the field of belles-lettres, I want to emphasize that this story was published in 1898, that is, before Freud's *Interpretation of Dreams* appeared. Henry James was therefore not applying any acquired analytic knowledge when he created *The Turn of the Screw*.

You will agree that we need a certain idea to direct us in our investigation. Yet we do not possess anything that can serve as a platform from which to start. We find ourselves in the same situation as at the beginning of an analysis. Accordingly let us listen to what James has to tell us, and use our minds as our instruments of observation. That is, we will let ourselves be guided by whatever feelings and thoughts the story may arouse in us.

Let me start, therefore, with my first impression. I felt that Henry James was trying to communicate a nightmare to his reader. Is the French saying, *"Les premiers sentiments sont toujours les meilleurs,"* also applicable to this impression? I may bring, in support, the associations of some of my patients after they read this book. They insisted that they did not feel any anxiety, but rather were bored. Nevertheless, to their great amazement, their associations went back to their own childhood nightmares.

What does Henry James himself have to say about this subject? Already on the first page we are introduced to a scene in which a little boy, who is sleeping in the same room with his mother, wakes her up in terror. This type of introduction certainly convinces me of the correctness of my impression that James had a nightmare in mind when he wrote *The Turn of the Screw*.

In the past, literary people have stressed the anxiety-arousing quality of the story. For instance, Heywood Broun writes that for days and days he saw the ghostlike face of Peter Quint behind the window.

At this point we are justified in asking whether it was James's aim to arouse anxiety in the reader. More than thirty years ago there was an analytic rule, not at all incorrect even today, that "the result reveals the intention" (*"was erreicht wird, war auch die Absicht"*). Thus, if James succeeds in making his reader afraid, we may be sure that James wanted to do so. If you want a confirmation, let us turn to James himself:

> In calling *The Turn of the Screw* "the most powerful, the most nerve-shattering ghost story I have ever read," Phelps is merely giving expression to a universal verdict. [Phelps is one of the literary critics who wrote about James.] It seems that no one has ever written about this story without frankly confessing to the fear and horror it aroused in him. When Phelps told James that it "made my blood chill, my spine curl, and every individual hair to stand on end," James declared that he was very happy to learn that it had affected him in this way, because, he said, "I meant to scare the whole world with that story; and you had precisely the emotion that I hoped to arouse in everybody. When I wrote it, I was too ill to hold the pen; I therefore dictated the whole thing to a Scot stenographer. I was glad to try this experiment, for I believed that I should be able to judge of its effect on the whole world by its effect on the man who should hear it first. Judge of my dismay, when from first to last page, this iron Scot betrayed not the slightest shade of feeling! I dictated to him sentences that I thought would make him leap from his chair; he short-handed them as tho they had been geometry, and whenever I paused to see him collapse, he would enquire in a dry voice, 'What next?' "[1]

[1] Kunitz, Stanley J., ed. *Authors Today and Yesterday*. New York: H. W. Wilson, 1933.

Having obtained confirmation from James, our next question is: why did he want to frighten everybody? Here we are on much firmer ground. Especially those of you who treat children will immediately know at what I am hinting. If a child, for instance, experiences strong anxiety during examination by a doctor, we may be sure that some hours later, or the next day, we will see him playing with friends a game in which he repeats this examination. But instead of now being the passive victim, he becomes active: he is the doctor and tries to make the other child feel all the anxiety that he himself suffered during the real examination.

Thus we may conclude that James is doing here the sort of thing that children do. He wants to instill anxiety in everybody because he has so much anxiety himself. He wants to get rid of his anxiety by discharging it onto others. And he tries to achieve this by using infantile mechanisms.

Here we touch upon a very intricate problem. Is art neurotic? We may say simply that we do not know what art is.[2] If infantile mechanisms are used in art, this does not mean that for that reason art is neurotic. We may say of the neurotic that infantile conflicts disturb the normal functioning of his ego. In contradistinction, the ego of the artist uses infantile mechanisms for the purpose of a higher aim, namely, to create a product that we call art. The artist or author, through his creation, tries to obtain mastery of a problem. I have already pointed out how great a role the reader plays in James's attempt; namely, James wants to unload his anxiety upon the reader. James wants to draw the reader in, to arouse in him similar conflicts, and to look with him for a solution. Therefore, we may ask: does the author offer any solution?

We know how the story ends. The girl turns against the governess; and the boy, just when the governess thinks she has saved him, dies. Thus we may say that this is a ghost story without a solution. All the attempts of the governess to ferret out the secret which the children keep hidden lead to disaster. When the little boy finally surrenders the name of the tormenting ghost, he dies from this admission. *Our conclusion is that if this story reflects James's own*

[2] Here I would refer the reader to the beautiful book by Ernst Kris, in which he so brilliantly treats the subject of art (*Psychonalytic Explorations in Art*. New York: International Universities Press, 1952).

anxiety, he must at a certain period of his life have had secrets which arouses in him mortal terror!

It becomes clear that James, in order to cope with this terror, appealed liberally to the sense of terror in the reader. This terror must have been the focal point of James's personality. Since he had never found a proper solution for it, he did not want his reader to find a solution, either.

But is not this conclusion, that the story fails to offer a solution, at odds with our previous statement that James already on the first page reveals that a nightmare must have been the original source for his story. Indeed, it may be considered a weakness that James already betrays so much at the very beginning. However, from that point on, James does his best to neutralize this early revelation. After all, James does not speak of a nightmare, for he changes what seems to be a child's bad dream into an event of supernatural character. A little boy sees an apparition, and the mother sees it too. This story causes somebody else—his name is Douglas—to narrate a story of the same kind, only this second story surpasses the first in horror: not one but two children take part in it. The involvement of two children means that it takes that many turns of the screw to effect the story; the title is thus explained.

The division into two separate stories, told by two different persons, points not to one but to a number of events which are closely associated with one another (for instance, Henry's sharing the bedroom alone with his mother as well as in the company of another child).

It will be of interest to find out at what age James's crucial nightmares started. The boy and the girl in the story are latency children. In James's attempt to disguise the underlying events, he may have distorted the ages of the children as well. Latency is not exactly the period in which one expects nightmares to occur for the first time. There is another cue which perhaps will lead to more correct information about the time element. Douglas, the narrator, during the summer after his second year at Trinity, fell in love with the governess, who was ten years his senior. The supernatural events, the written account of which she sent him, took place when she was twenty. We may assume that Douglas, when he went home that summer for his vacation, was then the same age. Thus the apparitions must have appeared ten years before he met her. Since Douglas kept quiet about the affair for forty years more, we may place the original events fifty years back. *The Turn of the Screw* was published in 1898, when James was fifty-five years old. It was written, of course, somewhat earlier. If we may trust our deductions, the traumatic events in James's life which caused his nightmares took place before and around the time when he was about five years old.

We may assume that James, in order to create the proper atmosphere for a ghost story and even more in order to deny the autobiographical origin, created a very complicated chain of events to explain how the story became known.

Having laid the groundwork, we may now tackle the ghost story itself. Let us start with a question: is this a love story? The introductory chapter hints at the love of a young student for a woman ten years older. This is only a beginning, for it cannot escape us that *The Turn of the Screw* is filled with love. First, there is the love between the ghosts. But this is not the only love affair. There is the love of the twenty-year-old governess for the bachelor in London, and from this love we see develop the governess's love for the two orphan children whom she has been hired to take care of. So these two types of love—or three types of loves—are intimately interwoven.

Let us look at the first love story, the love between the ghosts. This love is revealed through hallucinations. French psychiatrists have called a delusion shared by two *"une folie à deux."* Consequently, if a hallucination is shared by three, as is hinted at in this story, we may speak of *"une hallucination à trois."*

You know, when the governess sees the ghosts in the presence of the children, she is convinced that the children see them too. When the ghost of Miss Jessel appears for the first time, the governess has Flora with her. The reaction which the governess had expected from the child does not come about. Instead, Flora picks up "a small flat piece of wood, which happened to have in it a little hole that had evidently suggested to her the idea of sticking in another fragment that might figure as a mast and make the thing a boat. This second morsel, as I watched her, she was very markedly and intently attempting to tighten in its place." Nobody can escape the meaning of the child's action: it is the symbol of sexual intercourse. The author purposely leaves it indefinite whether Flora has seen the apparition or not. According to the description, the little girl behaves as if she has not seen anything. Nevertheless, the warded-off comes out, for her play-acting betrays through its symbolism what she wants to keep secret.

In the ensuing chapters we obtain more information about this point. There is a very simple but lovable woman, Mrs. Grose, who confirms what the governess suspects after seeing the apparitions, namely, that these two ghosts, Peter Quint and Miss Jessel (the previous governess), had had sexual relations together. And Mrs. Grose says that the two were infamous, that there was everything between them in spite of the difference in their rank, that Peter Quint did what he wished, and that Miss Jessel did what she wished.

In Chapter VIII the governess, speaking of Flora, tries "once more to describe the portentous little activity by which she sought to divert my attention—the perceptible increase of movement, the greater intensity of play, the singing, the gabbling of nonsense, and the invitation to romp." Indeed, what great self-experience of denial must have been present in James for him to word his observations in this precise way!

Thus, despite their denial, both children—for Miles also acts similarly—betray through their behavior that they are aware of the sexual relationship between the former valet and the former governess. When the present governess discovers that the children know, she thinks they are lost. So, if we may take the words of the governess as being James's own, they have this meaning: if, as a child, you have witnessed intercourse between the parents or their substitutes, and if you cannot get rid of these impressions but under their influence you get "in cahoots" with another child, you are lost. This is a terrible secret which the child has to carry with him. Thus we may say that James suffered from the traumatic effects of primal-scene observations.

The sexual relationship between Peter Quint and Miss Jessel is pictured as a sinful act which cannot go unpunished. Mrs. Grose stresses this point by her remark about the previous governess: "Poor woman—she paid for it." And although Mrs. Grose professes to know nothing, she lets slip that, after what had happened, "she couldn't have stayed," and finally hints at what she imagined the end had been: "And what I imagine is dreadful." The inference is that

Miss Jessel committed suicide and that Peter Quint had to die too.

Next in the story the governess forces Mrs. Grose to tell more about these former employees who now appear as ghosts—how the valet, Peter Quint, had a very intimate relationship with the little boy, and how she, Mrs. Grose, tried to destroy the influence of the valet upon the boy. But the boy lies to Mrs. Grose: he conceals the sexual relationship between the man and Miss Jessel, and he refuses to give up his own relationship with the valet. When Mrs. Grose reminds Miles that Peter Quint was only a low menial hand and certainly no fit company for him, the boy becomes accusative and replies, "You are one, too." And with this he silences Mrs. Grose.

From the description of the relationship between Peter Quint and Miles, as well as that between Miss Jessel and Flora, it becomes clear why the ghosts appear. These dead persons manifest themselves in order to retain their influence upon the children so that the children will not reveal the secret. Mrs. Grose also supplies further corroboration: "the children saw more things, terrible and unguessable, that came from passively watching intercourse in the past." I think James's choice of words speaks for itself.

Despite the children's denial, their behavior betrayed that they had seen the ghosts. This ambiguity adds greatly to the already-existing veil of secrecy.

I have said that there are many love stories in this short story by James. Let us leave the love between the ghosts and turn to another love affair. When the governess visited the children's guardian in London, she immediately fell in love with this bachelor. This is the reason why she agreed to fulfill the role of a mother to the two orphan children. You will remember that the guardian had stipulated that she should not ask him anything; he wanted nothing to do with any part of the children's upbringing, and the governess should follow her own inclinations. Only love can prevail upon a young, inexperienced girl to accept such an impossible task. It does not take very much imagination to figure out the resulting fantasies of this twenty-year-old girl. Namely, the bachelor is the father, and she is the mother, of these two orphan children. Of course, it would be naïve to think that the governess's fantasy life would stop here. In short, she sees herself sexually related to the bachelor.

Let us follow the governess on her walk through the woods,

absorbed in her own thoughts. "Someone would appear there at the turn of the path and would stand before me and smile and approve." On that occasion, when she looks back at the house, her imagination seems to have "turned real": someone does stand there, on top of the tower. Then comes the shock of discovering that it is not the bachelor. It is another man. At that moment the whole world around her turns dead; the birds no longer make any sound. James indeed had an imagination—an imagination which conceived a picture very close to the description of hallucinations as they occur in our patients.

During the entire time that the apparition is present, the man on top of the tower does not take his eyes off the governess. You know, Freud very early in his analytic career described a woman who suffered from the delusion of being watched. Already in this very early stage of his development Freud deducted that this psychotic feature of being watched is the projection of a normal function of the conscience—of the superego, as he later called it. The superego watches the ego, and as such exerts a moral pressure upon it.

Let us apply Freud's discovery to James's story. At the moment when the sexual fantasies about her beloved threaten to become conscious to this Victorian parson's daughter, she does not become aware of a resulting feeling of guilt. Instead, her ego hallucinates the appearance of a stranger, which hallucination produces the necessary inhibiting effect. The blow dealt at her forbidden fantasies is beautifully turned into the sensation that the world has become a solitude.

But there is still more. The governess describes to Mrs. Grose the apparition of Peter Quint. Although his clothes were those of a gentleman, he himself certainly was not. Mrs. Grose confirms the governess's impression: the master missed certain clothing!

What does this mean? If, in our dream analysis, a figure is described as looking like A. but having a coat that belongs to B., we may conclude that in the dream a condensation of these two figures occurred, stressing a certain identity between them. Accordingly, when James describes an asexual bachelor and the bachelor's very sexual, morally low valet, James is bringing out a relationship between these two figures—between the bachelor and Peter Quint. Thus we may say that Peter Quint and the bachelor are two sides of one and the same person, that James has split a person into two parts, a good part and a bad part, and that the good part becomes the asexual bachelor, and the bad part the villain, possessed of base sexuality.

Such a split has a great advantage: each of the two parts becomes available for separate use. This newly acquired insight affords us a much better understanding of the content of the hallucination. The governess's superego condemns her sexual wishes and therefore paints the bachelor—namely, the object of her desires—as being a villain. Her ego is obedient to the superego's demands and forms a hallucination about this villain in order to ward off the sexual attraction of the bachelor. This process is typical of the hysterical hallucination!

Then comes the second hallucination. When the governess and Mrs. Grose are on their way to church one Sunday afternoon, the governess discovers that she has left her gloves behind on a chair in the living room, and she goes back to get them. When she looks up, there is the face of Peter Quint pressed against the window. This second apparition lasts only a few seconds: "it was as if I had been looking at him for years and had known him always." This utterance proves that the figure represents somebody whom she has always known, presumably her father! At that moment she does not know that the apparition is Peter Quint, the former valet. (Mrs. Grose identifies him later as such.) Nevertheless, the ominous character of this figure foreshadows subsequent events.

There is a striking difference between this second hallucination and the first one. Whereas in the first hallucination the ghost stares at the governess, this time he stares not only at her. She knows immediately that he is looking for someone else. During her talk with Mrs. Grose, it dawns upon her that Peter Quint had been looking for Miles, that he wanted the boy to see him.

Why does Peter Quint's gaze in the second hallucination switch from the governess to the little boy? When we discussed the love affair between Peter Quint and Miss Jessel, we closed that part of our discussion with the deduction that the ghosts appear in order to prevent the children from betraying the secret. But with the occurrence of the second hallucination, the governess is still completely unaware of the fact that the children know. Therefore, when she becomes upset because Peter Quint is looking for Miles, we can only conclude that this change in hallucinations must represent some change within herself. You know, in the governess's unconscious fantasies, the bachelor and she herself are the father and the mother of the two orphans. Thus the second hallucination shows that the governess's forbidden fantasies now include Miles also. Later we shall see how intense her sexual interest in Miles has become.

The governess grows desperate following her discovery that Peter Quint wants to reveal himself to Miles. She forms the plan of protecting the children by offering herself as the sole subject of this experience (the hallucination): "by accepting, by inviting, by surmounting it all, I should serve as an expiatory victim and guard the tranquillity of my companions." Thus she still hopes to prevent the children from becoming involved in sexual excitement. But in doing so, her inner tension rises tremendously, and, with that, her guilt feelings increase proportionately. "The more I saw, the less they would. I began to watch them in a stifled suspense, a disguised excitement that might well, had it continued too long, have turned to something like madness."

A new development prevents the governess from breaking down under the strain of her superego's exciting accusation. There is a turn of the screw now, for a new hallucination appears. We have already mentioned this; namely, the governess, in Flora's presence, sees an apparition of Miss Jessel, and the little girl pretends not to see it. Such hallucinations convince the governess that the children are lost, for they obviously deny that they see such apparitions. Thus the governess discovers that the children have full knowledge of the sexual relationship between the former governess and the valet. The primal-scene material that is conscious in the children's minds corresponds exactly with the unconscious fantasies of the governess, in which she sees herself linked sexually to the bachelor. In her unconscious, she is not very different from Miss Jessel. Accordingly all three—the governess and the two children—have fantasies about the primal scene, or about scenes derived therefrom. And, what is worse, all three are sexually excited by this common fantasy. So now the meaning of the hallucinations has been turned back into fantasy life. Since all three persons share a certain sexual fantasy, we may call it *"une phantasie à trois."*

This discovery of the children's knowledge causes the governess to change her attitude. Until now she had hoped, by absorbing the hallucinations herself, to keep the secret hidden from the children. From this point on she can only try, as far as she herself is concerned, to keep her own fantasies fully repressed. Yet she still strives to obtain a confession from the children in order to free them from the power of the ghosts. Basically, this is a sound attitude, for it means that through this confession she will be able to relieve them of the guilt which they undoubtedly have. The ghosts are the result not only of the guilty conscience of the governess but also of the guilty consciences of the children!

It is time to focus our attention on the significance of the letter written by the headmaster of Miles's school. This letter determines the course of the story from beginning to dramatic end!

You will remember that the governess's new position contained the provision that under no condition is she to bother the guardian. Soon after starting, namely, on the second day, she receives a letter from her employer, "enclosing another, addressed to himself, with a seal still unbroken. 'This, I recognise, is from the head-master, and the head-master's an awful bore. Read him, please; deal with him; but mind you don't report. Not a word. I'm off.'" The headmaster has written a brief note to the effect that Miles has been expelled from school, without adding why such an extreme disciplinary measure is necessary.

What would any sensible woman have done under such circumstances? Immediately we become aware of a number of things that she should have done. First of all, she should have told the guardian that it might be all very well for him not to want to be bothered with various trivia, but that this time he *had* to be bothered about the matter. Second, she should of course have requested more information from the principal. And third, when the boy himself did not speak of it, she should have asked him what had happened. However, nothing of this kind is done by our heroine.

The grave punishment suggests that Miles must have behaved very badly indeed. His guardian, without taking notice of the letter but obviously sensing that something was wrong, turns the entire matter over to the young governess, who in turn decides not to act upon it. Thus we find ourselves confronted with the problem of why the very two persons who should know better refrain from doing the right thing. After pondering over this question, we are struck with the recognition that *if either of these two had behaved sensibly, the story would never have been written.* The secret would then have been out in the open, and the whole complex conglomeration of supernatural happenings would have been without a foundation. Did James therefore conceive of this letter, and the lack of action on the part of both the guardian and the governess, as a trick to make the whole story possible? If that were the case, James would be a very facile writer, but he certainly would not deserve a place among the great authors of modern times. Is it possible that what seems on the surface to be a trick is, in fact, well founded upon psychological principles?

This consideration leads us to examine the eventual motivations behind the bachelor's behavior, as well as the conspicuous refusal of this otherwise very active young woman to attack the problem.

In the past, when the ghosts were still living persons, the bachelor had visited the children many times. Now that these persons are dead and the children need the bachelor's guidance more than ever, he does not want to have anything to do with them. What other conclusion can we draw than that these dramatic events have frightened him and that as a result he withdraws from the situation, that he shies away from the ideas which are already shared by the governess and the children? Thus the bachelor is—and this causes us no small surprise—the fourth participant in what then becomes *"une phantasie à quatre."* He runs away from the obscure stirrings of the oedipal feelings which have so strongly aroused the other three. Clearly, the bachelor is modeled after the illustrious example of the author himself.

As far as the governess is concerned, we may be brief. She lets herself be convinced by the angelic appearance of the girl and by the persuasion of that good woman, Mrs. Grose, that she should not take any action. She has not yet even met the boy. Here, at least, there is no obscurity. These motivations serve only as a cover for the fact that the governess, for reasons of her own, wants to be convinced that the boy is not bad. For if she should bother the bachelor, she would lose whatever chance there might be that some day he would respond to her love.

The great change comes when Miles rebels. One Sunday morning, on his way to church with the governess, he tells her that he no longer wants to be pinned to her skirts. He wants to be with other boys and therefore asks to be sent back to school. It is time for his uncle to take control of things, and Miles, with youthful bravado, is determined to make him come to Bly. We may say that this is a masculine protest of little Miles, a masculine protest such as undoubtedly James himself must have made when he was growing up. We understand fully the impact of Miles's demands. *The governess*, figuratively speaking, *is placed with her back against the wall, for now she will have to face the issue with the guardian.* Therefore we are not amazed that at this point she leaves the boy and is tempted to run away. Everybody is at church, a circumstance which would make her flight easy. From the churchyard, where she has been sitting on a tombstone, she goes home to collect her belongings. At the foot of the staircase she collapses. But the memory of what she had seen there a month ago—"just so bowed with evil things . . . the spectre of the most horrible of women"—makes her go further. When she opens the door of the schoolroom, the ghost of Miss Jessel is sitting at her desk, "dishonored and tragic." The hint that the governess's own mood corresponds with the impression of the recently perceived apparition leads us to the interpretation that the specter of Miss Jessel is the governess's projected self, the self that the governess would be if she should abandon the children. Thus we are not surprised to read that after the apparition has vanished, "there was nothing in the room the next minute but the sunshine and a sense that I must stay." The decision to fight it out causes the governess to write to the guardian, which fact of course means that she has abandoned all hope of winning the guardian's love.

From here on, the governess can concentrate only on freeing the children from the ghosts. Her efforts increase. She tries to get the children to confess their secret. What James is describing here is indeed a form of psychotherapy. We must say that James betrays a great deal of intuitive insight.

The outcome of the therapeutic endeavors by the governess is already known: she is highly unsuccessful. In her attempts to wrest the secret from the children, she becomes increasingly excited. She tries to force herself upon the children. In fact, she becomes as possessive and seductive as are the ghosts. More and more she acquires the character of Miss Jessel.

In the final scene with Flora, Mrs. Grose is also present. The ghost of Miss Jessel appears. The governess wants to use this apparition as a proof that the truth can no longer be denied. But Mrs. Grose does not see any apparition. Flora shatters any hope that the governess might have had of curing her. Not only does Flora deny having seen anything, she accuses the governess of cruelty and wants nothing more to do with her.

It does not require much explanation to understand why Mrs. Grose does not see the apparition. She is portrayed as being only a motherly figure, who does not harbor any incestuous fantasies. She cannot even write or read. Her defenses do not need hallucinations to fall back upon. And yet Mrs. Grose is a necessary link between the past and the present. She has to identify the ghosts for the governess.

Flora presents a more intricate problem. She turns against the very person who wants to save her. In her hysterical delirium that follows, of which Mrs. Grose is the informant, it turns out that Flora uses shocking language and accuses her present governess of terrible things.

We see that James betrays again an uncanny intuition regarding psychotherapeutic principles. For, in general, if the therapist, in his efforts to free the patient from certain thoughts, becomes too excited himself, then therapy becomes impossible. Interpretation cannot work under such circumstances. The patient is then in danger of also becoming too excited. He can no longer rely on the therapist for help in mastering his excitement. As a result, he either runs away or turns directly against the therapist.

In the story something similar happens. When the governess thinks she finally has Flora in a position where the little girl no longer can deny the truth, at that very moment the child turns against her. The child wants nothing to do with her any more. For if Flora had admitted the truth, the governess would have had her in her power. Instead of gaining her freedom, Flora would simply have exchanged her former dependency upon Miss Jessel for a similar dependency upon the present governess.

Flora does not stop at simply removing herself from the influence of the governess. In the subsequent hysterical outburst she accuses the governess of everything that Miss Jessel had done in reality, thus identifying her present governess, not without reason, with the dead governess. In this way Flora makes it clear that the governess has, at least in fantasy, the same sexual desires as Miss Jessel had. Thereupon they can no longer continue in each other's presence, and Flora is taken by Mrs. Grose to London.

Only the little boy and the governess now remain. After all, their relationship was by far the strongest. Listen to the description of the meal that the governess and Miles have together. "We continued silent while the maid was with us—as silent, it whimsically occurred to me, as some young couple who, on their wedding-journey, at the inn, feel shy in the presence of the waiter. He turned round only when the waiter had left us. [Miles said] 'Well—so we're alone!' " You see how incestuous the scene has become through its comparison with a honeymoon.

One final task remains. The governess still has to try to save Miles from the grip of the demoniacal power. The incident of the letter which she had written to the guardian comes up. The boy confesses his guilt: he stole the letter, for he was afraid of what the governess might have told the guardian. The governess had asked only for an appointment with the guardian. Then Miles admits he had said things, while still at school, to other boys whom he liked, and these friends told the masters, and the headmaster thought these things too terrible to write home. He could write only that the boy had been dismissed.

So near the final outcome, when Miles gives the appearance of innocence, the governess suddenly acquires a ray of insight. She says, "For if he *were* innocent, what then on earth was I?" If the boy had not had any of her fantasies, it would become clear how pathological the governess was.

It turns out completely differently. For a split second the governess may have had a certain insight into her own morbid desires, but it was only for a second, for at the end, when the apparition appears again and she tries to make the boy aware of it, he asks, "Is it he?" Governess: "Whom do you mean by 'he'?" Miles: "Peter Quint—you devil!" So finally the governess obtains Miles's admission. The governess thinks she has saved him, but at that moment the boy dies.

Through the interference by the governess, the boy has been saved from the ghost, but now he is exposed to an even greater danger. It is obvious, after the description of the intense incestuous feelings between the governess and the boy, that exposure to the influence of this woman would arouse him too strongly sexually. In order to understand what it would mean to be in Peter Quint's power, we have only to think of Mrs. Grose's hinting remarks. It means that the boy had a homosexual dependency upon Peter Quint. This power of Peter Quint's extends even after the valet's death. Yet this relation with Peter Quint protects him against the dangerous attachment to a mother figure. When the governess destroys Peter Quint's influence, she turns the clock back. The warded-off exciting oedipal relationship comes again to the fore. Out of necessity the boy has to die, for James had no other solution left. It was this dramatic ending through which James hoped to prevent the reader from having any discharge of the castration anxiety that James intended to arouse.

I have already explained why I think that infantile nightmares served as an example for James's ghost story. These terrifying dreams were based upon traumatic events of his childhood. The way in which James tried to discharge his anxiety onto his reader is too obvious for us not to accept the idea that James, in his story, is giving a distorted fantasy of important events in his life which gave rise to anxiety.

According to the introduction, little Henry suffered from nightmares when he shared the bedroom with his mother. The manifest content of these nightmares is irrelevant; we would not be able to reconstruct this dream content, anyway. Fortunately, the story contains enough material for us to acquire insight into the successive developmental steps which led to the outbreak of the nightmares.

In the story, primal-scene material is abundant. The parents are dead, as though James wanted to impress upon us that they were not involved in any sexual events. Considering this as an attempt at denial of what actually happened, I assume that James's earliest observations were made in his parents' bedroom, and it is highly possible that later he obtained similar impressions from the relations he observed between members of the servant staff.

The story shows clearly that another child shared the secret of the primal-scene observations with Henry. According to *The Turn of the Screw*, Henry's nightmares must also have contained evidence of how much the feelings aroused in the two children by what went on had influenced the relationship between them!

What was this relationship between the children like? Was it only one of sharing a bedroom secret, or did it go further? James remains very secretive about it. Miles could not remember what he had told the boys at school. According to our understanding, he might have talked to them about many things. It might have been about what happened between Miss Jessel and Peter Quint, or about Miles's own contact with the valet, or about the relationship between himself and Flora. It is even possible that he only used vile language. Yet his guilt feelings spoke loudly, for otherwise he would not have stolen the governess's letter in order to find out what she had written to his guardian. Clearly, we do not have evidence to say exactly what it was that occurred between the two children.

Next, the mother's interference complicates the situation. In the story the governess becomes aware, through the apparitions, of a plot between the two children. Real life, however, does not concur with the supernatural. Therefore, we have to eliminate the supernatural and look for a more prosaic way of obtaining information. The governess, who, as we have seen, was already in her fantasy life taking on the mother role, may simply be interpreted as standing for Henry's mother. The bachelor is then, of course, a substitute for his father.

Henry's mother, not through supernatural events but in one way or another having become suspicious of some kind of exciting inter- play between the children, must have tried to force the truth out of them. James spares no trouble to make it clear how excited his mother became during this quest of hers. In the story, the insight which the governess developed for a split second into her own morbidity may very well have been derived from Henry's original accusation of his mother's behavior. For her methods exposed him to the danger of overstimulation and, as a result, losing control of himself.

At this point Henry must have felt a great need for his father's protection against his mother's overbearing attitude. The story emphasizes the great extent to which the father failed to live up to such an expectation. We remember that before events took an unfortunate turn, the bachelor had shown great interest in the wel- fare of the children. He had sent them to his house in the country, as the proper place for them to live, "going down himself, whenever he might." But when things went wrong, he had divorced himself completely from the situation, had sent Miles away to school, and had insisted that the governess assume full responsibility for the children. Therefore, we may conclude that Henry accused his father, although for different reasons, no less than his mother.

We should be well aware that primal-scene observations leading to interplay with another child would in themselves never cause such traumatic effects as the story emphasizes. These effects result from a summation of stimuli, the main source of which seems to have been the relentless prodding by the mother.

One should really not be amazed that the little boy, sleeping in the same room as his mother, reacted, on the basis of these various experiences, with nightmares.

What prompted James, at the age of fifty-five, to write about this traumatic period of his early life poses a problem that we do not have to solve now.

But we are not yet at the end of our questions. If this construction comes close to the truth, which one of the two children does Henry James use to portray himself as a little child? This question is certainly not easy to answer and leads to a deeper probing into the story. At a certain point in this discussion I said that the whole supernatural occurrence was based upon *une phantasie à quatre*. The bachelor, the governess, and the two children all have a single sexual theme in common, and each of them deals with the ensuing conflicts in his or her own special way.

These various personalities that are so intimately interwoven with one another impress me—at times quite clearly, at other times more obscurely—as betraying glimpses of certain aspects of James himself. From this impression the conclusion can be easily drawn that not only do three of these four characters portray those persons who once figured in the author's past, but that these portrayals in turn contain as well the imprint of characteristics of James himself. In view of the different ages of the four, we may conceive of them as depicting four successive stages in James's ego development. Each one of these stages represents, in chronological sequence, a different ego attempt to master the conflict which is at the center of the story.

Let us take Flora first. Her angelic appearance concealed a "wild life" of forbidden thoughts and actions. She could not admit the truth, for this would have put her completely in the power of her governess. From this we may construe that young Henry's experiences made him afraid to assume the masculine role and therefore he wanted to be a girl. However, we may further deduct that the complete surrender of his masculinity would go too far, that it would bring him too much under the domination of his mother.

This brings us, then, to the second figure. Fortunately, the boy in Miles is not absent at all. Although he is pictured on the surface as being a sweet, almost feminine little boy, his other side is too strong not to break through the veneer of girlishness. You will remember that he puts up a masculine protest to his governess: he wants to associate with men and to shake off the influence of being dominated by women. But we have seen that the castration fears connected with his heterosexuality were too strong to afford this tendency the slightest chance of prevailing later in adult life in relation to women.

I now turn to the adult figures. From the introductory chapter, we might have expected that the little boy, who was the one who saw the apparitions first, would be the narrator. To our surprise, however, in the story proper it is the mother figure who sees the apparitions first, without the children being present, and who now tells the story. James writes as if he were identifying with this dominating mother figure. During the unfolding of the story, the governess emerges more and more as a person who has the same dominating qualities as the demoniacal Miss Jessel. The governess, in her incestuous love for the little boy, tries to possess him completely. James, in his mother identification, loved a little boy who was the picture of himself at an early age.

We are well acquainted with this type of mechanism. Freud described it already very early. When the time comes for the boy to exchange his incestuous love for his mother for the permissible love of a girl of his own age, he is unable to do so. Instead, his ego identifies with the mother, and now, as the mother, he loves other boys who represent himself at that early period of his life.

Thus we may conclude that James, at the end of his adolescence, tried to find a solution through a feminine identification. From the story we may reconstruct the fate of this identification. The sexual side of the identification is abolished and can appear only in the form of Miss Jessel's ghost. Nevertheless, this solution could not keep the identification with the asexual mother figure (the governess) free from the warded-off sexual trends. Perhaps the strongest dramatic effects of the story occur when James shows how the governess became possessed of the same characteristics which doomed Miss Jessel. Thus the feminine identification is stranded on its sexual implications.

James was unable to accept active masculinity in his adult personality, and simultaneously he forbade the appearance of overt homosexual features in his life. Nothing else remained for him, therefore, but to become a man who looked at life from a distance, a man who could create from his unconscious only those figures which he could never realize in actuality. He became the bachelor.

Thus, in my "Causerie" I have added another turn to the already sufficiently turned screw of the story. But my additional turn is different from James's. If James has "turned" autobiography into a ghost story, I have tried to "return" his production to its origin.

At this point, of course, we strike a new problem. Unable to obtain James's confirmation or denial—would his repression have permitted him to give either?—we can only make a new turn. James's charming autobiography keeps his answer hidden. Here lies our new task: to "unturn" the "turns" of James's autobiography, to wrest the answer from his secretiveness!

CONTENTS OF PREVIOUS VOLUMES

CONTENTS OF PREVIOUS VOLUMES

VOLUME III/IV, 1949

VOLUME V, 1950

VOLUME VI, 1951

VOLUME VII, 1952

VOLUME VIII, 1953

VOLUME IX, 1954

VOLUME X, 1955

VOLUME XI, 1956

VOLUME XII, 1957

VOLUME XIII, 1958

VOLUME XIV, 1959

VOLUME XV, 1960

VOLUME XVI, 1961